Foreword

This year marks the fortieth anniversary of the introduction of free second-level education in 1967. The time-series analysis presented in this report reveals the immediate impact of that policy reform and the hunger for learning that this unlocked in the Irish population. The number of Leaving Certificate candidates quadrupled before the twenty-fifth anniversary of the initiative in 1982. This move together with our subsequent investment in higher education has resulted in a remarkable improvement in the educational profile of the Irish population over those forty years.

Sé Sí provides a very thorough evaluation of gender and education in Ireland. Boys are significantly more likely than girls to leave school early and to demonstrate low levels of attainment in education. Although our gender differences in examination performance would appear to be moderate in an international context, these gender differences are substantial and they have increased slowly but steadily over time. Females now outnumber males among students of higher education and this gap has increased steadily over the last decade. The rapidly improving educational profile of women in Ireland has added significantly to the pool of skills in the Irish labour market.

Gender is one of a range of factors that impact on educational attainment. The international data demonstrate that home background characteristics and community characteristics have the most significant impacts on the extent to which individuals derive benefit from education systems here and elsewhere. How we deal with diversity in our education system will be a critical determinant of our future success as a society. Maintaining and continuing to improve quality in the context of ever-increasing diversity is at the heart of our aspirations towards the universal provision of educational opportunities.

This points to the importance of innovation in teaching and learning and we are fortunate with the quality of our teachers and with the continuing high regard for teaching as a profession in Ireland. In an era when mass participation and world-class quality in education are pre-requisites for economic competitiveness, this report also highlights the effectiveness of education systems where all schools and educational institutions embrace the diversity of their community.

I would like to take this opportunity to pay tribute to the principals and staff of our schools and staff of our further and higher education institutions whose work in reporting data on an annual basis to the Department and other state agencies has made the analysis in this report possible. We look forward to your continued support in our efforts to further improve the quality and policy-relevance of our evidence-base in Irish education.

If there is a key message from the time-series analysis presented in this report, it is that significant challenges remain in the context of our educational ambitions as a country. By encouraging more young people to finish school and ensuring much greater second chance and further education opportunities for those who leave school early, we can continue to address these challenges.

It is my sincere hope that this report will be a catalyst for reflection, dialogue and research on key issues relating to education and to gender in Irish society.

Mary Hanafin

Mary Hanafin T.D.
Minister for Education and Science
July 2007

Table of Contents

Table of Appendices

Sé Sí

Inscne in Oideachas na hÉireann

PRIMARY LEVEL

SECOND LEVEL

JUNIOR CERTIFICATE

LITERACY IN INTERNATIONAL CONTEXT

LEAVING CERTIFICATE

FURTHER EDUCATION & TRAINING

HIGHER EDUCATION

EDUCATIONAL PERSONNEL

OVERVIEW OF THE POPULATION

RANNÓG STAITISTIC
STATISTICS SECTION

AN ROINN
OIDEACHAIS
AGUS EOLAÍOCHTA

DEPARTMENT OF
EDUCATION
AND SCIENCE

Cúlra

Tá bunús le Sé Sí sa mhachnamh agus sna hathbhreithnithe ar chaighdeán agus ábharthacht le polasaí na sonraí riaracháin laistigh den Roinn Oideachais agus Eolaíochta. D'éirigh sé seo ina chuid d'athbhreithniú níos leithne ar fud na Státseirbhíse a thionscnaigh an Príomh Oifig Staidrimh agus Roinn an Taoisigh sa bhliain 2002.[1] Léirigh na hathbhreithnithe seo teorainneacha tromchúiseacha le caighdeán na sonraí riaracháin a bhí ann, atá fós ag cur bac ar fhorbairt pholasaí bunaithe ar fhianaise, ach go háirithe faoi mar a bhaineann sé leis na staitisticí ar a bhféadfaí staitisticí sóisialta agus comhionannais a thabhairt orthu. Cé gur aithin siad an gá le caighdeán na sonraí riaracháin a fheabhsú ar fud na státseirbhíse agus na seirbhíse poiblí, cuireadh béim shuntasach freisin ar an riachtanas le húsáid níos fearr a bhaint as sonraí a bhí ann cheana.

Laistigh den Roinn Oideachais agus Eolaíochta léirigh iniúchadh inmheánach de riachtanais agus foinsí sonraí a deineadh ag an am na teorainneacha leis na sonraí a bhí ann ach freisin léirigh sé go raibh easpa feasachta ann faoin méid eolais a bhí ar fáil ó fhoinsí riaracháin. Mar thoradh ar na tátail seo thosaigh Rannóg na Staitisticí ag machnamh ar an gcaoi ina bhféadfaí eolas staitisticiúil a chur ar fáil níos fearr do lucht déanta beartas. Dá bhrí sin bhí béim athnuaite ar shoiléire agus ábharthacht le polasaí ár n-oibre. Ag tosú le smaoineamh simplí, is é sin Tuairiscí Bliantúla Staitisticí uilig na Roinne a chur le chéile, aithníodh go raibh forbairt ar staitisticí amshraithe ina chéad chéim thábhachtach le héascacht úsáide ár dtuairiscí staitisticí a fheabhsú. Ar chloisteáil dóibh faoin obair ar staitisticí amshraithe léirigh an tAonad Comhionannais Inscne suim láidir i bhfoilseachán a fhorbairt ar staitisticí inscne in oideachas. Thug sé seo fócas don obair laistigh de Rannóg na Staitisticí. Toradh is ea Sé Sí ar ghníomhaíocht leathan bhuainteoireachta sonraí a rinne foireann Rannóg na Staitisticí thar cúig samhradh.

Cuspóirí na tuarascála

Tá sé de chuspóir ag Sé Sí forbhreathnú cuimsitheach a thabhairt ar staitisticí oideachais imdhealaithe de réir inscne. Thar aon ní eile dhírigh an obair ar shonraí oideachais a thiomsú agus a scaipeadh chun leasa na hainilíse pholasaí fianaise-bhunaithe. Cé gur foilsíodh cuid mhór de na sonraí cheana i dTuairiscí Bliantúla Staitisticí na roinne, tá cuid mhór de na táscairí a thugtar i Sé Sí nua, toisc go bhfuil na sonraí forbartha anois ina staitisticí amshraithe. Cinntíonn buainteoireacht na sonraí ó réimse leathan d'fhoinsí go bhfuil Sé Sí cuimsitheach ó thaobh réimse de, agus tá sé i gceist go gcuideoidh tiomsú na staitisticí amshraithe le machnamh agus plé ar threonna thar am in oideachas agus foghlaim na hÉireann.

Leagan amach na tuarascála

Cuireann Sé Sí forbhreathnú i láthair ar ghné na hinscne in oideachas na hÉireann i léargas ar feadh an tsaoil, ó bhreith go bás. Go ginearálta leagtar an cháipéis amach de réir ama, ón bhunleibhéal go dtí oideachas dara leibhéal agus tríú leibhéal. Tugtar sonraí ar bhreisoideachas agus ar phearsanra oideachais freisin. Baintear úsáid as sonraí daonra ón bPríomh Oifig Staidrimh le hathchoimriú a dhéanamh ar threonna, agus, nuair is féidir, cuirtear scéal na hÉireann i gcomhthéacs le sonraí cuí idirnáisiúnta.

---

[1] Ag eascairt as an Tionscnamh Bainistíochta Straitéisí (SMI), thosaigh tionscnamh idir-rannach le caighdeán agus ábharthacht le polasaí na sonraí riaracháin a fheabhsú sa bhliain 2002. Do thuilleadh eolais féach An Bord Náisiúnta Staitisticí, *Strategy for Statistics, 2003–2008* (2003) ag http://www.nsb.ie/pdf_docs/StrategyforStatistics2003-2008.pdf; freisin [SGSES] *Report of the Steering Group on Social and Equality Statistics* (2003) ag http://www.taoiseach.gov.ie/attached_files/Pdf%20files/SocialAndEqualityStatisticsReport.pdf, agus *The [SPAR] Report on the Statistical Potential of Administrative Records* (2003) ag http://www.cso.ie/releasespublications/documents/other_releases/spar.pdf.

Agus an tuairisc seo á fhorbairt, tugadh aire ar leith do chur i láthair na sonraí ar bhealach soiléir agus oibiachtúil. Cuireann aguisín mionsonraithe táblaí sonraí ar fáil atá ag teacht leis na cairteanna i gcorp na tuarascála mar thaca agus spreagadh le breis anailíse ar na hábhair ag lucht acadúil, mic léinn agus saoránaigh eile leasmhara.

Príomhthátail

Ó tharla gur deineadh líon suntasach taighde ar inscne in oideachas, tá an chuid is mó de na tátail agus torthaí aonair ar eolas go forleathan cheana féin. Mar sin féin, ceadaíonn Sé Sí anailís an-chuimsitheach ar scéal na hinscne in oideachas thar am. Ní dhéantar iarracht ar na tátail a achoimriú sa réamhrá seo, toisc go bhfuil sé i gceist go bhfeidhmeodh an cháipéis uilig mar achoimre ar na sonraí staitisticiúil atá ar fáil maidir le hinscne agus foghlaim in Éirinn. Mar sin féin, tugtar rogha de na príomhthátail thíos.

Feabhas suntasach thar am

Tá sé an-deacair do pháistí scoile na linne seo agus fiú do chéimithe ollscoile tuiscint a bheith acu ar leathnú na ndeiseanna oideachais a baineadh amach in Éirinn le glúine beaga anuas. I measc ghlúin a seantuismitheoirí, chríochnaigh leath de phobal na scoile a n-oideachas ag an mbunleibhéal, agus bhí dhá dtrian críochnaithe faoin Teastas Sóisearach . Níor éirigh ach le duine as gach triúr leibhéal na hArdteistiméireachta a shroicheadh, agus chuaigh thart ar dhuine as gach deichniúr ar aghaidh chuig an ardoideachas. Ní raibh rogha an ardoideachais ann ar chor ar bith do 90 faoin gcéad dá seantuismitheoirí.

Bhí feabhas mór tagtha ar an scéal faoin am go raibh glúin a dtuismitheoirí ag freastal ar scoil; ach bheadh comparáid an-bhocht ann idir phróifíl oideachais dhaonra na hÉireann agus a chomhpháirtithe ar an Mór-Roinn ag an am. Tháinig cinneadh stát na hÉireann le hoideachas dara leibhéal a chur ar fáil go forleathan dos na saoránaigh uilig déanach a dhóthain i gcomhthéacs pholasaí sóisialta iarthar na hEorpa. I dtíortha cóngaracha tugadh oideachas dara leibhéal saor isteach i ndiaidh an chogaidh; in Éirinn d'fhógair an tAire Oideachais, Donogh O'Malley, tabhair isteach an oideachais dara leibhéal saor sa bhliain 1967. Is féidir an tionchar a bhí ag an gcinneadh sin láithreach bonn, chomh maith le fonn an phobail don fhoghlaim a nochtaigh sé, a fheiceáil i gcaibidil 2 den tuarascáil seo, áit a mhéadaigh líon iomlán na n-iarrthóirí Ardteistiméireachta faoi cheathair, dáiríre, sna fiche cúig bliana a lean.[2]

Sa lá atá inniu ann tá bunoideachas uilíoch againn, críochnú 82 faoin gcéad d'oideachas dara leibhéal uachtarach, 55 faoin gcéad iontráil san ardoideachas, agus réimse suntasach de dheiseanna breisoideachais. Go hidirnáisiúnta, tá Éire i measc na dtíortha is mó a rinne dul chun cinn thar am le próifíl oideachais an daonra a fheabhsú. Mar sin féin, tá dúshláin ríthábhachtacha ann fós de réir mar a bhíonn tábhacht níos mó ag an oideachas agus ag an bhfoghlaim sa tóraíocht ar fholláine aonair, pobail agus náisiúnta. Bhí coinneáil agus críochnú scoile go leibhéal na hArdteistiméireachta mar ghné lárnach i bpolasaí oideachais na hÉireann agus fanann an scéal amhlaidh.

---

[2] Féach figiúirí agus táblaí 2.11a agus 2.11b.

Coinneáil agus críochnú scoile

Tá fás ag teacht ar an tábhacht a bhaineann le cáilíochtaí dara leibhéal uachtarach a fháil i dtíortha uilig an AE agus ECFE, de réir mar a thagann fás rialta ar éileamh do scileanna i margadh an tsaothair. Is é críochnú an oideachais dara leibhéal uachtarach anois an príomhbhealach le páirtíocht leanúnach foghlama a bheith ann. Maidir leis seo, aithnítear go bhfuil coinneáil go críochnú an oideachais dara leibhéal mar chuspóir lárnach i bpolasaí oideachais a bhfuil impleachtaí díreacha aige do rannpháirtíocht i mbreisoideachas agus ardoideachas agus do pholasaithe níos leithne a bhaineann le hiomaíochas eacnamaíochta agus cuimsitheacht shóisialta.

Faoi láthair tá thart ar 82 faoin gcéad ar an iomlán de dhaltaí dara leibhéal a thógann an Ardteistiméireacht. Ó leathnú na rannpháirtíochta dara leibhéal sna 1960í déanacha, tá rátaí níos airde de choinneáil scoile léirithe go rialta ag cailíní. Buachaillí is ea beagnach dhá dtrian de na daltaí a fhágann oideachas dara leibhéal roimh an Ardteistiméireacht agus dhá dtrian díobh siúd a fhágann gan cáilíochtaí ar bith.[3]

Gach uile bhliain in Éirinn ó thosaigh taifid oifigiúla in 1864, rugtar beagán níos mó de bhuachaillí ná cailíní, agus mar thoradh air seo, faoi láthair, mar shampla, tá thart ar 1,800 níos mó de bhuachaillí 17 mbliana d'aois ná de chailíní 17 mbliana d'aois. Tá difir cosúil leis seo ann idir dhaoine 16 bliana d'aois, 15 bliana d'aois srl.[4] D'ainneoin an chúlra déimeagrafaigh seo, le deich mbliana anuas tá líon na gcailíní atá ina n-iarrthóirí don Ardteistiméireacht gach uile bhliain níos mó ná líon na mbuachaillí de bhreis agus 2,400 go 3,300. Agus comparáid á dhéanamh againn idir líon na n-iarrthóirí Ardteistiméireachta scoil-bhunaithe leis an daonra ag aois 17 go 18 mbliana feicimid nár shuigh thart ar 6,900 buachaillí an Ardteistiméireacht sa bhliain 2005, i gcomparáid le thart ar 3,000 cailíní. Sa bhliain chéanna, bhí thart ar 1,350 buachaillí nach ndearna an Teastas Sóisearach, i gcomparáid le thart ar 350 cailíní.[5]

Glacadh ábhair in oideachas dara leibhéal

Tá an-chuid den díospóireacht ar chúrsaí inscne in oideachas na hÉireann dírithe ar ghlacadh ábhair ag an dara leibhéal agus ina dhiaidh sin. Léiríonn an forbhreathnú ar phatrúin ghlacadh ábhair atá ar fáil i Sé Sí go bhfuil difríochtaí suntasacha inscne ann, a d'fhan gan athrú thar am, a bheag nó a mhór. Ón dara leibhéal luath ar aghaidh, cloíonn daltaí go dlúth le steiréitíopaí traidisiúnta inscne sna hábhair a ndéanann siad staidéar orthu. Tá i bhfad níos mó buachaillí ná cailíní a ghlacann na "hábhair phraiticiúla," innealtóireacht, líníocht theicniúil agus staidéir foirgníochta mar shampla, agus i bhfad níos mó cailíní ná buachaillí in eacnamaíocht bhaile, ceol, ealaíon agus teangacha Eorpacha.

Go ginearálta, tá cosúlachtaí suntasacha idir na patrúin ghlacadh ábhair in oideachas dara leibhéal luath agus glacadh ábhair de réir inscne i mbreisoideachas agus ardoideachas. Is deacair a rá an é go léiríonn sé seo claonadh dúchasach i dtreo réimsí éagsúla d'ábhar nó go léiríonn sé na haisfhuaimnithe fadtéarmacha de ghlacadh ábhair ag tús an oideachais dara leibhéal. Faraor, mar thoradh ar bhrú ama, ní dhéantar an réimse de chúrsaí suimiúla a bhaineann le soláthar na n-ábhar i scoileanna dara leibhéal a chíoradh sa tuarascáil seo.

---

3 Féach figiúirí agus táblaí 2.11b, 2.12, 2.13, agus 2.14.

4 Príomh Oifig Staidrimh, *Census 2002: Principal Demographic Results (2003)*, tábla 10, lch. 56. Thangthas ar an bhfigiúr 1,800 tré shlánú a dhéanamh ar an mheándifir i líon na mbuachaillí agus cailíní idir 15 agus 17 mbliana d'aois.

5 Is iad na foinsí dos na meastacháin seo ná an Phríomh Oifig Staidrimh, *Census 2002: Principal Demographic Results (2003)*, tábla 10, lch. 56, agus an Roinn Oideachais agus Eolaíochta, *Annual Statistical Report, 2004/05* (le foilsiú), tábla 5.1. Díorthaíodh na meastacháin tré chomparáid a dhéanamh idir líon na n-iarrthóirí scoilbhunaithe sna scrúduithe don Teastas Sóisearach agus Ardteistiméireacht (ath-iarrthóirí as an áireamh) leis na cohóirt aoise cuí i ndaonáireamh 2002 (lúide 3 bliana). I dtéarmaí cheatádáin, bhí thart ar 22 faoin gcéad de bhuachaillí nár shuígh scrúdú na hArdteistiméireachta, i gcomparáid le 10 faoin gcéad de chailíní, agus níor shuígh 4.6 faoin gcéad de bhuachaillí scrúdú an Teastais Sóisearaigh, i gcomparáid le 1.3 faoin gcéad de chailíní.

Sa mheasúnú de ghlacadh ábhair de réir inscne in oideachas na hÉireann, is fiú a mheabhrú go bhfuil thart ar 36 faoin gcéad de dhaltaí dara leibhéal in Éirinn sa lá atá inniu ann ag freastal ar scoileanna aonghnéis. I dtromlach na dtíortha Eorpacha níl aon scoileanna aonghnéis ann, agus sna tíortha eile níl ach mionlach an-bheag de dhaltaí ag freastal ar oideachas aonghnéis. Faraor, níl sonraí atá inchomparáide go hidirnáisiúnta ar dhifríochtaí inscne i nglacadh ábhair ag an dara leibhéal ar fáil go fóill. Bheadh sé an-suimiúil sonraí idirnáisiúnta a fhorbairt sa réimse seo toisc go bhfuil sainiúlacht ag Éirinn i measc na dtíortha Eorpacha, ó tharla go bhfuil céatadán chomh mór sin de scoileanna aonghnéis inti.

Na heolaíochtaí

Thaispeáin an díospóireacht phoiblí ar inscne in oideachas le blianta beaga anuas go bhfuil suim ar leith sa ghlacadh ábhair sna hábhair eolaíochta agus innealtóireachta. Laistigh den churaclam dara leibhéal, múintear agus meastar eolaíocht mar ábhar aontaithe ag an dara leibhéal íochtarach sula dtairgtear cúrsaí ar leith i mbitheolaíocht, fisic agus ceimic do dhaltaí ag tosú sa dara leibhéal uachtarach. Is í an bhitheolaíocht is mó i bhfad a ghlactar mar ábhar eolaíochta san Ardteistiméireacht, agus is iad cailíní is mó a ghlacann í, dhá oiread na mbuachaillí (68 faoin gcéad in aghaidh 32 faoin gcéad). Tá níos mó cailíní ná buachaillí ina n-iarrthóirí do scrúdú na Ardteistiméireachta sa cheimic freisin, (54 faoin gcéad in aghaidh 46 faoin gcéad). Os a choinne sin, iad buachaillí is mó a ghlacann fisic, trí oiread líon na gcailíní (75 faoin gcéad in aghaidh 25 faoin gcéad).

Agus na hábhair eolaíochta san Ardteistiméireacht ar fad á nglacadh le chéile, tá an coibhneas inscne i bhfábhar na gcailíní (55 faoin gcéad cailíní, 45 faoin gcéad buachaillí). Malartú is ea é seo ar an gcoibhneas a fheictear in eolaíocht sa Teastas Sóisearach, áit a bhfuil níos mó buachaillí na cailíní (53 faoin gcéad in aghaidh 47 faoin gcéad). Mar sin féin, d'ainneoin an choibhnis iomláin i bhfábhar na gcailíní sna heolaíochtaí ag an dara leibhéal uachtarach, tá imní láidir sa phobal maidir le glacadh an-íseal san fhisic i measc chailíní. Creidtear gur ghné amháin is ea í seo a chuireann le glacadh íseal ar an innealtóireacht ina dhiaidh sin i measc na mban in ardoideachas. Tá sé suimiúil gurb í an fhisic an t-ábhar is mó ina n-éiríonn le cailíní níos fearr ná buachaillí i scrúduithe Ardteistiméireachta le tamall anuas.

Bunmhatamaitic "do chailíní amháin"

Tá scéal na matamaitice a thagann ón anailís a deineadh do Sé Sí thar a bheith suimiúil. Go traidisiúnta bhí matamaitic mar ábhar inar éirigh níos fearr le buachaillí ná le cailíní i dtéarmaí choibhneasa na ndaltaí ag fáil onóracha ardleibhéal i scrúduithe dara leibhéal. Mar sin féin, éiríonn anailís na feidhmíochta sa mhatamaitic thar am casta mar thoradh ar stair na héagóra i soláthar na matamaitice ag ardleibhéal do chailíní. Sa bhliain 1932 (nuair nár fhan ach codán beag den daonra ar scoil go dtí an Ardteistiméireacht), roghnaigh 21 faoin gcéad d'iarrthóirí fireann an páipéar matamaitice ag an ardleibhéal, i gcomparáid le 3 faoin gcéad de chailíní. Bhí coibhneas na n-iarrthóirí baineann Ardteistiméireachta a ghlac an páipéar ardleibhéal an-íseal go deo i lár na fichiú haoise, ag titim faoi bhun 2 faoin gcéad idir na 1940í lár agus na 1960í lár. Mar shampla, i scrúdú matamaitice na bliana 1952 ghlac níos lú ná 1 faoin gcéad de chailíní an páipéar ardleibhéal, i gcomparáid le 26 faoin gcéad de bhuachaillí.

I dTuairiscí Bliantúla Staitisticí idir na 1930í agus 1968, cuireadh "uimhríocht–cailíní amháin" agus ina dhiaidh sin "bunmhatamaitic (do chailíní amháin)" ar thaifead mar ábhair Meánteistiméireachta ar leith, scartha ón mhatamaitic ardleibhéal. Tá sé le tuiscint go soiléir ó thuairiscí staitisticiúla na linne sin go raibh bunmhatamaitic ann do chailíní, nach raibh oiriúnach do mhatamaitic ag an ardleibhéal, glacadh leis. Do thromlach na ndaltaí baineann sa timthriall sóisearach agus sinsearach ag an am sin, ní raibh matamaitic ardleibhéal ann mar rogha a tugadh dóibh ar chor ar bith ar scoil.

Nuair a chuirtear líon na n-iarrthóirí baineann Ardteistiméireachta sa mhatamaitic i gcomparáid le líon na n-iarrthóirí ag dul faoin scrúdú Béarla, is léir go bhfuil mionlach suntasach de chailíní (thart ar 15–20 faoin gcéad) nár ghlac páipéar matamaitice ar bith i scrúdú na hArdteistiméireachta idir na 1930í luatha agus na 1970í lár. De na cailíní a rinne páipéar matamaitice, bhí fíorbheagán a rinne an páipéar ardleibhéal. Lean an éagothroime seo sna coibhneasa a ghlacann matamaitic ardleibhéal thar am.

I 1991 fós bhí sé a dhá oiread níos dóchaí do bhuachaillí ná do chailíní an páipéar ardleibhéal a ghlacadh (16.1 faoin gcéad i gcoinne 8.2 faoin gcéad). Mar sin féin, d'éirigh le cailíní an bhearna in fheidhmíocht a mhaolú go suntasach tré líon i bhfad níos mó a bheith ag glacadh matamaitice ag an ardleibhéal le blianta beaga anuas. Is fiú a mheabhrú, i measc na ndaoine a ghlacann páipéir ardleibhéal, gur sháraigh cailíní feidhmíocht na mbuachaillí go rialta ó 1996 i leith. Mar sin féin, toisc go bhfuil níos mó buachaillí ag glacadh an pháipéir ardleibhéal go fóill, leanann coibhneas iomlán na mbuachaillí a fhaigheann onóracha sa mhatamaitic ardleibhéal de bheith níos airde ná coibhneas coibhéiseach na gcailíní.

Ag an dara leibhéal íochtarach, tá níos mó onóracha ardleibhéal sa mhatamaitic faighte ag cailíní ó 1993 i leith. Tá níos mó dóchúlachta ann anois go nglacfaidh cailíní scrúdú an Teastais Shóisearaigh ag an ardleibhéal, agus tá níos mó dóchúlachta ann go bhfaighidh siad onóracha ná a macasamhla fireann. Cé go bhfuil na difríochtaí inscne i bhfeidhmíocht matamaitice beag i gcomparáid le réimsí ábhair eile, tá sé suimiúil go bhfeidhmíonn buachaillí Éireannacha níos fearr ná cailíní sna measúnuithe PISA (de dhaoine 15 bliana d'aois) agus níos measa ná cailíní i scrúdú matamaitice an Teastais Shóisearaigh. D'fhéadfadh go dtarlaíonn na difríochtaí seo idir mheasúnuithe náisiúnta agus idirnáisiúnta mar thoradh ar an mbéim láidir atá ar chur chuige a bhaineann leis an bhfíor-shaol i PISA, i gcomparáid, ar bhealach, le béim na hÉireann ar mhodhanna, coincheapa teibí agus cruthúnais.

Mar achoimre, tá feidhmíocht níos fearr ag buachaillí ná cailíní go rialta i matamaitic na hArdteistiméireachta ó na 1930í luatha agus roimh sin i leith. Mar sin féin, bhog cailíní beagán chun tosaigh ar bhuachaillí i matamaitic an Teastais Shóisearaigh ó na luath-1990í ar aghaidh agus d'éirigh leo an bhearna i bhfeidhmíocht na hArdteistiméireachta a laghdú go suntasach le blianta beaga anuas. Maidir le feidhmíocht na gcailíní a ghlacann matamaitic ardleibhéal don Ardteistiméireacht, atá go han-mhaith go ginearálta, tugtar le fios go gcuirfeadh méaduithe breise ar líon na cailíní a roghnaíonn an mhatamaitic ardleibhéal le 'caipiteal matamaitice' na tíre. Braitheann an-chuid ar ár gcumas chun feidhmiú ar an stáitse idirnáisiúnta sa mhatamaitic, sna heolaíochtaí, agus, go háirithe, in airgtheacht. Léirítear ríthábhacht na ndisciplíní seo d'ár straitéis náisiúnta eacnamaíochta sa Strategy for Science, Technology and Innovation (2006) agus sa Phlean Forbartha Náisiúnta.

Feidhmíocht i scrúduithe stáit ag an dara leibhéal

Caitheadh tromlach an ama d'ullmhúchán Sé Sí ar anailís na feidhmíochta i scrúduithe stáit. Tugann Caibidlí 3 agus 5 anailís mhionsonraithe ar scrúduithe an Teastais Shóisearaigh agus na hArdteistiméireachta maidir le feidhmíocht iomlán thar am. Toisc gur iondúil do dhaoine le suim ghinearálta san oideachas "grá" speisialta a bheith acu d'ábhar nó dhó ar leith, críochnaíonn na caibidlí seo le forbhreathnú ar fheidhmíocht de réir ábhair idir 1992 agus 2002.

Ó thaobh na staitisticí de, tugann na sonraí riaracháin a ghineann scrúdú an Teastais Shóisearaigh an anailís is cirte ar fheidhmíocht de réir inscne. Tá staitisticí, mar dhisciplín, bunaithe ar ghrúpaí samplacha a úsáid le heolas a ríomh faoi dhaonra níos iomláine inspéise. Díríonn cuid mhór den díospóireacht a leanann sa litríocht shóisialta agus eolaíochta ar an gcaoi ina bhfuil difríochtaí a fheictear sa taighde ar ghrúpaí samplacha ina léiriú ar fhíordhifríochtaí sa daonra níos iomláine inspéise. Tá sé de bhuntáiste ag torthaí an Teastais Shóisearaigh go dtugann siad sonraí ar an daonra inspéise ar fad, beagnach. Agus idir 95 agus 97 faoin gcéad de dhéagóirí Éireannacha ag glacadh scrúdú an Teastais Shóisearaigh gach uile bhliain, tugann na torthaí léargas ar chroí an scéil maidir le feidhmíocht scrúdaithe de réir inscne. Léiríonn difríochtaí a fheictear i bhfeidhmíocht sa Teastas Sóisearach fíordhifríochtaí inscne, atá dúchasach, b'fhéidir, sna scileanna agus intleachtaí atá á measúnú againn. Freisin tá sé de bhuntáiste ag an Ardteistiméireacht go gclúdaítear cuid mhór den daonra agus tugtar léargas breise ar fheidhmíocht i scrúduithe sna déaga déanacha.

Taispeánann an anailís ar fheidhmíocht thar am sna scrúduithe Teastais Shóisearaigh agus Ardteistiméireachta araon go bhfuil feidhmíocht níos fearr ag cailíní ná ag buachaillí go rialta sna scrúduithe. Ní eisceacht í Éire ar chor ar bith sa chomhthéacs seo, agus mar a tharlaíonn sé tugann na sonraí atá ar fáil le fios go bhfuil na difríochtaí inscne anseo réasúnta measartha. Mar sin féin, tá bearna na hinscne san fheidhmíocht i scrúduithe an Teastais Shóisearaigh agus na hArdteistiméireachta suntasach, agus léiríonn an anailís amshraithe gur leathan sé go rialta le blianta beaga anuas.

Feidhmíonn cailíní níos fearr ná buachaillí i mbreis agus 80 faoin gcéad d'ábhair Ardteistiméireachta; agus go comhthitimeach, in 80 faoin gcéad d'ábhair tá an difríocht i bhfábhar chailíní méadaithe ó na luath-1990í i leith. Tá difríochtaí inscne an-suntasacha ann i bhfábhar chailíní i réimse leathan d'ábhair, lena n-áirítear Béarla, Gaeilge, fisic, ceimic, ealaíon agus nuatheangacha Eorpacha. Áirítear innealtóireacht agus staidéir foirgníochta i measc an fhíorbheagáin ábhar Ardteistiméireachta ina mbíonn feidhmíocht níos fearr ag buachaillí ná ag cailíní go fóill. Ag tús na deich mbliana seo freisin bhí feidhmíocht beagán níos fearr ag buachaillí ná ag cailíní sa mhatamaitic agus sa chuntasaíocht. Ach faoi 2005 bhí feidhmíocht níos fearr ag cailíní ná ag buachaillí sa chuntasaíocht agus bhí an difríocht i bhfábhar na mbuachaillí sa mhatamaitic laghdaithe go 1.5 pointe céatadáin. Má leanann na treonna atá tugtha faoi deara leis na deicheanna de bhlianta anuas, beidh cailíní chun tosaigh ar bhuachaillí i matamaitic na hArdteistiméireachta go han-luath.

Ón anailís stairiúil shínte ar fheidhmíocht sa Ghaeilge agus sa Bhéarla, is léir nach bhfuil aon rud ró-nua ag baint le cailíní ag feidhmiú níos fearr ná buachaillí. Sa Ghaeilge, tá feidhmíocht níos fearr ag cailíní ná ag buachaillí go rialta ó lár na 1930í, agus sa Bhéarla tá feidhmíocht níos fearr acu ó na luath-1960í agus bhí feidhmíocht níos fearr acu ná ag buachaillí go minic i mblianta níos luaithe. Mar sin féin, tá fairsinge na ndifríochtaí inscne a chonacthas sna hábhair seo ó lár na 1990í i leith gan fasach. Cé go raibh difríochtaí thart ar 4 go 5 faoin gcéad sa Bhéarla agus 8 go 9 faoin gcéad sa Ghaeilge coitianta idir na 1930í agus na 1980í, shroich na difríochtaí i bhfábhar chailíní 14 faoin gcéad i mBéarla agus Gaeilge araon sa bhliain 2002. Nuair a scrúdaímid treonna i bhfeidhmíocht Ardteistiméireachta ar an iomlán feicimid gur leathnaigh an bhearna inscne i bhfábhar chailíní ó 4.1 pointe céatadáin sa bhliain 1990 go 9.0 pointe céatadáin sa bhliain 2002.[6] Bhí an bhearna seo ag 10.4 pointe céatadáin in Ardteistiméireacht na bliana 2005.

Ardoideachas

Ó tharla go bhfuil feidhmíocht níos airde ag cailíní i scrúdú na hArdteistiméireachta, ní haon iontas é go bhfuil níos mó ban ná fir in ardoideachas. Le fírinne, ó tharla go raibh feidhmíocht níos airde san Ardteistiméireacht go rialta ag cailíní le deicheanna de bhlianta anuas, is é an rud is iontaí ná nár thosaigh líon na mban ag sárú líon na bhfear san ardoideachas go dtí lár na 1990í. Ag féachaint ar an gcoibhneas inscne i measc na mac léinn lánaimseartha ar fad in ardoideachas feicimid go raibh líon na bhfear níos airde ná líon na mban idir 1980 agus 1994/95. Thar na mblianta ina dhiaidh sin tá ráta rannpháirtíochta na mban ardaithe ag luas i bhfad níos tapúla ná ráta rannpháirtíochta i measc na bhfear, agus tá bearna inscne i bhfábhar na mban tagtha anois. Sa bhliain 2002/03 ba é an coibhneas i measc na mac léinn lánaimseartha ná 46 faoin gcéad fireann in aghaidh 54 faoin gcéad baineann. Tá an méadú sa rannpháirtíocht bhaineann ag an tríú leibhéal an-suntasach go deo in earnáil na n-ollscoileanna, áit a raibh 12,500 níos mó de mhná i measc na mac léinn lánaimseartha sa bhliain 2003 (42 faoin gcéad fireann in aghaidh 58 faoin gcéad baineann).

Léiríonn comparáid de chéimithe sa bhliain 1993 leis an mbliain 2003 athruithe suntasacha sa chomhdhéanamh inscne san ardoideachas thar na 1990í. I measc chéimithe na bliana 2003, bhí níos mó de mhná ná d'fhir ag gach leibhéal de cháilíocht, ó theastas agus dioplóma go leibhéal PhD. Méadaíonn coibhneas na mban de réir mar a ardaíonn leibhéal na cáilíochta trí leibhéil NQAI 6 go 9 (teastais go céimeanna máistreachta). Mar sin féin, ní raibh na difríochtaí chomh suntasach sin ag leibhéal 10 (leibhéal PhD), áit a bhfuil líon cothrom de chéimithe fireann agus baineann, a bheag nó a mhór, sa bhliain 2003.

Chomh maith leis an anailís ar rannpháirtíocht, tugann caibidil 7 forbhreathnú ar fheidhmíocht scrúdaithe chéimithe ollscoile sa bhliain 2004. Go ginearálta, is cosúil go bhfuil feidhmíocht na bhfear agus na mban in ollscoileanna na hÉireann cothrom, a bheag nó a mhór, agus ní fheictear na héagsúlachtaí nochta a chonacthas i scrúduithe stáit ag an dara leibhéal i measc chéimithe ollscoile. Ag leibhéal na bhfochéimithe, bronnadh níos mó céimeanna céad onóracha ar fhir. Ach tá feidhmíocht na mban ar an iomlán níos fearr i dtéarmaí céimeanna onóracha a bhaint amach, agus léirítear é seo sna réimsí staidéir uilig ag leibhéal na bunchéime. Ag leibhéal na hiarchéime, áit a raibh 3,943 céimí fireann agus 6,416 céimí baineann sa bhliain 2004, bhí fir beagán chun tosaigh ar mhná i bhfeidhmíocht scrúdaithe.

[6] Féach figiúr agus tábla 5.10.

Athraíonn an cothromas inscne i measc chéimithe ardoideachais go mór idir na réimse éagsúla staidéir, le mná sa bhreis ar na fir i 70 faoin gcéad de na disciplíní éagsúla. Is iad na réimsí ina bhfuil na mná sa bhreis ar na fir don mhéid is mó ná na heolaíochtaí sóisialta, eolaíochtaí sláinte, agus oiliúint mhúinteoirí. Is iad an dá chatagóir is mó de chéimithe sa réimse ginearálta staidéir ar a dtugtar na heolaíochtaí sláinte nó sláinte agus leas ná altranas (92 faoin gcéad baineann) agus leigheas (58 faoin gcéad baineann).[7] Freisin is tromlach iad na mná de chéimithe i réimse leathan de achair eile, lena n-áirítear tréidliacht, ealaíona agus daonnachtaí, gnó, dlí, na heolaíochtaí beatha, agus na heolaíochtaí fisiciúla. Ach amháin sna heolaíochtaí fisiciúla, mhéadaigh an bhearna i bhfábhar na mban idir 1993 agus 2003 sna disciplíní seo ar fad. Bhí na fir de bhreis ar na mná don mhéid is mó i measc chéimithe innealtóireachta agus ailtireachta agus freisin sa mhatamaitic, ríomhaireacht agus talmhaíocht.

Tá na hathruithe suntasacha seo i bpatrúin bhaint amach céime ardoideachais le sonrú cheana i staitisticí dhaonra na Príomh Oifige Staidrimh, áit ar mhéadaigh próifíl oideachais ban ag luas níos tapúla ná luas na bhfear le blianta beaga anuas. Faoi 2005, bhí cáilíocht ardoideachais ag 44 faoin gcéad de mhná idir 25 agus 34 bliana d'aois, i gcomparáid le 35 faoin gcéad d'fhir.[8] Agus machnamh á dhéanamh ar threonna atá ag fás i gclárú agus i mbaint amach céime, tá sé beagnach cinnte go leanfaidh an bhearna inscne i bhfeidhmíocht ardoideachais in Éirinn sna blianta beaga atá romhainn ar a laghad.

Breisoideachas

Bunphrionsabal de pholasaí oideachais AE is ea foghlaim ar feadh an tsaoil ó bhí an t-uachtaránacht ag Éire sa bhliain 1996. Mar sin féin tá éagsúlacht shuntasach ann sa chaoi inar éirigh le ballstáit rannpháirtíocht i bhfoghlaim ar feadh an tsaoil a bhaint amach. Tá na rátaí rannpháirtíochta is airde bainte amach ag na tíortha Lochlannacha, agus sa tSualainn meastar go raibh níos mó ná trian de na haosaigh uilig páirteach in oideachas nó oiliúint sa bhliain 2004. Tá leibhéil réasúnta ard bainte amach freisin ag an mBreatain, an tSlóivéin, an Ísiltír agus, do leibhéal níos lú, an Ostair, i rannpháirtíocht i bhfoghlaim ar feadh an tsaoil. Sna ballstáit AE eile ar fad bhí ráta rannpháirtíochta i bhfoghlaim ar feadh an tsaoil faoi bhun 10 faoin gcéad i 2004. Bhí ráta rannpháirtíochta de 7.2 faoin gcéad i measc aosaigh na hÉireann, a bhí faoi mheán an AE, 9.9 faoin gcéad.[9]

Toisc go bhfuil raon an-leathan agus an-éagsúil de ghníomhaíochtaí foghlama iar-dara leibhéal agus easpa sonraí riaracháin sa réimse seo, bhí sé deacair achoimre a sholáthar ar bhreisoideachas agus oiliúint in Éirinn. Tá líon i bhfad níos mó de mhná ná d'fhir i gcúrsaí iar-Ardteistiméireachta agus sa réimse iomlán de chúrsaí eile breisoideachais agus aosoideachais a chuirtear ar fáil tríd an Roinn Oideachais agus Eolaíochta (agus na Coistí Gairmoideachais). Ach tugann na gradaim FETAC pictiúr níos cothroime ó thaobh inscne de d'oideachas agus oiliúint dearbhaithe, toisc go gcuimsíonn siad freisin oiliúint eagraithe ag gníomhaireachtaí eile, ar nós FÁS agus Teagasc. Laistigh de raon iomlán de ghradaim FETAC sa bhliain 2005 bhí coibhneas inscne de 53 faoin gcéad baineann i aghaidh 47 faoin gcéad fireann ann.

---

[7] Díorthaítear comhréirí na mban a thuariscítear anseo idir lúibíní ó shonraí curtha ar fáil ag Rannóg na Staitisticí san ÚAO ar chéimithe na bliana 2006.

[8] Féach figiúr agus tábla 7.19.

[9] Féach figiúr agus tábla 9.10.

Tá difríochtaí soiléire inscne ann i nglacadh chúrsaí, agus ag leibhéal ginearálta bíonn na cineálacha de cháilíocht bhreisoideachais a leantar ag teacht go dlúth leis na steiréitíopaí inscne clasaiceacha. Tá sé seo fíor ach go háirithe d'fhir, a choinníonn a rannpháirtíocht sa bhreisoideachas, a bheag nó a mhór, d'oiliúint atá gairmiúil agus, go háirithe, dírithe ar fhoirgníocht. Bíonn printíseacht, sainoiliúint scileanna agus cúrsaí oiliúna talmhaíochta ag Teagasc fireann go hiomlán, beagnach. Is gnách go mhná páirt níos leithne a ghlacadh sa bhreisoideachas, ó oiliúint sa ghnó, scileanna oifige agus cúram go healaíona, ceird agus cúrsaí san oideachas leantach.

Maidir le foghlaim ar feadh an tsaoil, léiríonn mná Éireannacha fonn níos mó agus níos buaine d'oideachas ná fir thar timthriall an tsaoil. Léirítear é seo go maith ina leibhéil níos airde rannpháirtíochta i gcúrsaí bhreisoideachais agus aosoideachais. Tá díograis níos mó na mban don oideachas soiléir freisin sa ról lárnach atá acu ag an leibhéal áitiúil i dtionscnamh na hoibre oideachais pobail i bpobail atá faoi mhíbhuntáiste ó na 1980í i leith.

Ina choinne sin, is cosúil go laghdaíonn rannpháirtíocht na bhfear in oideachas agus oiliúint thar timthriall an tsaoil. Nuair a scrúdaítear é i gcomhthéacs an tsaoil, tá sé tábhachtach a mheabhrú gur cúrsaí iarscoile de ghnáth iad na cláracha bhreisoideachais ina bhfuil na fir chun tosaigh a d'fhéadfaí a rannú mar chríoch le hoideachas agus oiliúint tosaigh murab ionainn agus oideachas leantach nó aosoideachas. Tá tromlach na bprintíseach sna déaga déanacha nó sna luath-fichidí, agus tá tromlach na ndaoine atá páirteach i sainoiliúint scileanna faoi bhun fiche cúig bliana d'aois.

Críochnú rathúil is ea an príomhábhar eile is mó a bhíonn idir lámha d'fhir in Oideachas na hÉireann. Tá sé seo taifeadta go maith ag an dara leibhéal, ach anois leanann thart ar 25 faoin gcéad d'fhir óga in Éirinn breisoideachas agus oiliúint tré chlárú i gcúrsaí printíseachta.[10] Tugann comparáid thapa díobh siúd ag tosú agus ag críochnú printíseachtaí go dtiteann breis agus 40 faoin gcéad d'oiliúnaithe amach sula gcríochnaíonn siad go rathúil. Ar an bhfianaise seo, is cosúil go bhfuil fadhb thromchúiseach ann le coinneáil d'fhir i mbreisoideachas chomh maith leis an oideachas dara leibhéal. San ardoideachas freisin tá dóchúlacht níos mó d'fhir ná do mhná nach n-éireoidh leo a gcúrsa staidéir a chríochnú. Is é seo is cúis le staid aisteach ag leibhéil na dteastas agus dioplóma, nuair atá fir chun tosaigh ar na mná i líon na gclárúchán ach ní i measc na gcéimithe.

Pearsanra oideachais

I gcaibidil 8 gluaiseann fócas na hainilíse ó mhic léinn agus foghlaimeoirí go scrúdú ar an bpearsanra atá freagrach as soláthar agus riarachán an oideachais in Éirinn. Tá a fhios go forleathan go bhfuil i bhfad níos mó ban ná fir i measc bhunmhúinteoirí sa lá atá inniu ann. Taispeánann an anailís amshraithe a chuirtear i láthair i Sé Sí go raibh líon níos mó de mhná ann go rialta le seachtó bliain anuas ar a laghad. Mhéadaigh coibhneas na mbunmhúinteoirí baineann ó 58 faoin gcéad i 1930 go 83 faoin gcéad sa bhliain 2005. Cé gur mhéadaigh líon iomlán na múinteoirí ag bunleibhéal faoi dhó sna blianta sin, níor athraigh líon na mbunmhúinteoirí fireann mórán thar am.

10 Seán McDonagh agus Vivienne Patterson, *The Institutes of Technology and Future Skills (2006)*.

Tá coibhneas inscne na múinteoirí dara leibhéal anois ag druidim i dtreo 60-40 i bhfábhar na mban. San ardoideachas, mná ab ea 32 faoin gcéad d'fhoireann acadúil in institiúidí teicneolaíochta agus 40 faoin gcéad d'fhoireann acadúil in ollscoileanna faoi 2003. In Éirinn agus i dtíortha eile ECFE tá patrún suntasach ina dtiteann coibhneas na mban de réir mar ghluaistear ó bhunoideachas go hoideachas dara leibhéal agus ar aghaidh go hardoideachas. Go hidirnáisiúnta, mná is ea 82 faoin gcéad de phearsanra múinteoireachta ag bunleibhéal, 60 faoin gcéad ag an dara leibhéal, agus 36 faoin gcéad ag an tríú leibhéal. Tá na coibhneasa in Éirinn iontach cosúil leis na meáin idirnáisiúnta seo ag gach ceann de na trí leibhéil.

Is léir go bhfuil ceisteanna ann maidir le hionadaíocht ban i bpoist shinsearachta i bhforais oideachais. Tá sé seo soiléir ag bunleibhéal agus an dara leibhéal, áit a bhfuil gannionadaíocht thromchúiseach ag mná ag leibhéal an phríomhoide scoile. Mná is ea 83 faoin gcéad den fhoireann uilig ag bunleibhéal ach díreach 53 faoin gcéad de phríomhoidí scoile. Ag an dara leibhéal, áit ar mhná iad 60 faoin gcéad den fhoireann uilig, tá dhá oiread d'fhir ina bpríomhoidí scoile.

D'ainneoin an mhéadaithe mhóir i bhfoireann acadúil bhaineann le deich mbliana anuas, faightear na difríochtaí inscne is suntasaí i bhforais ardoideachais. In ollscoileanna faoi láthair tá níos mó ban ná fir ag na leibhéil acadúla ísle de léachtóir cúnta agus foireann mhúinteoireachta "eile". De réir mar a théimid in airde trén ordlathas acadúil laghdaíonn coibhneas na mban go tréan. Sna hinstitiúidí teicneolaíochta agus sna hollscoileanna tá patrún soiléir le feiceáil ina mhéadaíonn coibhneas na bhfear le sinsearacht an phoist acadúil.

Is ag na leibhéil is airde, ollamh agus ollamh comhlach, is géire atá gannionadaíocht na mban i measc na foirne acadúla ollscoile. I 2003/04 bhí 8 faoin gcéad de phoist ollaimh agus 12 faoin gcéad de phoist ollaimh comhlaigh ag mná. Tá patrúin éagothroime den chineál céanna le fáil ag na leibhéil is airde d'fhoireann acadúil sna hinstitiúidí teicneolaíochta. Ach tá thart ar dhá oiread de líon na mban ag na leibhéil acadúla is sinsearaí sna hinstitiúidí teicneolaíochta agus atá sna hollscoileanna; mar sin tá fairsinge na héagothroime inscne i measc an luchta acadúla níos géire in earnáil na n-ollscoileanna.

Léargas cosúil leis sin, a bheag nó a mhór, a thagann ón anailís ar phearsanra riaracháin. Cé gur mhná iad dhá dtrian den fhoireann ar fad sa státsheirbhís, tá ró-ionadaíocht acu ag na leibhéil ísle agus gannionadaíocht thromchúiseach ag an dtaobh is airde de speictream na sinsearachta. Le fírinne, laghdaíonn coibhneas na mban go tréan de réir mar a ardaíonn sinsearacht an ghráid. Taispeánann an t-amharcléiriú ar inscne de réir an ghráid sa státsheirbhís an rud a d'fhéadfaí staighre clasaiceach na héagothroime inscne a thabhairt air. Mná is ea 80 faoin gcéad de bhaill na foirne ag leibhéil na n-oifigeach cléireachais agus n-oifigeach foirne agus beagnach dhá dtrian ag grád an oifigigh feidhmiúcháin. Cé gur mhná iad breis agus leath de na hoifigigh riaracháin ar fad, mná is ea níos lú ná leath de na hardoifigigh feidhmiúcháin, trian de phríomhoifigigh cúnta, cúigiú de phríomhoifigigh, deichiú d'ard-rúnaithe cúnta agus sciar níos lú fós de phoist mar ard-rúnaithe.

Cé go raibh na patrúin éagothroime inscne ar an iomlán sa Roinn Oideachais agus Eolaíochta cosúil leo sin, mná is ea codán níos mó de bhaill na foirne ag leibhéal an ardoifigigh feidhmiúcháin agus leibhéal an phríomhoifigigh sa roinn seo ná mar a bheadh sa státsheirbhís go ginearálta. Ag féachaint siar ar na deich mbliana a chuaigh thart feicimid méaduithe seasta agus substaintiúil ar choibhneasa na mban sna grádanna meáin go hard sa roinn. Mar sin féin, fanann coibhneas na mban i bpoist shinsearachta íseal, agus leantar de ghannionadaíocht na mban ag na leibhéil is airde i gcoibhneas lena n-uimhreacha san iomlán. Críochnaíonn caibidil 8 le forbhreathnú ar choibhneasa inscne na mball foirne agus comhaltaí na mbord i gcnuasach de ghníomhaireachtaí tábhachtacha oideachais.

Mar chríoch

Tá sonraí i Sé Sí ar riachtanais speisialta oideachais, áit a bhfuil a dhá oiread de bhuachaillí, agus ar réimse de nithe eile lena n-áirítear rannpháirtíocht i gcláracha laistigh den churaclam dara leibhéal agus feidhmíocht na mac léinn Éireannacha i measúnuithe litirtheachta idirnáisiúnta PISA. Taispeánann úsáid leathan na sonraí idirnáisiúnta ar fud na tuarascála gur ceisteanna iad difríochtaí inscne i rannpháirtíocht agus feidhmíocht oideachais a chuireann dúshlán ar na tíortha forbartha uilig, beagnach.

San anailís níos cuimsithí de na sonraí idirnáisúnta, tá inscne ar cheann de réimse de thréithe cúlracha a bhfuil an chuma orthu go mbíonn tionchar acu ar fheidhmíocht na ndaltaí sna measúnuithe litearthachta. Cé go bhfuil an chuma ar an scéal gur ghné shuntasach í inscne, ach go háirithe i bhfeidhmíocht dhaltaí i léitheoireacht, iad na gnéithe is tábhachtaí a théann i gcion ar fheidhmíocht ná stádas socheacnamaíochta agus tréithe teaghlaigh cúlracha na ndaltaí.

Ag bogadh thar tréithe an ndaltaí aonair go struchtúr agus eagrú chórais scoile, is iad na tíortha a bhaineann na caighdeáin is airde litearthachta amach de ghnáth ná na cinn ina bhfuil córais scoile gan mórán de roghnú agus deighilt ghníomhach, áit a nglacann scoileanna go réidh le hilchineálacht a bpobal áitiúil. Ceann de na tátail is suimiúla a tháinig as na measúnuithe leantacha PISA ná gur éirigh le an-chuid de na tíortha is airde feidhmíochta feidhmíocht ard ar an iomlán a cheangal go rathúil le leibhéil arda cothroime i dtorthaí oideachais. Os a choinne sin, is iad na tréithe atá ag córais oideachais ina bhfuil leibhéil arda éagothroime (go minic in éineacht le leibhéil ísle d'fheidhmíocht ar an iomlán) ná roghnú agus sruthú luath, srathú idir chineálacha scoileanna, agus carnadh de mhíbhuntáiste i scoileanna agus ceantair ar leith. Taispeánann na tátail ghinearálta seo nach bhfuil "cothroime agus feabhas comheisiatach in oideachas. I bhfírinne, is léir gur féidir leis an dá chuspóir pholasaí oideachais a bheith comhlántach go hiomlán."[11]

Le foilsiú na tuarascála seo, tá súil ag an Roinn Oideachais agus Eolaíochta cuidiú le díospóireacht phoiblí oilte agus le machnamh, plé agus tuilleadh taighde a spreagadh ar cheisteanna oideachais agus inscne.

---

[11] An Roinn Oideachais agus Eolaíochta, *Supporting Equity in Higher Education: A Report to the Minister for Education and Science*, 2003, p. 7–8.

Foclóirín

A

ability to perform	cumas feidhmithe
academic staff	foireann acadúil
accessible	inrochtana
adaptability	solúbthacht
administrative data	sonraí riaracháin
administrative personnel	foireann riaracháin
administrative sources	foinsí riaracháin
aggregated results	torthaí comhiomlána
agricultural science	eolaíocht thalmhaíochta
analysis	anailís
anomaly	aimhrialtacht
anti-poverty initiative	tionscnamh frithbhochtaineachta
applied mathematics	matamaitic fheidhmeach
apprenticeship	printíseacht
approximately	beagnach
area partnership	páirtíocht cheantair
arithmetic	uimhríocht
art, craft, and design	ealaín, ceird, agus dearadh
assessment	measúnacht
autism	uathachas
autonomous	neamhspleách
average	meán

B

background characteristics	tréithe cúlra
beauty therapy	teiripe scéimhe
breakdown	miondealú
business studies	staidéar gnó

C

candidates	iarrthóirí
capitation	ceannsraith
certification	deimhniú
certified further education and training programmes	cláir dheimhnithe breisoideachais agus oiliúna
challenges	dúshláin
chemistry	ceimic
civil service	státseirbhís
clear and objective	soiléir agus oibiachtúil
clustering of disadvantage	cnuasú míbhuntáiste
co-educational schools	scoileanna comhoideachais
cohort analysis	miondealú cohórt
community and comprehensive sector	earnáil phobail agus chuimsitheach
community education	oideachas pobail
community education facilitators	éascaitheoirí oideachais phobail

comparability	comparáideacht
compared to	i gcomparáid le
comprehensive	cuimsitheach
compulsory subjects	ábhair riachtanacha
computing	ríomhaireacht
considerable	suntasach
consistency	comhsheasmhacht
construction studies	staidéir tógála
contextualised	curtha i gcomhthéacs
contractor plant operation	oibriú gléasra conraitheora
core skills	croí-scileanna
core subjects	croí-ábhair
correlation	comhghaolmhaireacht
Council of Directors of Institutes of Technology	Comhairle Stiúrthóirí na nInstitiúidí Teicneolaíochta
counterparts	comhpháirtithe
cradle to grave	breith go bás
craftsperson	ceardaí
cross-curricular	traschuraclaim

D

data	sonraí
data-base	bunachar sonraí
data needs	riachtanais sonraí
data sources	foinsí sonraí
decade	deich mbliana
decreased	laghdaithe/íslithe
demographics	déimeagrafaic
dentistry	fiaclóireacht
designated trades	ceirdeanna sonraithe
disability groups	grúpaí míchumais
disadvantaged	faoi mhíbhuntáiste
disadvantaged areas	ceantair faoi mhíbhuntáiste
diversity	ilghnéitheacht
drop-out	éirí as
Dublin Institute of Technology	Institiúid Teicneolaíochta Bhaile Átha Cliath

E

economic competitiveness	iomaíochas eacnamaíochta
educational disadvantage	míbhuntáiste oideachais
educational institutions	forais oideachais / institiúidí oideachais
educational opportunities	deiseanna oideachais
educational profile	próifíl oideachais
Educational Research Centre	Lárionad Taighde Oideachais
elaboration strategies	straitéisí mionsaothraithe
electrical installation	insuiteáil leictreachais
elementary mathematics	bunmhatamaitic
emerging trends	treonna atá ag teacht chun cinn

empowering	cumhachtú
engineering	innealtóireacht
enrolment [action]	cur ar rolla
enrolment [total number]	líon ar rolla
enterprise and business skills	scileanna fiontair agus gnó
environmental and social studies	staidéir imshaoil agus shóisialta
equality	comhionannas
equity	cothromas
equivalent	coibhéis
Established Leaving Certificate	Ardteistiméireacht Bhunaithe
European languages	teangacha Eorpacha
European Union	Aontas Eorpach
evidence-informed policy	polasaí fianaise-bhunaithe
examination performance	feidhmíocht scrúdaithe
expansion	leathnú
ex-prisoners' groups	grúpaí iarphríosúnacha

F

factor	gné
farm management	bainisteoireacht feirme
flexible part-time learning opportunities	deiseanna solúbtha páirtaimseartha foghlama
full-time students	mic léinn lánaimseartha
further and continuing education	breisoideachas agus oideachas leantach
further education and training	breisoideachas agus oiliúint

G

gender	inscne
gender differences	difríochtaí inscne
gender gap	bearna inscne
gender ratios	coibhnis inscne
graduates	céimithe
graduation	bronnadh céimeanna

H

hard-to-reach groups	grúpaí atá doiligh a theagmháil
health-care support	tacaíocht chúram sláinte
hierarchy	ordlathas
higher education	ardoideachas
higher level	ardleibhéal
historical time-series analysis	anailís amshraithe stairiúil
home economics	eacnamaíocht bhaile
horticulture	gairneoireacht
humanities	daonnachtaí

I

implication	impleacht
improve	feabhsú
increased	méadaithe / ardaithe
index of control strategies	innéacs straitéisí smachta
indicator	táscaire
individualised student data-bases	bunachair shonraí aonánacha daltaí
inequity	míchothromas
information and communications technology	teicneolaíocht faisnéise agus cumarsáide
information processing	próiseáil eolais / próiseáil faisnéise
initiative	tionscnamh
innate	dúchasach
innate disposition	méin inbheirthe / méin dhúchasach
insight	léargas
institutes of technology	institiúidí teicneolaíochta
intelligences	intleachtaí
interdisciplinary	idirdhisciplíneach
international context	comhthéacs idirnáisiúnta
international data	sonraí idirnáisiúnta
interpersonal skills	scileanna idirphearsanta
inventiveness	airgtheacht

J

Junior Certificate	Teastas Sóisearach
junior cycle	timthriall sóisearach
juvenile liaison	idirchaidreamh don óige

K

key findings	príomhthátail
knowledge-based economy	geilleagar eolasbhunaithe

L

labour force	lucht saothair
law	dlí
learners	foghlaimeoirí
learning strategies	straitéisí foghlama
Leaving Certificate	Ardteistiméireacht
Leaving Certificate–Applied	Ardteistiméireacht Fheidhmeach
Leaving Certificate candidates	iarrthóirí Ardteistiméireachta
Leaving Certificate Vocational Programme	Gairmchlár na hArdteistiméireachta
life cycle	saolré
lifelong learning	foghlaim feadh saoil
life sciences	eolaíochtaí beatha
likelihood	dealraitheacht
link modules	nascmhodúil
literacy	litearthacht
literacy attainment	gnóthachtáil litearthachta
logistics	lóistíocht

long-term reverberations   aisfhuaimnithe fadtéarmacha
lower second level   dara leibhéal íochtarach
low take-up   glacadh íseal

M

marginalised   imeallaithe
masters' degrees   céimeanna máistir
materials technology   teicneolaíocht ábhar
materials technology (woodwork)   teicneolaíocht ábhar (adhmadóireacht)
mean [value]   meán
median   airmheán
member-state   ballstát
memorisation strategies   straitéisí glanmheabhraithe
metalwork   miotalóireacht
mild general learning disability   deacracht éadrom ghinearálta foghlama
moderate general learning disability   deacracht mheasartha ghinearálta foghlama
modular assessment   measúnacht mhodúlach
monitoring   monatóireacht

N

National Craft Certificate   Teastas Ceirde Náisiúnta
National Development Plan   Plean Forbartha Náisiúnta
National Framework of Qualifications   Creat Náisiúnta Cáilíochtaí
needs-directed learning   foghlaim riachtanais-dírithe
non-completion   neamhchríochnú
numeracy   uimhearthacht

O

odds-ratio basis   bonn corr-chóimheasa
off-the-job training   oiliúint ar láthair eile
official records   taifid oifigiúla
one-to-one tuition   teagasc duine le duine
on-the-job competence testing   tástáil cumais ar an láthair
ordinary level   gnáthleibhéal
origins   foinsí
outnumber   líon níos mó a bheith ann
outperform   sáraigh
overview   forbhreathnú

P

participation   rannpháirtíocht
participation rate   ráta rannpháirtíochta
part-time students   mic léinn páirtaimseartha
pedagogy   múinteoireacht
percentage   céatadán
percentile   peircintíl
performance   feidhmíocht
performance in state examinations   feidhmíocht i scrúduithe stáit

personal development	forbairt phearsanta
person-centred	duinelárnach
perspective	dearcadh
physical sciences	eolaíochtaí fisiciúla
physics	fisic
policy-relevance	bainteacht le polasaí
portfolio	punann
positions of seniority	poist shinsearachta
postgraduate courses	cúrsaí iarchéime
postgraduate degrees	iarchéimeanna
post-Leaving Certificate (PLC) courses	cúrsaí iar-Ardteistiméireachta
potential	lánacmhainneacht
primary degrees	bunchéimeanna
proficiency	cumas
Programme for International Student Assessment (PISA)	Clár Measúnacht Idirnáisiúnta Daltaí
progression opportunities	deiseanna dul ar aghaidh
proportion	comhréir / coibhneas
public debate	díospóireacht phoiblí
pupil-centred approach	cur chuige daltalárnach

Q

qualifications	cáilíochtaí
Quarterly National Household Survey	Suirbhé Teaghlaigh Ráithiúil Náisiúnta

R

ranking	grádú
ratio	cóimheas
reading achievement	gnóthachtáil léitheoireachta
reading profiles	próifílí léitheoireachta
Records of Achievement	Taifid Ghnóthachtála
reflect and evaluate	machnamh agus meastóireacht a dhéanamh
remedial assistance	cúnamh feabhais
representation	ionadaíocht
retention rates	rátaí coinneála
reveal	léirigh
review	athbhreithniú

S

school expectancy	ionchas scoile
school completion	críochnú scoile
school population	daonra scoile
science	eolaíocht
secondary voluntary sector	meánearnáil shaorálach
second-chance education	oideachas dara áiméar
segregation	deighilt
self-directed learning	foghlaim féindírithe
self-funded part-time adult education courses	cúrsaí oideachais féinmhaoinithe páirtaimseartha do dhaoine fásta

senior cycle	timthriall sinsearach
senior Traveller training centre	lárionad oiliúna sinsir don Lucht Siúil
Senior Traveller Training Programme	Clár Oiliúna Sinsir don Lucht Siúil
sensory	céadfach
severe general learning disability	deacracht throm ghinearálta foghlama
sex	gnéas
[a] significant minority	mionlach suntasach
[a] significant proportion	codán suntasach
similarities	cosúlachtaí
skew	sceabh
skills	scileanna
single-sex schools	scoileanna aonghnéis
social awareness	feasacht shóisialta
social exclusion	eisiatacht shóisialta
social inclusion	cuimsitheacht sóisialta
social policy	polasaí sóisialta / beartas sóisialta
social statistics	staitisticí sóisialta
socio-economic status	stádas socheacnamaíoch
special educational needs	riachtanais speisialta oideachais
specific learning disability	sain-mhíchumas foghlama
Specific Skills Awards	Duais Sainscileanna
speech and language disorder	easláinte teanga agus urlabhra
standards	caighdeáin
stark differences	difríochtaí suntasacha
statistically significant	tábhachtach i daobh staitisticí
stereotypes	buanchruthanna
strategy	straitéis
stratification	srathú
streaming	sruthú
structure of the school system	struchtúr an chórais scoile
students	mic léinn
subject take-up	tógáil ábhar
summary	achoimre

T

teachers	múinteoirí
technical graphics	grafaic theicniúil
technology	teicneolaíocht
teleservices	teilisheirbhísí
time-series analysis	anailís amshraithe
time-series data	sonraí amshraithe
time-series statistics	staitisticí amshraithe
tourism, culinary and hospitality skills	scileanna turasóireachta, cócaireachta, agus féile
transition year	idirbhliain
Traveller Community	Lucht Siúil
Traveller groups	grúpaí Lucht Siúil
trends	treonna

tuition	teagasc
tutors	teagascóirí
twice as likely	dhá oiread an dóchúlacht

U

undergraduate degrees	fochéimeanna
under-represented	gannionadaithe
universal	uilíoch
upper second level	dara leibhéal uachtarach

V

veterinary medicine	tréidliacht
vocational education committee	coiste gairmoideachais
Vocational	
Preparation and Training Programme	Clár Ullmhúchán agus Oiliúint Ghairme
vocational sector	earnáil ghairmoideachais

W

web design	dearadh gréasáin
work experience	taithí oibre
work-and-study format	formáid oibre agus staidéir

Y

young offenders' groups	grúpaí ciontóirí óga

Introduction

Background

Sé Sí has its origins in reflections and reviews of the quality and policy-relevance of administrative data within the Department of Education and Science. This became part of a broader review throughout the civil service initiated by the Central Statistics Office and the Department of the Taoiseach in 2002.[1] These reviews identified serious limitations in the quality of existing administrative data, which continue to undermine the development of evidence-informed policy, particularly in relation to what could be broadly termed social and equality statistics. While they recognised the need to improve the quality of administrative data throughout the civil service and public service, significant emphasis was also placed on the need to make better use of existing data.

Within the Department of Education and Science an internal audit of data needs and data sources carried out at that time identified the limitations of existing data but also revealed a lack of awareness about the extent of the information that was available from administrative sources. In the light of these findings the Statistics Section began to reflect on how we could better communicate statistical information to policy-makers. This led to a renewed emphasis on the clarity and policy-relevance of our work. Beginning with the simple idea of stringing all the department's Annual Statistical Reports together, the development of time-series statistics was identified as an important first step in improving the ease of use of our statistical reports. On hearing of the work on compiling time-series statistics, the Gender Equality Unit expressed a strong interest in developing a publication on gender statistics in education. This provided a focus for the work within the Statistics Section. Sé Sí is the product of an extensive data-harvesting exercise undertaken over five summers by the staff of the Statistics Section.

Aims of the report

Sé Sí aims to provide a comprehensive overview of education statistics disaggregated by gender. The overriding emphasis of the work has been to compile and disseminate clear and accessible data on education in the interests of evidence-informed policy analysis. While much of the data have been previously published in the department's Annual Statistical Reports, many of the indicators presented in Sé Sí are new, in the sense that the data have now been developed into time-series statistics. The harvesting of data from a broad range of sources ensures that Sé Sí is comprehensive in scope, and the compiling of time-series statistics is intended to facilitate reflection and discussion on trends over time in Irish education and learning.

---

[1] Arising out of the Strategic Management Initiative (SMI), an inter-departmental initiative to improve the quality and policy-relevance of administrative data began in 2002. For more information see National Statistics Board, Strategy for Statistics, 2003–2008 (2003) at http://www.nsb.ie/pdf_docs/StrategyforStatistics2003-2008.pdf; also The [SGSES] Report of the Steering Group on Social and Equality Statistics (2003) at http://www.taoiseach.gov.ie/attached_files/Pdf%20files/SocialAndEqualityStatisticsReport.pdf, and The [SPAR] Report on the Statistical Potential of Administrative Records (2003) at http://www.cso.ie/releasespublications/documents/other_releases/spar.pdf.

Layout of the report

Sé Sí presents an overview of the issue of gender in Irish education in a lifelong – cradle to grave – perspective. The layout of the document is generally chronological from primary level through second and third-level education. Data on further education and educational personnel are also presented. Population data from the Central Statistics Office are used to summarise trends and the Irish experience is contextualised whenever possible using relevant international data.

Many of the time-series charts end in the 2002/03 academic year. Readers should note that, in almost all cases, the underlying data required for further updates are published in the annual statistical reports of the Department of Education and Science.

Principal findings

Given the considerable amount of research that has been done on the issue of gender in education, most of the individual findings and results are already widely known. Nevertheless, Sé Sí allows for the emergence of a comprehensive analysis of the issue of gender in education over time. A summary of the findings is not attempted in this introduction, because the entire document is intended to serve as a summary of available statistical data on gender and learning in Ireland. Nevertheless, a selection of the principal findings is presented below.

Remarkable improvement over time

It is very difficult for today's schoolchildren and even university graduates to appreciate the extent of the expansion of educational opportunities that has been achieved in Ireland over the last few generations. Among their grandparents' generation, half the school population finished their education at the primary level, and two-thirds were finished by the Junior Certificate. Only one in three got to the Leaving Certificate level, and roughly one in ten progressed to higher education. Higher education was simply not an option for 90 per cent of their grandparents.

The situation had improved substantially by the time their parents' generation attended school; but the education profile of the population of Ireland would have compared extremely poorly with its Continental counterparts at that time. The decision of the Irish state to make second-level education freely available to all citizens was relatively late in the context of western European social policy. In neighbouring countries the introduction of free second-level education was a post-war initiative; in Ireland the introduction of free second-level education was announced by the Minister for Education, Donogh O'Malley, in 1967. The very immediate impact of that decision, and the public appetite for learning that it uncovered, can be seen in chapter 2 of this report, where the total number of Leaving Certificate candidates in effect quadrupled over the following twenty-five years.[2]

[2] See figs. and tables 2.11a and 2.11b.

Today we have universal primary education, 82 per cent completion of upper second-level education, 55 per cent[3] entry to higher education, and a significant range of further-education opportunities. Internationally, Ireland is among the countries that have made most progress over time in improving the education profile of the population. However, important challenges remain as education and learning assume increasing importance in the pursuit of individual, community and national well-being. School completion and retention to the Leaving Certificate level has been and remains a central issue in Irish education policy.

Retention and school completion

The attainment of upper second-level qualifications has acquired growing importance in all EU and OECD countries, against the background of steadily rising skill demands in the labour market. Completion of upper second-level education has become the main gateway to continuing engagement with learning. In this regard, retention to the completion of second-level education is widely recognised as a central objective of education policy that has direct implications for participation in further and higher education and for broader policies relating to economic competitiveness and social inclusion.

At present the total proportion of second-level pupils who take the Leaving Certificate is approximately 82 per cent. Since the expansion of second-level participation in the late 1960s, girls have demonstrated consistently higher rates of school completion. Boys account for almost two-thirds of the pupils who leave second-level education before the Leaving Certificate and two-thirds of those who leave without any qualifications at all.[4]

Every year in Ireland since official records began in 1864, slightly more boys are born than girls, with the result that today, for example, there are approximately 1,800 more 17-year old boys than 17-year old girls. A similar difference exists among 16-year-olds, 15-year-olds, etc.[5] Despite this demographic backdrop, over the last ten years girls have outnumbered boys by between 2,400 and 3,300 among candidates for the Leaving Certificate each year.

Comparing the number of school-based Leaving Certificate candidates with the numbers in the population at 17 to 18 years of age we see that approximately 6,900 boys did not sit the Leaving Certificate in 2005, compared with approximately 3,000 girls. In the same year the number of boys not sitting the Junior Certificate was approximately 1,350, compared with approximately 350 girls.[6]

---

[3] This 2004 entry rate to higher education is calculated as the total number of new entrants to higher education (including mature students), divided by the total numbers in the population at typical age of entry (17-18 year olds).

[4] See figs. and tables 2.11b, 2.12, 2.13, and 2.14.

[5] Central Statistics Office, Census 2002: Principal Demographic Results (2003), table 10, p. 56. The figure of 1,800 was derived by rounding the average difference in the number of boys and girls aged 15 to 17 years.

[6] The sources for these estimates are Central Statistics Office, Census 2002: Principal Demographic Results (2003), table 10, p. 56, and Department of Education and Science, Annual Statistical Report, 2004/05 (forthcoming), table 5.1. The estimates were derived by comparing the numbers of school-based candidates in the 2005 Junior Certificate and Leaving Certificate examinations (excluding repeats) with the relevant age cohorts in the 2002 census (minus 3 years). In percentage terms, approximately 22 per cent of boys did not sit the Leaving Certificate examination, compared with 10 per cent of girls, and 4.6 per cent of boys did not sit the Junior Certificate examination, compared with 1.3 per cent of girls.

Subject take-up in second-level education

Much of the debate on gender issues in Irish education has focused on the issue of subject take-up at second level and beyond. The overview of subject take-up patterns provided in Sé Sí reveals substantial gender differences that have remained largely unchanged over time. From early second level onwards, pupils conform closely to the traditional gender stereotypes in terms of the subjects they study. Boys far outnumber girls in the take-up of "practical subjects," such as engineering, technical drawing, and construction studies and girls far outnumber boys in home economics, music, art and European languages.

In general, there are notable similarities between the subject take-up patterns in early second-level education and the subject take-up by gender in further and higher education. It is difficult to assess the extent to which this reflects innate dispositions towards different subject areas and the extent to which it arises as a consequence of socialisation and social conditioning. In any event, these trends in subject take-up patterns highlight the long-term reverberations of subject take-up at the beginning of second-level education. Regrettably, due to time pressures, the range of interesting issues relating to choice and the provision of subjects across second-level schools remains unexplored in this report.

In assessing subject take up by gender in Irish education, it is worth remembering that approximately 36 per cent of second-level pupils in Ireland today attend single-sex schools. In a majority of European countries, there are no single sex schools and only a very small minority of pupils attend single sex education in the remaining countries. Unfortunately, internationally comparable data on gender differences in subject take-up at second level do not yet exist. It would be interesting to develop international data in this area because of Ireland's distinctiveness among European countries in having such a significant proportion of single-sex schools.

The sciences

Public debate on gender in Irish education over recent years has conveyed a particular interest in the take-up of science and engineering subjects. Within the second-level curriculum, science is taught and assessed as a unified subject at the lower second level before pupils beginning the upper second level are offered distinct courses in biology, physics, and chemistry. Biology, which is by far the most popular of the Leaving Certificate science subjects, is dominated by girls, who outnumber boys by 2 to 1 (68 per cent to 32 per cent). Girls also outnumber boys among Leaving Certificate examination candidates in chemistry (54 per cent to 46 per cent). Physics, on the other hand, is dominated by boys, who outnumber girls by 3 to 1 (75 per cent to 25 per cent).

Taking all the Leaving Certificate science subjects together, the gender ratio is in favour of girls (55 per cent girls, 45 per cent boys). This is a reversal of the ratio observed in Junior Certificate science, where boys outnumber girls (53 per cent to 47 per cent). However, despite the overall ratio in favour of girls in the sciences at the upper second level, there is considerable public concern about the low take-up of physics among girls. It is believed that this is one factor that contributes to the subsequent low take-up of engineering among women in higher education. Interestingly, physics is the subject in which girls most outperform boys in recent Leaving Certificate examinations.

Further education

Lifelong learning has been a core principle of EU education policy since the Irish presidency in 1996. However, there is considerable variation in the extent to which member-states have succeeded in achieving participation in lifelong learning. The Scandinavian countries have achieved the highest participation rates, and in Sweden it is estimated that more than a third of all adults were engaged in education or training in 2004. Britain, Slovenia, the Netherlands and, to a lesser extent, Austria have also achieved relatively high levels of participation in lifelong learning. In all other EU member-states the participation rate of adults in lifelong learning was below 10 per cent in 2004. The participation rate among Irish adults was 7.2 per cent, which was below the EU average of 9.9 per cent.[10]

Given the broad and diverse range of post-secondary learning activities and the patchiness of administrative data in this area, it was difficult to provide a summary of further education and training in Ireland. Women substantially outnumber men in post-Leaving Certificate courses and in the full range of other further and adult education courses provided through the Department of Education and Science (and the VECs). However, the FETAC awards provide a more gender-balanced picture of certified further education and training, because they also include training organised by other agencies, such as FÁS and Teagasc. Within the full range of FETAC awards in 2005 the gender ratio was 53 per cent female to 47 per cent male.

There are clear gender differences in the take-up of courses, and at a general level the types of further-education qualification pursued correspond closely to the classic gender stereotypes. This is especially true of men, who largely confine their engagement in further education to vocationally oriented and especially construction-related training. Apprenticeship, specific skills training and Teagasc agricultural training courses are almost exclusively male. Women tend to engage more broadly with further education, from training in business, office skills and caring to arts, craft and continuing education courses.

With regard to lifelong learning, Irish women display a much greater and more sustained appetite for education than men over the life cycle. This is well illustrated in their higher levels of participation in further and adult education courses. Women's greater lifelong enthusiasm for education is also evident in the central role they have played at the local level in initiating community education work in disadvantaged communities since the 1980s.

In contrast, men's participation in education and training appears to diminish rapidly over the life cycle. When it is examined in a lifelong perspective, it is important to note that the male-dominated further education programmes are generally post-school courses that could legitimately be considered the end of initial education and training rather than as continuing or adult education. The great majority of apprentices are aged between their late teens and early twenties, and most participants in specific skills training are under twenty-five.

The other major recurring issue for males in Irish education is successful completion. This is well documented at second level but approximately 25 per cent of young men in Ireland now pursue further education and training by enrolling in apprenticeship programmes.[11] A quick comparison of entrants and graduates in Apprenticeship suggests that more than 40 per cent of trainees drop out prior to successful completion. On this evidence, retention appears to be a serious issue for males in further education as well as in second-level education. In higher education also, males are less likely than females to successfully complete their course of study. This gives rise to a peculiar situation at NFQ levels 6 and 7 (certificate and diploma) where males outnumber females among overall enrolments but not among graduates.

Educational personnel

In chapter 8 the focus of the analysis shifts from students and learners to an examination of the personnel responsible for the provision and administration of education in Ireland. It is widely known that nowadays women far outnumber men among primary teachers. The time-series analysis presented in Sé Sí demonstrates that women have continually outnumbered men among primary teachers over the last seventy years at least. The proportion of female primary teachers increased steadily from 58 per cent in 1930 to 83 per cent in 2005. While the total number of teachers at the primary level has more than doubled over those years, the actual number of male primary teachers has not changed much over time.

The gender ratio of second-level teachers is now approaching 60-40 in favour of women. In higher education, women accounted for 32 per cent of academic staff in institutes of technology and 40 per cent of academic staff in universities by 2003. In Ireland and in other OECD countries there is a noticeable pattern whereby the proportion of women declines as one moves from primary through secondary to higher education. Internationally, women account for 82 per cent of teaching personnel at the primary level, 60 per cent at the second level, and 36 per cent at the third level. The ratios in Ireland are remarkably similar to these international averages at each of the three levels.

Clearly there are issues concerning the representation of women in positions of seniority in educational institutions. This is evident at the primary and second levels, where women are seriously under-represented at the school principal level. Women account for 83 per cent of all staff members at the primary level but only 53 per cent of school principals. At the second level, where women now account for 60 per cent of staff members, men outnumber women by 2 to 1 among school principals.

Notwithstanding the significant increase in female academic staff over the last decade, the most striking gender differences are found in higher-education institutions. In universities women now outnumber men at the lower academic levels of assistant lecturer and "other" teaching staff. However, as we move up through the academic hierarchy the proportion of women declines steadily. In institutes of technology and the universities a clear pattern is observable whereby the proportion of men increases with the seniority of the academic position. At the time of going to print, women accounted for 3 of the 14 directors of institutes of technology and none of the 7 university presidents.

[11] Seán McDonagh and Vivienne Patterson, The Institutes of Technology and Future Skills (2006).

The under-representation of women among university academic staff members is most severe at the highest levels of professor and associate professor. In 2003/04 women accounted for 8 per cent of professor posts and 12 per cent of associate professor posts. Similar patterns of imbalance are also found at the highest levels of academic staff in the institutes of technology. However, there are approximately twice as many women at the most senior academic levels in the institutes of technology as there are in the universities; therefore the extent of gender imbalance among senior academics is most severe in the university sector.

A broadly similar picture emerges from the analysis of administrative personnel. Although women account for two-thirds of all staff members in the civil service, they are over-represented at the lower grades and quite severely under-represented at the higher end of the seniority spectrum. In fact the ratio of women declines steadily as the seniority of the grade rises. The visual representation of gender by grade in the civil service depicts what could be referred to as the classic staircase of gender inequality. Women account for 80 per cent of staff members at the clerical officer and staff officer levels and almost two-thirds at the executive officer grade. Although they account for more than half of all administrative officer posts they comprise fewer than half the higher executive officers, one-third of assistant principal officers, one-fifth of principal officers, one-tenth of assistant secretaries-general, and an even smaller share of secretary-general posts.

Although the overall patterns of gender imbalance were similar within the Department of Education and Science, women account for a larger proportion of staff members at the higher executive officer and principal officer level in this department than is typical in the civil service generally. Looking back over the last decade we see steady and substantial increases in the ratios of women in the middle to higher grades in the department. However, the proportion of women in positions of seniority remains low, and women continue to be under-represented at the highest levels relative to their total numbers. Chapter 8 concludes with an overview of the gender ratios of staff members and board members in a selection of important education agencies.

Finally

Sé Sí includes data on special educational needs, where boys outnumber girls by 2 to 1, and on a range of other issues including programme take-up within the second-level curriculum and the performance of Irish students in the PISA international literacy assessments. The extensive use of international data throughout the report demonstrates that gender differences in educational participation and performance are issues that present challenges to almost all developed countries.

In the fuller analysis of the international data, gender is one of a range of background characteristics that appear to affect pupils' achievement in the literacy assessments. While gender appears to be a significant factor, particularly on the performance of pupils in reading, the most significant factors affecting performance are the socio-economic status and home background characteristics of pupils.

Moving beyond individual pupils' characteristics to the structure and organisation of school systems, countries that achieve the highest standards of literacy tend to have school systems with little active selection and segregation, where schools embrace and accommodate the diversity of their local communities. One of the most interesting findings to emerge from the continuing PISA assessments is that many of the highest-performing countries have successfully combined high overall performance with high levels of equity in educational outcomes. On the other hand, characteristics of education systems that have high levels of inequity (often accompanied by low levels of overall performance) include early selection and streaming, stratification between school types, and the clustering of disadvantage in specific schools and geographical areas. These general findings show that "equity and excellence are not mutually exclusive in education. In fact, it is clear that these two educational policy objectives can be entirely complementary." [12]

In publishing this report, the Department of Education and Science hopes to contribute to informed public debate and to stimulate reflection, discussion and further research on educational and gender issues.

[12] Department of Education and Science, Supporting Equity in Higher Education: A Report to the Minister for Education and Science, 2003, p. 7–8.

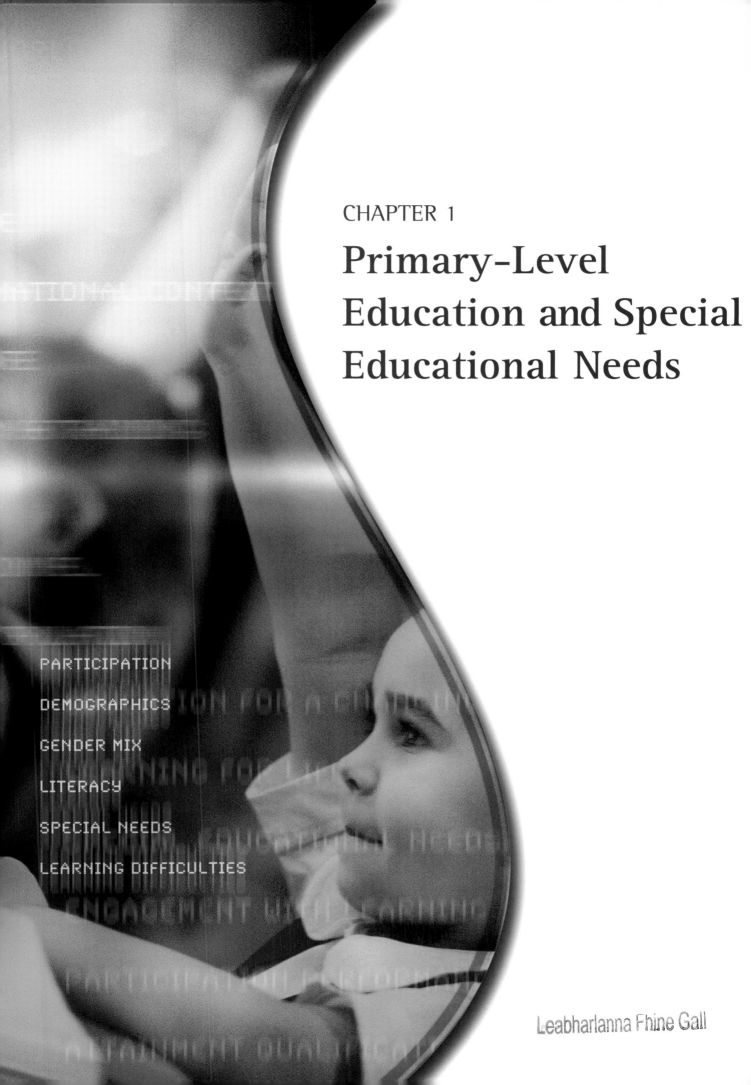

CHAPTER 1

Primary-Level Education and Special Educational Needs

PARTICIPATION

DEMOGRAPHICS

GENDER MIX

LITERACY

SPECIAL NEEDS

LEARNING DIFFICULTIES

Leabharlanna Fhine Gall

Primary-Level Education and Special Educational Needs

Participation and demographics

Fig. 1.1 presents the total enrolment of pupils in "ordinary classes" in national schools between 1980 and 2002/03. The total number of pupils in primary-level education declined steadily between the mid-1980s and the turn of the millennium. Over the course of the 1990s total enrolment at primary level dropped by more than 100,000, from 532,000 pupils at the beginning of the decade to 423,000 in 2000/01. Since that year, pupil numbers in primary education have begun to increase once again and will increase steadily into the near and medium future, as a result of increases in births since 1995 and of immigration in more recent years.

Another notable feature of enrolment at the primary level is the consistently larger number of male pupils. In 2002/03, for example, there were 219,000 boys in primary schools, compared with 208,500 girls. Altogether, between 1980 and 2003 the gender ratio in ordinary classes at the primary level has been 51.3 per cent male to 48.7 per cent female. Bearing in mind that we have achieved 100 per cent participation at the primary level, this gender ratio is the direct result of demographics.

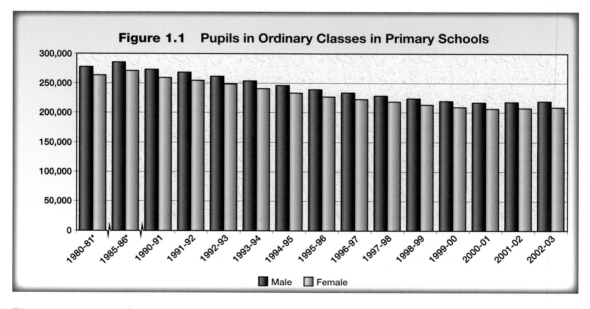

Fig. 1.2 presents a historical overview of births in Ireland by sex, with annual average births per decade between 1871 and 1990 and annual births per year between 1991 and 2003. This figure illustrates the decline in births that occurred during the 1980s and early 1990s, as well as the more recent increases in births, which will result in steady increases in primary-level enrolment over the next decade. Fig. 1.2 also demonstrates the fact that more boys are born than girls. The ratio of births since 1921 has been 51.4 per cent male to 48.6 per cent female. This is consistent with patterns observed internationally, and it explains why boys outnumber girls among primary-level enrolments.

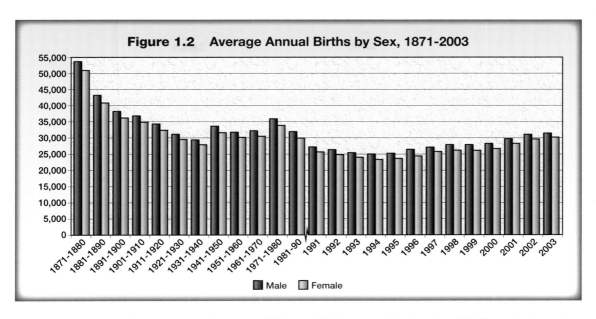

Figure 1.2   Average Annual Births by Sex, 1871-2003

Fig. 1.3 presents data on enrolments within publicly provided early-childhood education under the "Early Start" pre-school pilot programme.[1] While enrolments by sex have varied from year to year, the overall male-female ratio among Early Start pupils has been 51:49 since the programme began in 1995/96.

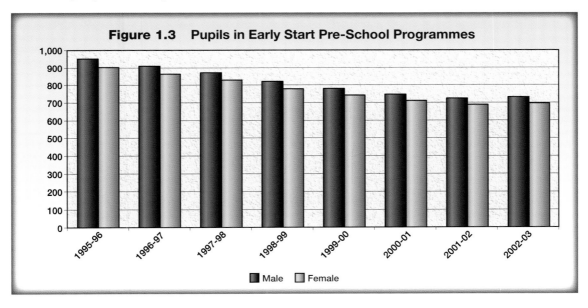

Figure 1.3   Pupils in Early Start Pre-School Programmes

Gender mix in primary schools

Over recent years there has been an increase in the proportion of primary pupils who are educated in mixed classes. This proportion rose from 65 per cent in 1985 to 74 per cent in 2002/03. Conversely, there has been an equivalent decline in the proportion of pupils educated in single-sex classes, as outlined in Fig. 1.4. Single-sex primary education remains slightly more popular among girls, as seen in the continually higher proportion of female pupils in single-sex classes over recent decades.

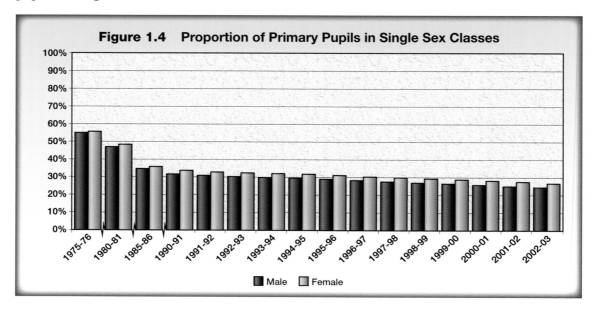

Figure 1.4   Proportion of Primary Pupils in Single Sex Classes

Literacy: Sample surveys

Although comprehensive literacy attainment data are not available at present to the Department of Education and Science through administrative data sources, the department has commissioned national sample surveys on literacy attainment among primary-level pupils. A report published by the Educational Research Centre in 2000[2] provides a detailed analysis of the 1998 survey of literacy among fifth-class pupils as well as comparisons with an earlier survey carried out in 1993. An equivalent survey of literacy was carried out in 2004 which examined literacy among first class pupils as well as fifth class pupils.[3]

In the assessments of reading achievement conducted in 1993 there was no difference in the average performance of boys and girls. However, the 1998 assessment found small but significant differences, with girls performing better, on average, than boys. This suggests that gender differences in average reading achievement may have increased between 1993 and 1998. The 2004 survey of literacy also found that girls performed significantly better than boys on the reading test at both first class and fifth class. The gender difference in favour of fifth-class girls was broadly equivalent to that found in 1998 survey. There were small (but not statistically significant) gender differences in favour of girls in the proportions of pupils performing at the very high and very low end of the reading spectrum.[4]

[2] Cosgrove, J., Kellaghan, T., Forde, P., Morgan, M., *The 1998 National Assessment of English Reading (with Comparative Data from the 1993 National Assessment)*, Dublin: Educational Research Centre, 2000.

[3] Eivers, E., Shiel, G., Perkins, R., Cosgrove, J., *Succeeding in Reading?* Reading standards in Irish Primary Schools, Educational Research Centre, 2005

[4] Judith Cosgrove et al., T*he 1998 National Assessment of English Reading (with comparative data from the 1993 National Assessment)*, Educational Research Centre, 2000, pp. 32-35.

These literacy assessments were accompanied by a survey of teachers, in which they were asked to rate the reading proficiency and coping ability of pupils included in the sample survey. Fig. 1.5 provides an overview of pupils' reading standard as judged by their teachers.

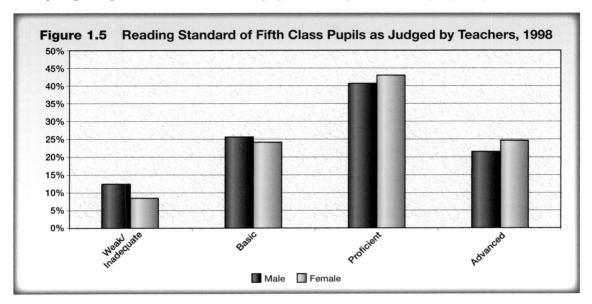

Figure 1.5   Reading Standard of Fifth Class Pupils as Judged by Teachers, 1998

In general, boys received less positive ratings from their teachers than did girls. In response to further questions, the teachers rated the coping ability of girls significantly higher than boys, particularly in their ability to cope with the reading and writing demands of post-primary education.[5] These gender differences were also reflected in the fact that a significantly higher number of boys than girls had received remedial assistance.

> These findings complement those of another study in Irish primary schools which revealed considerable differences in teachers' perceptions of boys and girls on a variety of behavioural and achievement-related characteristics (Lewis & Kellaghan, 1993). Girls themselves expressed more positive attitudes to school and to reading than did boys and they also had higher aspirations and expectations regarding the length of time they would stay in the education system.[6]

In 2003 the Department of Education and Science asked the Educational Research Centre to carry out a sample survey of reading literacy in designated disadvantaged primary schools. This study looked at reading achievement among first-class, third-class and sixth-class pupils. In first class and third class, girls obtained significantly higher reading achievement scores than boys. Among third-class pupils, twice as many boys as girls (13 per cent versus 6 per cent) scored at or below the 10th percentile, indicating very low achievement. However, among sixth-class pupils, boys scored slightly (but not significantly) higher than girls, and a higher proportion of boys than girls scored at or above the 90th percentile, indicating very high achievement.[7]

---

[5] Ibid., p. 38–40.

[6] Ibid., p. 105.

[7] Eivers, E., Shiel, G., Shortt, F., Sofroniou, N., *Reading Literacy in Disadvantaged Primary Schools*, ERC 2004, p. 49.

In an international assessment of primary pupils' achievement in mathematics conducted in 1995 among third-class and fourth-class pupils, gender differences in mathematical achievement were found to be "small or essentially non-existent."[8] In the small number of countries where statistically significant differences did exist they tended to favour boys. Among Irish pupils, girls performed slightly better than boys in both third and fourth class, although neither of these differences was statistically significant. In examining pupils' attitudes towards mathematics, this study found broadly equivalent levels of enthusiasm for the subject between the sexes. However, in Ireland (and in Scotland), girls reported liking mathematics better than did boys.

Special educational needs and learning difficulties

An examination of gender and the issue of learning difficulties at the primary level is constrained by the absence of comprehensive national information on the literacy attainment of all primary-level pupils. Nevertheless, data on the total number of pupils retained at the same grade level for consecutive years can provide a useful indicator of pupils experiencing difficulty in progressing through primary-level education. These data are presented in fig. 1.6. There has been a steady decline in the total number of pupils retained at the same grade level, from 16, 691 in 1990 to 4,811 in 2002/03. The practice of retaining pupils has been discouraged by the Inspectorate over recent years and is being replaced by the promotion of continuity through primary school accompanied by specialist assistance for children with learning difficulties or special educational needs.

Looking at the gender ratio among pupils retained, fig. 1.6 demonstrates that male pupils are consistently more likely to be retained than female pupils. Between 1990 and 2002/03 the overall male-female ratio was 57:43.

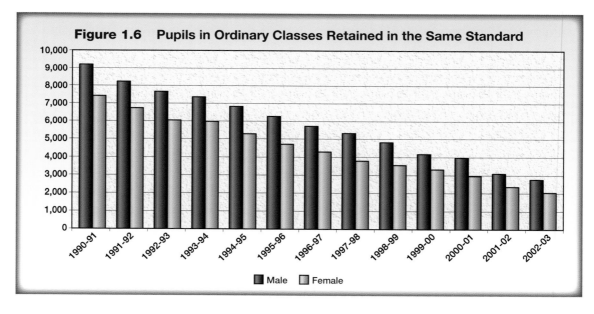

Figure 1.6 Pupils in Ordinary Classes Retained in the Same Standard

8 International Association for the Evaluation of Educational Achievement, *Mathematics Achievement in the Primary School Years: Third International Mathematics and Science Study*, Amsterdam: IEA, 1997, p. 3.

In Ireland, pupils with special educational needs are educated either within ordinary[9] national schools or within special schools. Fig. 1.7 provides details of the number of pupils identified as having special educational needs who are educated within ordinary national schools.[10] Over the course of the 1990s, and particularly during the late 1990s, there was a considerable and steady increase in the total number of pupils identified as having special educational needs in national schools. The number almost doubled, from approximately 1,800 in 1994/95 to approximately 3,500 in 2002/03. This increase in overall numbers was accompanied by increases in the proportions of boys identified as having special educational needs. By 2002/03, boys outnumbered girls by almost 2 to 1 in the number of children with special educational needs in primary schools.

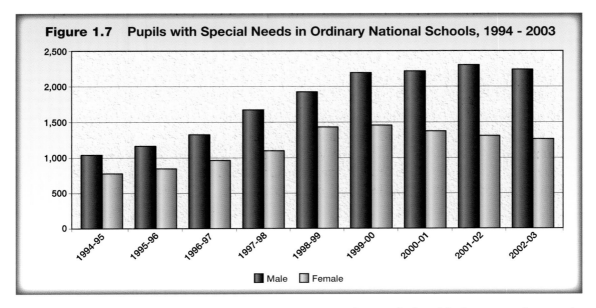

Figure 1.7   Pupils with Special Needs in Ordinary National Schools, 1994 - 2003

Taking fig. 1.6 and fig. 1.7 together, there appears to be a relationship between the steady decline over time in the total number of pupils being retained in the same grade level and the simultaneous increase in the number of pupils identified as having special educational needs in ordinary national schools. It is also important to take account of the fact that boys slightly outnumber girls in overall enrolment in ordinary national schools (see fig. 1.1). To take account of all these factors, figs. 1.8 (a) and 1.8 (b) combine the numbers of pupils retained and identified as having special educational needs and present these figures as a proportion of total enrolments.

[9] The terms 'ordinary' and 'special' are becoming increasingly outdated, as descriptions of educational needs, classes and educational institutions. However, they are the terms used in the official statistics which constitute the primary data sources for the time-series data compiled and presented in this publication. Therefore, in order to ensure clarity in presentation, these terms are used in this publication.

[10] In the Annual Census of Primary Schools, administrative data (for the years shown in fig. 1.7) on children from the Traveller community were collected on the same forms as data on children with special educational needs in ordinary national schools. The forms were designed in this way for administrative reasons, relating to the payment of additional capitation to schools on behalf of both sets of children. For the purposes of calculating the gender ratio of pupils identified as having special educational needs in ordinary national schools, the male-female ratio of Travellers in national schools is assumed to be 50:50. The Annual Census forms have since been amended to provide separate information for children from the Traveller community.

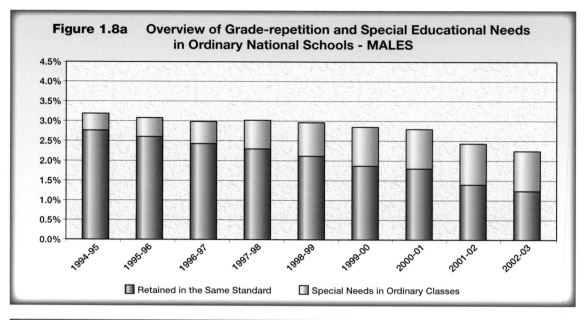

Figure 1.8a   Overview of Grade-repetition and Special Educational Needs in Ordinary National Schools - MALES

■ Retained in the Same Standard   □ Special Needs in Ordinary Classes

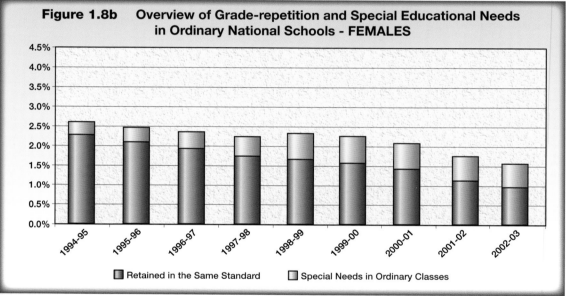

Figure 1.8b   Overview of Grade-repetition and Special Educational Needs in Ordinary National Schools - FEMALES

■ Retained in the Same Standard   □ Special Needs in Ordinary Classes

Taken together, the combined proportions of pupils retained in the same grade and identified as having special educational needs has declined for both boys and girls since 1994. Throughout that period, higher proportions of boys than girls have been retained and have been identified as having special educational needs. For example, in 2002/03, 1.2 per cent of boys were retained, compared with 1.0 per cent of girls, and 1.0 per cent of boys were identified as having special educational needs, compared with 0.6 per cent of girls.

Fig. 1.9 provides an overview of the range of special educational needs among pupils in ordinary national schools in 2002/03.[11] More than two-thirds (68 per cent) of all pupils with special educational needs in ordinary national schools are classified as having a mild general learning disability. The next-highest category of special educational need is children with a speech and language disorder (12 per cent); these are followed by children with autism (7 per cent), children with a specific learning disability (6 per cent), and children with a moderate general learning disability (4 per cent).

[11]   As data on special needs are collected at the aggregated (school) level, it is not possible at present to provide a gender breakdown within each of the identified special educational needs described in fig. 1.9.

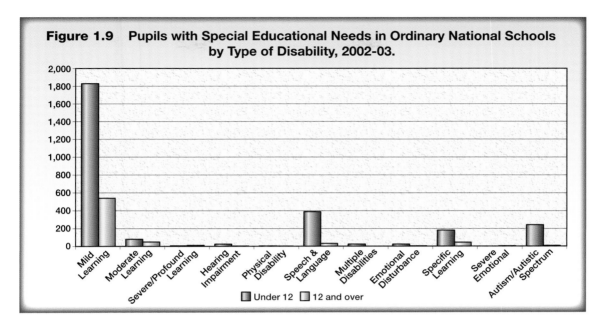

Figure 1.9 Pupils with Special Educational Needs in Ordinary National Schools by Type of Disability, 2002-03.

Special schools

The numbers of pupils in special schools between 1980 and 2002/03 are given in fig. 1.10. There has been a slow but steady decline in the total number of pupils in special schools, corresponding with (demographic) trends in total primary enrolment over that period. The number of pupils in special schools as a proportion of all pupils has remained constant at between 1.5 and 1.6 per cent over that period. As with special educational needs in ordinary national schools, boys outnumber girls by almost 2:1 among pupils in special schools. The proportion of boys has increased from 59 per cent in the early 1980s to 64 per cent in 2002/03.

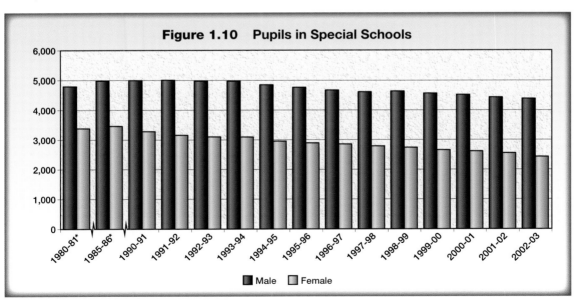

Figure 1.10 Pupils in Special Schools

Fig. 1.11 provides an overview of the number of pupils enrolled in special schools by age and gender. This illustrates the fact that special schools cater for the educational needs of pupils from early primary school age to early adulthood. In 2002/03, 60 per cent of all pupils enrolled in special schools were aged twelve or over.

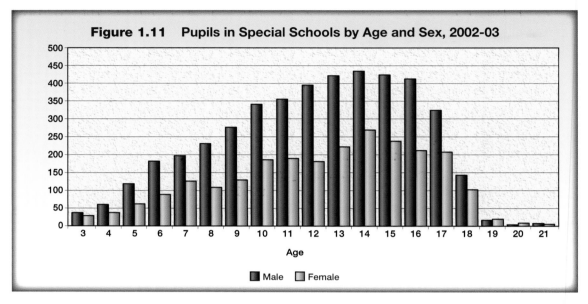

An overview of the range of disabilities and special educational needs of pupils in special schools is provided in fig. 1.12. Once again the largest category is mild general learning disability. At 38 per cent, however, it accounts for a considerably smaller proportion of pupils in special schools than of pupils with special needs in ordinary national schools. The data presented in fig. 1.12 suggest that a wider range of disabilities is catered for in special schools. Enrolment in special schools includes significant numbers of pupils with moderate and severe general learning disabilities as well as those with a range of physical, sensory or other learning disabilities.

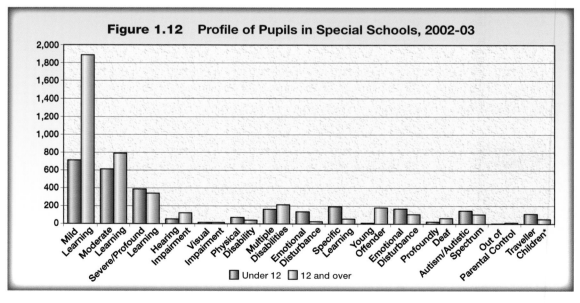

This chapter has provided an overview of available data relating to primary-level education and children with special educational needs. Chapter 2 focuses on issues of enrolment and participation in second-level education.

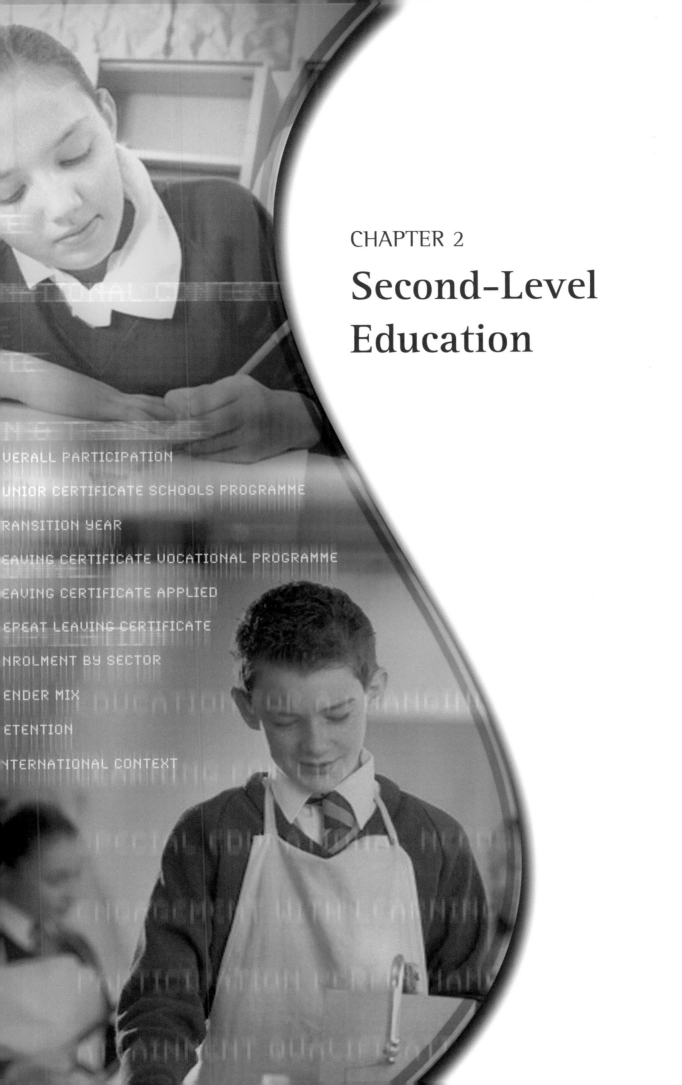

CHAPTER 2

Second–Level Education

Second-Level Education

Overall participation in second-level education

The total number of pupils enrolled in the junior cycle of second-level education between 1980 and 2002/03 is shown in fig. 2.1. Following demographic and enrolment trends at the primary level observed in chapter 1, total enrolment in the junior cycle has declined steadily since 1993. Another notable feature of enrolment at the primary level was the consistently larger number of male pupils. This is also apparent in the junior-cycle enrolments, although it is less pronounced at this level. This suggests that boys are more likely to leave school before completing the Junior Certificate than girls.

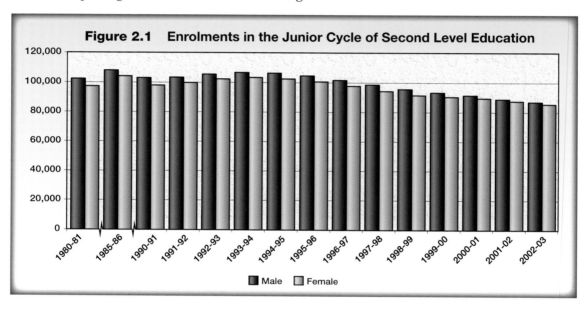

Fig. 2.2[1] presents an overview of enrolments at the senior-cycle level between 1980 and 2002/03. Enrolments at the senior-cycle level began to decline from 1997 onwards. Given the trends observed at earlier levels, total enrolments at this level will continue to decline until the end of the present decade.

[1] The data presented in fig. 2.2 include transition year pupils, pupils in all the various Leaving Certificate programmes and repeat Leaving Certificate pupils in public institutions.

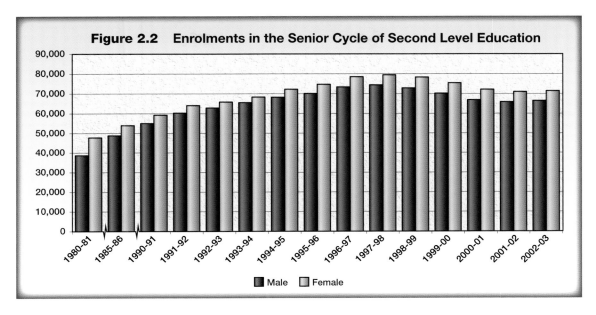

Figure 2.2   Enrolments in the Senior Cycle of Second Level Education

Girls have consistently outnumbered boys among senior-cycle enrolments. The average ratio since 1990 has been 48:52, with girls outnumbering boys to a greater extent in the 1980s. This contrasts with the ratio observed at earlier levels and again suggests that boys are more likely to leave second-level education before the Leaving Certificate. (The issue of retention throughout second-level education is explored in more detail later in this chapter.)

Participation in particular programmes at the second level

The Junior Certificate School Programme (JCSP)

The JCSP is a national programme of the Department of Education and Science within the Junior Certificate, aimed at pupils who may leave school early. Through the provision of a support framework that adopts a pupil-centred approach, the JCSP aims to ensure that each participating pupil experiences success and progression within an accessible and relevant curriculum and assessment framework. The JCSP is not an alternative to the Junior Certificate: it is a support framework that aims to ensure that all participating pupils sit the same Junior Certificate examination as their peers in as many subjects as they can succeed in.[2] The programme is now operating in approximately 150 schools throughout the country, and in 2002/03 JCSP pupils accounted for 2.8 per cent of all junior-cycle pupils.[3]

---

[2] This information on the JCSP is taken from the web site www.jcsp.ie, where more details on the programme are available.

[3] Department of Education and Science, *Tuarascáil Staitistiúil, 2002/03: Annual Statistical Report*, Dublin: DES, 2004, p. 41, table 3.3.

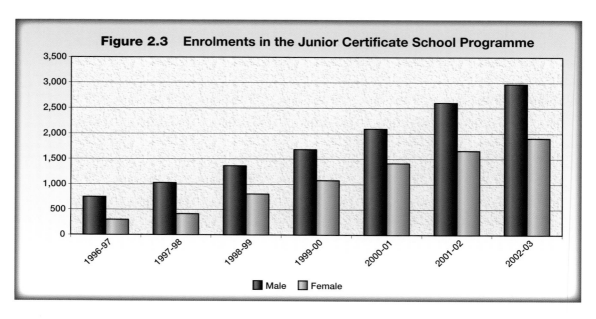

Figure 2.3   Enrolments in the Junior Certificate School Programme

Fig. 2.3 provides an overview of the numbers of pupils enrolled in the JCSP between 1996/97 and 2002/03.[4] In that period the total participation in the programme rose from just over 1,000 to almost 5,000 pupils. Boys have consistently outnumbered girls among participating pupils. In 2002/03 the ratio was approximately 60:40 in favour of boys. In that year 3.4 per cent of boys and 2.2 per cent of girls in the junior cycle participated in the JCSP.

Transition year

The transition year is an optional year available to pupils after they have completed the Junior Certificate course and before they begin one of the three Leaving Certificate courses. Schools have considerable autonomy in designing their own transition year programme within the framework of a national curriculum. The national framework emphasises personal development, social awareness and the promotion of interdisciplinary, self-directed learning through the development of general, technical and academic skills. Education through the experience of adult and working life is also strongly promoted in the transition year programme.[5]

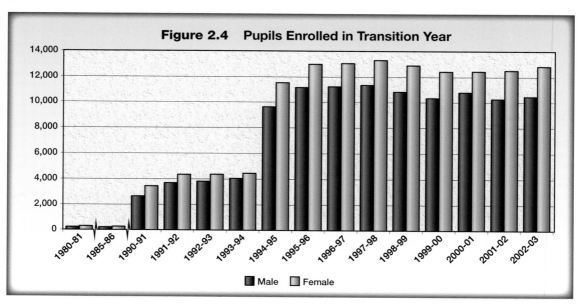

Figure 2.4   Pupils Enrolled in Transition Year

---

[4] Pupils enrolled in the JCSP are included among the total enrolments in the junior cycle presented in fig. 2.1.

[5] For additional detail on the transition year programme see DES guidelines, "The Senior Cycle in Second-Level Schools" (p. 3–4) at http://www.education.ie/servlet/blobservlet/senior_cycle_options.pdf?language=EN

Just over 70 per cent of schools now provide a transition year programme as part of their curriculum. In some schools it is policy that all pupils take the programme; in others it is taken by a selection of pupils. Total enrolment in the transition year programme increased from over 21,000 in 1994/95 to almost 24,000 in 2002/03. Fig. 2.4 shows that girls outnumber boys among those taking a transition year. In 2002/03 the ratio (male to female) was 45:55.

At the end of the transition year, pupils begin a two-year Leaving Certificate programme. Those who do not participate in the transition year begin a two-year Leaving Certificate course immediately after completing the junior cycle. Three different options are available to pupils within the Leaving Certificate programme: the Established Leaving Certificate, the Leaving Certificate Vocational Programme, and the Leaving Certificate Applied.

Leaving Certificate Vocational Programme (LCVP)

The LCVP is a Leaving Certificate programme with a strong vocational element. This is included through two link modules, on enterprise education and preparation for the world of work, which participating pupils take in addition to at least five Leaving Certificate subjects. These link modules are designed to be combined flexibly with each other and with learning in relevant (vocational) subjects taken by the pupil. The link modules are examined through a combination of a written examination and a portfolio of coursework. The Leaving Certificate subjects offered through the LCVP are arranged in groups, which give pupils an insight into a particular vocational area.[6]

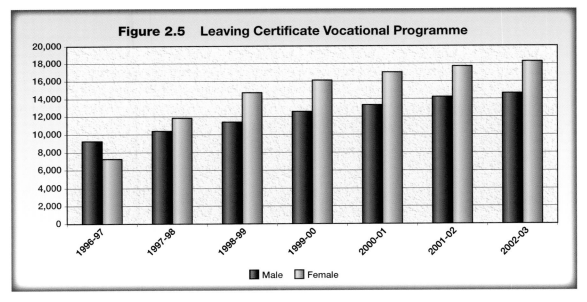

Figure 2.5 Leaving Certificate Vocational Programme

Enrolment in the LCVP has doubled over recent years, from 16,500 in 1996/97 to almost 33,000 in 2002/03, against the background of a decline in total senior cycle enrolment (see fig. 2.2). In 2002/03 pupils participating in the LCVP accounted for 29 per cent of all Leaving Certificate pupils.[7] Since 1997 girls have outnumbered boys, leading to a ratio (boys to girls) of 45:55 in 2002/03.

---

[6] For additional details on the LCVP see DES guidelines, 'The Senior Cycle in Second-Level Schools," at http://www.education.ie/servlet/blobservlet/senior_cycle_options.pdf?language=EN, p. 10–12.

[7] The term "Leaving Certificate pupils" includes fifth-year, sixth-year and repeat Leaving Certificate pupils within all three Leaving Certificate programmes. It does not include transition-year pupils.

Leaving Certificate Applied (LCA)

The LCA is a distinct, self-contained two-year Leaving Certificate programme that aims to prepare pupils for adult and working life. It is a person-centred programme, incorporating a cross-curricular approach rather than a subject-based structure. The LCA offers courses in vocational education, in general education and in vocational preparation, in which work experience is an essential element. The programme is characterised by educational experiences of an active and practical nature. "It is innovative in the way students learn, in *what* they learn and in *how* their achievements are assessed."[8]

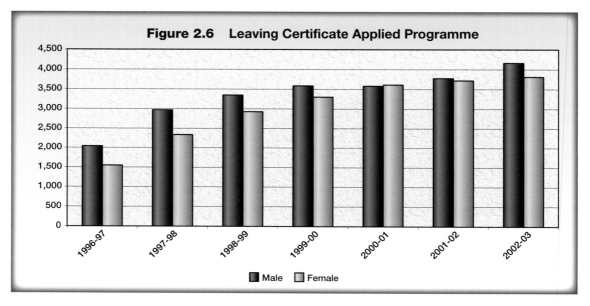

Figure 2.6   Leaving Certificate Applied Programme

There has been a steady increase in the number of pupils participating in the LCA over recent years, particularly among girls. In 2002/03, LCA pupils accounted for 7 per cent of all Leaving Certificate pupils, and boys slightly outnumbered girls, with a ratio of 52:48.

8 DES guidelines, "The Senior Cycle in Second-Level Schools," p. 6–9, available at
   http://www.education.ie/servlet/blobservlet/senior_cycle_options.pdf?language=EN

Repeat Leaving Certificate

There has been a considerable reduction in the total number of pupils repeating the Leaving Certificate in public second-level schools. This reduction is particularly notable since 1996/97. Within public institutions, boys have traditionally outnumbered girls among repeat Leaving Certificate pupils. However, the gap has narrowed in recent times and was evenly balanced in 2002/03 at 50:50.

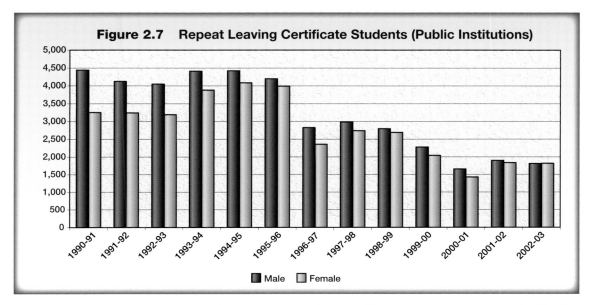

Figure 2.7 Repeat Leaving Certificate Students (Public Institutions)

The overview of participation in the various Leaving Certificate programmes provided in fig. 2.8 demonstrates that in 2002/03, 61 per cent of all pupils participated in the Established Leaving Certificate programme, 29 per cent in the LCVP, and 7 per cent in the LCA, with those repeating the Leaving Certificate accounting for the remaining 3 per cent. Looking at gender differences, it can be seen that a higher proportion of boys participate in the Established Leaving Certificate and in the LCA; in contrast, girls have higher participation rates in the LCVP.

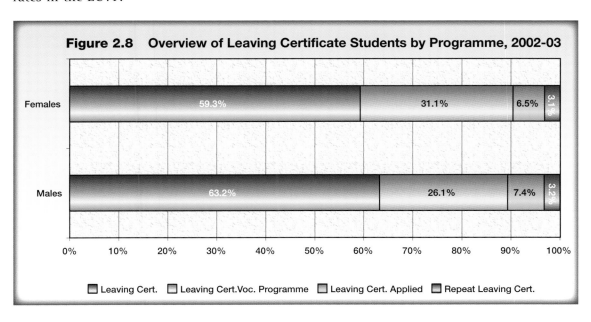

Figure 2.8 Overview of Leaving Certificate Students by Programme, 2002-03

Enrolment by school sector

In Irish second-level education there are three different school sectors: the secondary voluntary sector, the vocational sector, and the community and comprehensive (C&C) sector. While the three sectors have their own distinct local management structures and have traditionally had differing emphases in curricular provision, all sectors now aim to provide a broad curriculum for their pupils.

The largest and oldest sector is the secondary voluntary sector, whose schools were established by religious orders and other denominational groups. At the beginning of the 1980s, 70 per cent of all second-level pupils attended secondary voluntary schools; by 2003 the proportion had declined to 60 per cent. Over that period the proportion of second-level pupils enrolled in the vocational sector increased slightly, from 21 per cent to 23 per cent, and there was a significant increase in the proportion of pupils attending C&C schools, from 9 per cent in 1981 to 16 per cent in 2003.

Fig. 2.9 provides an overview of the enrolment of male and female second-level pupils by school sector between 1981 and 2003. As noted above, the largest proportion of pupils attend secondary voluntary schools, and this is particularly true of female pupils. In 1981, 79 per cent of female second-level pupils were enrolled in secondary schools, compared with 62 per cent male pupils. Since that time there has been a steady decrease in the proportion of girls in secondary voluntary schools (to 65 per cent in 2003), and this has been accompanied by increases in the proportion of girls attending vocational and C&C schools. The proportion of male second-level pupils in vocational schools has remained relatively constant over that period. The increasing female enrolment in vocational schools has resulted in an improved gender balance in vocational schools, from a situation where boys outnumbered girls by more than 2 to 1 in 1981 to a ratio of 57:43 in favour of boys in 2003. Girls continue to outnumber boys in the secondary voluntary sector, where the ratio in 2003 was 45:55 in their favour.

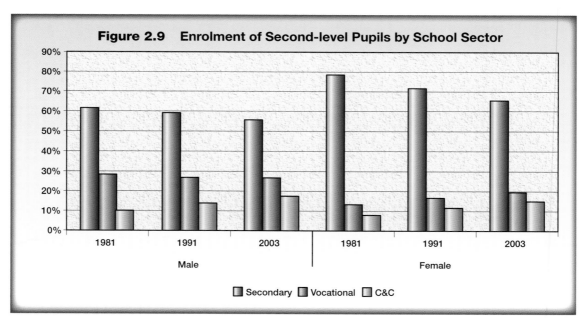

Figure 2.9   Enrolment of Second-level Pupils by School Sector

Gender mix in second-level schools

Looking at the enrolment statistics for second-level schools, we see a clear pattern of increase in the proportion of pupils receiving second-level education in mixed schools. At the beginning of the 1980s a majority of second-level pupils (58 per cent) attended single-sex schools. Since that time the proportion has declined steadily and consistently, and by 2003 it was 38 per cent. The proportion of second-level pupils in single-sex schools in Ireland is very high by international standards. In fact in a majority of European countries there are no single-sex schools at second level. In the remaining countries only a very small minority of pupils (at the age of fifteen) attend single-sex schools—fewer than 5 per cent altogether.[9] Ireland has therefore by far the highest proportion of pupils in single-sex education in Europe.

Fig. 2.10 provides an overview of the declining proportion of pupils attending single-sex second-level schools between 1980 and 2003. The proportion of girls in single-sex schools has remained considerably higher than the corresponding figure for boys, showing that boys are more likely to attend mixed schools. The higher proportion of girls in single-sex schools is linked to the fact that girls are more likely to attend schools in the secondary voluntary sector (see fig. 2.9). Unlike the vocational and C&C sectors, where almost all schools are mixed, approximately two-thirds of schools in the secondary voluntary sector are single-sex schools. The increase over time in the number of second-level pupils in mixed schools is related to the increasing enrolment in vocational schools among girls and the steady overall increase in enrolments in C&C schools among all pupils.

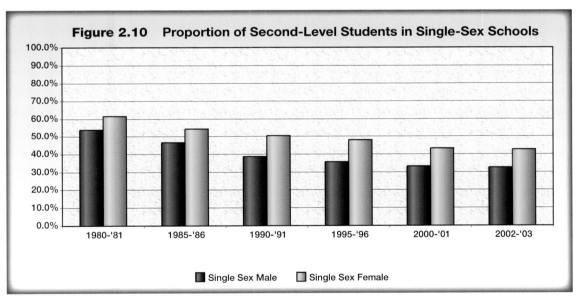

Figure 2.10   Proportion of Second-Level Students in Single-Sex Schools

[9]   Source: Department of Education and Science, *Education Trends: Key Indicators on Education in Ireland and Europe* (forthcoming). Indicator 4.11 (Data sourced from OECD PISA 2003 data-base).

Retention through second-level education

In Ireland, as in many other countries, qualifications obtained at the end of second-level education provide an important platform for participation in higher education and for future engagement with learning through further and continuing education and training. The promotion of continued participation and engagement with second-level education up to the Leaving Certificate has been a central goal of Irish education policy for many years. The rapid advances in information and communications technologies (ICTs) and the emergence of the "knowledge-based economy" over recent years have further reinforced the importance of upper second-level education.

This general increase in skill demands over time has resulted in a steady and severe decline in the labour market opportunities available to those who leave school before completing upper second-level education. Early school-leaving is therefore an important indicator of educational disadvantage and of social exclusion. The intensive policy debates on the subject of lifelong learning have also drawn attention to the vital importance of initial education as a foundation for continuing participation in education and engagement with learning as a lifelong activity.

> The link between initial levels of educational attainment and likely participation in further and continuing education is evident right across the OECD and is particularly marked in countries with low levels of overall public provision of adult and second-chance education. It is estimated that Irish adults with third-level qualifications are four times more likely to participate in continuing education than their peers with less than upper second-level qualifications.[10]

To set this analysis of retention through second-level education in historical context, figs. 2.11(a) and 2.11(b) use information on the number of Junior/Intermediate and Leaving Certificate English examination candidates as indicators of participation and attainment in second-level education. These charts provide data extending back to the early 1930s and provide a good insight into lower and upper secondary completion among boys and girls over time. The data show very low levels of participation in second-level education between the early 1930s and the late 1960s. The charts also highlight the very considerable increases in participation at second-level that occurred since the introduction of free second-level education in the late 1960s. Up to that point, the numbers sitting the Intermediate (ie. Junior) Certificate and the Leaving Certificate were low.

[10] Department of Education and Science, *Supporting Equity in Higher Education: A Report to the Minister for Education and Science*, 2003, p. 7—referring to OECD, *International Adult Literacy Survey*, and evidence from the CSO's Quarterly National Household Survey.

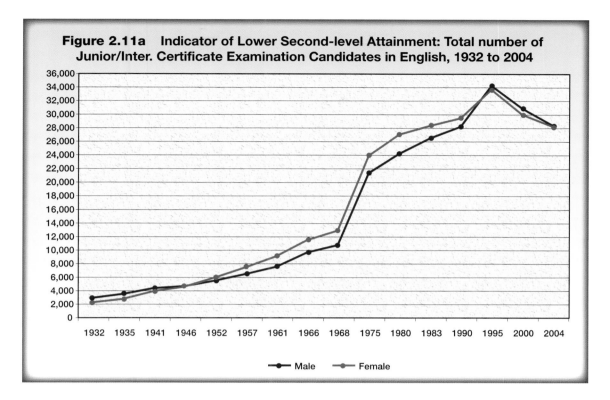

Figure 2.11a   Indicator of Lower Second-level Attainment: Total number of Junior/Inter. Certificate Examination Candidates in English, 1932 to 2004

It is interesting to note that girls outnumbered boys among Intermediate Certificate candidates from about 1950 onwards.[11] Between 1950 and the late 1960s, the number of girls taking the Intermediate Certificate increased at a faster rate than for boys. In fact, the gender balance in favour of girls was most pronounced during the 1960s. The introduction of free second-level education resulted in very rapid increases in the numbers of boys and girls completing lower secondary education and also resulted in a narrowing of the gender gap that was emerging during the 1960s. The educational work of religious orders throughout the country over many years contributed to the relatively high levels of participation among girls in Irish second-level education.

---

[11] The fact that boys begin to outnumber girls from 1995 reflects almost full participation in lower second level together with the higher number of boys in the population (see Figure 1.2). Even since 1995, a higher proportion of girls complete the Junior Certificate than boys.

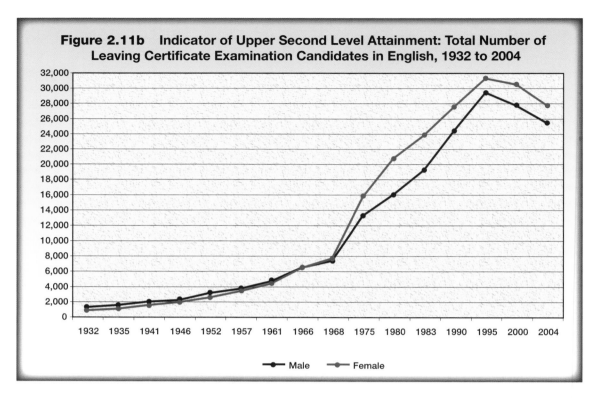

Figure 2.11b   Indicator of Upper Second Level Attainment: Total Number of Leaving Certificate Examination Candidates in English, 1932 to 2004

The numbers of male and female Leaving Certificate candidates were broadly equivalent between the 1930s and the late 1960s, albeit with males slightly outnumbering females during that period. From the late 1960s onwards, female participation in upper second-level education accelerated at a faster pace than among males. Since that time to the present day, girls have consistently outnumbered boys among Leaving Certificate candidates.

Fig. 2.12 provides a comparison of retention rates by gender since 1980, using data from the ESRI School-Leavers' Surveys.[12] The proportion of second-level pupils leaving school having sat the Leaving Certificate increased steadily throughout the 1980s, from 66 per cent in 1982 to 80 per cent in 1993. Improvements were more gradual between 1993 and 2002, when approximately 82 per cent sat the Leaving Certificate.

[12] Source: published results of ESRI School-Leavers' Surveys for the years shown, tables 2A and 2B.

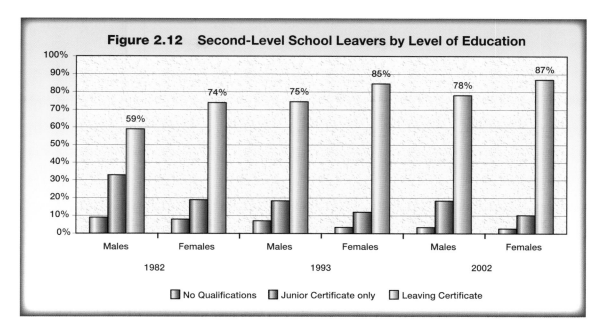

Figure 2.12 Second-Level School Leavers by Level of Education

Boys have consistently been more likely to leave second-level school before the Leaving Certificate than girls. The difference in retention up to Leaving Certificate between girls and boys was very large in the early 1980s (15 percentage points) and remains substantial (at 9 percentage points). Looking at the same data in a different way, fig. 2.13 shows the gender ratio among school-leavers at the different levels of education over time.[13]

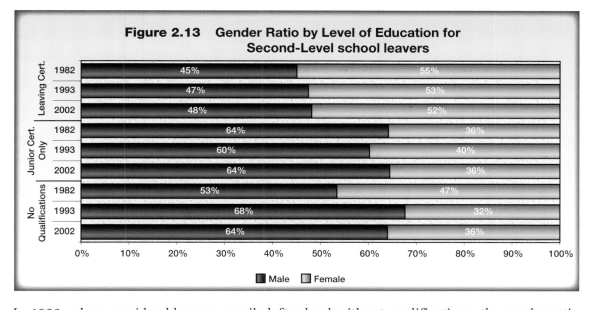

Figure 2.13 Gender Ratio by Level of Education for Second-Level school leavers

In 1982, when considerably more pupils left school without qualifications, the gender ratio among early school-leavers was relatively even, at 53:47 (male to female). In more recent years boys outnumber girls by 2 to 1 among pupils leaving second-level education without any qualification (i.e. before the Junior Certificate). Boys have consistently outnumbered girls by a similar margin among those pupils who sit the Junior Certificate but subsequently leave school before the Leaving Certificate. At the upper end, the gender gap among pupils completing second-level education has narrowed since 1983. At that time boys accounted

13 Source: published results of ESRI School-Leavers' Surveys for the years indicated, tables 2A and 2B.

35

for 45 per cent of school-leavers who sat the Leaving Certificate; by 2002, 48 per cent of those completing second-level education were boys.

In the early 1990s the Department of Education and Science introduced a Post-primary Pupil Database to record administrative data on second-level schools at the level of the individual pupil. Cohort analysis of these data allow for a more detailed look at the issue of retention through second-level education.[14] Fig. 2.14 refers to the 69,103 pupils who entered first year in publicly aided second-level schools in 1994. Allowing for participation in the transition year and for repeating the Leaving Certificate, all these pupils would have completed their schooling or have left school by the year 2000. Fig. 2.14 quantifies the number of these pupils who left school before sitting the Leaving Certificate on a roughly year-by-year basis.

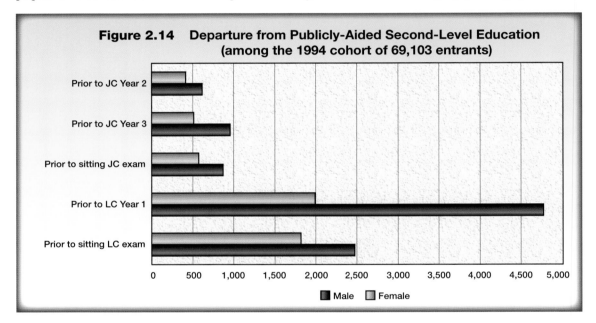

Figure 2.14   Departure from Publicly-Aided Second-Level Education (among the 1994 cohort of 69,103 entrants)

This cohort analysis demonstrates steady levels of early school-leaving throughout the junior cycle and confirms the fact that boys outnumber girls among early school-leavers. Altogether, 3,942 pupils (5.7 per cent) of the 1994 cohort had left second-level education before the Junior Certificate (i.e. without any qualifications). The proportion of boys leaving with no qualifications was 6.9 per cent, compared with 4.4 per cent of girls.

There is a considerable increase in the number of departures from second level after the Junior Certificate, and this increase is particularly sharp among boys. Boys account for 70 per cent of those who leave school after the Junior Certificate but before the beginning of fifth year. A number of those leaving second-level education at this point would be pursuing other forms of education and training, through apprenticeship courses and VPT II (PLC) courses; others may depart to continue their studies in private colleges. In the absence of individualised data-bases covering further and higher education it is not possible to quantify the proportions of second-level school-leavers who pursue further education and training.[15] To summarise retention among the 1994 entrants to second level, 27.5 per cent of boys left school before sitting the Leaving Certificate, compared with 15.7 per cent of girls.

---

[14] For more details on this cohort analysis of retention through second-level education see Department of Education and Science, "Report on Retention of Pupils in Post-Primary Schools," at http://www.education.ie/servlet/blobservlet/pp_retention_1994_report.doc (2003).

[15] Chapter 6 of this publication provides an overview of participation in further and continuing education. The point being made here is that, in the absence of individualised student data-bases in further and higher education, we cannot link the data in a way that would make possible quantification of the proportions that continue to participate in education and training.

Data on the retention rates of pupils who began their second-level education over the following two years (1995 and 1996) are now available from the Department of Education and Science. These cohorts would have completed their schooling or left school by the years 2001 and 2002. Taken together, these cohort studies demonstrate a very stable rate of overall retention across a series of cohorts beginning second-level education between 1992 and 1996.

Taking stock of the variety of data sources on school completion over time, we began with incremental increases before a period of sustained and steep growth between the late 1960s and the early 1990s. This period was followed by little or no improvement in overall retention rates between the mid 1990s and 2003 when the overall completion rate plateaued at 81-82 per cent.

People tend to get confused with the variety of data sources on school completion and with the variations in the way that it is estimated and measured. At the risk of adding to the already complex range of indicators on the subject, one relatively simple way to gauge the level of school completion is to compare the number of Leaving Certificate candidates to the overall numbers of 17-18 year olds in the country in a given year. Comparing the number of school-based Leaving Certificate candidates to the numbers in the population at 17 to 18 years of age, approximately 6,900 males did not sit the Leaving Certificate in 2005 compared to approximately 3,000 girls. In the same year, the number of boys not sitting the Junior Certificate was approximately 1,350 compared to approximately 350 girls.[1] Although these numbers remain substantial, this indicator suggests that overall school completion rates have moved beyond the 82 per cent mark in recent years. The estimated 10,000 teenagers not sitting their Leaving Certificate in 2005 compares with estimates of the order of 13,000 to 14,000 per annum at the beginning of the current decade.

The final point on retention relates to those who leave school early but who achieve qualifications equivalent to upper secondary completion through further educational routes. This equivalence is determined through the National Framework of Qualifications (NFQ) and refers to qualifications achieved at NFQ levels 4 and 5. Data from the Central Statistics Office demonstrate that the take-up of further education opportunities by some of those who leave school early results in an additional 2 or 3 per cent of the Leaving Certificate cohort achieving equivalent qualifications through further education and training before the end of their early 20s.

---

[1] Data sources for these estimates are the CSO (2003) Census 2002: Principle Demographic Results, Table 10, p.56 and Department of Education and Science Annual Statistical Report 2004/05 (forthcoming) Table 5.1. The estimates were derived by comparing the numbers of school based candidates in the 2005 Junior and Leaving Certificate examinations (excluding repeats) with the relevant age cohorts in the 2002 Census (minus 3 years). In percentage terms, approximately 22 per cent of males did not sit the Leaving Certificate compared to 10 per cent of females and 4.6 per cent of males did not sit the Junior Certificate compared to 1.3 per cent of females.

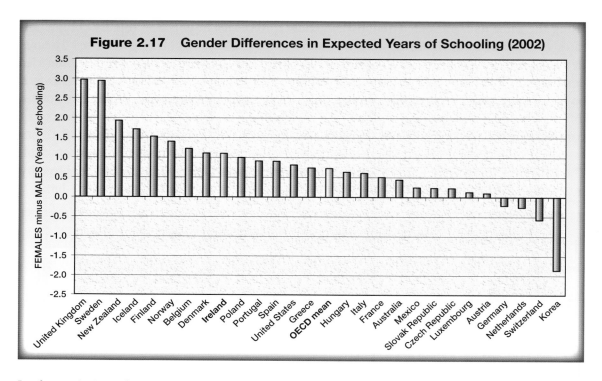

Figure 2.17   Gender Differences in Expected Years of Schooling (2002)

In the majority of countries, girls remain in education for longer periods than boys, and on average in OECD member-countries they can expect to receive 0.7 more years of initial formal education than boys. Contrary to international norms, boys in South Korea, Switzerland, the Netherlands and Germany have higher school expectancy averages than girls. Elsewhere, girls remain in education for longer. In Ireland, where girls receive 1.1 years more education than boys, the gender difference in school expectancy is above the international average.

This chapter has provided an overview of trends in participation in second-level education over recent years. In the chapters to follow, the emphasis moves from participation to an analysis of subject take-up and performance in state examinations. This is complemented in chapter 4 by an analysis of the performance of Irish second-level pupils in international assessments of literacy. Chapter 3 provides a detailed examination of subject take-up and performance in the Junior Certificate.

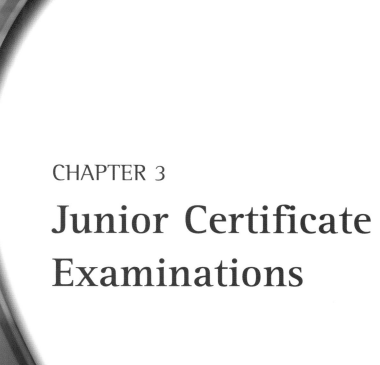

CHAPTER 3

Junior Certificate
Examinations

EXAM CANDIDATES

SUBJECT TAKE-UP

HIGHER AND ORDINARY LEVEL

OVERALL PERFORMANCE

OVERVIEW BY SUBJECT

IRISH, ENGLISH, MATHS . . .

Junior Certificate Examinations[1]

Junior Certificate examination candidates

This chapter examines the Junior Certificate examination and presents time-series data on participation, subject take-up and performance by candidates. To begin with, fig. 3.1 provides an overview of the total number of Junior Certificate examination candidates between 1991 and 2003. While gradual improvements over time in retention would have some minor impact on the number of candidates, the total number of candidates is primarily determined by demographics. Between 1992 and 2000 there was a demographic swell in the number of Junior Certificate examination candidates, corresponding to increases in births in Ireland fifteen to sixteen years earlier.

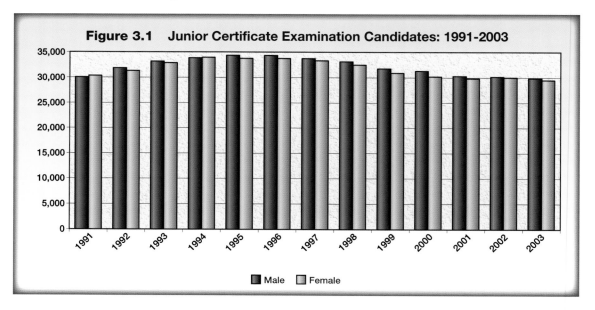

Figure 3.1 Junior Certificate Examination Candidates: 1991-2003

Subject take-up

An analysis of the gender ratio among Junior Certificate examination candidates reveals striking differences in the subject take-up patterns of boys and girls in lower second-level education. Fig. 3.2 shows the ratio of examination candidates in the various subject areas.[2] As expected, we find broadly equivalent numbers of boys and girls in the compulsory subjects, notably in Irish, English, and mathematics. At the extremes we find that lower second-level pupils continue to conform closely to the traditional gender stereotypes. Boys far outnumber girls in the take-up of metalwork, technical graphics, materials technology (woodwork), and technology; girls outnumber boys to the greatest extent in home economics and in music. Girls also have higher levels of participation in modern European languages and in art.

---

[1] For readers not familiar with the education system in Ireland, the Junior Certificate examination is taken by second-level pupils after three years of second-level education. The Junior Certificate marks the end of lower second level (ISCED level 2), and the average age of candidates is between fifteen and sixteen.

[2] In figures 3.2 to 3.5, subjects with fewer than 1,000 examination candidates are denoted by an asterisk. Subjects with fewer than 100 candidates have been omitted from this chart but are included in the corresponding appendix tables.

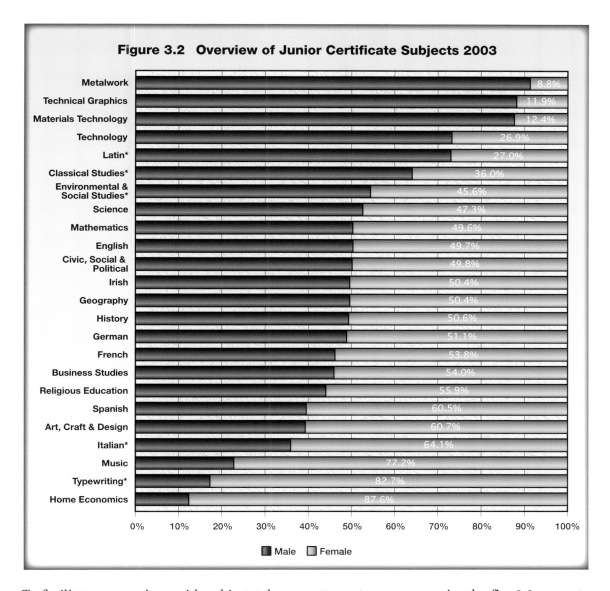

Figure 3.2   Overview of Junior Certificate Subjects 2003

Subject	Female %
Metalwork	8.8%
Technical Graphics	11.9%
Materials Technology	12.4%
Technology	26.9%
Latin*	27.0%
Classical Studies*	36.0%
Environmental & Social Studies*	45.6%
Science	47.3%
Mathematics	49.6%
English	49.7%
Civic, Social & Political	49.8%
Irish	50.4%
Geography	50.4%
History	50.6%
German	51.1%
French	53.8%
Business Studies	54.0%
Religious Education	55.9%
Spanish	60.5%
Art, Craft & Design	60.7%
Italian*	64.1%
Music	77.2%
Typewriting*	82.7%
Home Economics	87.6%

■ Male □ Female

To facilitate comparison with subject-take up patterns ten years previously, fig. 3.3 presents equivalent data from the 1993 Junior Certificate examination. The most striking feature of the comparison between the 1993 and 2003 examinations is the similarity over time and the almost identical overall ranking of subjects as between boys and girls. At the extremes there is some evidence of a slight improvement in the take-up of materials technology, metalwork and technical graphics among girls and in home economics among boys. Otherwise, beyond a reduction in the take-up of Spanish and an increase in the take-up of German among boys, the picture is one of consistency over time.

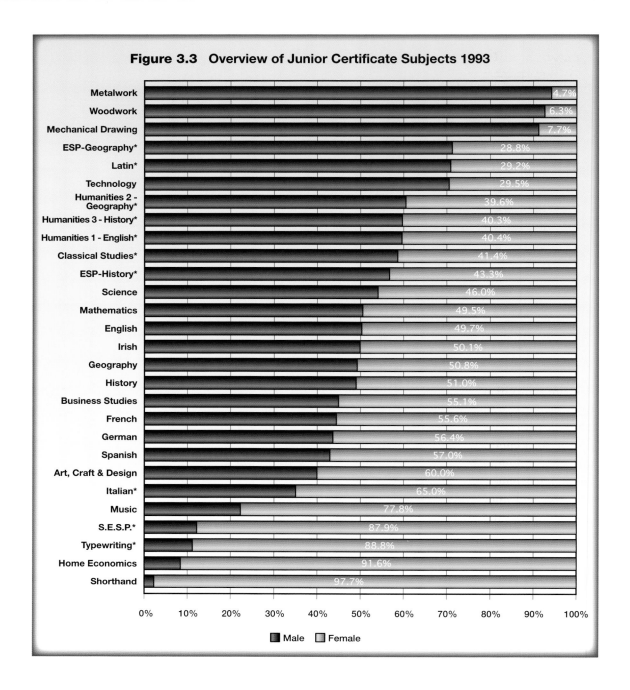

Figure 3.3 Overview of Junior Certificate Subjects 1993

Subject	Female %
Metalwork	4.7%
Woodwork	6.3%
Mechanical Drawing	7.7%
ESP-Geography*	28.8%
Latin*	29.2%
Technology	29.5%
Humanities 2 - Geography*	39.6%
Humanities 3 - History*	40.3%
Humanities 1 - English*	40.4%
Classical Studies*	41.4%
ESP-History*	43.3%
Science	46.0%
Mathematics	49.5%
English	49.7%
Irish	50.1%
Geography	50.8%
History	51.0%
Business Studies	55.1%
French	55.6%
German	56.4%
Spanish	57.0%
Art, Craft & Design	60.0%
Italian*	65.0%
Music	77.8%
S.E.S.P.*	87.9%
Typewriting*	88.8%
Home Economics	91.6%
Shorthand	97.7%

■ Male □ Female

Higher-level and ordinary-level examinations

In the Junior Certificate examination, candidates can choose between a higher-level examination paper (for honours-level grades) and an ordinary-level paper. Fig. 3.4 shows the proportions of total male and female candidates in the 2003 examination who chose to sit higher-level papers. Subjects are ranked on an odds-ratio basis according to the strength of the gender differences in the likelihood of sitting the higher-level paper. (See appendix, table 3.4, for more detail.) In summary, Italian is on the far left of this chart because this is the subject where the difference in favour of girls is largest in the proportions sitting higher-level papers in 2003.

As a way of summarising trends, fig. 3.9 also presents the average gender difference over time for the eight most popular Junior Certificate subjects. This average difference in favour of girls increased steadily, from less than 8 per cent in 1992 to just over 10 per cent in 2002. This shows that gender differences in performance increased between 1992 and 2002.

Summarised overview of performance by subject

Another important question that arises in this analysis of gender differences in Junior Certificate examination performance is, In which subjects do we find the greatest differences? This question is analysed in fig. 3.10, which presents subjects ranked according to the strength of the gender difference in the Junior Certificate examination results. Subjects are ranked according to average gender differences in examinations between 2000 and 2002. Equivalent average gender differences in earlier examinations (1992 to 1994) are also presented in order to provide information on trends.

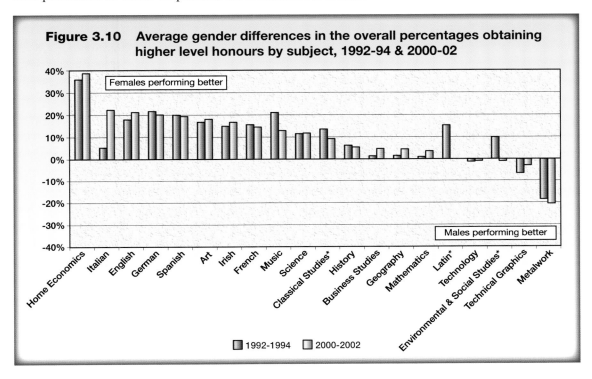

Figure 3.10   Average gender differences in the overall percentages obtaining higher level honours by subject, 1992-94 & 2000-02

This ranking of subjects by the strength of gender differences in examination results shows that girls outperform boys in more than three-quarters of Junior Certificate examination subjects. The most severe differences are found in home economics, where the proportion of girls obtaining higher-level honours is 38 percentage points higher than the corresponding proportion of boys. There are also considerable differences in favour of girls in English, Irish, art, music, and the full range of modern European languages. At the other end of the spectrum of gender differences, boys strongly outperformed girls between 2000 and 2002 in metalwork. Boys performed fractionally better in technical graphics, environmental and social studies, and technology.

Detailed overview of performance by subject

The remainder of this chapter is devoted to the presentation of time-series statistics that provide details of performance in the Junior Certificate examination for individual subjects between the early 1990s and 2002. It is often the case that educational professionals and those with a general interest in educational issues have a particular interest in a specific subject area or in a number of specific subject areas. Therefore, the results shown in fig. 3.11 (a)–(u) provide information on performance over time in individual subjects.

Each of these charts presents details on the number of candidates obtaining grade C or above in higher-level papers as a percentage of all candidates in the subject in question. As with all the charts in this publication, a corresponding table in the appendix provides the actual data underlying the chart, as well as additional data of interest. In the case of the appendix tables corresponding to fig. 3.11(a)–(u), the additional detail provided is considerable and will be of interest to teachers and others with a specific interest in particular subjects. In respect of each individual subject, the appendix tables provide the following information, all disaggregated by gender:

(1) the total number of Junior Certificate candidates taking the subject
(2) the percentages taking the subject at the higher level
(3) the percentage of higher-level candidates obtaining grade C or above
(4) the number of candidates obtaining grade C or above at the higher level as a percentage of all candidates taking the subject.

The data referred to at no. 4 above are used as a basis for the individual subject charts that follow. The subjects are presented in the following order:

(a) Irish
(b) English
(c) Mathematics
(d) History
(e) Geography
(f) French
(g) German
(h) Spanish
(i) Italian
(j) Science
(k) Business studies

(l) Home economics
(m) Environmental and social studies
(n) Materials technology
(o) Metalwork
(p) Technical graphics
(q) Technology
(r) Art, craft, and design
(s) Music
(t) Latin
(u) Classical studies

Following this detail on individual Junior Certificate subjects, chapter 4 draws from recent international assessments of literacy among fifteen-year-old pupils to examine the performance of Irish pupils in the international context. A detailed analysis of performance in the Leaving Certificate is then presented in chapter 5.

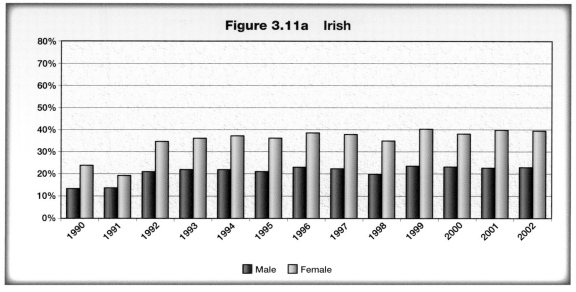

Figure 3.11a   Irish

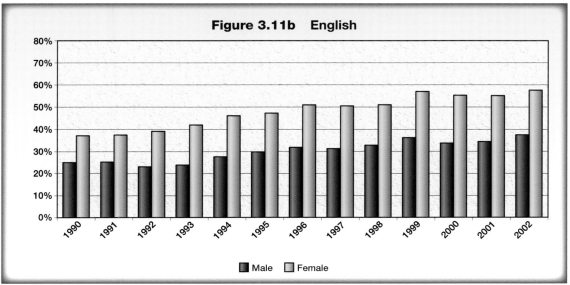

Figure 3.11b   English

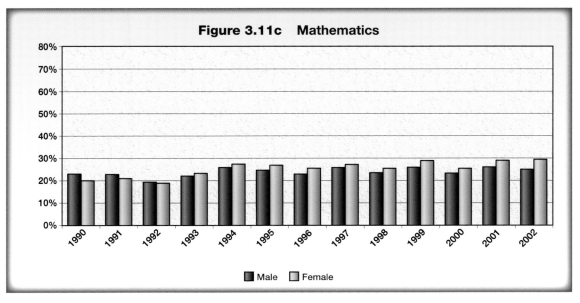

Figure 3.11c   Mathematics

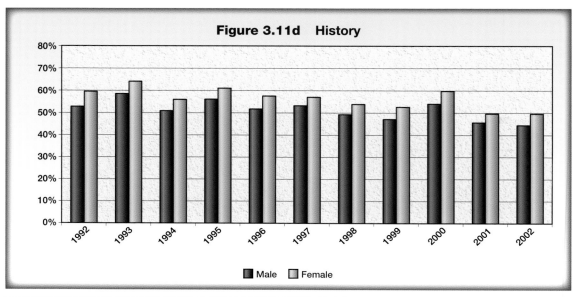

Figure 3.11d   History

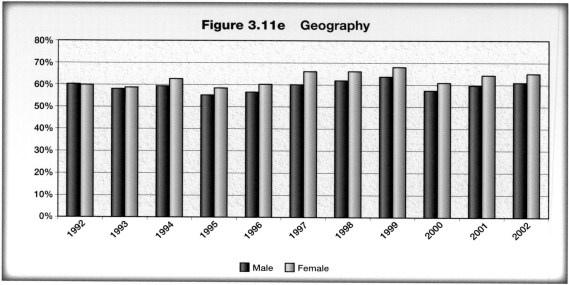

Figure 3.11e   Geography

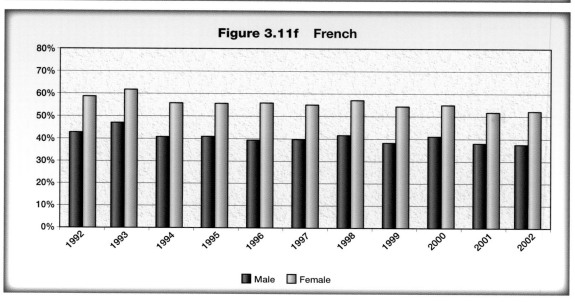

Figure 3.11f   French

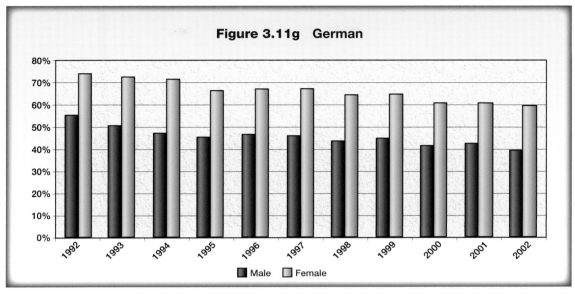

Figure 3.11g   German

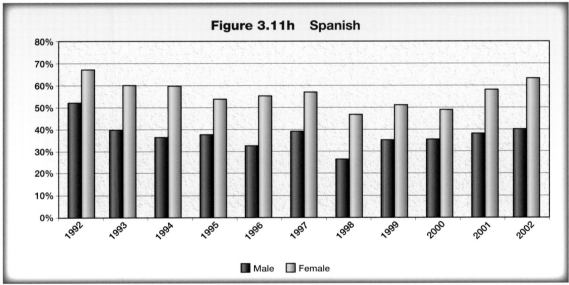

Figure 3.11h   Spanish

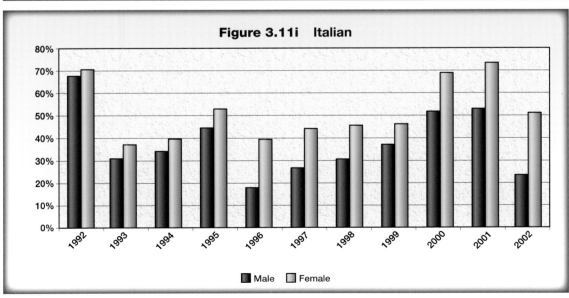

Figure 3.11i   Italian

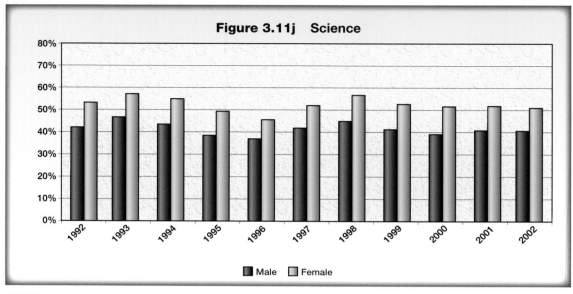

Figure 3.11j   Science

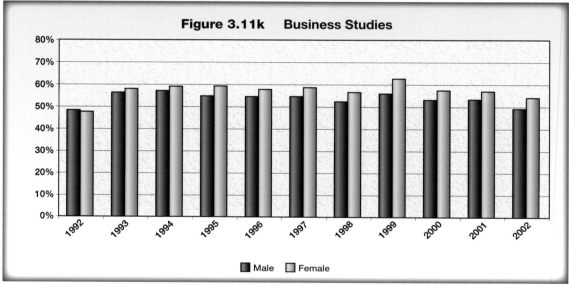

Figure 3.11k   Business Studies

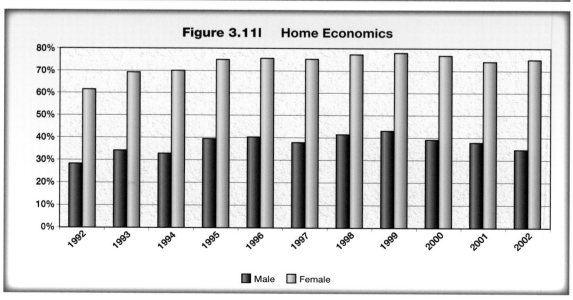

Figure 3.11l   Home Economics

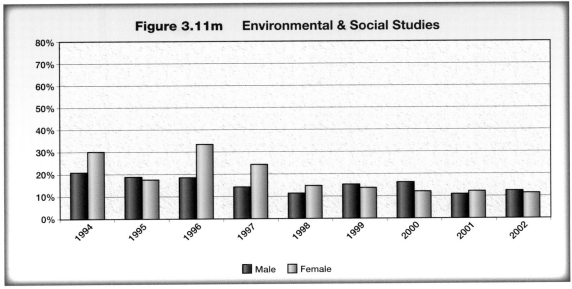

Figure 3.11m   Environmental & Social Studies

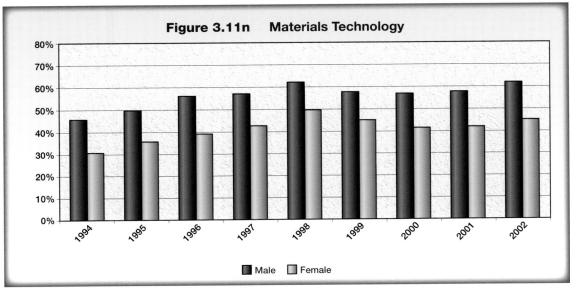

Figure 3.11n   Materials Technology

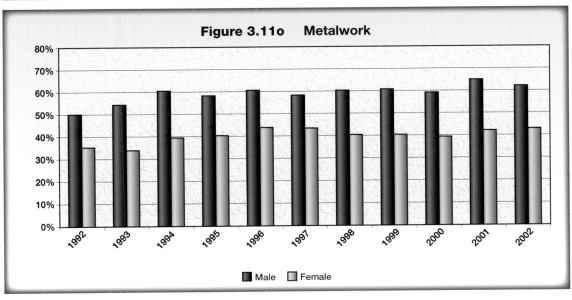

Figure 3.11o   Metalwork

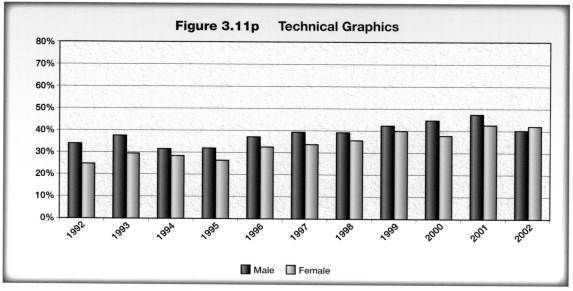

Figure 3.11p Technical Graphics

■ Male ■ Female

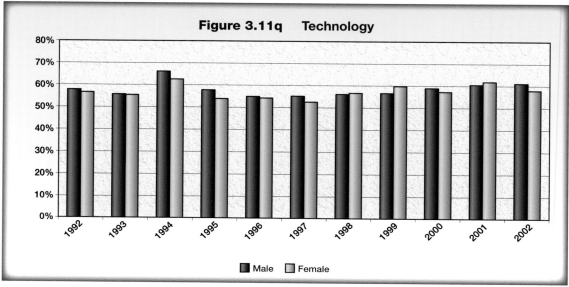

Figure 3.11q Technology

■ Male ■ Female

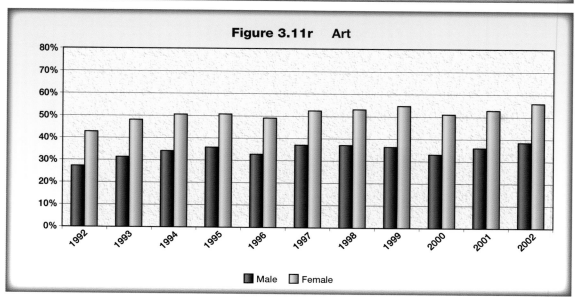

Figure 3.11r Art

■ Male ■ Female

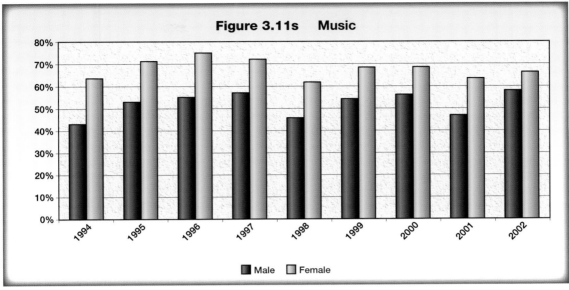

Figure 3.11s   Music

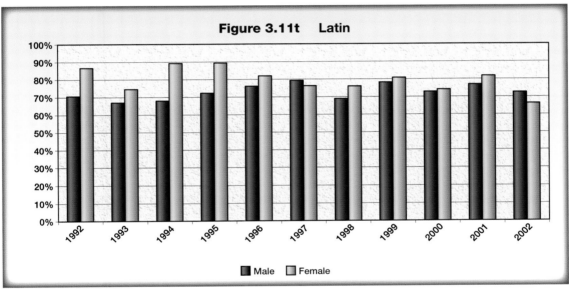

Figure 3.11t   Latin

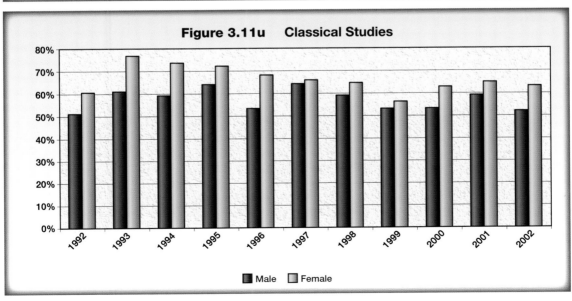

Figure 3.11u   Classical Studies

CHAPTER 4

Literacy in International Context

Literacy in International Context

Programme for International Student Assessment

In this chapter the literacy achievements of Irish second-level pupils are examined in the international context. This analysis is made possible through Ireland's participation in the Programme for International Student Assessment (PISA). This is a three-yearly survey, beginning in 2000, that aims to assess the knowledge and skills of fifteen-year-olds. Specifically, the survey carries out assessments of reading, mathematical and scientific literacy. The PISA assessments aim to interpret knowledge and the acquisition of skills for real-life challenges, rather than the outcomes of specific school curriculums. This work represents a unique collaboration among governments to monitor educational outcomes. The scheme is co-ordinated by the OECD, and Ireland's participation is managed by the Educational Research Centre on behalf of the Department of Education and Science.[1]

In addition to the assessments of knowledge and skills among fifteen-year-olds, data on the characteristics of individual pupils, of schools and of school systems are also collected. The literature that has emerged so far on the basis of the PISA 2000 and PISA 2003 assessments provides a rich source of data on gender differences in pupils' performance in the international context.

Reading literacy

In the first PISA study, conducted in 2000, the main assessment domain was reading literacy, while mathematical literacy and scientific literacy were minor domains. As noted above, the PISA surveys have adopted an understanding of "literacy" that refers to the application of knowledge and skills to real-life settings and challenges.

> Reading literacy is the ability to understand, use and reflect on written texts in order to achieve one's goals, to develop one's knowledge and potential, and to participate effectively in society. This definition goes beyond the notion that reading means decoding written material and literal comprehension.[2]

Fig. 4.1 provides an overview of reading literacy performance in OECD countries from the PISA 2000 survey.[3] Participating countries are ranked according to the mean score achieved by all pupils in each country. Irish pupils performed extremely well in the PISA 2000 reading literacy assessments, achieving a mean score that was significantly above the OECD average.

---

[1] For more information on PISA see www.pisa.oecd.org and www.erc.ie/pisa

[2] Organisation for Economic Co-operation and Development, *Education at a Glance: OECD Indicators*, Paris: OECD, 2004, p. 98.

[3] Source: Organisation for Economic Co-operation and Development, *Knowledge and Skills for Life: First Results from PISA 2000*, Paris: OECD, 2001, table 5.1a (p. 276).

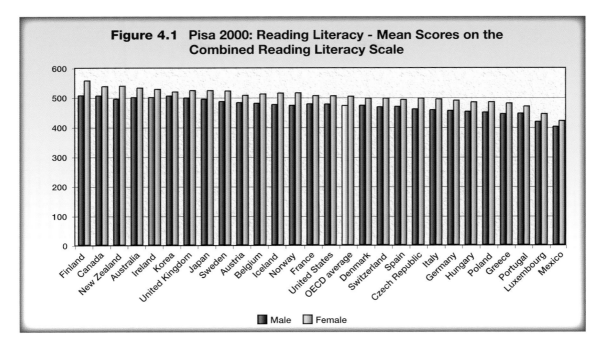

Figure 4.1 Pisa 2000: Reading Literacy - Mean Scores on the Combined Reading Literacy Scale

The gender differences in reading literacy have been quantified in fig. 4.2 by simply subtracting the mean score achieved by boys in each country from the mean score achieved by girls. The positive scores for all countries demonstrate that girls performed better on average than boys in every country that participated in PISA 2000. At 32 points, the average gender gap in reading performance within the OECD countries is substantial. This finding was confirmed in the reading assessments conducted in PISA 2003, when the average OECD gender gap was estimated at 34 points, in favour of girls.[4] Fig. 4.2 demonstrates a considerable variation between countries in the size of gender differences in reading literacy. In 2000, the difference among Irish pupils was slightly below the OECD average, at 29 points.

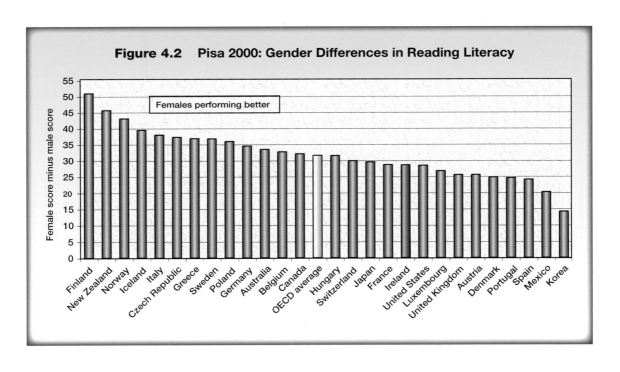

Figure 4.2 Pisa 2000: Gender Differences in Reading Literacy

---

[4] Appendix tables 4.1 (b), 4.2 (b) and 4.3 (b) provide results from the reading assessments conducted in PISA 2003 equivalent to those presented here in respect of PISA 2000.

The PISA reading literacy assessments measure proficiency in reading at five levels, representing tasks of increasing complexity and difficulty, with level 5 being the highest. Pupils proficient at a particular level are required and expected to demonstrate not only the knowledge and skills associated with that level but also the proficiencies defined by all lower levels. For instance, pupils proficient at level 4 are also proficient at levels 3, 2, and 1.

Level 1 pupils are capable only of the least complex reading tasks, such as finding a single piece of information, identifying the main theme of a text, or making a straightforward link with everyday knowledge. Those unable to routinely perform tasks associated with the most basic knowledge and skills that PISA seeks to measure are described as performing "below level 1." "This does not mean that they have no literacy skills," but "such students have serious difficulty in using reading literacy as an effective tool to advance and extend their knowledge and skills in other areas."[5]

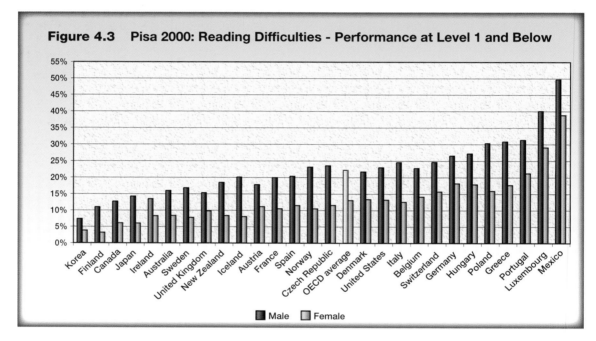

Figure 4.3   Pisa 2000: Reading Difficulties - Performance at Level 1 and Below

Fig. 4.3 shows the proportions of boys and girls in OECD countries who performed at level 1 or below in PISA 2000.[6] Once again, countries are ranked according to the proportion of pupils performing at these low levels. The overall ranking of countries is similar to that presented in fig. 4.1, because countries with a high overall performance in reading literacy tend to have lower proportions of pupils performing at level 1 and below. In all OECD countries, boys are significantly more likely than girls to demonstrate a poor level of literacy performance. On average within the OECD countries, 22.3 per cent of boys performed at level 1 or below, compared with 13.1 per cent of girls.

In Ireland, 12.7 per cent of all pupils performed at level 1 or below in the PISA 2000 reading assessments. The same gender differences observed throughout the OECD are evident among Irish pupils, with 13.5 per cent of boys registering poor performance, compared with 8.3 per cent of girls. Fig. 4.4 provides an overview of the proportions of Irish pupils and all OECD pupils performing at each of the proficiency levels on the PISA 2000 combined reading literacy scale.[7] This illustrates the relatively strong performance of Irish pupils compared

---

[5] OECD, *Knowledge and Skills for Life*, p. 48. See also OECD, Education at a Glance, p. 96–100.

[6] Source: OECD, *Knowledge and Skills for Life*, table 5.2a (p. 278).

[7] Sources: Gerry Shiel et al., *Ready for Life?: The Literacy Achievements of Irish 15-Year-Olds with Comparative International Data*, Dublin: Educational Research Centre, 2001, p. 59; OECD, Education at a Glance, p. 105; OECD, *Knowledge and Skills for Life*, table 5.1a (p. 278).

with international averages. It also illustrates the extent of the gender differences in performance throughout the OECD in favour of female pupils.

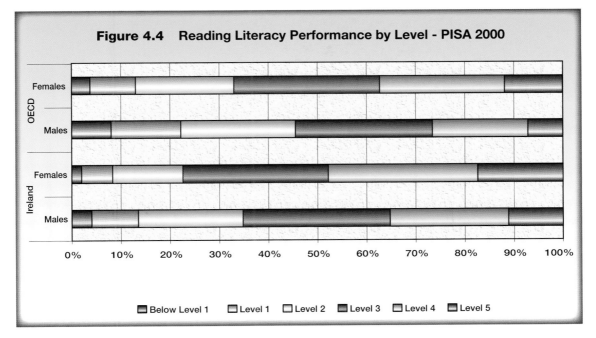

In Ireland, the gender differences are striking at both ends of the reading proficiency spectrum. At the lower end, more than a third of boys have a reading proficiency of level 2 or below, compared with approximately a fifth of girls. At the upper end, almost half the Irish female pupils performed at level 4 or 5, compared with roughly one in three of the male pupils.

In the PISA 2003 reading assessment[8] the proportion of Irish pupils registering poor performance dropped to 11.0 per cent. However, the proportion of boys performing at level 1 or below in 2003 is estimated to be 14.3 per cent, suggesting a disimprovement in performance among fifteen-year-old boys and a further widening of the gender gap in reading literacy among Irish pupils.

Reading profiles and learning strategies

Drawing from a rich source of background data, the literature on PISA provides an interesting analysis of the relationship between background characteristics and reading literacy. As one might expect, there is a strong link between a pupil's level of interest in and engagement with reading and their achievement in reading literacy. In all OECD countries, girls recorded higher levels of engagement and interest in reading than boys. Girls throughout the OECD spend more time "reading for enjoyment" than boys, and they read a more diversified range of material. In Ireland, 42.4 per cent of boys and 24.5 per cent of girls reported not reading for enjoyment.[9]

The PISA 2000 survey revealed considerable differences in the reading profile of boys and girls at the age of fifteen, with boys primarily interested in newspapers, magazines, and comics, while the more highly diversified reading of girls also included reading books

---

[8] See appendix, tables 4.1 (b), 4.2 (b) and 4.3 (b) for PISA 2003 results on reading literacy.
[9] OECD, *Knowledge and Skills for Life*, p. 280.

(particularly fiction). While girls outperformed boys in all aspects of the PISA reading literacy assessment, their performance on assessment items involving continuous text was particularly strong, and they performed most strongly in the "reflect and evaluate" reading sub-scale.

The PISA 2000 surveys also provide profiles of pupils' learning strategies that reveal consistent differences in the strategies reported by male and female pupils. Girls throughout the OECD report an emphasis on memorisation strategies, and this is particularly true of girls in Ireland.[10] Girls report spending more time on homework, and tend to study in a more strategic and self-controlled way, than their male counterparts. Again the gender differences on this "index of control strategies" are more pronounced in Ireland than the OECD average.[11]

In general, boys throughout the OECD report using "elaboration strategies" more often than girls. Elaboration strategies involve learning through working out how new material fits in with what has already been learnt and working out how the information might be useful in the real world.[12] This particular learning strategy was used less frequently by Irish pupils than by pupils in most other OECD countries. In Ireland, contrary to the international trend, girls were slightly more likely than boys to use elaboration strategies.[13]

In addition to their low levels of enthusiasm for reading, a substantial proportion of teenage boys in Ireland and throughout the OECD lack the strategic skills and the motivation to actively engage in learning.

Mathematical literacy

In PISA 2003 the main assessment domain was mathematical literacy, while reading literacy and scientific literacy were minor domains. (As noted above, the PISA surveys have adopted an understanding of "literacy" that refers to the application of knowledge and skills to real-life settings and challenges.) The mathematical assessments in PISA 2003 concentrated primarily on "real-world" situations and on "the capacities of students to analyse, reason, and communicate ideas effectively as they pose, formulate, solve and interpret mathematical problems in a variety of situations."[14]

Fig. 4.5 provides an overview of mathematical literacy performance in OECD countries from the PISA 2003 survey. As before, the participating countries are ranked according to the mean score achieved by all pupils in each of the countries. Irish pupils performed at a level equivalent to the OECD average.[15]

---

[10] See OECD, *Knowledge and Skills for Life*, p. 270.

[11] See OECD, *Knowledge and Skills for Life*, p. 269.

[12] For more detail on the index of elaboration strategies used in PISA 2000 see OECD, *Knowledge and Skills for Life*, p. 224.

[13] This slight difference is not statistically significant. Source: OECD, *Knowledge and Skills for Life*, table 4.7 (p. 271).

[14] Organisation for Economic Co-operation and Development, *The PISA 2003 Assessment Framework: Mathematics, Reading, Science and Problem Solving Knowledge and Skills*, Paris: OECD, 2003, p. 24. For more detail on the framework for the PISA 2003 mathematical literacy assessments see Judith Cosgrove et al., *Education for Life: The Achievements of 15-Year-Olds in Ireland in the Second Cycle of PISA*, Dublin: Educational Research Centre, 2005, p. 4–11.

[15] Source: Organisation for Economic Co-operation and Development, *Learning for Tomorrow's World: First Results from PISA 2003*, Paris: OECD, 2004, table 2.5c (p. 356).

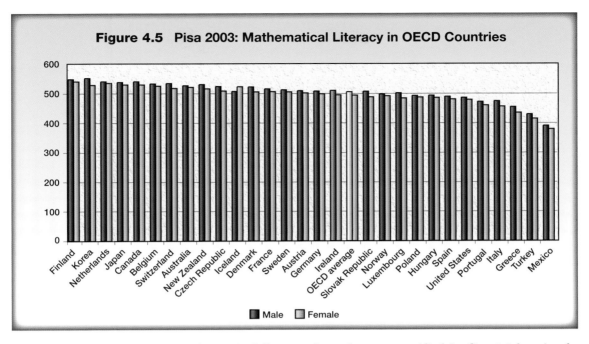

Figure 4.5   Pisa 2003: Mathematical Literacy in OECD Countries

The gender differences in mathematical literacy have been quantified in fig. 4.6 by simply subtracting the mean score achieved by boys in each country from the mean score achieved by girls. The negative scores demonstrate that boys performed better on average than girls in all countries, except Iceland, in PISA 2003. At –11 points, the average gender gap in mathematics is approximately a third of the gap that was found in reading literacy throughout the OECD. An equivalent gap was found in the earlier mathematical assessments conducted as part of PISA 2000.[16] At –15 points, the gap in favour of boys in Ireland was greater than that found in most other OECD countries.

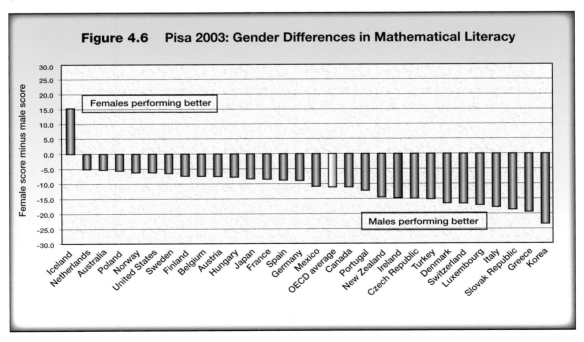

Figure 4.6   Pisa 2003: Gender Differences in Mathematical Literacy

[16] Appendix tables 4.5 (b) and 4.6 (b) provide results from the reading assessments conducted in PISA 2000 equivalent to those presented here in respect of PISA 2003.

In a similar fashion to the results for reading literacy in the PISA 2000 assessments, the OECD also analysed the performance of pupils in mathematics in accordance with proficiency levels in PISA 2003. Fig. 4.7 presents the proportions of pupils in each OECD country that performed at the lowest level (level 1) or below.[17] Pupils performing at this level display very low achievement in mathematical literacy and are likely to experience severe difficulties in applying mathematical concepts to "real-world" problems. In all countries, with the exception of Finland and South Korea, more than 10 per cent of pupils performed at level 1 or below. On average in all OECD countries more than one in every five pupils (21.4 per cent) performed at level 1 or below. At 16.8 per cent, the proportion of Irish pupils at these low levels of performance was less than the international average.

Looking at the gender breakdown, we see that in general girls are slightly more likely than boys to perform at level 1 or below. In two-thirds of the participating countries the proportion of girls demonstrating low levels of performance was higher than that of boys. This is consistent with the higher average performance of boys in the PISA 2003 mathematical assessments. (See fig. 4.5.)

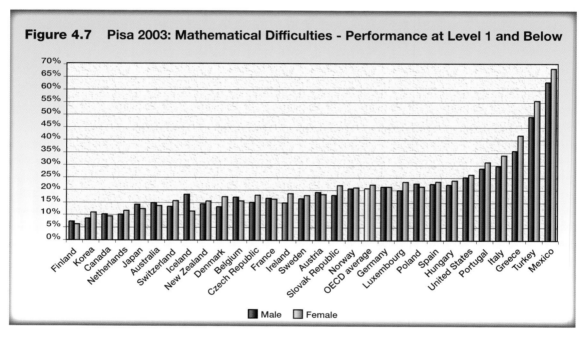

Figure 4.7   Pisa 2003: Mathematical Difficulties - Performance at Level 1 and Below

An overview of the performance of Irish pupils and all OECD pupils in all the proficiency levels in the combined mathematical literacy scale is provided in fig. 4.8.[18]

[17] Source: OECD, *Learning for Tomorrow's World*, table 2.5a and table 2.5b (p. 354–355).
[18] Source: Cosgrove et al., *Education for Life*, p. 101; OECD, *Learning for Tomorrow's World*, p. 354–355.

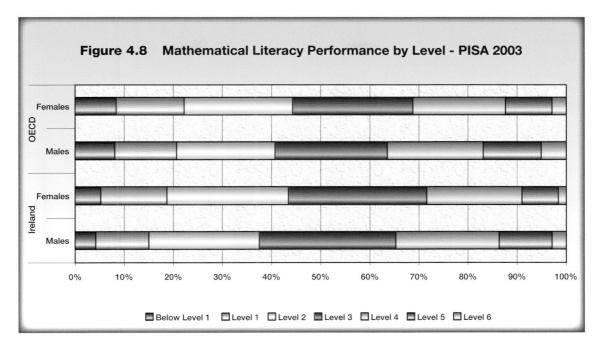

Figure 4.8 Mathematical Literacy Performance by Level - PISA 2003

As noted above, a smaller proportion of Irish pupils performed at the lowest levels of mathematical literacy compared with the international averages. However, at the other end of the proficiency spectrum Ireland lagged behind international averages, with smaller proportions of pupils displaying a performance at the very highest proficiency level (level 6). 2.2 per cent of Irish pupils achieved level 6, compared with 4 per cent of pupils throughout the OECD.

> Ireland's average performance is characterised by comparatively high performance at the lower end of the achievement scale and comparatively low performance at the upper end.[19]

The gender differences in performance among Irish pupils were broadly similar in pattern to those observed in the OECD averages. However, the differences in favour of boys that were observed internationally in the PISA mathematical assessments are slightly more pronounced among Irish pupils.

The better performances of male pupils in Ireland in the PISA mathematical assessments raises interesting questions when they are contrasted with the performance of pupils in the Junior Certificate mathematics examination. As reported in chapter 3, girls have consistently outperformed boys in Junior Certificate mathematics since 1993. (See fig. 3.11(c) and the corresponding appendix table.) Although the difference in favour of girls is small when compared with other examination subjects, girls are more likely to take the Junior Certificate mathematics examination at the higher level, and they are more likely to obtain honours than their male counterparts.

In the Irish national reports on the PISA 2000 and 2003 assessments the Educational Research Centre undertook a detailed analysis of the comparability of the international assessments with relevant subjects in the Junior Certificate examinations.[20] In its analysis the ERC noted that while the broad objectives of the Irish and international mathematics

---

[19] Cosgrove et al., *Education for Life*, p. 189.

[20] For a detailed comparison of the Junior Certificate and PISA 2003 assessments of mathematics see Cosgrove et al., *Education for Life*, p. 161–168, and the rest of chapter 6. See also the earlier national report, Shiel et al., *Ready for Life?*, p. 141 and 163.

assessments are similar, there are also notable differences. The essential differences appear to be the way in which mathematical problems are contextualised. These differences arise from the strong emphasis on the real-life approach to mathematics in PISA, which contrasts to a certain extent with the Irish emphasis on procedures, abstract concepts, and proofs.

> In the Junior Certificate Examination papers, questions are usually presented in a purely mathematical and abstract context, almost always without redundant information. In the PISA assessments, on the other hand, questions are often embedded in rich real-life contexts, accompanied by texts and diagrams. In PISA, students are often required to discriminate between necessary and redundant information, as well as to actually formulate the problem, in order to solve it.[21]

Although the gender differences in mathematical performance are small when compared with other subject areas, it is interesting that Irish boys perform better than girls in the PISA assessments and worse than girls in the Junior Certificate mathematics examination.

Scientific literacy

Scientific literacy was assessed as a minor domain in the first two rounds of PISA, conducted in 2000 and 2003. It will receive more thorough and comprehensive examination in the forthcoming PISA study (2006), in which it will feature as the major assessment domain. Drawing from the PISA 2003 data, fig. 4.9 reports the performance of fifteen-year-olds in scientific literacy, with countries ranked in order of their national average scores.

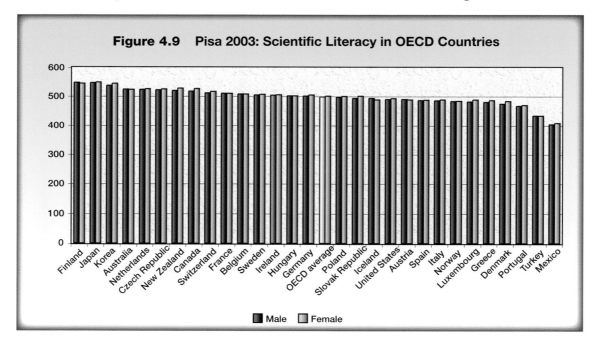

Figure 4.9   Pisa 2003: Scientific Literacy in OECD Countries

[21] Cosgrove et al., *Education for Life*, p. 165.

CHAPTER 5

Leaving Certificate Examinations

Leaving Certificate Examinations[1]

Leaving Certificate examination candidates

This chapter provides a detailed analysis of participation, subject take-up and performance in the Leaving Certificate examination. The structure of the chapter is modelled on the analysis of Junior Certificate examinations undertaken in chapter 3. In addition, at the end of this chapter some historical time-series analysis of Leaving Certificate performance in selected subjects is presented.

To begin with, fig. 5.1 provides an overview of the total number of Leaving Certificate examination candidates between 1991 and 2003. The first thing to note is that, whereas boys slightly outnumbered girls among Junior Certificate candidates (see fig. 3.1), girls consistently outnumber boys among Leaving Certificate candidates. For example, in the 2003 Leaving Certificate examination, female candidates outnumbered male candidates by approximately 2,500. This reversal in the gender ratio of candidates between the Junior and Leaving Certificate examinations is a direct result of the substantially higher rates of early school-leaving among boys. (See fig. 2.13.)

With regard to trends in the number of Leaving Certificate candidates, the total number of candidates has declined since 1998. This is primarily a direct result of demographic circumstances. The total number of Leaving Certificate candidates is likely to continue to edge downwards for another year or two, after which it will begin to increase steadily, in line with a demographic swell among seventeen and eighteen-year-olds and improvements in school completion rates.

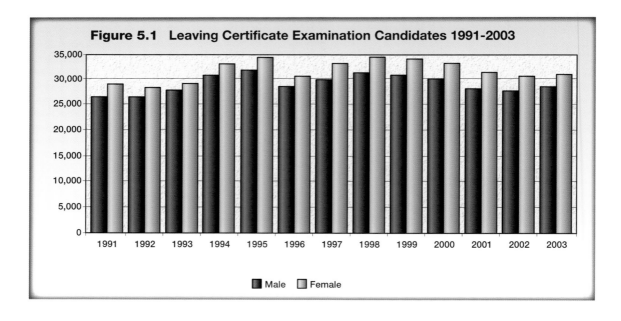

Figure 5.1 Leaving Certificate Examination Candidates 1991-2003

Subject take-up

Fig. 5.2 shows the gender ratio among examination candidates in the various subjects.[2] The striking differences in the subject take-up patterns of boys and girls that were observed in the junior cycle are also apparent among Leaving Certificate candidates. At the extremes we find that upper second-level pupils continue to conform closely to the traditional stereotypes. Boys far outnumber girls in the take-up of "practical subjects," such as engineering, technical drawing, and construction studies. Entirely consistent with the patterns observed at the lower second level, girls in the Leaving Certificate outnumber boys to the greatest extent in home economics and in music. In modern European languages and in art the ratio in favour of girls in the Leaving Certificate is even greater than that observed in the Junior Certificate.

An interesting split in the gender ratio is observed throughout the science subjects. While science is taught and assessed as a unified subject at the lower second level, pupils in the upper second level are offered distinct courses in biology, physics, and chemistry. Biology, which is by far the most popular of the Leaving Certificate science subjects, is dominated by girls, who outnumber boys by 2 to 1 (68 per cent to 32 per cent). Girls also outnumber boys among Leaving Certificate examination candidates in chemistry (54 per cent to 46 per cent). Physics, on the other hand, is dominated by boys, who outnumber girls by 3 to 1 (75 per cent to 25 per cent).

Taking all the Leaving Certificate science subjects together, the gender ratio is in favour of girls (55 per cent girls, 45 per cent boys). This is a reversal of the ratio observed in Junior Certificate science, where boys outnumber girls (53 per cent to 47 per cent). However, despite the overall ratio in favour of girls in the sciences at the upper second level, there is considerable concern about the very low take-up of physics among girls. It is believed that this is one factor that contributes to the subsequent low take-up of engineering among girls in higher education.

[2] In figures 5.2 to 5.5, subjects with fewer than 1,000 examination candidates are denoted by an asterisk. Subjects with fewer than 100 candidates have been omitted from the charts but are included in the corresponding appendix tables.

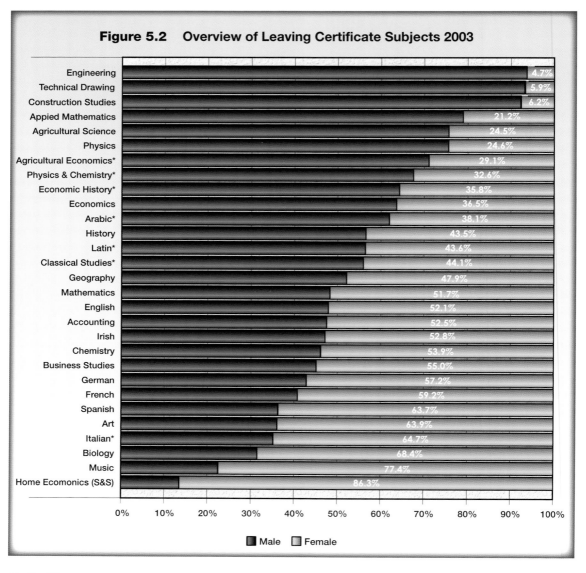

Figure 5.2 Overview of Leaving Certificate Subjects 2003

Subject	Male/Female split (Female %)
Engineering	4.7%
Technical Drawing	5.9%
Construction Studies	6.2%
Appied Mathematics	21.2%
Agricultural Science	24.5%
Physics	24.6%
Agricultural Economics*	29.1%
Physics & Chemistry*	32.6%
Economic History*	35.8%
Economics	36.5%
Arabic*	38.1%
History	43.5%
Latin*	43.6%
Classical Studies*	44.1%
Geography	47.9%
Mathematics	51.7%
English	52.1%
Accounting	52.5%
Irish	52.8%
Chemistry	53.9%
Business Studies	55.0%
German	57.2%
French	59.2%
Spanish	63.7%
Art	63.9%
Italian*	64.7%
Biology	68.4%
Music	77.4%
Home Ecomonics (S&S)	86.3%

■ Male □ Female

To facilitate comparison with subject-take up patterns ten years previously, fig. 5.3 presents equivalent data from the 1993 Leaving Certificate examination. As with the earlier analysis of the Junior Certificate, the most striking feature of the comparison between the 1993 and 2003 examinations is the similarity over time and the almost identical overall ranking of subjects by gender.

The most dramatic change has occurred in chemistry, where the gender ratio among examination candidates has been reversed. In 1993 boys outnumbered girls in Leaving Certificate chemistry, with a ratio of 56 per cent boys to 44 per cent girls. By 2003 the ratio in chemistry was 44 per cent boys to 56 per cent girls. The ratio in physics remained remarkably stable over that period and was also stable in biology, although with a slight increase in the proportion of girls taking the examination. Among the other subjects—beyond minor increases in the take-up of German and Spanish among boys and minor increases in the take-up of economics, construction studies and engineering among girls—the picture is one of consistency over time.

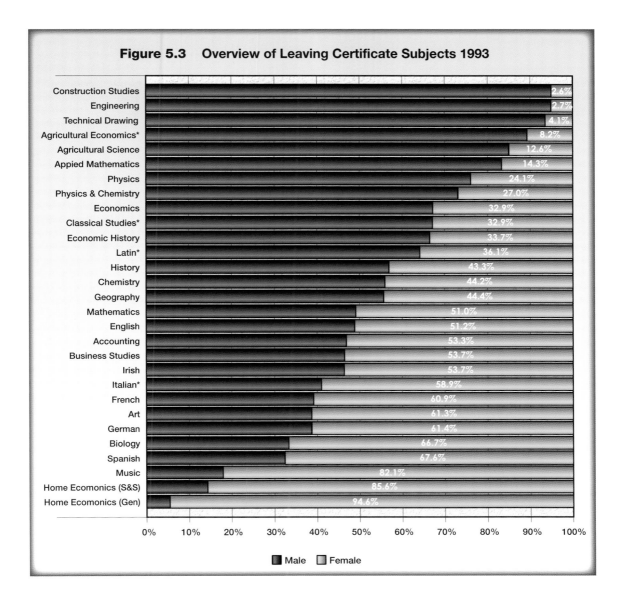

Figure 5.3   Overview of Leaving Certificate Subjects 1993

Subject	Female %
Construction Studies	2.6%
Engineering	2.7%
Technical Drawing	4.1%
Agricultural Economics*	8.2%
Agricultural Science	12.6%
Appied Mathematics	14.3%
Physics	24.1%
Physics & Chemistry	27.0%
Economics	32.9%
Classical Studies*	32.9%
Economic History	33.7%
Latin*	36.1%
History	43.3%
Chemistry	44.2%
Geography	44.4%
Mathematics	51.0%
English	51.2%
Accounting	53.3%
Business Studies	53.7%
Irish	53.7%
Italian*	58.9%
French	60.9%
Art	61.3%
German	61.4%
Biology	66.7%
Spanish	67.6%
Music	82.1%
Home Ecomonics (S&S)	85.6%
Home Ecomonics (Gen)	94.6%

■ Male   □ Female

Higher-level and ordinary-level examinations

In the Leaving Certificate examination, candidates can choose between a higher-level paper (for honours-level grades) and an ordinary-level paper. Fig. 5.4 shows the proportions of total male and female candidates in the 2003 examination that chose to sit higher-level papers. Subjects are ranked on an odds-ratio basis according to the strength of the differences in the proportions of male and female candidates sitting the higher-level paper. (See appendix, table 5.4, for more detail.) In summary, Irish is on the far left of this chart because this is the subject in which the difference in favour of girls is largest in the proportions sitting higher-level papers in 2003.

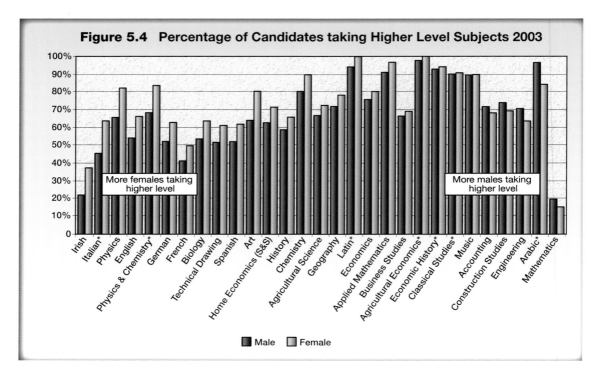

Figure 5.4 Percentage of Candidates taking Higher Level Subjects 2003

Girls are more likely to sit higher-level papers in more than 80 per cent of all Leaving Certificate subjects, from Irish to music. Among the few remaining subjects in which boys are more likely to choose the higher-level paper (to the right of music), the difference in favour of boys is strongest in mathematics, in which almost 20 per cent of boys take the higher-level paper, compared with just over 15 per cent of girls. This is a reversal of the situation in Junior Certificate mathematics, in which girls are more likely to take the higher-level paper than boys.

While the few subjects in which boys are more likely to take the higher-level paper correspond broadly to those subjects in which there is a ratio in subject take-up in favour of boys, there are some notable exceptions. For example, in physics, where boys outnumber girls by 3 to 1 in subject take-up, girls are substantially more likely than boys to choose the higher-level paper. The same is true of technical drawing and to a lesser extent of history, agricultural science, and economics.

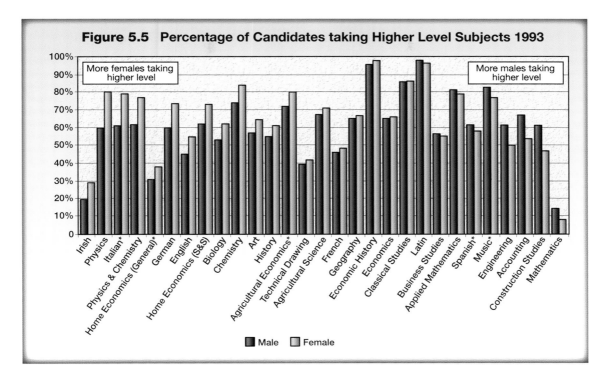

Figure 5.5 Percentage of Candidates taking Higher Level Subjects 1993

Fig. 5.5 provides equivalent data on the proportions of examination candidates choosing higher-level papers in the 1993 Leaving Certificate examination. (The more detailed appendix tables, 5.4 and 5.5, allow for a detailed comparison of trends over time in the particular subject areas.) By way of overall trends, there appears to have been a general increase over time in the proportions of pupils opting for higher-level papers in a wide range of subjects, including mathematics, English, and Irish. In the average for all subjects (with more than 100 candidates) the proportion taking higher-level papers has risen from 63 per cent in 1993 to 70 per cent in 2003. Over that period there is evidence of an increase in the gender difference in favour of girls in the numbers taking higher-level papers.

Overall performance in the Leaving Certificate examination

The Department of Education and Science publishes detailed breakdowns of performance in the Leaving Certificate examination by subject and by gender in its Annual Statistical Reports.[3] As with the analysis of Junior Certificate examination performance in chapter 3, we begin here with summaries of performance at the high and the very low end of the spectrum of achievement. The proportion of pupils achieving the high levels of performance is shown in fig. 5.6.

---

[3] These data have traditionally been compiled and supplied to the Statistics Section by the Examinations Branch of the Department of Education and Science. The responsibility for state examinations has recently been transferred to the State Examination Commission, which is now the official source for examination statistics.

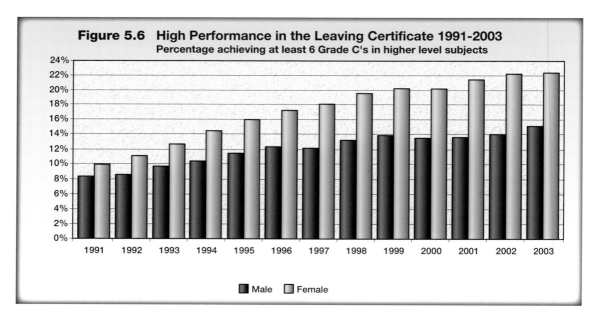

Figure 5.6 High Performance in the Leaving Certificate 1991-2003
Percentage achieving at least 6 Grade C's in higher level subjects

Girls have consistently outnumbered boys among candidates achieving a high overall performance in the Leaving Certificate examination. Indeed, between 1991 and 2003 the difference in favour of girls at the higher levels of performance appears to have increased. This has occurred against the background of an increase in the proportions of both boys and girls achieving very high results.

Turning our attention to the opposite end of the performance spectrum, we see in fig. 5.7 the proportion of pupils who achieve fewer than five grade Ds at any level in the Leaving Certificate examination. The overall proportion of pupils performing at this level decreased over the period 1991–2003. As in the Junior Certificate examination, boys have consistently outnumbered girls among those with very low levels of performance.

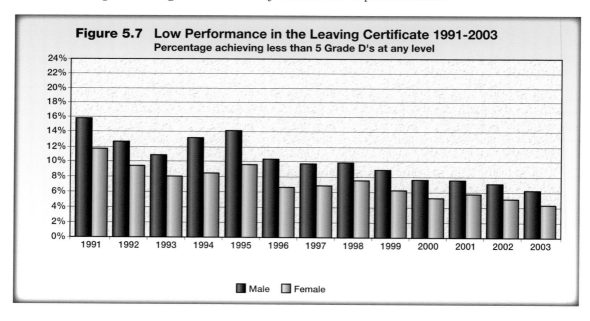

Figure 5.7 Low Performance in the Leaving Certificate 1991-2003
Percentage achieving less than 5 Grade D's at any level

The charts above show that girls consistently outnumber boys at the highest levels of performance, and that boys consistently outnumber girls at the lowest levels of performance. Looking at the 2003 Leaving Certificate examination, we see in fig. 5.8 an overview of the spectrum of performance. At the upper end of the performance spectrum (the top half of fig. 5.8) girls consistently outnumber boys. Conversely, boys outnumber girls throughout the lower half of the performance spectrum, showing that girls comprehensively outperformed boys in the 2003 examination.

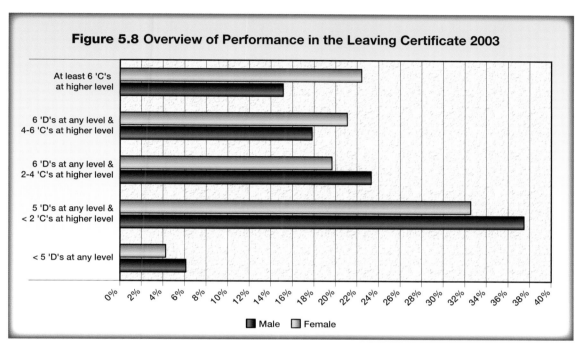

Figure 5.8 Overview of Performance in the Leaving Certificate 2003

A good way to examine overall performance in the Leaving Certificate examination is through the total number of CAO (Central Applications Office) points obtained by candidates.[4] Fig. 5.9 presents an overview of the performance of male and female candidates in the 2005 examination.[5] Once again this demonstrates considerable gender differences in overall performance in the Leaving Certificate examination. The statistical distributions of performance are significantly different for male and female candidates, "with clearly different medians and skews."[6] Girls outnumber boys in all the categories above 300 points, and boys outnumber girls in each of the categories at the lower end of the performance spectrum. Fig. 5.9 illustrates clearly the extent to which girls outnumber boys among the high-achievers in the Leaving Certificate. A third of all girls scored more than 400 points in the 2005 examination, compared with less than a quarter of all boys.

[4]   Examination candidates receive CAO points according to their performance in their six best subjects.
[5]   McDonagh and Patterson, *Discipline Choices and Trends for High Points CAO Acceptors*, p. 3. Data source: Central Applications Office.
[6]   Seán McDonagh and Vivienne Patterson, *Discipline Choices and Trends for High Points CAO Acceptors*, 2005, p. 3.

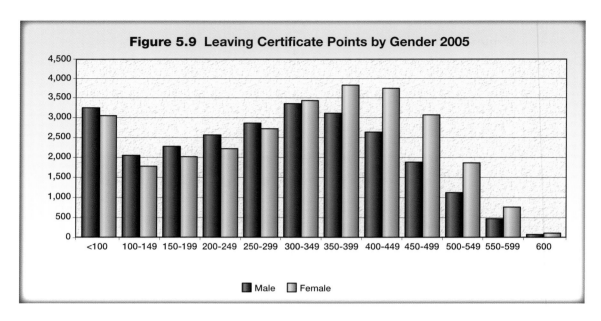

Figure 5.9 Leaving Certificate Points by Gender 2005

Having established that girls are more likely to take higher-level papers in the Leaving Certificate, and that girls have consistently outperformed boys in the examination over recent years, we turn our attention to trends in the gender differences in performance over time. The question that arises at this point is, Are the gender differences in Leaving Certificate performance increasing or decreasing over time? To explore this important issue, fig. 5.10 presents gender differences in performance in the eight most popular Leaving Certificate subjects between 1990 and 2002.

The gender difference in performance (as used here) is simply the difference between the proportion of girls that obtained grade C or above in the higher-level paper and the equivalent proportion of boys. By way of illustration, of all female candidates in the 2002 Leaving Certificate English examination, 52.1 per cent obtained grade C or above at the higher level; the corresponding figure for boys was 38.2 per cent. Therefore the gender difference in performance for this examination is 13.9 per cent (52.1 per cent minus 38.2 per cent). Given the way that this indicator is calculated (girls minus boys), a positive figure corresponds to a difference in favour of girls and a negative figure shows a difference in favour of boys. For example, in the 2002 mathematics examinations, in which 13.9 per cent of boys obtained grade C or above at the higher level, compared with 11.4 per cent of girls, the gender difference is –2.5 per cent (11.4 per cent minus 13.9 per cent). A nil result (0 per cent) would indicate equivalence or gender balance in performance.

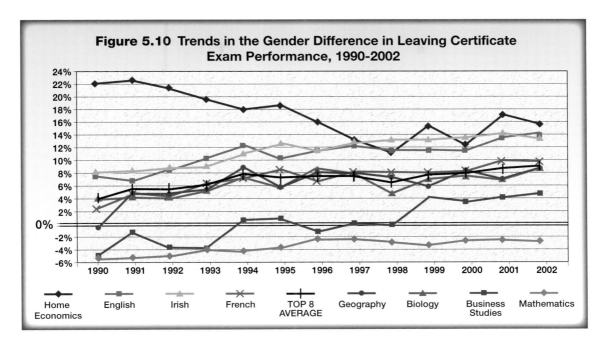

Figure 5.10 Trends in the Gender Difference in Leaving Certificate Exam Performance, 1990-2002

The first thing to note about fig. 5.10 is that almost all the figures are positive (i.e. above 0 per cent). This indicates a difference in favour of girls in seven of the eight most popular subjects. The one exception is mathematics, where boys continued to outperform girls in the 2002 Leaving Certificate examination. Between 1990 and 2002 the gender difference in mathematics narrowed from −5.4 per cent to −2.5 per cent. In business studies the difference in performance was reversed, from −4.9 per cent (in favour of boys) in 1990 to +4.9 per cent (in favour of girls) in 2002.

In all the other most popular subjects, girls outperformed boys. The difference in favour of girls is strongest in home economics, English, and Irish. Interestingly, while the most severe differences are found in home economics, this is the only one of the eight most popular subjects in which we find a reduction over time in the extent of the difference in favour of girls. In all the other subjects the gender difference in Leaving Certificate performance in favour of girls is clearly increasing over time. This trend is summarised by the average for the eight subjects, where the difference in favour of girls more than doubled, from 4.1 per cent in 1990 to 9.0 per cent in 2002. This gap was 10.4 per cent in the 2005 Leaving Certificate.

Summarised overview of performance in the Leaving Certificate examination by subject

A further important question that arises in this analysis of gender differences in Leaving Certificate performance is, In which subjects do we find the greatest gender differences? This question is examined in fig. 5.11, which presents subjects ranked according to the strength of the gender difference in the Leaving Certificate examination results. Subjects are ranked according to the average gender difference in examinations between 2000 and 2002. Equivalent average differences in examinations ten years earlier are also presented in order to provide information on trends.

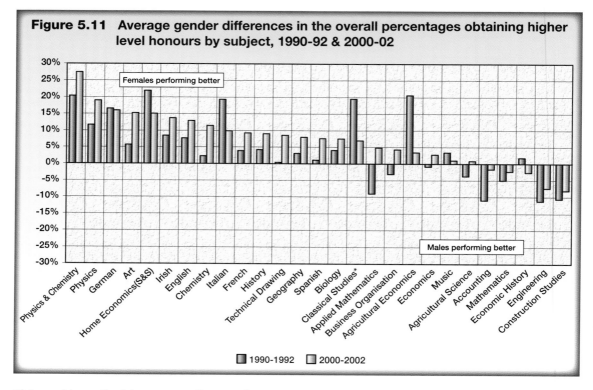

Figure 5.11   Average gender differences in the overall percentages obtaining higher level honours by subject, 1990-92 & 2000-02

This ranking of subjects according to the strength of gender differences in examination results shows that girls outperform boys in more than 80 per cent of Leaving Certificate examination subjects. The most severe differences are found in "physics and chemistry" and in physics, where the proportion of girls obtaining higher-level honours is 27 percentage points and 19 percentage points, respectively, higher than the corresponding proportion of boys. There are considerable gender differences in favour of girls in a wide range of subjects, including English, Irish, chemistry, art, and modern European languages. At the other end of the spectrum of gender differences, the subjects in which boys outperformed girls between 2000 and 2002 are construction studies, engineering, economic history, mathematics, and accounting.

The difference in performance in favour of girls increased between the years 1990–92 and 2000–02 in more than 80 per cent of Leaving Certificate subjects. This increase is often very substantial, as for example in art, chemistry, technical drawing, Spanish, and applied mathematics. In a small minority of subjects, boys have improved their relative performance: this has occurred in Italian, classical studies, agricultural economics, music, and economic history. In general, however, the difference in favour of girls is substantial, and the time-series analysis shows that it has increased steadily over recent years.

Extended time-series analysis in core subjects

To place this analysis of Leaving Certificate examination performance in its historical context, the time-series analysis has been extended back to the 1930s in a selection of core subjects—Irish, English, and mathematics—using the Annual Reports and Annual Statistical Reports of the Department of Education of Science. Readers should exercise caution in interpreting these data, because of changes to the Leaving Certificate over time and because the proportions of seventeen to eighteen-year-olds sitting the examination was substantially lower than it is today. Nevertheless the historical analysis of performance in Leaving Certificate Irish, English and mathematics presented here is useful and interesting in the context of our analysis of gender in Irish education.

As regards Irish and English, the first thing we learn from the historical analysis, as shown in fig. 5.12 (a) and (b), is that there is nothing particularly new about girls outperforming boys in these subjects. In Irish, girls have consistently outperformed boys since the mid-

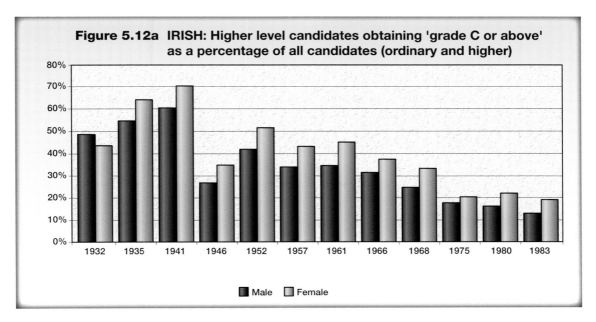

Figure 5.12a IRISH: Higher level candidates obtaining 'grade C or above' as a percentage of all candidates (ordinary and higher)

1930s, and in English they have consistently outperformed boys since the early 1960s and frequently also in earlier years. However, the extent of the differences observed in these subjects since the mid-1990s, as shown in fig. 5.13 (a) and (b), is unprecedented. While gender differences in the range 4–5 per cent in English and 8–9 per cent in Irish were common between the 1930s and the 1980s, the difference in favour of girls reached 14 per cent in both English and Irish in 2002.

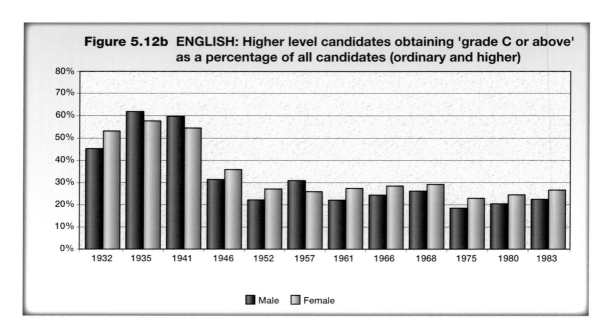

Figure 5.12b ENGLISH: Higher level candidates obtaining 'grade C or above' as a percentage of all candidates (ordinary and higher)

■ Male ☐ Female

The historical analysis of performance in mathematics is particularly interesting. Readers will recall that mathematics was the only one of the more popular Leaving Certificate subjects in which boys outperformed girls consistently during the 1990s. Fig. 5.12 (c) shows that boys have consistently been more likely to obtain grade C or above in higher-level mathematics since the early 1930s. The greater detail provided in the corresponding appendix tables is relevant in examining mathematics in the historical context. When this is compared with the total numbers of female candidates sitting the Leaving Certificate English examination, it is clear that a significant minority of girls (approximately 15–20 per cent) did not sit a mathematics paper at all in the Leaving Certificate examination between the early 1930s and the mid-1970s. Of the girls who did sit a mathematics paper, very few sat the higher-level paper.

The proportion of girls sitting higher-level mathematics was particularly low between the mid-1940s and early 1960s. For example, in the 1952 mathematics examination less than 1 per cent of girls sat the higher-level paper, compared with 26 per cent of boys. There is clearly a historical inequity in the provision of higher-level mathematics to girls. In fact in Annual Statistical Reports between the 1930s and 1968, "arithmetic–girls only" and later "elementary mathematics (for girls only)" were recorded as separate Intermediate Certificate subjects–crucially distinct from higher-level mathematics. The clear implication from reports of that era is that elementary mathematics was for girls, who, it was assumed, were unsuitable for higher-level mathematics. For most female pupils in the junior and senior cycle at that time, higher-level mathematics was simply not an option that they were offered at school.

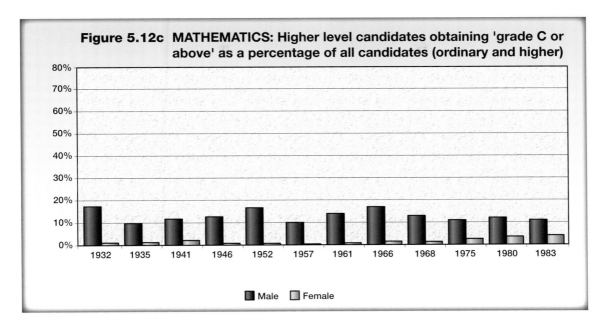

Figure 5.12c **MATHEMATICS: Higher level candidates obtaining 'grade C or above' as a percentage of all candidates (ordinary and higher)**

The gender imbalance in the proportions taking higher-level mathematics has persisted over time. In 1991 boys were still twice as likely as girls to sit the higher-level paper (16.1 per cent versus 8.2 per cent). However, girls have managed to considerably narrow the gap in performance by taking higher-level mathematics in far greater numbers over recent years. Among those who do take higher-level papers, girls have in fact outperformed boys consistently since 1996. However, because more boys continue to take the higher-level paper, the overall proportion of boys obtaining honours in higher-level mathematics continues to be higher than the equivalent overall proportion of girls.

Detailed overview of recent performance in the Leaving Certificate examinations by subject

The remainder of this chapter is devoted to the presentation of more recent time-series statistics that provide details on performance in the Leaving Certificate examination for individual subjects between 1990 and 2002. As noted in chapter 3, educational professionals and those with a general interest in educational issues often have a particular interest in a specific subject area or in a number of specific subject areas. Therefore, the results shown in fig. 5.13 (a)-(z) provide information on performance over time in individual subjects.

Each of these charts presents details on the number of candidates obtaining grade C or above in higher-level papers as a proportion of all candidates in the subject in question. As with all the charts in this publication, a corresponding table in the appendix provides the actual data underlying the chart, as well as additional data of interest. In the case of the appendix tables corresponding to fig. 5.13 (a)–(z) the additional detail provided is considerable and will be of interest to teachers and others with a specific interest in particular subjects. In respect of each individual subject, the appendix tables provide the following information, all disaggregated by gender:

(1) the total number of Leaving Certificate candidates taking the subject
(2) the proportions taking the subject at the higher level
(3) the proportions of higher-level candidates obtaining grade C or above
(4) candidates obtaining grade C or above at the higher level as a percentage of all candidates taking the subject.

The data referred to at no. 4 above are used as a basis for the individual subject charts that follow. The subjects are presented in the following order:

(a) Irish
(b) English
(c) Mathematics
(d) Applied mathematics
(e) History
(f) Geography
(g) French
(h) German
(i) Spanish
(j) Italian
(k) Physics
(l) Chemistry
(m) Physics and chemistry
(n) Biology
(o) Agricultural science
(p) Business studies
(q) Economics
(r) Accounting
(s) Agricultural economics
(t) Home economics
(u) Construction studies
(v) Engineering
(w) Technical drawing
(x) Art
(y) Music
(z) Classical studies

Figure 5.13a Leaving Certificate Irish

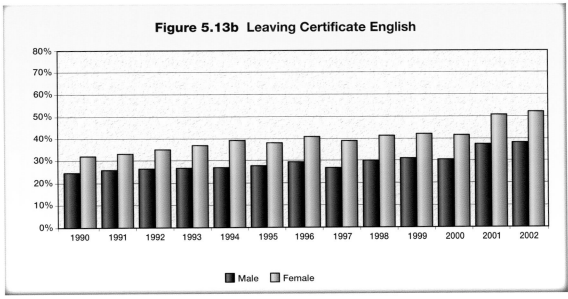

Figure 5.13b Leaving Certificate English

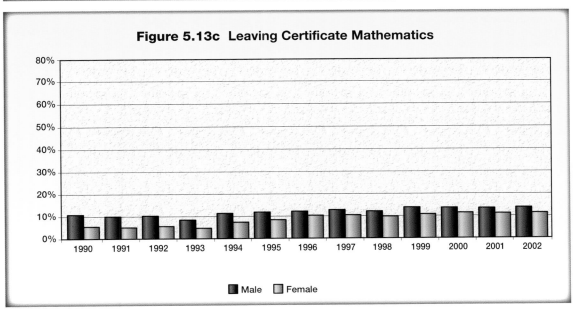

Figure 5.13c Leaving Certificate Mathematics

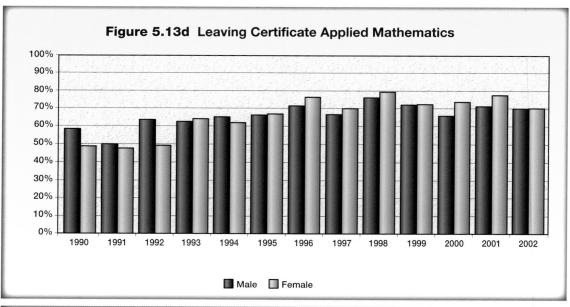

Figure 5.13d Leaving Certificate Applied Mathematics

Figure 5.13e Leaving Certificate History

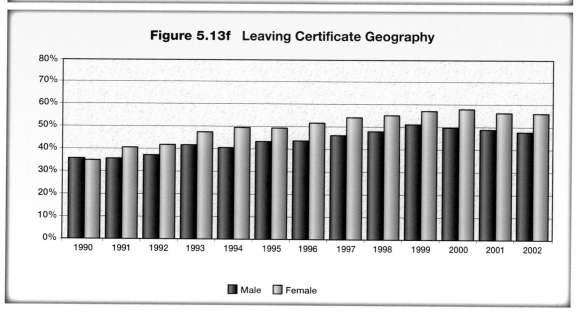

Figure 5.13f Leaving Certificate Geography

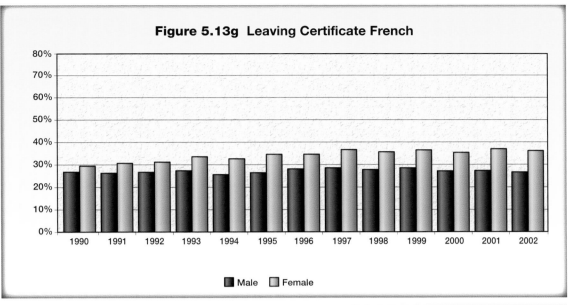

Figure 5.13g Leaving Certificate French

■ Male ☐ Female

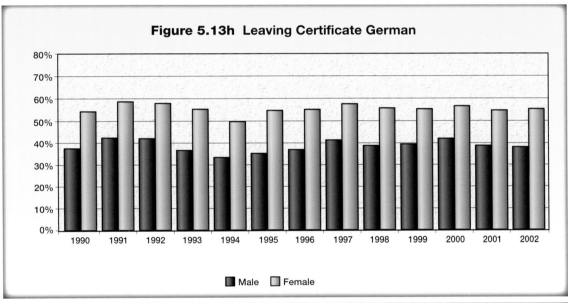

Figure 5.13h Leaving Certificate German

■ Male ☐ Female

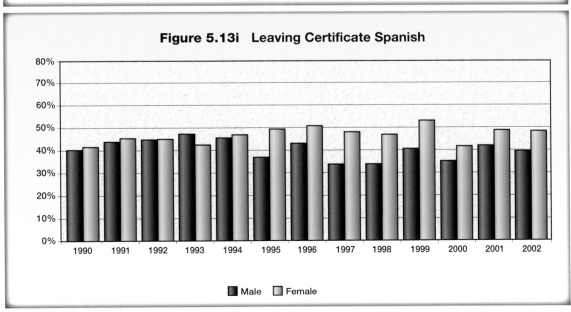

Figure 5.13i Leaving Certificate Spanish

■ Male ☐ Female

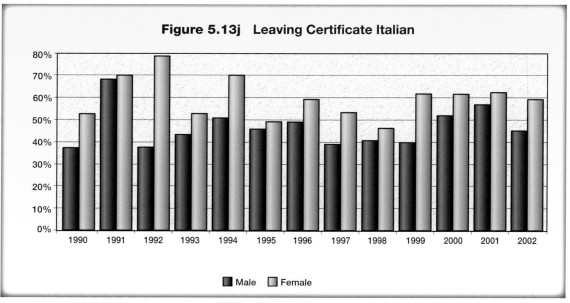

Figure 5.13j Leaving Certificate Italian

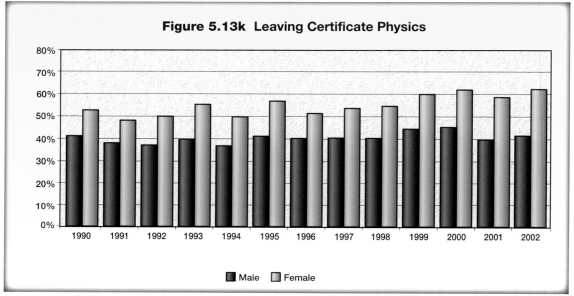

Figure 5.13k Leaving Certificate Physics

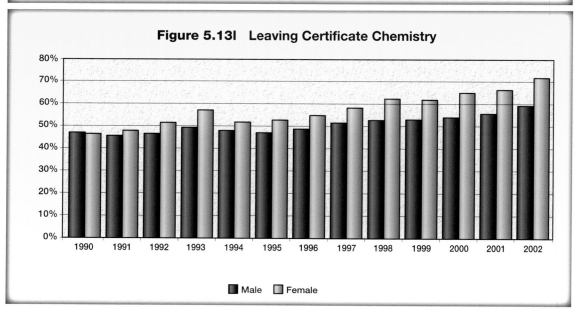

Figure 5.13l Leaving Certificate Chemistry

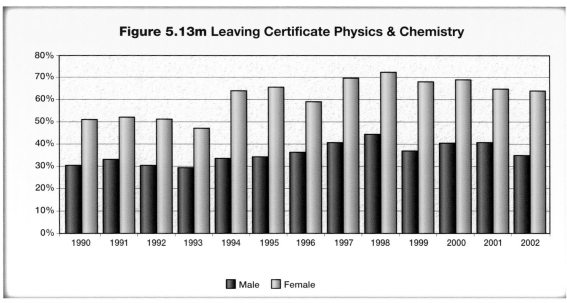

Figure 5.13m Leaving Certificate Physics & Chemistry

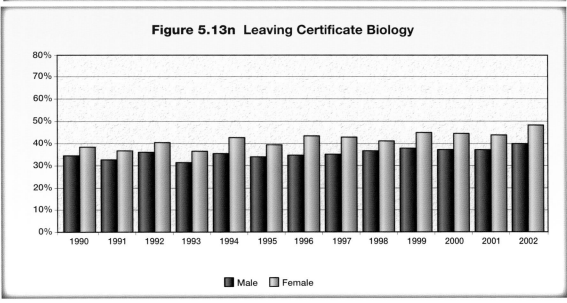

Figure 5.13n Leaving Certificate Biology

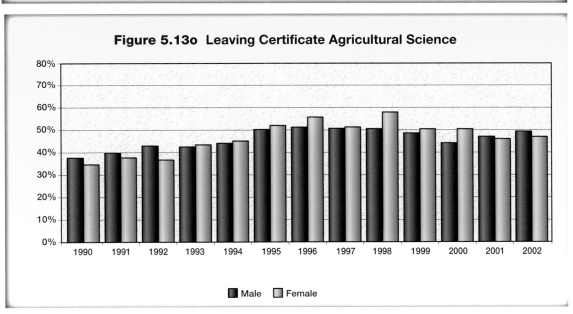

Figure 5.13o Leaving Certificate Agricultural Science

Figure 5.13p Leaving Certificate Business Organisation

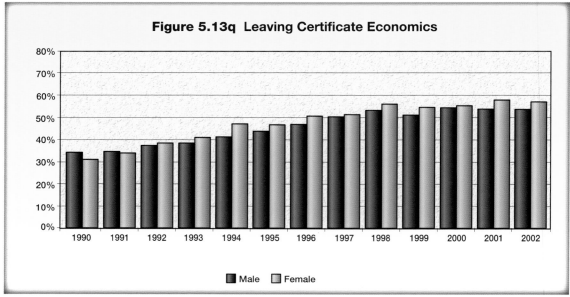

Figure 5.13q Leaving Certificate Economics

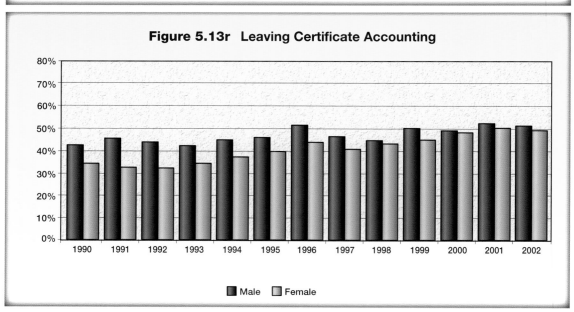

Figure 5.13r Leaving Certificate Accounting

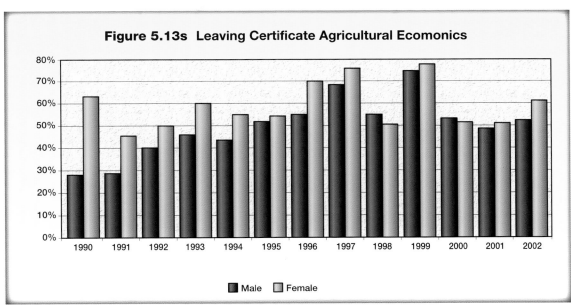

Figure 5.13s Leaving Certificate Agricultural Ecomonics

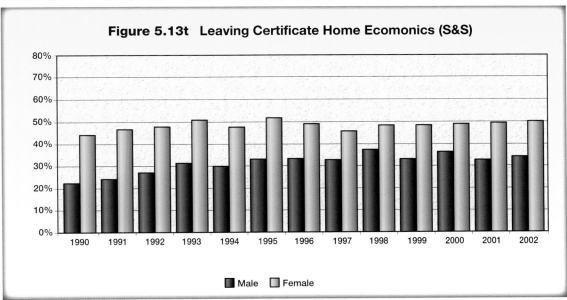

Figure 5.13t   Leaving Certificate Home Ecomonics (S&S)

Figure 5.13u Leaving Certificate Construction Studies

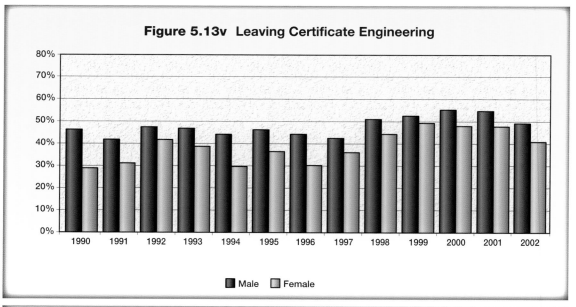

Figure 5.13v Leaving Certificate Engineering

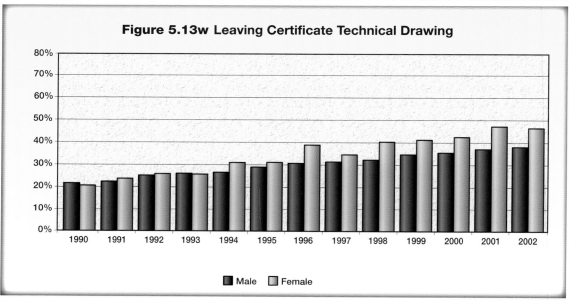

Figure 5.13w Leaving Certificate Technical Drawing

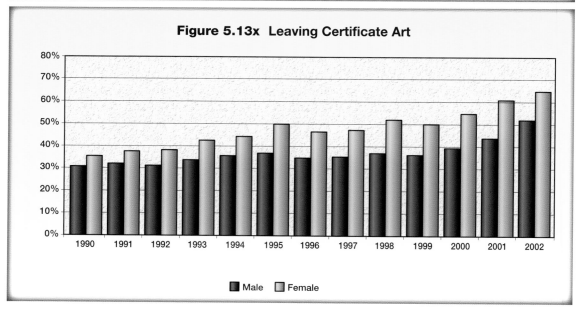

Figure 5.13x Leaving Certificate Art

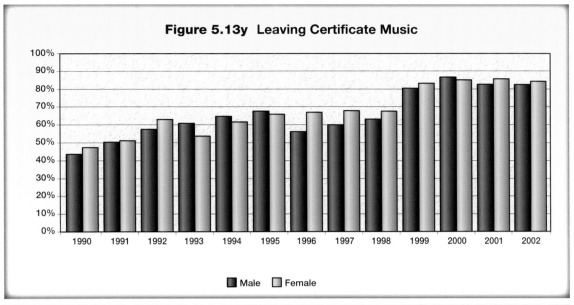

Figure 5.13y Leaving Certificate Music

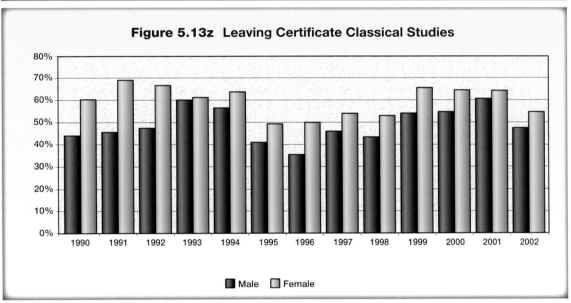

Figure 5.13z Leaving Certificate Classical Studies

CHAPTER 6

Further Education & Training

Further Education and Training[1]

The term "further education and training" covers a broad range of education and training that occurs after second-level schooling but that is not part of the third-level system. A distinctive feature of further education generally is its diversity and breadth of provision, as well as its links with other services, such as employment, training, area partnership, welfare, youth, school, juvenile liaison, justice, community and voluntary interests. The Department of Education and Science provides for programmes such as

- post-Leaving Certificate (PLC) courses
- the Vocational Training Opportunities Scheme (VTOS) for the unemployed
- Youthreach for early school-leavers
- senior Traveller training centre programmes for young and adult Travellers who have left school early
- adult literacy
- the Back-to-Education Initiative
- community education
- self-funded part-time adult education programmes.

These further education programmes are generally provided locally by the vocational education committees and by second-level schools. Programmes at this level are also provided through other Government departments by a range of training agencies, such as FÁS, CERT, and Teagasc, and by community organisations. National certification is provided by the Further Education and Training Awards Council (FETAC), and programmes can also be offered that lead to awards under the Junior or Leaving Certificates.

This chapter aims to provide an overview of participation in the various further education and training programmes now in operation.

Post-Leaving Certificate courses

The Post-Leaving Certificate programme, or Vocational Preparation and Training Programme, was introduced in 1985 to provide appropriate vocational training for young people to bridge the gap between school and work. The programme integrates training for vocational skills in particular disciplines and the development of general skills necessary in all jobs, such as interpersonal skills, adaptability, and initiative. It also includes work experience to give relevance to the skills learnt and to provide an appreciation of working life. Post-Leaving Certificate courses are full-time, of one or two years' duration, and offer integrated general education, vocational training and work experience for those who seek further training to enhance their chances of gaining employment. The programme is aided by the European Social Fund. The courses cover an extensive range of options, including business and secretarial skills, computer studies, child care and community care, art, theatre, tourism, teleservices, and horticulture. Fig. 6.1 provides details on the number of students enrolled in PLC programmes from 1991 to 2003.

---

[1]   The information provided in this chapter on specific further education programmes draws on the Further Education and Training section of the Department of Education and Science web site. For more details see
http://www.education.ie/home/home.jsp?pcategory=10815&ecategory=11345&language=EN

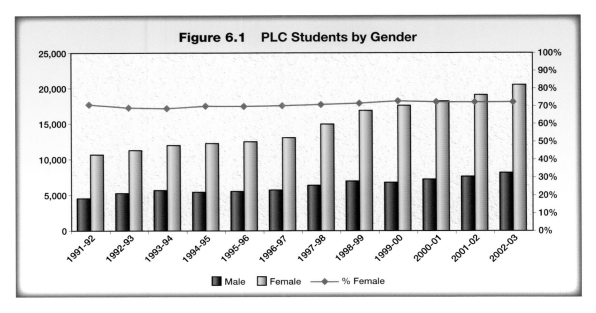

Figure 6.1   PLC Students by Gender

The number of PLC students increased from 15,200 in 1991/92 to 28,650 in 2002/03. Women have consistently outnumbered men on PLC programmes, and the ratio has remained stable through the substantial growth in numbers that was achieved over recent years. In 2002/03 the ratio was 72 per cent female to 28 per cent male.

The Vocational Training Opportunities Scheme

The Vocational Training Opportunities Scheme (VTOS) is a "second chance" education and training programme that provides courses for unemployed people. To be eligible for the scheme one must be over twenty-one, be unemployed, and have been receiving specific social welfare payments for at least six months. The courses, which are provided free of charge, are full-time and can last up to two years, with thirty hours' attendance per week. The scheme has proved successful in opening up learning and progression opportunities for people who have been marginalised by unemployment. VTOS trainees can pursue subjects in the Junior or Leaving Certificate programmes or modules or awards certified by the Further Education and Training Awards Council. Participants may also acquire a portfolio of qualifications in line with their needs and interests. Fig. 6.2 provides an overview of students enrolled in VTOS courses between 1995 and 2004.

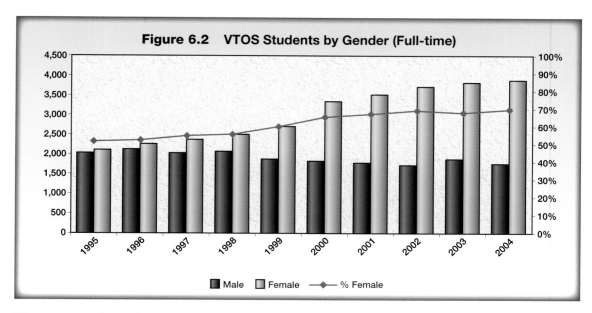

Figure 6.2 VTOS Students by Gender (Full-time)

Male Female % Female

The total number of students enrolled on VTOS courses has increased from 4,100 in 1995 to 5,600 in 2004. This increase in total numbers has been driven by substantial increases in female enrolment on VTOS courses. In fact over that period there has been a slow but steady decrease in male participation. In 1995 the ratio was close to 50:50, but in 2004 women outnumbered men by more than 2 to 1.

Youthreach[2]

The Youthreach programme is designed for unemployed early school-leavers aged between fifteen and twenty. The programme adopts a learner-centred approach, which aims to engage young people as equals and to facilitate them in returning to learning and preparing them for employment and adult life. The programme is full-time and operates in centres that are distributed throughout the country, generally in disadvantaged areas. The Youthreach programme concentrates on the holistic development of the individual and combines education, training and youth-work methods in an interdisciplinary approach. Courses are now structured in the form of an engagement phase, a foundation phase, and a progression phase. Fig. 6.3 provides an overview of students enrolled in Youthreach by age and gender in 2003.

[2] The description of the Youthreach programme provided here is condensed from the Youthreach web site, www.youthreach.ie, where substantial additional information is available.

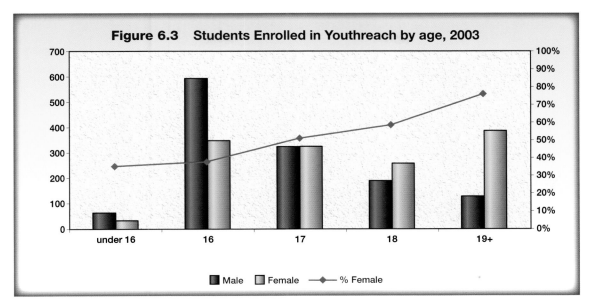

Figure 6.3   Students Enrolled in Youthreach by age, 2003

Male   Female   ◆ % Female

Among the 2,600 students enrolled in Youthreach in 2003 the gender ratio was 51 per cent female to 49 per cent male. Looking at the breakdown of participants by age, we note that although boys outnumbered girls among those aged sixteen and below, girls increasingly outnumbered boys among the older teenagers. This arises because girls tend to stay in second-level school longer than boys, but it also reflects the fact that within the Youthreach programme girls are more likely to pursue the course beyond the foundation level to the progression levels.

Senior Traveller Training Programme

The aim of the Senior Traveller Training Programme is to provide Travellers with the knowledge and skills required to successfully make the transition to work and to participate fully in their communities. The programme is aimed at young and adult Travellers who have left school early. There is no upper age limit, and a particular effort is made to encourage parents to join the programme, given the influence this can have on their children's subsequent participation in schooling. The programme is provided through a network of twenty-nine centres throughout the country and is aided by the European Social Fund.

Programmes place a particular emphasis on the core skills of literacy, numeracy, communications and new technology while providing a range of vocational options allied with work experience. The programme is designed to be flexible and to respond to the needs, talents and interests identified by Travellers. The courses are typically provided over two years, but this period can be extended to facilitate access to the Leaving Certificate or equivalent qualifications. The certification by FETAC (NCVA awards) of all courses provided in senior Traveller training centres now ensures a range of progression opportunities for participants. Fig. 6.4 provides an overview of students enrolled in senior Traveller training courses in 2003 by age group and gender.

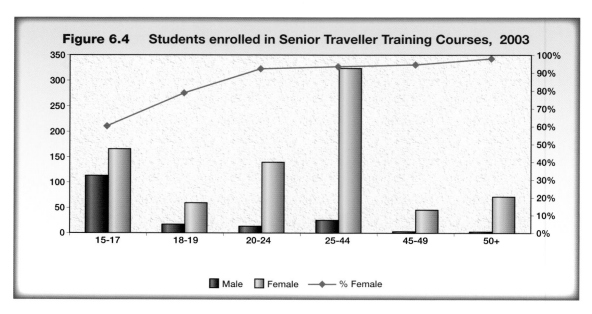

Figure 6.4   Students enrolled in Senior Traveller Training Courses, 2003

In 2003 a total of 981 students were enrolled in senior Traveller training courses. Women outnumbered men by more than 4 to 1, with an overall ratio of 82 per cent female to 18 per cent male. The analysis of participation by age group shows substantial levels of participation among women aged twenty-five and over. However, the participation of men appears to evaporate as we move through the older age groups, suggesting severe difficulties in engaging adult male Travellers in education and training.

Adult literacy

The publication of the International Adult Literacy Survey (IALS) results for Ireland in 1997[3] demonstrated that Ireland lagged significantly behind other European countries in the literacy skills of the adult population. The survey found that approximately 25 per cent of the adult population performed at the lowest of four levels of literacy[4]. This gave rise to very serious concerns among policy-makers and provided the impetus for the increased priority given to adult education as a whole. In 2000 the White Paper on Adult Education[5] was published, and the National Development Plan, 2000–2006, provided for a significant expansion of the adult literacy service.

Adult literacy services are provided through the vocational education committees and are funded by the Department of Education and Science, with assistance from the European Social Fund, as part of the National Development Plan. Each VEC employs adult literacy organisers to organise services in its area. Tuition is provided by paid tutors to groups, and volunteers have also been trained to provide one-to-one tuition. The service is free, and confidential. Fig. 6.5 provides an overview of participants in adult Literacy programmes between 2000 and 2004.

---

[3]   Mark Morgan et al., *Education 2000: International Adult Literacy Survey: Results for Ireland*, Dublin: Government Publications, 1997.

[4]   The International Adult Literacy Survey did not find evidence of very substantial gender differences in literacy levels in Ireland or in other participating countries. Females in Ireland performed slightly better than males in prose literacy and males performed better in the case of both document and quantitiative literacy. Gender differences favouring males were greatest in the case of quantitative literacy. See IALS, p.45

[5]   Department of Education and Science, *Learning for Life: White Paper on Adult Education*, Dublin: Government Publications, 2000.

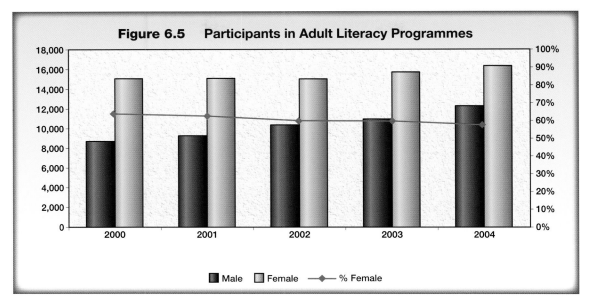

Figure 6.5   Participants in Adult Literacy Programmes

The total number of participants in adult literacy programmes increased from 23,800 in 2000 to 28,650 in 2004. Once again women outnumber men among students of literacy, and in 2004 women accounted for 57 per cent of all participants. However, there has been a steady improvement in the participation of men in adult literacy programmes, from 8,750 in 2000 to 12,300 in 2004, and their share of the total number of participants has risen from 37 to 43 per cent over that period.

Back-to-Education Initiative

The Back-to-Education Initiative (BTEI) was another central element in the lifelong learning strategy outlined in the White Paper on Adult Education. It aims to build on existing further education programmes and to facilitate a significant expansion of flexible part-time options within these programmes. The BTEI is intended to make further education more accessible, and it places a considerable emphasis on engaging with "hard-to-reach" groups—those that are more difficult to engage in the formal (and full-time) learning process. The programme aims to increase the participation of young people and adults with less than upper second-level education in a range of flexible part-time learning opportunities. An important function of the BTEI is ensuring that progression opportunities are available to students from the Adult Literacy Service, and there is also provision for entry at higher levels. Under the BTEI, 10 per cent of places are exclusively for the community sector. Fig. 6.6 provides an overview of BTEI participants in 2004.

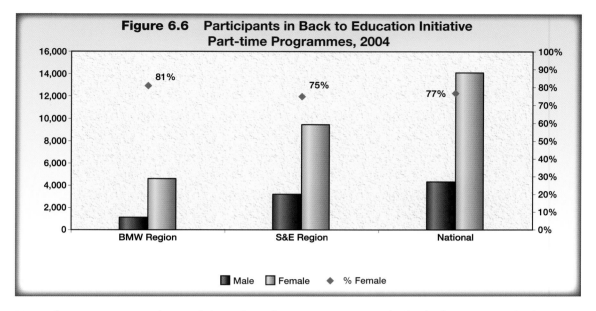

Figure 6.6 Participants in Back to Education Initiative Part-time Programmes, 2004

More than 18,400 people participated in the BTEI in 2004, of which the great majority were female. Women outnumbered men by 3 to 1 in the South and East Region and by 4 to 1 in the Border, Midlands and Western Region. When we combine full-time participants in PLC, VTOS, Youthreach, Traveller Training and Adult Literacy, the overall gender ratio is 64 per cent female to 36 per cent male (in 2004). However, in the part-time options that the BTEI provides within these further education programmes the ratio is 77 per cent female to 23 per cent male. This amounts to considerably higher participation by women than we find on the full-time further education programmes and indicates a huge appetite for part-time education among women in Ireland.

Apprenticeship[6]

Apprenticeship is the recognised means by which people are trained to become craftspersons in Ireland. Apprenticeship is organised by FÁS (the National Training Agency), in co-operation with the Department of Education and Science, employers, and unions. The apprenticeship training programme adopts a work-and-study format over a four-year period. Provision of the programme takes place in seven phases, which alternate between on-the-job training in the work-place and off-the-job training in FÁS training centres and institutes of technology. Standards to be achieved in each trade are measured through on-the-job competence testing, together with modular assessment and formal examinations for the off-the-job elements.

Apprenticeships have proved extremely popular over recent years, with between six and eight thousand new registrations each year between 1998 and 2003. The number of new registrations in 2004 exceeded 8,200. Apprenticeship operates primarily in a number of designated trades, including engineering, construction, motor, electrical, printing, and furniture. While there are twenty-six craft trades in total, three trades linked to the construction industry—carpentry/joinery, electrical installation, and plumbing—accounted for 65 per cent of all registrations in 2005. This proportion was an increase over the figure of 54 per cent in 1998.[7] Fig. 6.7 provides data on total enrolment in apprenticeship in 2003/04.[8]

---

[6] Information on apprenticeships is available on the FÁS web site at www.fas.ie/services_to_businesses/apprenticeship.html.

[7] The information used in this paragraph is FÁS data included in Seán McDonagh and Vivienne Patterson, *The Institutes of Technology and Future Skills* (2006), p. 20.

[8] The figures here use data supplied by FÁS on the gender breakdown of Apprentices applied on a pro-rata basis to the total number on Apprentices of 27,935 - as published in the 2004 FÁS Annual Report - http://www.fas.ie/annual_report/annual_report04/appendices2.htm

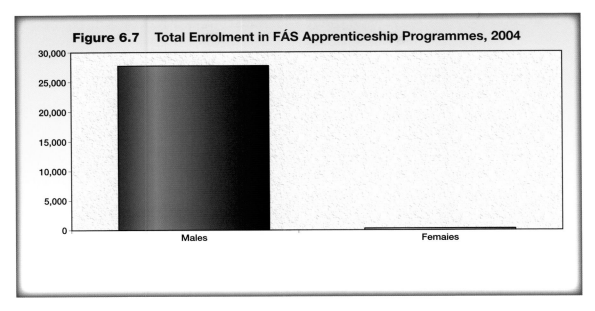

Figure 6.7   Total Enrolment in FÁS Apprenticeship Programmes, 2004

When we look through the range of further education programmes presented earlier in this chapter, the central question that arises is - where are the boys? Bearing in mind in particular that boys significantly outnumber girls among those who leave school early, there is a certain hope and expectation that boys will avail of further education and training opportunities in large numbers. With the data on enrolment in apprenticeship presented in fig. 6.7 we have identified a substantial number of males. Almost all the 28,000 apprentices registered with FÁS on the 31st of December 2004 were male, and it is estimated[9] that 25 per cent of young men now pursue further education and training by enrolling in apprenticeship programmes.

Apprenticeship builds on the more practical subjects of the second-level curriculum (which are male-dominated), and the success of the programme demonstrates the effectiveness of the work-and-study format in securing the continued participation of men in education and training. Successful completion of an apprenticeship course leads to a National Craft Certificate; in the National Framework of Qualifications this is a level 6 award. However, the present lack of progression opportunities for those who successfully complete an apprenticeship is an issue in the context of national efforts to facilitate and encourage lifelong learning.

> Apprenticeship is a valuable format conferring very important craft skills and qualifications and employment opportunities. In a National Qualification Framework (NQF) promoting progression it is, however, a cul-de-sac qualification.[10]

[9] Estimated in Seán McDonagh and Vivienne Patterson, *The Institutes of Technology and Future Skills* (2006), p. 20.
[10] McDonagh and Patterson, *The Institutes of Technology and Future Skills*, p. 21.

Overview of FETAC awards, 2005

To provide an overview of the range of certified further education and training programmes, fig. 6.8 presents data on all FETAC qualifications awarded in 2005.[11] The information is ranked according to the gender ratio of recipients within each category of award. Apprentices graduating with National Craft Certificates (NCC) are at the extreme left of the chart. In 2005 men accounted for 99.5 per cent of such recipients. Although substantial, the figure of 4,500 people who completed an apprenticeship in 2005 compares poorly with the 8,000 entrants four years earlier, suggesting serious issues of drop-out and non-completion within apprenticeship programmes.

In addition to the apprenticeship programmes, FÁS also provides a comprehensive range of specific skills training in a wide range of occupational areas. This is a large programme, accounting for almost 35,800 FETAC awards in 2005. By far the largest course within this programme is that entitled "Construction–Contractor Plant Operation," which had more than 14,300 award recipients, of whom again 99.9 per cent were male. With such a significant component devoted to training for the construction industry, it is perhaps not surprising that men accounted for three-quarters of all Specific Skills Awards in 2005. However, the range of courses on offer extends far beyond the construction industry, to include health and safety, logistics, and web design. Although women comprise a minority within the Specific Skills Awards, they outnumber men in a number of courses relating to computer skills, office skills, enterprise and business skills, hairdressing, and caring.

Men accounted for 86 per cent of the 2,800 students completing Teagasc (Agriculture and Food Development Authority) programmes in 2005. The training provided includes courses in farm management, agriculture, and horticulture.

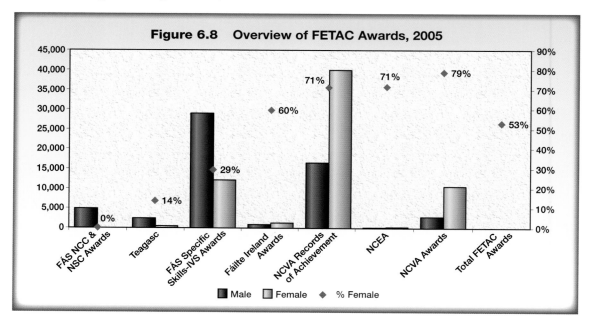

Figure 6.8   Overview of FETAC Awards, 2005

[11] Data supplied by FETAC. The Department of Education and Science acknowledges the very comprehensive and detailed files provided by FETAC on the range of awards conferred in 2005. Additional details on FETAC and its awards are available at www.fetac.ie

Women make up a majority of recipients within the other categories of further education and training awards. Among the 2,100 Fáilte Ireland awards relating to tourism, culinary and hospitality skills the ratio is 60 per cent female to 40 per cent male. A similar ratio was found in the FÁS Introductory Vocational Skills awards. The ratio was closer to 70:30 (female to male) in the small number of FÁS National Skill Certificate Awards. Again a wide range of well-regarded vocational courses is available within this programme, but the most popular courses relate to child care and care of the elderly. Courses are also available in office administration, beauty therapy, and assistance to lawyers, dentists, and pharmacists.

The largest category of qualification awarded by FETAC in 2005 was Records of Achievement in NCVA courses. There were almost 56,500 recipients in 2005, with women accounting for 40,000 (71 per cent). Records of Achievement are awarded for completion of modules within the NCVA range of courses and can be accumulated in pursuit of full NCVA awards. FETAC awarded almost 13,400 full NCVA awards in 2005. These were the most female-dominated awards in 2005, with women accounting for 79 per cent of all recipients. A broad range of courses is provided within the NCVA programme. The most popular courses include child care, business studies, health-care support, information processing, and art, craft, and design. Although men accounted for roughly a fifth of all recipients they tended to outnumber women in the more technological courses within this award category also.

Within the full range of FETAC awards in 2005 the gender ratio was 53 per cent female to 47 per cent male. There are clear gender differences in the take-up of courses, with men generally opting for practical and trade-oriented training and women opting for training in business, office skills and caring as well as the more educationally oriented programmes. In general there are notable similarities between the subject take-up in further education and the subject take-up by gender in early second-level education. It is difficult to assess the extent to which this reflects innate dispositions towards different subject areas and the extent to which it arises as a consequence of socialisation and social conditioning. In any event, these trends in subject take-up patterns highlight the long-term reverberations of subject take-up at the beginning of second-level education.

The diversity and breadth of provision within further education and training was noted at the beginning of this chapter, and this is reflected in the range of FETAC awards described above. Before concluding this chapter's overview of further education it is important to refer to community education and to "self-funded" part-time adult education courses. Given the variety of data sources used in this chapter on further education, it is not clear whether, or to what extent, participation in these strands of adult education is reflected in the FETAC (NCVA) awards described above. Another important element of further education relates to the continuing vocational training of employees. A brief overview of international data relating to this type of training follows the discussion of community education and adult education.

Community education

Community education is a significant strand within adult education that emerged over recent decades from community development and anti-poverty initiatives at the local level. Women's community education groups began with very little Government support in the 1980s but have since been supported through a range of funding schemes, including the Community Development Programme (CDP), the New Opportunities for Women (NOW) Programmes, and the Women's Education Initiative (WEI), which has since been expanded into the Education Equality Initiative (EEI).

> Initiatives like NOW, WEI and EEI were successful because of the particular attention paid to the provision of comprehensive supports, including childcare, allowances and mentoring, to participants in the scheme. Such supports are essential features of Community Education.[12]

The community education sector was officially recognised in the White Paper on Adult Education (2000), in which it was described as "amongst the most dynamic, creative and relevant components of Adult Education provision in Ireland."[13] The White Paper provided additional funding for community education through the BTEI (Back-to-Education Initiative) and an infrastructure of additional resources through the appointment of regionally based community education facilitators in VECs. Community education is an innovative and empowering approach to education and is gaining recognition as a strategy that has considerable potential for addressing the systematic causes of poverty and educational disadvantage.

> While educational disadvantage is often perceived as individual failure, it is typically mediated through the local community in which one lives. In this sense, poverty and disadvantage are as much about the experiences of communities as about the experiences of individuals. This implies that the elimination of educational disadvantage requires an approach which combines both individual and community development. Community Education strategies have proven very effective in reaching out to non-traditional learners and are purposely designed to build up and maintain resources within communities. By focusing on the empowerment of marginalised groups, Community Education enables learners to make connections between local problems and the wider structures in society—economic, social, political and cultural—which create and perpetuate marginalisation. It is this process of linking the individual to the community and understanding both in the context of broader social structures that gives Community Education its transformative potential and which makes it of particular benefit to those who are disadvantaged.[14]

The principle of needs-directed learning is a central principle of the community education approach. This refers to the importance of learners determining the nature and timing of educational provision, in the light of their own needs and interests. Needs-directed learning applies equally to community needs and can be identified through a systematic social analysis in which learners participate collectively. This enhances the relevance of education for individuals and communities and can assist in overcoming difficulties in securing the involvement of those who are "most in need" and "hardest to reach" in lifelong learning.[15]

---

[12] AONTAS, *Community Education 2004*, Dublin: AONTAS, 2004, p.10. This report, which provides a comprehensive overview of the development of community education in Ireland, can be downloaded from www.aontas.com/download/pdf/community_ed_04.pdf.

[13] Dept. of Education and Science, *Learning for Life*, p. 112.

[14] CORI Education Commission, *Learning for Life: White Paper on Adult Education: An Analysis*, Dublin: CORI, 2001, p. 17.

[15] CORI, *Learning for Life*, p. 8.

While the emphasis on communal values is a distinctive feature of community education, the commitment to matching curriculum and pedagogy with the needs and interests of learners is also guiding reform of the broader range of further education programmes.

Accurate and comprehensive statistics on the numbers participating in community education groups are not readily available.[16] Community education is undoubtedly a significant strand of adult education that has succeeded in reaching large numbers of non-traditional learners in disadvantaged settings. While it has traditionally been far more successful in engaging women in learning than men, the range of groups involved in community education activities has expanded over recent years to include men's groups, disability groups, Traveller groups, ex-prisoners' and young offenders' groups, and others. The broadening appeal of community education as an approach to learning and the involvement of a wider range of groups have resulted in more men participating over recent years. Nevertheless, women still comprise a large majority of participants in community education.

Self-funded part-time adult education courses

A further important strand of further education refers to part-time adult education courses that take place in vocational, community and comprehensive schools. A substantial range of such part-time courses is on offer throughout the country, relating primarily to hobby, leisure and remedial learning. The courses are generally self-funded, which means that adults pay fees to attend. While participants may receive some form of certification at the conclusion of these courses, they will not, as a rule, be following a formal course of study. These courses have proved extremely popular and have consistently attracted large numbers of participants over the years.

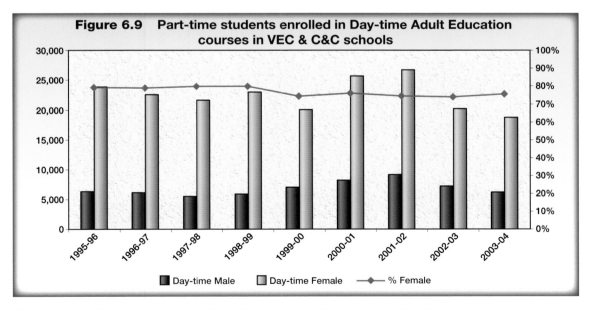

Figure 6.9   Part-time students enrolled in Day-time Adult Education courses in VEC & C&C schools

Fig. 6.9 provides an overview of participation in day-time adult education courses between 1995/96 and 2003/04. The total number of participants has declined from 30,000 in 1995 to 25,000 in 2003, with women outnumbering men by 3 to 1 among participants in these programmes. It is possible that the increased participation of women in the labour market may be affecting their participation in day-time courses.

---

16 AONTAS (The National Association of Adult Education) estimated that there were more than 40,000 participants in women's (community education) groups in 2004. Preliminary indications from a more recent AONTAS survey to collate information on community education activity in each VEC area suggests that approximately 45,000 or more adults were involved in 2005. It is unclear whether, and to what extent, these numbers reported to Aontas overlap with learners on the variety of other adult and further education programmes.

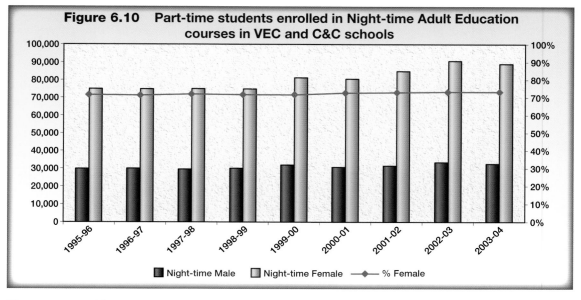

Figure 6.10 Part-time students enrolled in Night-time Adult Education courses in VEC and C&C schools

Fig. 6.10 provides an overview of participation in night-time adult education courses and illustrates the high levels of participation in such courses over recent years. The total number of participants in night classes rose from 105,000 in 1995 to almost 122,000 in 2003. This growth in numbers, particularly among women, more than compensates for the recent decline in day-time courses. As with the day-time courses, the gender ratio has remained relatively stable over recent years, with women outnumbering men by almost 3 to 1 in night classes.

Continuing vocational training of employees

One final element of further education and training that is important to consider is on-the-job training. Fig. 6.11 presents Eurostat data on the percentage of employees across all enterprises that participated in continuing vocational training (CVT) in 1999-2000. Countries are ranked according to the overall participation rates of their employees in CVT. The highest levels of participation were found in Scandinavian countries and in the United Kingdom. Participation in CVT varied considerably across countries from a high of 61 per cent in Sweden to a low of 10 per cent in Lithuania. On average across the European Union, 39 per cent of all employees participated in some form of CVT. At 41 per cent, Ireland is slightly above the EU average.

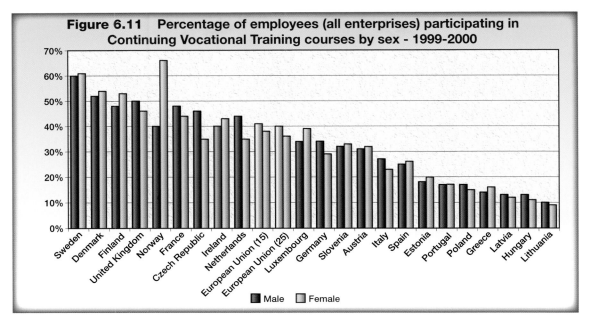

Figure 6.11 Percentage of employees (all enterprises) participating in Continuing Vocational Training courses by sex - 1999-2000

Looking at the gender differences, on average across the European Union, male participation in CVT (40 per cent) is higher than female participation (36 per cent). However, female employees in Ireland have higher levels of participation than their male counterparts (43 per cent versus 40 per cent). In general, the gender differences in CVT are small. However, in the Czech Republic and in the Netherlands, the gender differences in favour of males are substantial and the gender difference in favour of females in Norway is enormous. Appendix table 6.11 presents additional data on the average hours spent on training by male and females employees. Once again, the Irish results and the EU average do not suggest any great gender differences in the time spent on continuing vocational training.

Concluding remarks

Given the broad and diverse range of post-secondary learning activities and the patchiness of administrative data in this area, it is difficult to provide a summary of further education and training. Women substantially outnumber men in the full range of further education programmes provided through the Department of Education and Science (and the VECs). The one exception is Youthreach, where the ratio is close to 50:50. However, one would expect to have more boys in Youthreach, given that they outnumber girls by 2 to 1 within the target group of early school-leavers.

The overview of FETAC awards provides a more balanced picture of certified education and training, because it includes training organised by other agencies, such as FÁS and Teagasc. Apprenticeship, Specific Skills training and Teagasc agricultural training programmes all have very high levels of male participation; indeed apprenticeship is almost exclusively male. In general, the types of further education qualification pursued correspond closely to the classic gender stereotypes. This is especially true of men, who largely confine their engagement in further education to vocationally oriented and especially construction-related training. Women tend to engage in a broader range of courses. These trends in participation correspond with the findings of a study on gender and learning commissioned by Aontas in 2002, which identified gender differences in the motivation for learning. This study found that "men were more highly motivated when the outcome was project or vocationally orientated, and women were more prepared to explore wider options".[17]

When examined in a lifelong perspective, it is important to note that the male-dominated further education programmes are generally post-school courses that could legitimately be considered the end of initial education and training, rather than continuing education. The great majority of apprentices are aged between the late teens and early twenties, and most participants in Specific Skills training are under twenty-five. A quick comparison of entrants and those who complete their training suggests that more than 40 per cent of boys drop out of apprenticeship training. On this evidence, retention appears to be a serious issue for men in further education as well as in second-level education.

On the issue of continual engagement with learning over the life cycle, women display a much greater and more sustained appetite for education than men. Women tend to outnumber men by 3 to 1 in the range of courses directed at adults aged twenty-five and over. This is well illustrated in their high levels of participation in part-time adult education courses and indeed in their willingness to pay for such courses. Women's greater lifelong enthusiasm for education is also evident in their involvement in NCVA courses and in community education. In contrast, men's participation in education and training appears to diminish rapidly from the early to mid-twenties onwards. This pattern, which was observed earlier in relation to Traveller men, appears typical of Irish men more generally.

The synopsis of the 2002 study on gender and learning concludes as follows:

> In the context of the learning group, men were less likely to engage in questioning and in personal disclosure, for fear of ridicule, and the peer culture is a more significant form of social control for them. Women, on the other hand, are more likely to support each other and to engage in the wider learning environment, and to perceive adult education as a more holistic developmental experience. Because women have more networks within the community, they are more likely to become involved in educational activities, while disadvantaged men tended to experience much more isolation, and were consequently, less likely to access whatever provision there was. Once adult learners became engaged in the learning process, their needs were strikingly similar, pivoting on a learner-centred approach by the tutors and providers.[18]

[17] King, O'Driscoll & Holden (2002), *Gender and Learning,* Shannon Curriculum Development Centre – Commissioned by AONTAS and Department of Education and Science.

[18] King, O'Driscoll & Holden (2002), *Gender and Learning.*

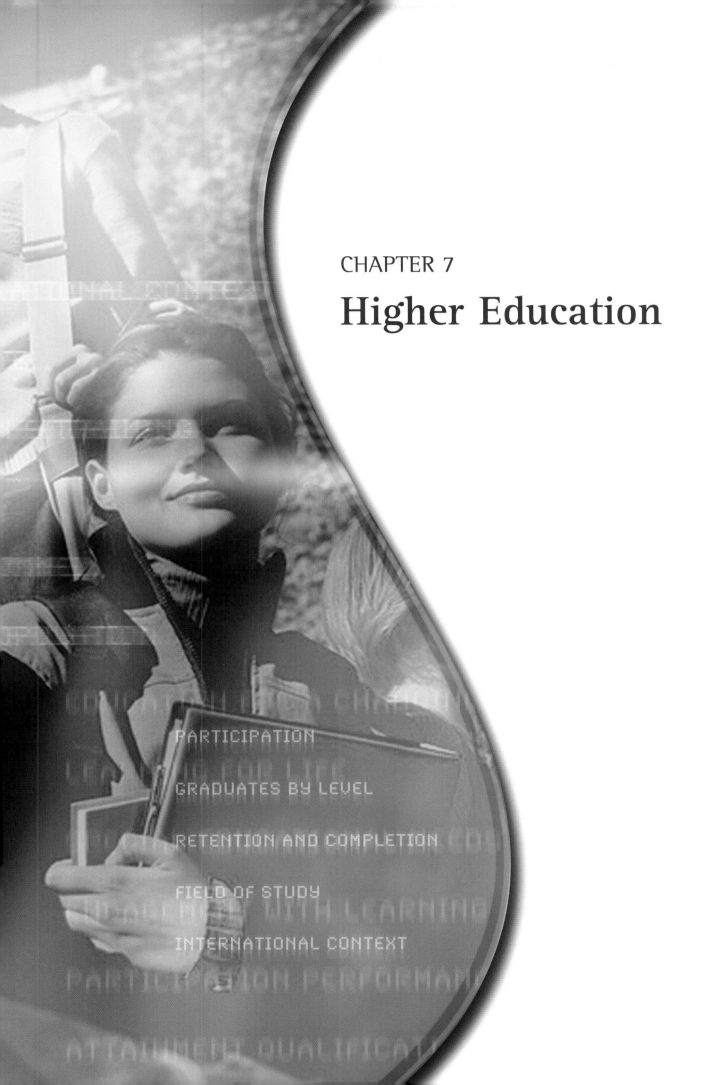

CHAPTER 7

Higher Education

PARTICIPATION

GRADUATES BY LEVEL

RETENTION AND COMPLETION

FIELD OF STUDY

INTERNATIONAL CONTEXT

Higher Education*

The very substantial and steady increase in the number of places at third level over the last 20 years is one of the most remarkable developments in modern Irish education... This expansion of third-level places was one of the critical cornerstones of our overall national economic strategy throughout the difficult 1980s and early 1990s. The availability and supply of substantial numbers of highly qualified graduates with third-level qualifications contributed significantly to Ireland's much improved economic circumstances.[1]

In this chapter we examine the growth of third-level education in recent years, concentrating on issues of participation, graduation, subject take-up and performance by gender.

Participation in third-level education*

The analysis of participation in third-level education begins with fig. 7.1, which provides an overview of full-time enrolments in universities between 1980 and 2003. This illustrates well the substantial increase in total full-time enrolment, from approximately 26,500 to approximately 75,000, during that period. Although men outnumbered women in our universities throughout the 1980s, by 1990 a ratio of 50:50 was reached. Between 1990 and 2003 female enrolment has grown at a much faster rate than male enrolment. By 2003 women outnumbered men by more than 12,500 full-time students, and the ratio was 58 per cent women to 42 per cent men.

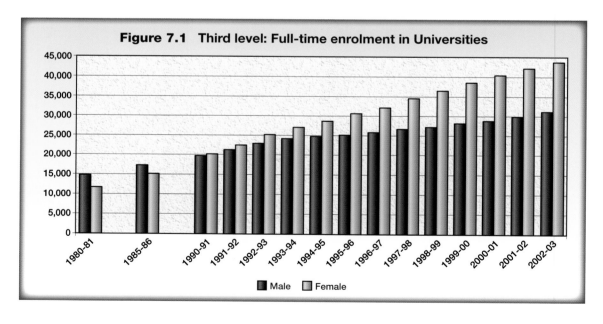

Figure 7.1 Third level: Full-time enrolment in Universities

* The terms 'higher education' and 'third-level education' are used interchangeably in this report

[1] Department of Education and Science, *Supporting Equity in Higher Education: A Report to the Minister for Education and Science*, 2003, p. 10.

[2] The institutes of technology are higher-education institutions (developed with the assistance of European Structural Funds) that traditionally have had a more technological and skills orientation than the universities. They are regionally dispersed throughout the country and have played a large role in upgrading the skills of the labour force. A majority of students in the institutes of technology are pursuing higher-education certificates or diplomas (ISCED level 5B), although an increasing number of degree and postgraduate courses have been offered in recent years.

Fig. 7.2 provides an equivalent overview of enrolment over time in the institutes of technology, including Dublin Institute of Technology (DIT).[2] Like the universities, the institutes of technology have expanded substantially in recent years, with total enrolments growing from approximately 11,000 full-time students in 1980 to 51,500 in 2003. Most of this growth occurred during the 1990s. With regard to the gender ratio of students, men have traditionally outnumbered women among enrolment in the institutes of technology, and this was still so in 2003. However, female enrolment has increased at a faster pace than enrolment among men, and the gap has narrowed significantly, from 59 per cent men in 1990 to 52 per cent men in 2002/03.

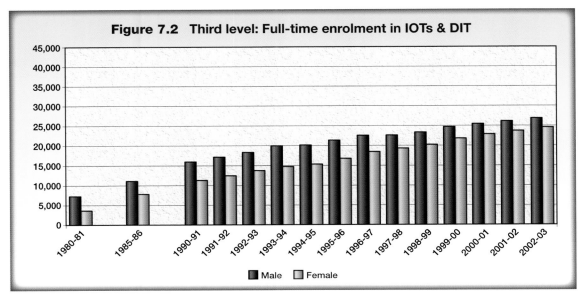

Figure 7.2 Third level: Full-time enrolment in IOTs & DIT

To provide an overview of full-time enrolment in all publicly aided third-level institutions, fig. 7.3 combines enrolments in universities and enrolments in institutes of technology, together with enrolments in other aided institutions and in institutions of higher education aided by other Government departments (Justice and Defence). Altogether, enrolment in higher education increased from fewer than 41,000 full-time students in 1980/81 to more than 130,000 in 2002/03. This very considerable expansion resulted in substantial increases in the proportion of Leaving Certificate pupils who entered higher education. In 1980, 20 per cent of the Leaving Certificate cohort entered higher education; this had increased to 44 per cent by 1998[3] and reached an estimated 55 per cent in 2004.[4]

Looking at the gender ratio among all full-time students in publicly aided institutions we see that men outnumbered women between 1980 and 1994/95. Over subsequent years the participation rate of women has risen at a much faster pace than the rate among men, and the gap in favour of women has widened significantly. In 2002/03 the ratio among full-time students in publicly aided institutions was 46 per cent male to 54 per cent female.

[3] Patrick Clancy, *College Entry in Focus*, Dublin: Higher Education Authority, 2001, table 25 (p. 68), as published in the Report of the Action Group on Access to Third-Level Education, 2001, p. 33.

[4] Philip O'Connell, David Clancy and Selina McCoy, *Who Went to College in 2004? A National Survey of New Entrants to Higher Education*, Dublin: Higher Education Authority, 2006, Table 3.8, p. 49.

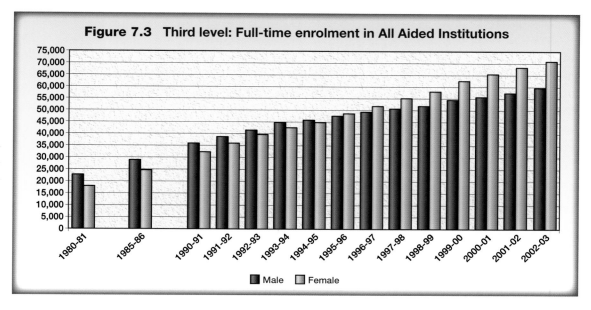

Figure 7.3   Third level: Full-time enrolment in All Aided Institutions

The Department of Education and Science also collects data on enrolment from private third-level colleges. Fig. 7.4 presents an overview of the data on enrolment in private colleges available to the department. Readers should exercise caution in interpreting these data, as private colleges are not under the same obligation to report data to the department as publicly aided institutions, and the data are therefore incomplete in terms of coverage from year to year. Nevertheless, the available (incomplete) data do suggest that, with regard to gender balance in participation, enrolment in private colleges has followed very similar patterns to that of public institutions, with women overtaking men in participation rates from the mid-1990s onwards.

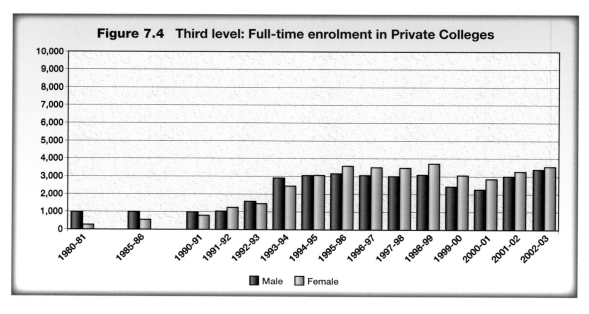

Figure 7.4   Third level: Full-time enrolment in Private Colleges

To complete this overview of participation in higher education, fig. 7.5 provides information on part-time enrolment in publicly funded higher education institutions between 1995/96 and 2002/03. Over this period, part-time enrolment increased from approximately 22,000 to approximately 35,500. While the part-time participation of women has increased steadily from year to year, the participation of men in part-time higher education did not increase between 1999/2000 and 2002/03. This resulted in a ratio among part-time students of 41 per cent male to 59 per cent female in 2002/03—a ratio that is more in favour of women than we find among full-time students. While men continued to outnumber women among full-time students in institutes of technology, even in this sector women outnumbered men among part-time students in 2002/03.

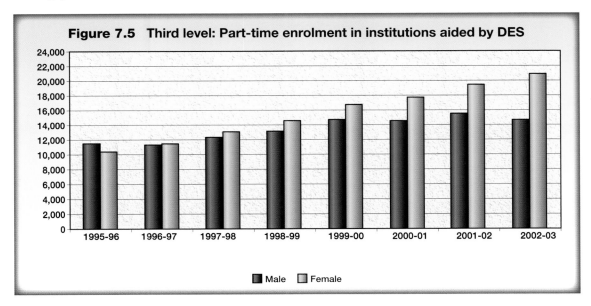

Figure 7.5 Third level: Part-time enrolment in institutions aided by DES

Analysis by level of qualification

Fig. 7.6 provides an overview of all those completing third-level education in 1993 by level or type of qualification obtained. The levels of third-level qualification range from certificates and diplomas up to doctorates. Among those completing third-level education in 1993, men outnumbered women among recipients of certificates, diplomas and postgraduate degrees and among the small number of PhD graduates; women outnumbered men in the attainment of undergraduate degrees.

---

[5] Readers should note that in the context of the implementation of the National Framework of Qualifications, Certificate awards are now known as Higher Certificates, Diplomas as Ordinary Bachelor Degrees and Undergraduate degrees as Honours Bachelor Degrees. See www.nqai.ie for more information.

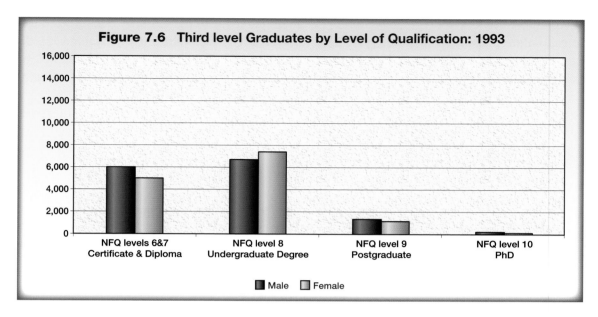

Figure 7.6   Third level Graduates by Level of Qualification: 1993

Fig. 7.7 provides an equivalent overview of those completing third-level education in 2003 and shows clearly that much had changed over that ten-year period. Firstly, the very significant expansion of higher education that we observed in the data on participation led to a dramatic increase in the total number of third-level qualifications awarded. Over those ten years the total number of annual qualifications nearly doubled, from less than 28,000 in 1993 to almost 54,000 in 2003. There was a particularly impressive increase in the number of postgraduate qualifications and very substantial increases also in the number of certificates, diplomas and undergraduate degrees awarded. The number of PhD graduates, however, remained relatively small.

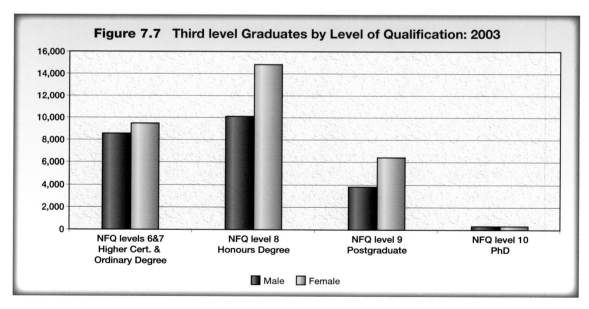

Figure 7.7   Third level Graduates by Level of Qualification: 2003

There are a number of striking changes in the gender composition of those completing third-level education when we compare the 1993 data with the 2003 data. Starting at the higher end, the gap in favour of men among PhD graduates that was evident in 1993 no longer existed in 2003. The situation among postgraduates was transformed over that period, with women moving from a less than equal share (46 per cent) in 1993 to 63 per cent of postgraduate qualifications in 2003. There is also clear evidence of an increasing gap in favour of women at undergraduate degree level that is consistent with the university enrolment patterns that emerged from the early 1990s up to the early years of the present decade. However, the fact that women outnumbered men among recipients of certificates and diplomas in 2003 is surprising and is not consistent with the enrolment patterns that we observed in the institutes of technology, where men continue to outnumber women in total enrolment. This anomaly suggests considerable gender differences in retention through higher education and in the successful completion of courses, particularly in the institutes of technology.

Retention and completion of third-level courses

Data on the extent to which students successfully complete their courses have been limited by the lack of individualised student data-bases in institutes of higher education[6]. However, two separate studies on non-completion, in institutes of technology and in undergraduate university courses, do provide some insights into this issue. Fig. 7.8[7] provides information on non-completion in institutes of technology by broad field of study and gender. This is based on a study of 1995 entrants that was carried out by the Educational Research Centre on behalf of the Council of Directors of Institutes of Technology.

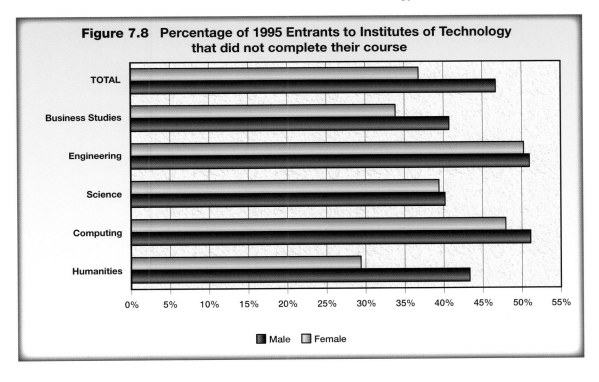

Figure 7.8 Percentage of 1995 Entrants to Institutes of Technology that did not complete their course

---

[6] This situation has been rectified to a large extent with the development of individualised student record systems in most higher education institutions over recent years. This will have many benefits, including the ability in the future to accurately monitor retention and completion rates in higher education from administrative data sources.

[7] Source: Mark Morgan, Rita Flanagan, and Thomas Kellaghan, *A Study of Non-Completion in Institute of Technology Courses*, Dublin: Higher Education Authority, 2000, table 5.1 (p. 17).

This study revealed very high rates of non-completion in institutes of technology, with a total of 43 per cent failing to complete their chosen course. The results also revealed a large gender gap in the rates of completion, with women a full 10 per cent more likely to complete their course than men. Altogether, 37 per cent of women did not complete their course, compared with 47 per cent of men. There were substantial differences in completion rates between different fields of study: in general, the poorest rates of completion were found in the disciplines in which the take-up by men was highest. (See appendix, table 7.8, for details.)

Non-completion rates were very high in all subject areas and were extremely high in both engineering and computing, where half the students who embarked on a course failed to complete it. The substantial drop-out rates, particularly among men, go a long way towards explaining the apparent anomaly noted above, where women outnumber men among recipients of certificates and diplomas, despite the fact that men continue to outnumber women among total enrolments in institutes of technology. In other words, while men enrol in greater numbers, women graduate in greater numbers, because of the considerably higher drop-out rate among men. A more up-to-date study of non-completion in institutes of technology and recent OECD estimates of completion in the sector, indicate that completion rates in institutes of technology have improved significantly in more recent years, rising to approximately 69% in overall terms by 2004.[8]

The Educational Research Centre also conducted a study of non-completion in undergraduate courses on behalf of the Higher Education Authority. This study dealt with new entrants to undergraduate courses in the academic year 1992/93 and provides the data that underlie fig. 7.9.[9]

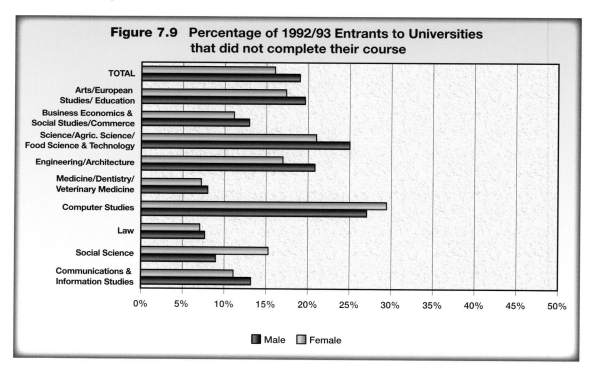

Figure 7.9   Percentage of 1992/93 Entrants to Universities that did not complete their course

8   See OECD (2006), *Education at a Glance, OECD Indicators 2006*, Table A3.2, p. 59.

9   Source: Mark Morgan, Rita Flanagan, and Thomas Kellaghan, *A Study of Non-Completion in Undergraduate University Courses*, Dublin: Higher Education Authority, 2001, table 5.1 (p. 30).

Although the data in fig. 7.9 are presented in a similar way to that on institutes of technology in fig. 7.8, readers should note that the two surveys are not comparable, and direct comparisons between the two sectors on the issue of retention are invalid. This lack of comparability arises because the HEA uses 1 March as the reference date for enrolments. In effect, all first-year students who have dropped out of their course before this date are simply not counted in the analysis of non-completion in universities. The reference date used by the Department of Education in obtaining enrolment data from the institutes of technology is 31 October. Therefore, the analysis of non-completion in institutes of technology is more comprehensive.

Bearing in mind the limitations described above arising from the reference date of 1 March, the study on non-completion in universities is useful in examining the issue by gender and by field of study. In general, the study found that women were more likely to complete their undergraduate courses than men. The proportion of women who did not complete was 15.5 per cent, compared with 18.4 per cent of men. The highest rates of non-completion were found in computer studies, the sciences, and engineering; the lowest rates of non-completion were found in law, medicine, dentistry, and veterinary medicine. With regard to the fields of study that displayed the highest rates of non-completion, there are broad similarities between the institutes of technology and the universities. The gender differences are also similar, with women more likely to complete courses that they embark on in both sectors. However, the extent of non-completion and the strength of the gender differences appear to be much more pronounced in the institutes of technology.

Analysis by field of study

Building on the analysis of subject take-up at second level presented in chapters 3 and 5, an analysis of graduations by field of study at third level is presented below. This analysis begins with fig. 7.10, which presents an overview of the gender ratio of all graduates in 1993 by field of study.[10]

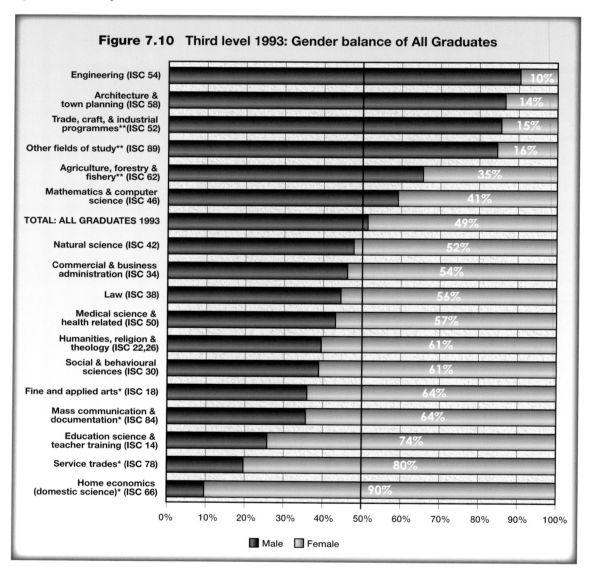

Figure 7.10 Third level 1993: Gender balance of All Graduates

In 1993 the gender ratio among all those completing third-level education was 51 per cent male to 49 per cent female. The ratio varied considerably within the different fields of study. Fig. 7.11[11] provides a similar overview of all those completing third-level education in 2003 by field of study to facilitate reflection on changes over that ten-year period.[12] By 2003 the overall gender ratio among graduates had changed substantially, to 42:58 (male to female), and women outnumbered men in 70 per cent of the various fields of study.

---

[10] Source: Department of Education and Science, Submissions of internationally comparable data on graduates to UNESCO, OECD and Eurostat (UOE returns) in respect of 1993. An asterisk indicates that there are fewer than 1,000 graduates in a particular category; two asterisks indicate that there are fewer than 100.

[11] Source: Department of Education and Science, Submissions of internationally comparable data on graduates to UNESCO, OECD and Eurostat (UOE returns) in respect of 2003. An asterisk indicates that there are fewer than 1,000 graduates in a particular category; two asterisks indicate that there are fewer than 100.

[12] Readers should note that the international classifications system for fields of study was revised in 1997, and therefore some headings have been changed. However, general comparisons by field of study between 1993 and 2003 remain useful and appropriate.

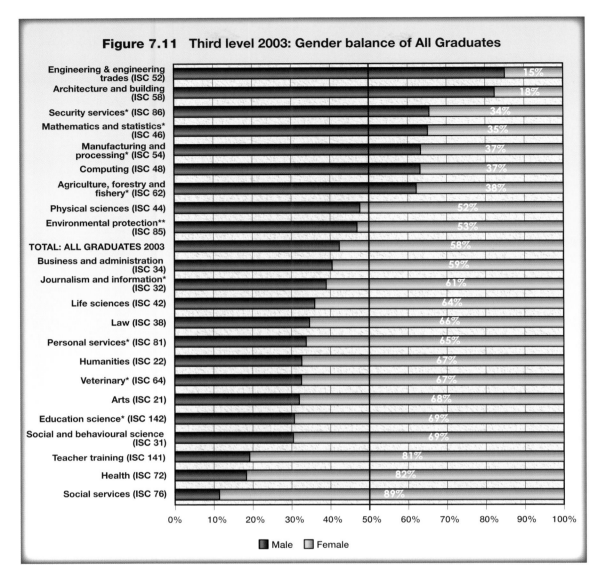

Figure 7.11 Third level 2003: Gender balance of All Graduates

The areas in which women most outnumber men are health and teacher training. In both these areas—as in many others—the ratio in favour of women increased significantly between 1993 and 2003. In the arts and humanities, women outnumbered men by 2:1. The ratio in veterinary medicine and in law was also similarly weighted towards female graduates. In fact the proportion of male graduates in law declined from 44 per cent to 35 per cent between 1993 and 2003. Women considerably outnumbered men (by almost 2:1) in the life sciences and even in the physical sciences, where the ratio among 2003 graduates was 48 per cent male to 52 per cent female.

Men continued to outnumber women in a range of more practically oriented and construction-related fields of study, most notably in engineering, architecture, and building. These areas remained the most male-dominated fields of study over the ten-year period, with men accounting for 85 per cent of engineering graduates and 82 per cent of architecture and building graduates in 2003. Men outnumbered women by approximately 2:1 in computing, mathematics, agriculture, manufacturing, and security services.

In general there appear to be some broad similarities between the subject take-up in higher education and the subject take-up by gender in early second-level education. It is difficult to say whether, or to what extent, this reflects innate dispositions towards different subject areas or whether it reflects the long-term reverberations of subject take-up at the beginning of second-level education.

To examine the gender ratio within fields of study at the different levels of higher education qualifications, fig. 7.12 to fig. 7.15 present separate summaries of information on fields of study for 2003 recipients of certificates and diplomas, undergraduate degrees, postgraduate degrees, and PhDs. As with all charts in this publication, additional detail is presented in the corresponding appendix tables, such as the total numbers of those completing third-level education in each field of study. Readers should note that the general category "science" as used here includes computing and mathematics as well as the more obvious life sciences and physical sciences.

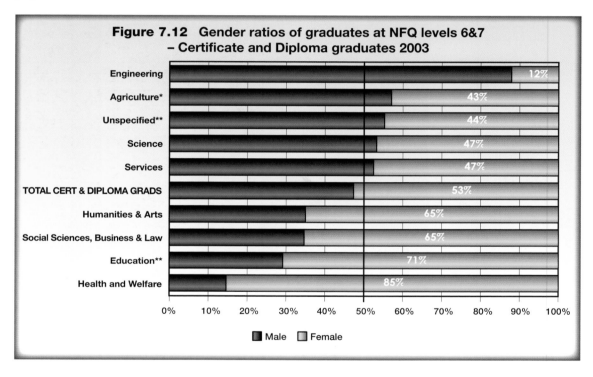

Figure 7.12   Gender ratios of graduates at NFQ levels 6&7 – Certificate and Diploma graduates 2003

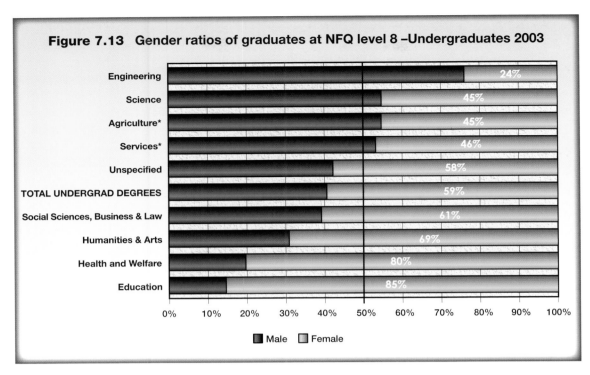

Figure 7.13   Gender ratios of graduates at NFQ level 8 –Undergraduates 2003

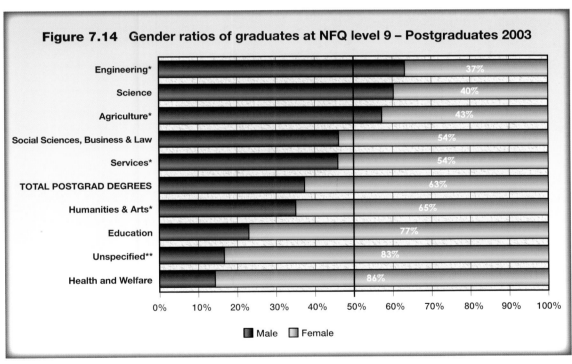

Figure 7.14   Gender ratios of graduates at NFQ level 9 – Postgraduates 2003

There is a very noticeable increase in the representation of women among those completing third-level education as the level of qualification increases, from certificates and diplomas towards postgraduate degrees. In engineering, for instance (which is the most male-dominated of all subject areas), the proportion of women rises from 12 per cent at certificate and diploma level to 24 per cent at undergraduate degree level and up to 37 per cent at postgraduate level. The extent to which medicine and the whole area of health and welfare are becoming increasingly female-dominated is apparent in the data presented in relation to undergraduate and postgraduate qualifications. This is also true of education and teacher training (an issue that will be further explored in the next chapter, on educational personnel).

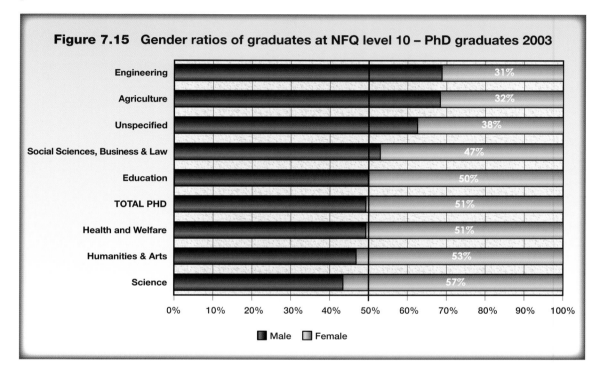

Figure 7.15   Gender ratios of graduates at NFQ level 10 – PhD graduates 2003

In comparison with lower-level qualifications, there are less dramatic gender differences at the PhD level, both in total numbers and within the different fields of study. Interestingly, it is in science that women most outnumber men at the PhD level; and science accounted for 45 per cent of all PhD graduates in 2003.

Performance in final university examinations

The higher entry rates of females together with their lower levels of drop-out explains the changes that we are witnessing in the gender balance of higher-education graduates over recent years. This was most apparent in the comparison of 1993 and 2003 in terms of the total graduates by level of award (figs 7.6 & 7.7). Although the 2004 results on performance presented in appendix table 7.16 refer solely to university graduates, the gender ratios of graduates at undergraduate degree and postgraduate degree level appear to have diverged by a further percentage point (in each direction) between 2003 and 2004. By 2004, females comprised 60 per cent of graduations at undergraduate level and 62 per cent at postgraduate level. This comparison is more difficult to interpret at PhD level where females comprised 51per cent of all PhD graduates in 2003 and 46 per cent of PhD graduates from universities in the following year. This type of fluctuation in gender ratios is a consequence of the comparatively low overall number of PhD graduates. Looking back over recent years, females accounted for 44 per cent of PhD graduates in 1998 and 1999, 47 per cent in 2000, 43 per cent in 2001 and 2002 before rising to 51per cent in 2003 and falling back to 46per cent in 2004.[13]

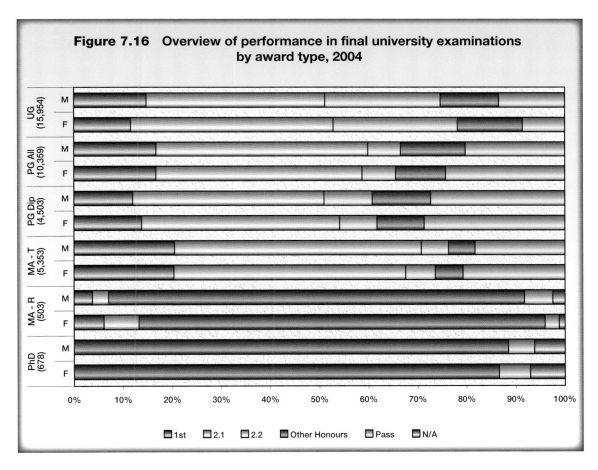

Figure 7.16 Overview of performance in final university examinations by award type, 2004

Fig. 7.16 presents an overview of the final examination performance of university graduates in 2004. Readers should note that these data refer only to those who successfully graduated, and therefore they provide no information on the number of final year students who did not pass their final year examinations. Among 2004 university graduates at undergraduate degree level, a higher proportion of males performed at the highest level with 15 per cent achieving 1st class honours (i.e. 1.1 awards) compared to 12 per cent of female graduates.

13 Source: Higher Education Authority (HEA) Statistics Section, see http://www.hea.ie/index.cfm/page/sub/id/702

However, the proportion of males performing at the lowest level of successful graduation is also higher than the equivalent proportion of females. 13 per cent of males achieved a pass undergraduate degree compared with 9 per cent of females. The 41 per cent of females achieving 2nd class honours, grade 1 (i.e. 2.1 awards) is substantially higher than the equivalent 36 per cent of males, and females outperform males in terms of the proportions of graduates who achieved "2.1 or 1.1 awards". In attempting to interpret the data on performance at undergraduate degree level, it is important to bear in mind that the number of female graduates (9,630) is one and a half times greater than the number of male graduates (6,324). This complicates any analysis and makes it difficult to arrive at general conclusions on gender and performance in university examinations.

The data indicate little or no gender differences in performance at postgraduate level. In fact, when all postgraduate awards (excluding PhD) are combined, there is a remarkable similarity in the levels of award achieved by males and females. As is evident from fig. 7.16, most research MA degrees and almost all PhDs have a marking system that differs from the undergraduate and taught postgraduate award format. Within these award types, the main awards are at honours level (in a general sense) and at pass level. Although the numbers graduating from universities with MA research degrees and PhDs is comparatively small, the available data suggest that females obtained higher-level awards at MA research level. Males performed somewhat better than females in taught MA degrees and were marginally more likely to obtain honours level PhDs in 2004.

In general, the performance of males and females in Irish universities appears to be broadly similar and the rather stark gender differences that were observed in state examinations at second level are not apparent among university graduates.

Fig. 7.17 attempts to summarise gender differences in the performance of university undergraduate degree graduates in 2004 by field of study. The bars in this chart correspond to the differences in the percentage of males and females who achieved '1.1 awards' and '2.1 awards and above' in each broad subject area. The bars reflect the percentage of females achieving at these levels minus the equivalent percentage of males. Therefore, positive results indicate better performance by females and negative results (less than 0 per cent) indicate better performance by males.

By way of example, looking at the results for total undergraduate degrees, 12 per cent of females achieved 1.1 awards compared to 15 per cent of males. The gender difference (females minus males) in terms of the achievement of 1st class honours is -3 per cent. However, 41per cent of females achieved 2.1 awards compared to 36 per cent of males. Therefore the gender difference in terms of the achievement of '2.1 awards and above' is [12 per cent+41 per cent] minus [15 per cent+36 per cent] which equals +2 per cent. This example illustrates that while males outperformed females in terms of the achievement of 1st class honours, the higher percentage of females obtaining 2nd class honours (grade 1) resulted in females outperforming males in terms of the achievement of awards at 2.1 or above. The results presented in fig. 7.17 are derived from the detailed overview of

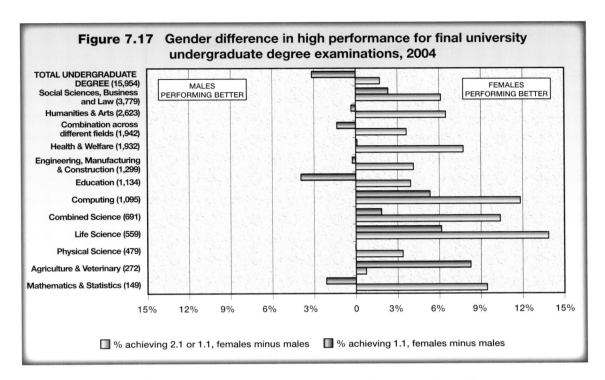

Figure 7.17   Gender difference in high performance for final university undergraduate degree examinations, 2004

□ % achieving 2.1 or 1.1, females minus males   ■ % achieving 1.1, females minus males

performance by grade level presented in the corresponding appendix table.

The analysis by field of study shows that a higher percentage of males achieved 1.1 awards in Education and in Mathematics & Statistics. Females outperformed males in terms of the achievement of 1.1 awards in Social Sciences, Business & Law, Computing, Combined Science, Life Science and Agriculture & Veterinary. In the remaining subject areas of Humanities & Arts, Health & Welfare, Engineering and the Physical Sciences, there were little or no gender differences in the achievement of the highest level of undergraduate award. When the percentages that achieved 1.1 and 2.1 honours are combined, fig. 7.17 illustrates that females outperformed males across all fields of undergraduate study in terms of the achievement of awards at '2.1 and above'. Interestingly, these gender differences in favour of females are most pronounced in the sciences, mathematics and computing areas. Females also outperformed males by between 6 and 8 percentage points in Health & Welfare, Humanities & Arts and in Social Sciences, Business and Law. Even in Engineering, Manufacturing & Construction studies, where three quarters of all graduates are male, females outperformed males by 4 percentage points in terms of the proportions obtaining '2.1 awards and above'.

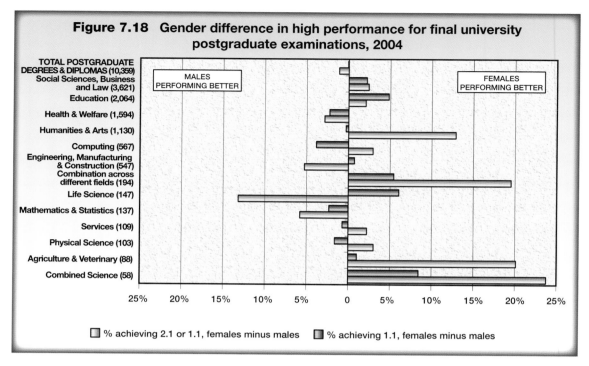

Figure 7.18 Gender difference in high performance for final university postgraduate examinations, 2004

Fig. 7.18 presents an equivalent summary overview of gender differences in performance at postgraduate degree and diploma level. As noted earlier, in overall terms there are remarkable similarities in the performance of males and females at postgraduate level in Irish universities. There is no gender difference at all in terms of the overall percentage of graduates obtaining 1.1 awards and males marginally outperformed females (by a single percentage point) in terms of the achievement of awards at '2.1 or above'. Readers should note that subject areas are ranked according to the overall number of graduates and should exercise some caution in the interpretation of differences observed in the smaller fields of study. Within the larger fields of study at postgraduate level, there are broad similarities in performance by gender. However, females outperform males in Social Sciences, Business & Law and in Education. Males outperform females in Health & Welfare studies at postgraduate level. In the Humanities & Arts, results are very even and there are mixed but generally even results for males and females in Computing, Services and the Physical Sciences. While females marginally outperformed males in terms of the achievement of 1.1 awards in Engineering, males outperformed females in terms of awards at '2.1 or above' within this field of study. Although the overall number of graduates is small in the Combined Sciences and in Agricultural & Veterinary studies, females strongly outperformed males at postgraduate level within these fields of study in 2004.

Third-level educational attainment in the international context

By way of conclusion, the final section of this chapter provides some recent data on the educational attainment of the (younger) Irish population in the European context. Before the European data are presented, fig. 7.19 uses recent data from the CSO's Quarterly National Household Survey to illustrate the steady improvement in the educational profile of 25 to 34-year-olds over recent years. This improvement is a direct result of the substantial improvements in participation in third-level education that have been achieved in recent years. In the seven-year period 1999–2005 the proportion of 25 to 34-year-olds with third-level qualifications increased from 27 per cent to almost 39 per cent. While the third-level educational attainment was similar for men and women in 1999, the gender differences in participation and in graduation documented in this chapter are now beginning to show in the educational profile of the 25 to 34-year-old age cohort. The educational profile of women has improved at a faster pace than that of men, and by 2005 there was a difference of 9 percentage points in the proportion of women with third-level qualifications compared with men in the same age cohort.

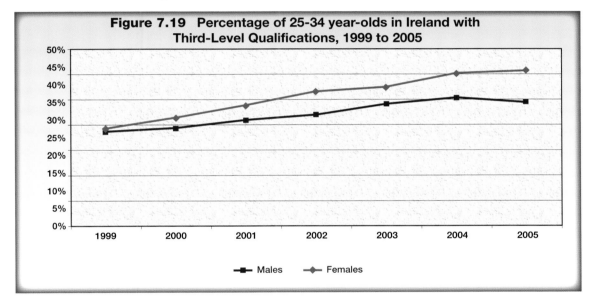

Fig. 7.20 provides an international comparison of higher-education attainment in 2004.[15] This chart illustrates the proportion of 25 to 34-year-olds in OECD countries who have third-level qualifications. Countries are ranked according to the proportion of those in that age cohort with higher education. Ireland ranked sixth of the twenty-four OECD countries in 2004 according to the educational profile of the 25 to 34-year-old age cohort. Data are presented for men and women in each country, and readers will note that the extent of the gender differences varies substantially between countries.

[14] Source: Central Statistics Office, Quarterly National Household Survey (QNHS), Special Module on Education, 1999–2003, table 5a, available at www.cso.ie/qnhs/documents/qnhseducation.xls. Data for 2004 and 2005 were also obtained from the QNHS, as reported on the CSO website.

[15] Data Source: OECD (2006), *Education at a Glance 2006*, Indicator A1.3a, A1.3b & A1.3c, p.39 (Gender breakdowns not published but available on the web at http://dx.doi.org/10.1787/701655207564). Equivalent details are provided in the corresponding appendix table in respect of the total adult population of 25-64 year olds.

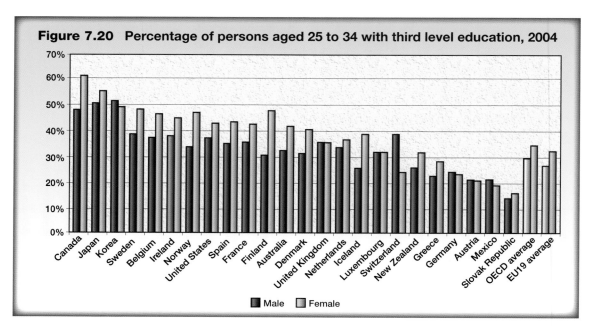

Figure 7.20 Percentage of persons aged 25 to 34 with third level education, 2004

■ Male ■ Female

The gender differences in the higher-educational attainment of 25 to 34-year-olds are quantified in fig. 7.21 simply by subtracting the proportion of men with higher education in each country from the equivalent proportion of women. The positive scores for most countries demonstrate that women have higher levels of third-level qualifications than men in seventeen of twenty-four countries. The gender differences are negligible in Luxembourg, the UK and Austria. Males have marginally higher levels of third-level qualifications in Germany, Mexico and Korea and substantially higher levels in Switzerland.

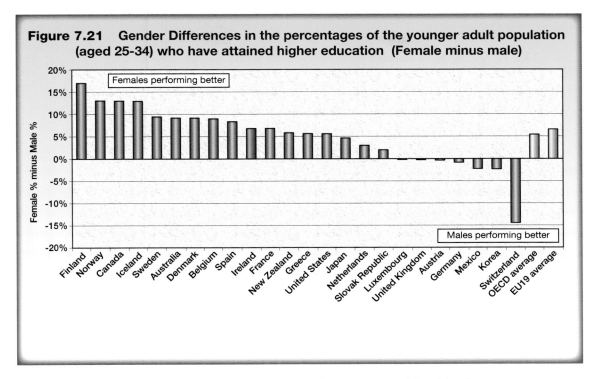

Figure 7.21 **Gender Differences in the percentages of the younger adult population (aged 25-34) who have attained higher education (Female minus male)**

The extent of the gender differences internationally varies considerably, from 17 percentage points in favour of women in Finland to 14 percentage points in favour of men in Switzerland. In general, women aged 25-34 have higher levels of third-level education than their male counterparts and this is illustrated in the international averages which are 5 percentage points in favour of women across the OECD and 6 percentage points in favour of women across the EU. The difference in favour of women in Ireland in 2004 was 7 percentage points (as published by the OECD[16]). This is higher than the international averages.

Taking stock of the full range of data that have been examined in this chapter, and the resultant trends that are already apparent in the educational profile of 25 to 34-year-olds in Ireland, it is certain that the gender gap in third-level educational attainment in Ireland will continue to increase into the near future at least.

---

[16] It is unclear why the international data on higher education attainment, as published by the OECD, differ from the national data, since they are both sourced from the CSO's Quarterly National Household Survey. It may be that Eurostat who process Ireland's international indicators use different weights to the CSO to map the sample survey to the Irish population.

SÉ SÍ   GENDER IN IRISH EDUCATION

Educational Personnel

Educational Personnel

In this chapter the focus shifts from students and learners to an examination of educational personnel by gender. The chapter provides an overview of teaching personnel at the primary, second and third level as well as of the personnel responsible for the administration and development of the education system in Ireland.

Primary teachers

Fig. 8.1[1] provides an extended time-series overview of teaching staff (including principals) at the primary level between 1930 and 2003. This demonstrates that women have continually outnumbered men among primary teachers over the last seventy years at least. The time-series data presented in fig. 8.1 shows that the proportion of female primary teachers increased steadily from 58 per cent in 1940 to 82 per cent in 2003. In fact while the total number of teachers at the primary level has doubled over the last fifty or sixty years, the number of male primary teachers in 2003 is broadly equivalent to the number of male teachers in the 1950s and 60s.

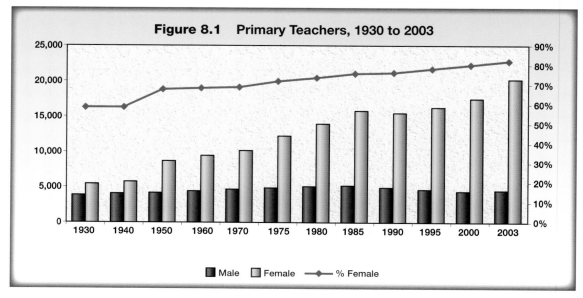

Figure 8.1 Primary Teachers, 1930 to 2003

To examine the gender ratio of primary teachers in an international context, fig. 8.2[2,3] provides an overview of the proportion of female teachers in member-states of the European Union and other selected countries. With the one exception of Turkey, women outnumber men by at least 2 to 1 among primary teachers in all other European countries. In fact women make up more than 80 per cent of teaching teachers at the primary level in the majority of European countries and more than 90 per cent in a number of central and eastern European countries, including Austria, Bulgaria, Italy, and Latvia. In 2003 women in Ireland accounted for 87 per cent of teaching teachers at the primary level. While Ireland is clearly not alone in having a severe gender imbalance among primary teachers, the imbalance in Ireland is relatively high by international standards.

---

[1] Source: Department of Education and Science, *Tuarascáil Staitistiúil: Annual Statistical Reports and Annual Reports*, various years, 1929/30 to 2002/03.

[2] Source: Eurostat web site, indicator on Educational Personnel - s06_2
     (http://epp.eurostat.cec.eu.int/portal/page?_pageid=0,1136184,0_45572595&_dad=portal&_schema=PORTAL), data updated 15
     September 2005, date of extraction 10 October 2005.

[3] Note that the data presented here refer to teaching teachers only (and therefore exclude principals who do not have teaching responsibilities).

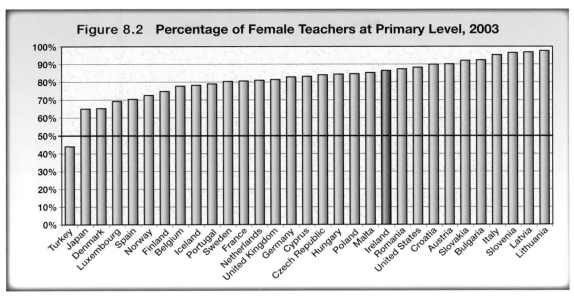

Figure 8.2 Percentage of Female Teachers at Primary Level, 2003

Fig. 8.3[4] provides a time-series overview of the gender ratio among principals, vice-principals and persons with posts of responsibility in Irish primary schools between 1990 and 2005. Although women have consistently outnumbered men among primary personnel, men outnumbered women among principals at the primary level until the year 2000, when the ratio was 50-50. While the proportion of female principals has increased over time, the continuing under-representation of women at the principal level is apparent in the present situation (2005), where women comprise 53 per cent of principals at a time when they account for 83 per cent of the total staff at the primary level. Therefore, in comparison with their total numbers in the primary teaching work-force, women continue to be quite severely under-represented at the school principal level.

4 Source: Data supplied by the Department of Education and Science, IT Unit (Athlone) and Primary Section.

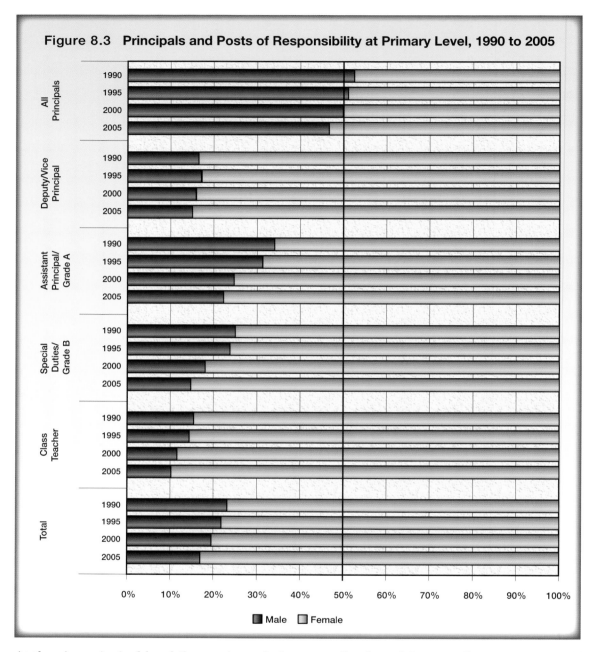

Figure 8.3 Principals and Posts of Responsibility at Primary Level, 1990 to 2005

At the vice-principal level the gender ratio is more reflective of the overall ratio among staff members. In fact women have been slightly over-represented at this level in comparison with their total numbers between 1990 and 2005. Among grade A and B posts of responsibility the percentage of women has increased steadily since 1990, and the ratio is now broadly equivalent to the overall gender ratio. When we look at the gender ratio throughout the range of posts of responsibility, the most striking feature is the continuing under-representation of women in principal posts relative to their total numbers among primary school personnel.

To examine the gender ratio of primary principals in an international context, fig. 8.4 presents the available Eurostat data on the percentage of female head teachers (principals) at the primary level. Unfortunately, these data were available only in respect of a limited number of countries, and readers should exercise caution in their interpretation of the Irish situation in the international context. In 10 of the 14 countries for which data were available, women outnumbered men among head teachers at the primary level in 2003.

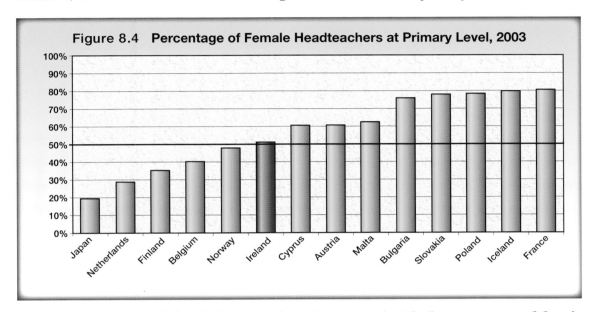

Figure 8.4   Percentage of Female Headteachers at Primary Level, 2003

When the percentage of female head teachers is compared with the percentage of female teachers (see appendix table 8.2 and 8.4), only in Iceland and in France do we find equivalence. In other words, the proportion of female principals in Iceland and France is equal to the overall proportion of female teachers at the primary level. Poland, Slovakia and Bulgaria also have a high proportion of female principals, which is relatively close to the gender ratio among primary teachers in those countries. In Ireland, where the overall proportion of female principals at the primary level appears to be lower than international averages, the gender ratio among principals is significantly out of line with the overall ratio among primary staff members.

5   Source: Eurostat web site, indicator on Educational Personnel - s01_2
(http://epp.eurostat.cec.eu.int/portal/page?_pageid=0,1136184,0_45572595&_dad=portal&_schema=PORTAL), data updated 15
September 2005, date of extraction 10 October 2005.

Second-level teachers

At the second level it as not possible to extend the time-series analysis back to before 1980, because teacher data published in the Department's Annual Statistical Reports were not disaggregated by gender. Fig. 8.5 presents an overview of second-level teachers by gender between 1985 and 2003. In 1985 the ratio among second-level teachers was almost exactly 50-50. However, in the intervening years the total number of female teachers has risen by approximately 3,500, while the total number of male teachers has declined by approximately 500. As a result the overall gender ratio is now approaching 60-40 in favour of women.

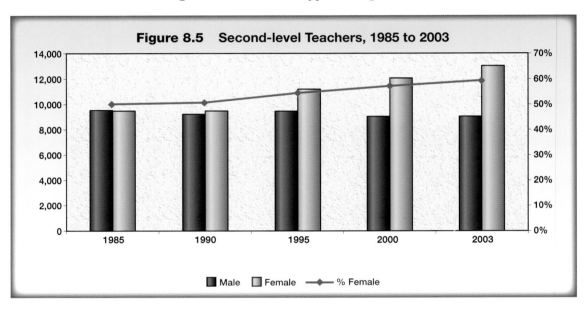

Additional detail on the gender ratio of teachers by second-level sector is provided in appendix table 8.5. This shows certain differences between the different second-level sectors, which have become less pronounced over time. The highest concentrations of female teachers are to be found in the secondary voluntary sector. Traditionally there were more male than female teachers in vocational schools and community and comprehensive schools. However, in these sectors women began to outnumber men from the mid to late 1990s onwards, and the ratio of 57 per cent female in 2003 is not too far from the 61 per cent now found in the secondary voluntary sector.

Fig. 8.6[6,7] uses the most recently available Eurostat data to provide an overview of the gender ratio of second-level teachers in an international context. At 60 per cent, Ireland is in the middle of the ranked listing of thirty countries in the percentage of female teachers at the second level and is very close to international averages in this regard. Women outnumber men among second-level teachers in 80 per cent of the countries listed, although the extent of the imbalance is not at all as severe as among primary teachers. With regard to the international country averages, women account for 82 per cent of primary teachers, compared with 61 per cent of teachers at the second level.

[6] Source: Eurostat web site, indicators on Educational Personnel - s06_3,4
      (http://epp.eurostat.cec.eu.int/portal/page?_pageid=0,1136184,0_45572595&_dad=portal&_schema=PORTAL), data updated 15
      September 2005, date of extraction 10 October 2005.

[7] As lower second-level and upper second-level education are provided in separate institutions in many European countries, the total second-
      level gender ratio of teachers has been calculated as an average of the ratio at the lower and upper second level to establish comparability
      with the Irish system.

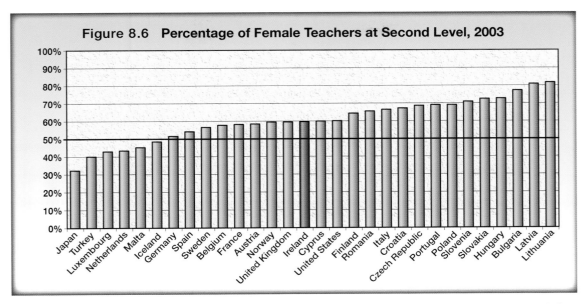

In examining the gender ratio among principals and holders of other posts of responsibility at the second level we are constrained by the limited availability of data. Firstly, readily accessible information on the detail of posts of responsibility in the vocational education sector is not available to the Department of Education and Science. Vocational schools are administered by the thirty-three vocational education committees, and at present no standardised system for recording such information exists among the various committees. A further constraint is the absence of comparable detail on the gender ratio of posts of responsibility going back in time. Notwithstanding these limitations, fig. 8.7[8] provides an overview of the gender ratio among principals, vice-principals and persons with posts of responsibility in the secondary sector and the community and comprehensive (C&C) sector in May 2005.[9]

Bearing in mind that the gender ratio among all teachers in secondary and C&C schools in 2003 was 60 per cent female to 40 per cent male, it is clear that women are under-represented from the level of A posts upwards. The higher the grade of teacher, the greater the extent of the under-representation. Once again the under-representation of women is most apparent at the level of principal, where men outnumber women by 2 to 1. In the C&C sector men outnumber women by 4 to 1 at the level of principal. (See appendix table 8.7.)

[8] Source: Department of Education and Science, Payroll Division (Primary Substitution and IT Liaison), Athlone.

[9] Of the 742 (publicly funded) second-level schools in Ireland in 2005, 54.3 per cent were secondary voluntary schools, 33.3 per cent were vocational and the remaining 12.4 per cent were in the community and comprehensive sector. Therefore, fig. 8.7 covers two thirds of all second-level schools in the country.

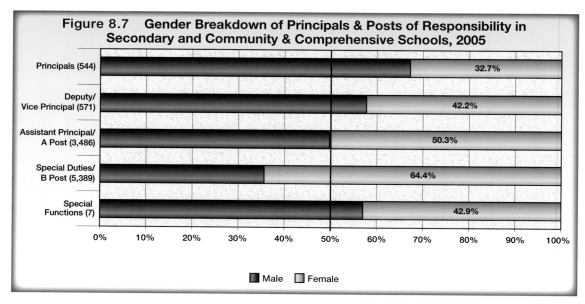

Figure 8.7   Gender Breakdown of Principals & Posts of Responsibility in Secondary and Community & Comprehensive Schools, 2005

Fig. 8.8[10,11] again uses recent Eurostat data on educational personnel to provide international data on the gender breakdown of school principals at the second level. Unfortunately, this information is available only in respect of a limited number of countries. Of the sixteen countries for which we have information, Ireland ranks in the middle and, at 32 per cent, is below the international average of 37 per cent. The underrepresentation of women at school principal level is a global phenomenon. Internationally, while women comprise a majority of second-level teachers (61 per cent), they account for only a little over 1 in 3 principals (37 per cent).

In all countries for which data are available, the proportion of female principals is lower than the proportion of female teachers. Only in France, Poland and Bulgaria does the representation of women among principals come close to their share of teaching positions at the second level. Interestingly, the international data suggest that many of the newer member-states of the European union have achieved greater levels of equality in principal posts than most of the older member-states.

[10] Source: Eurostat web site, indicators on Educational Personnel - s01_3 (http://epp.eurostat.cec.eu.int/portal/page?_pageid=0,1136184,0_45572595&_dad=portal&_schema=PORTAL), data updated 15 September 2005, date of extraction 10 October 2005.

[11] As lower second-level and upper second-level education are provided in separate institutions in many European countries, the total second-level gender ratio of principals has been calculated as an average of the ratio at the lower and upper second level to establish comparability with the Irish system.

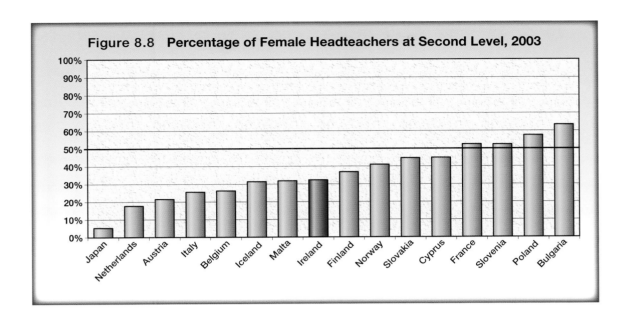

Figure 8.8   Percentage of Female Headteachers at Second Level, 2003

Higher education

Publicly funded higher education in Ireland has been provided primarily through two sectors—the institutes of technology and the universities. Up to now the universities have reported to the Higher Education Authority and the institutes of technology have traditionally reported directly to the Department of Education and Science. [12] Because of the different reporting arrangements, the level of detail available on educational personnel differs between the two sectors. Therefore, data on educational personnel for institutes of technology and universities will be presented separately in this section.

Institutes of technology[13]

Fig. 8.9[14] presents an overview of all staff members in the institutes of technology, divided broadly into academic staff, management and administrative staff, and support staff. Data are presented for 2003/04 and also for 1997/98 in order to provide an insight into developments over recent years. In 1997/98 men accounted for two-thirds of all staff members employed in the institutes of technology. However, the proportion of women has increased in the intervening years, and by 2003/04 women accounted for 42 per cent of all staff members.

---

[12] Following the enactment of the institutes of technology act, 2006, the funding and regulatory responsibilities for the institutes have been transferred from the Department of Education and Science to the Higher Education Authority (HEA), subject to overall Ministerial and government policy. The aim of this re-designation is to facilitate greater autonomy for the institutes of technology and to allow for the development of a unified and coherent policy and funding framework across the higher education sector.

[13] The analysis of educational personnel in the institute of technology sector presented here includes the Dublin Institute of Technology (DIT), the Tipperary institute (TRBDI) and the training college in Killybegs.

[14] Source: Department of Education and Science, Higher Education Technology and Training Section, Annual Returns from IOTs (THAS Reports).

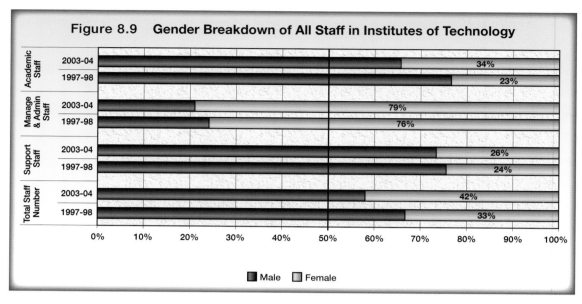

Figure 8.9 Gender Breakdown of All Staff in Institutes of Technology

While women account for a minority of the academic staff and a minority of the support staff,[15] they account for a substantial majority of personnel under the broad heading of management and administrative staff. Fig. 8.10[16] provides additional detail on the breakdown of staff members under this broad heading. A quick look at this information reveals that men strongly outnumber women in the area of management and that women strongly outnumber men in administration.

The largest category (accounting for 73 per cent of posts) is that labelled "other administrative staff," and women account for almost 90 per cent of staff members in this category. Women also make up three-quarters of library personnel, though their numbers diminish as we move up the management hierarchy. Only one-third of management personnel at the principal and assistant principal level are female, and women account for only 15 per cent of the senior management in the institutes of technology sector. This 15 per cent, however, is a considerable improvement on the situation in 1997/98, when 8 per cent of senior managers were female. Nevertheless, women continue to be severely under-represented at the senior management level relative to their total numbers in the broad category of management and administration in institutes of technology.

---

[15] "Support staff" refers to technical staff (599.5 posts, 76% male), students' services staff (81 posts, 83% female), and other support staff (491.5 posts, 80% male).

[16] Source: Department of Education and Science, Higher Education Technology and Training Section, Annual Returns from IOTs (THAS Reports).

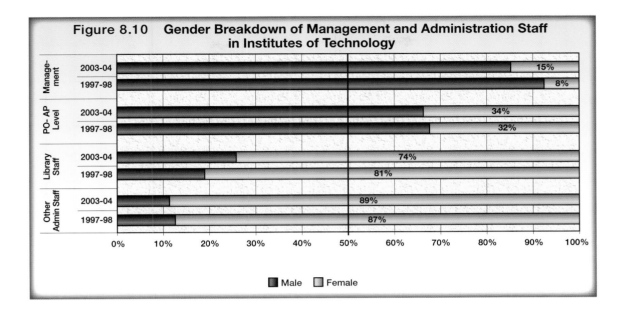

Figure 8.10 Gender Breakdown of Management and Administration Staff in Institutes of Technology

We know from fig. 8.9 that in 2003/04 men outnumbered women among academic staff members by 2 to 1 (66 per cent male). At 34 per cent, the proportion of women has improved considerably, from 23 per cent in 1997/98. Fig. 8.11[17] provides a more detailed breakdown of the academic staff in the institutes of technology and shows data from 1998/99 as well as from 2003/04. This shows that men outnumber women at all academic grades and that the proportion of women is particularly low at the senior lecturer level. At this level and among all the other academic grades there has been substantial improvement in the proportion of women in the short period between 1998/99 and 2003/04. Nevertheless, men continue to outnumber women among academic staff members in institutes of technology.

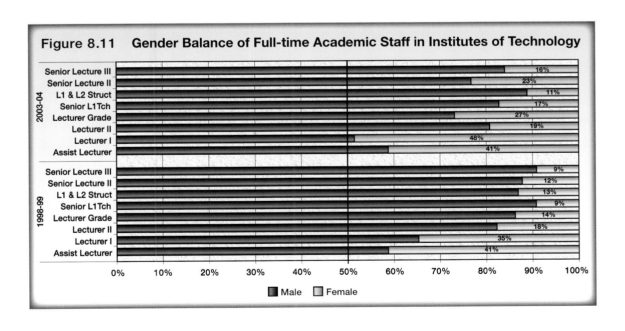

Figure 8.11 Gender Balance of Full-time Academic Staff in Institutes of Technology

[17] Source: Department of Education and Science, Higher Education Technology and Training Section, Annual Returns from IOTs (THAS Reports).

Universities

Regarding the breakdown of personnel in the university sector, data on management, administrative and support personnel are not available. However, the HEA has good information on academic personnel, and this provides the source for fig. 8.12,[18] which presents an overview of the gender breakdown of university academic personnel by grade for 1997/98 and 2003/04.

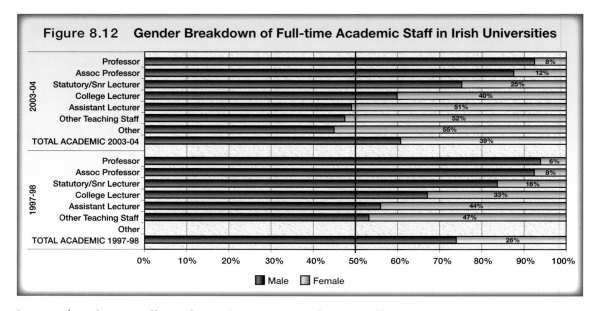

Figure 8.12   Gender Breakdown of Full-time Academic Staff in Irish Universities

In 2003/04 the overall gender ratio among academic staff in universities was 61 per cent male to 39 per cent female. This represented a considerable increase in the proportion of women from 1997/98, when women accounted for only 26 per cent of all academic staff. While in 1997/98 men outnumbered women in all the various academic grades, by 2003/04 women slightly outnumbered men at the lower levels of assistant lecturer, other teaching staff, and other (academic) staff. However, as we move up through the academic hierarchy the proportion of women declines steadily. This is very clear from fig. 8.12, where we can observe a clear pattern whereby the proportion of men increases with the seniority of the academic position.

The under-representation of women among university academic staff members is most severe at the highest levels of professor and associate professor. In 2003/04 women accounted for 8 per cent of professor posts and 12 per cent of associate professor posts. We have already observed similar patterns of imbalance at the highest levels of academic staff in the institutes of technology. However, there are approximately twice as many women at the most senior academic levels in the institutes of technology as there are in the universities; therefore the extent of gender imbalance among senior academics is most severe in the university sector.

[18] The data on which fig. 8.12 and appendix table 8.12 are based was supplied to the Department of Education and Science by the Higher Education Authority.

International data on academic personnel in higher education

To place these data on higher education personnel in an international context, fig. 8.13 provides an overview of the proportion of women among academic staff members in a range of (mostly European) countries. The countries with the lowest involvement of women academics are Switzerland, Japan, and the Netherlands, where fewer than one in five (20 per cent) of academic personnel are female; at the other end of the spectrum, Lithuania and Latvia have the highest level of participation by women. In contrast to all other countries for which we have data, women outnumber men among academic staff members in these two countries. Internationally, men outnumber women on average by 2 to 1 among academic staff members in higher education. With an overall female proportion of 36 per cent, Ireland is very close to the international average. Unfortunately, internationally comparable data are not available on the gender ratios that pertain within the hierarchy of academic grades.

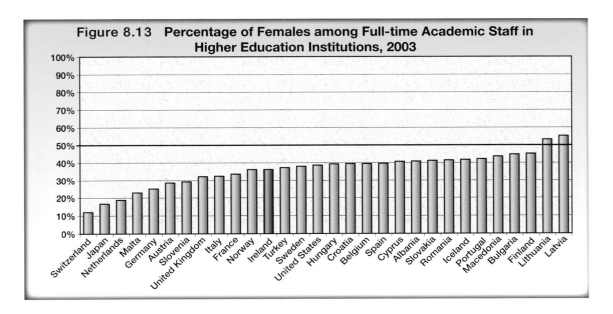

Figure 8.13 **Percentage of Females among Full-time Academic Staff in Higher Education Institutions, 2003**

Reflecting back on the range of data that has been presented on teaching personnel in educational institutions, we see a noticeable pattern whereby the proportion of women declines as one moves up through the various levels of education. Internationally, women account for 82 per cent of teaching personnel at the primary level, 60 per cent at the second level, and 36 per cent at the third level. The gender imbalance in Ireland is remarkably similar to these averages at each of the three levels. There are clear issues of imbalance among primary-level teachers that are also apparent to a lesser (and opposite) extent among teaching and academic personnel in higher education. There are also issues concerning the representation of women in positions of seniority in educational institutions. This is evident at the primary and the second level and was particularly striking in our analysis of seniority and academic hierarchy in higher education institutions.

19 Source: Eurostat web site, indicators on Educational Personnel - pers2_t
(http://epp.eurostat.cec.eu.int/portal/page?_pageid=0,1136184,0_45572595&_dad=portal&_schema=PORTAL), data updated 14 September 2005, date of extraction 21 December 2005.

The administration of the education system in Ireland

Having presented a comprehensive overview of teaching and management personnel in schools, colleges, and universities, the remaining section of this chapter deals with the personnel responsible for the administration of the education system. Given the large number of organisations involved in the development of education policy and in the provision of education services, the analysis presented will be confined to a number of important public agencies.

Department of Education and Science

We begin by looking at the staff of the Department of Education and Science, where the gender ratio among the 1,311 staff members is 35 per cent male to 65 per cent female. As with other Government departments, staff members in the Department of Education are divided into administrative and non-administrative grades. The majority of staff members (74 per cent) are in the administrative grade structure, and fig. 8.14 (a)[20] provides a gender breakdown of this staff. These data refer to the situation in April 2005, and the number of posts at each grade is given in parentheses.

Of the 968 administrative-grade staff members in the Department of Education and Science, 70 per cent are female. Looking at fig. 8.14 (a) above, we see clearly that women comprise an even higher proportion of staff members at the lower administrative grades of clerical officer (CO) and staff officer (SO). At the executive officer (EO) level the proportion of women (73 per cent) is close to their overall share of posts in the department. However, from the higher executive officer (HEO) level upwards the proportion of women diminishes substantially, from 60 per cent at the HEO level to 37 per cent at the assistant principal (AP) level and 31 per cent at the principal officer (PO) level.

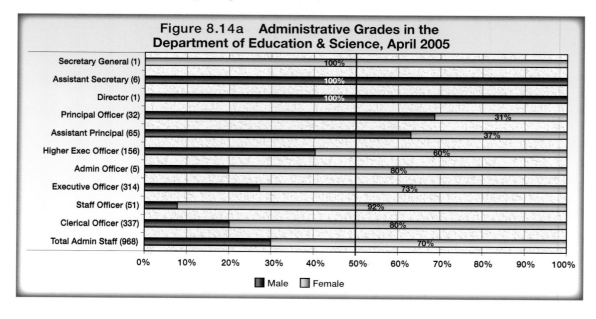

Figure 8.14a   Administrative Grades in the Department of Education & Science, April 2005

[20] Data supplied by Personnel Section, Department of Education and Science. For the full titles of each grade refer to appendix table 8.14.

In general, women are over-represented at the lower grades and under-represented at the higher administrative grades in the department relative to their total numbers. All six assistant secretary posts and the one director post were held by men in April 2005. However, the present secretary-general of the department is female.

There is a substantial diversity of posts among the remaining 343 staff members in the non-administrative grades. The largest category of non-administrative staff is that of inspectors. Fig. 8.14 (b)[21] presents a breakdown of staff members in the Inspectorate, which shows that there is a relatively even gender balance, with a small majority of men (54 per cent).

The Inspectorate is broadly divided between personnel who deal with primary education and those who deal with post-primary education. The district inspectors deal with primary schools, and they report to divisional inspectors. While a majority of district inspectors (58 per cent) are female, women account for only 30 per cent of divisional inspector posts. Similarly, at the post-primary level a majority of inspectors are female (60 per cent), although they constitute a minority of senior inspectors (PP), at 35 per cent. Women are substantially outnumbered by men at the highest levels of the Inspectorate, where the top three positions are all held by men and men account for two-thirds of the assistant chief inspector posts.

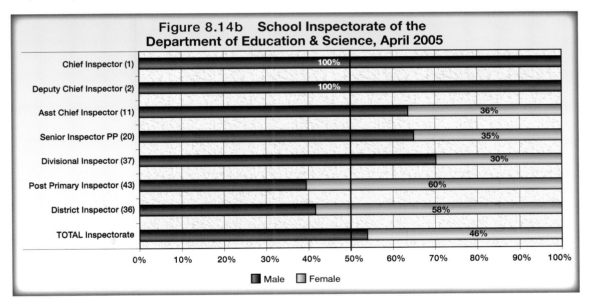

Figure 8.14b   School Inspectorate of the Department of Education & Science, April 2005

The second-largest category of non-administrative staff in the Department of Education and Science is that of psychologists employed in the National Educational Psychological Service (NEPS). Fig. 8.14 (c)[22] provides an overview of staff members in the NEPS, where women account for more than three-quarters (76 per cent) of all staff members. Men account for 19 per cent of psychologists, 30 per cent of senior psychologists, and 38 per cent of regional directors. Given their total numbers in the service, women make up a significant majority at all levels, and the acting director of the service is female. (All data refer to the position in April 2005.)

---

[21] Data supplied by Personnel Section, Department of Education and Science.
[22] Data supplied by Personnel Section, Department of Education and Science.

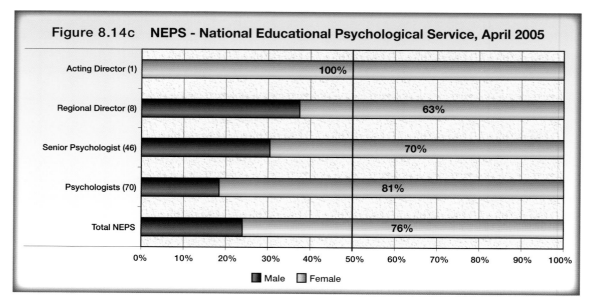

Figure 8.14c NEPS - National Educational Psychological Service, April 2005

As already noted, staff members in the non-administrative grades are a diverse group. Details on the remaining non-administrative grades are presented in appendix table 8.14. Here readers will find details on professional staff in the Building Unit, service grades and other professionals.

Department of Education and Science: 2005 data in context

To provide a context within which to examine the recent data on personnel in the Department of Education and Science, the charts below present equivalent data from ten years ago and an overview of staff members by grade from throughout the civil service. Fig. 8.15 provides an overview of all employees (in administrative grades) of the civil service with data relating to December 2003. Readers should note that this is sixteen months earlier than the data from April 2005 presented above on the Department of Education and Science.

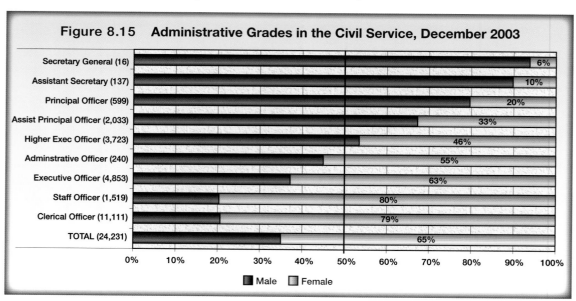

Figure 8.15 Administrative Grades in the Civil Service, December 2003

The visual representation of gender by grade in the civil service depicts what could be referred to as the classic staircase of gender inequality. Although women account for two-thirds of all administrative staff members in the civil service, they are over-represented at the lower grades and quite severely under-represented at the higher end of the seniority spectrum. In fact the ratio of women declines steadily as the seniority of the grade rises. Women account for 80 per cent of staff members at the clerical officer and staff officer levels and almost two-thirds at the executive officer grade. Although they account for more than half of all administrative officer posts they comprise fewer than half of the higher executive officers, one-third of assistant principal officers, one-fifth of principal officers, one-tenth of assistant secretaries-general, and an even smaller share of secretary-general posts.

Comparing the data from April 2005 on the Department of Education and Science with the general civil service data from December 2003, we see that the department has a higher proportion of women and a higher share at all grades except for the second-highest level of assistant secretary-general. Although the overall patterns of gender imbalance are similar, women account for a substantially larger proportion of staff members at the higher executive officer and principal officer level in the department than is typical in the civil service generally. At the assistant principal officer level the ratios are broadly similar. There were no female assistant secretaries-general in the Department of Education and Science in April 2005; this compares with a 10 per cent share by women at this grade in the civil service generally at the end of 2003. Readers should note that the current female secretary-general of the department was appointed after December 2003. All previous heads of the department were male.

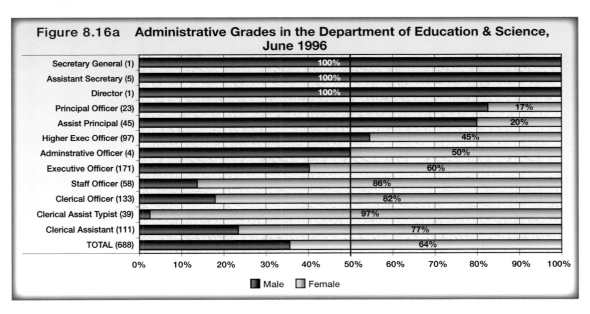

Figure 8.16a Administrative Grades in the Department of Education & Science, June 1996

To assess changes over time in the gender breakdown of staff members in the Department of Education and Science, fig. 8.16(a) provides an overview of administrative grades in the department in 1996. Over the nine-year period 1996–2005 the ratios of women in the middle to higher grades of the department increased. It rose from 45 to 60 per cent in the higher executive officer grade, from 20 to 37 per cent among assistant principal officers, and from 17 to 31 per cent among principal officers. The proportion of women among all administrative staff members also increased between 1996 and 2005, from 64 to 70 per cent. These general increases are reflected in the increases at all grades above the clerical officer level; at this level the ratio of women has remained at approximately 80 per cent over the last decade.

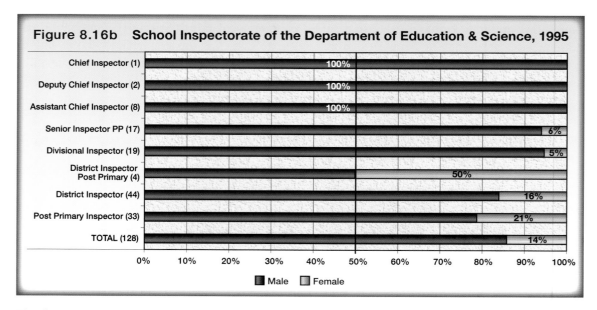

Figure 8.16b School Inspectorate of the Department of Education & Science, 1995

The last ten years have been a time of considerable change within the Inspectorate of the Department of Education and Science. Fig. 8.16(b) presents an overview of the gender breakdown of the Inspectorate in 1995. At that time women accounted for only 14 per cent of all inspectors; by 2005 this figure had risen to 46 per cent. The general increase in the number of female inspectors is apparent at both the primary and the post-primary level. Women now account for a majority of school inspectors and approximately one-third of middle-level Inspectorate posts. At the senior levels, where there were no women in 1995, women now account for more than one-third of assistant chief inspector posts. There were no changes in the gender ratios of the most senior posts between 1995 and 2005.

Education-related agencies

In addition to the Department of Education and Science, a wide range of public agencies have responsibilities for the administration and policy development of various aspects of education. It is beyond the scope of this publication to provide a full breakdown of every such agency. Nevertheless, it is appropriate to present an overview of the gender ratios of staff members and board members in a selection of important agencies.

Board membership of agencies and advisory committees

Appendix table 8.17 presents an overview of the board membership of forty different education-related agencies, advisory committees, and management committees, focusing in particular on the issue of gender balance. This list is a selection drawn from a more extended list maintained by the Gender Equality Unit of the Department of Education and Science. In addition to providing information on total board membership, appendix table 8.17 also presents information on Government or ministerial appointments to boards and committees and on the gender of the chairperson of the various groups. Summarising data on all forty agencies and committees listed in the appendix, we see that women accounted for 41 per cent of all appointments, 44 per cent of all Government and ministerial appointments, and 24 per cent of chairpersons. Fig. 8.17[23] presents the gender ratios on the boards of a small selection of education-related agencies. Additional details are provided in the corresponding appendix table.

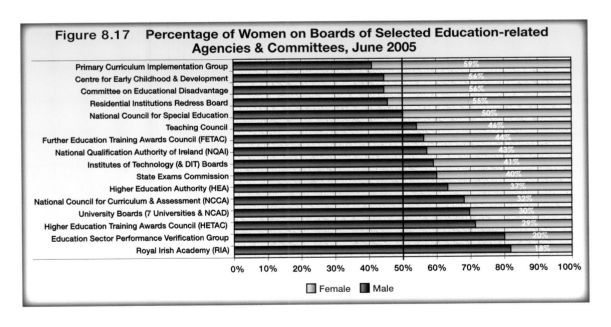

Figure 8.17   Percentage of Women on Boards of Selected Education-related Agencies & Committees, June 2005

Agency	%
Primary Curriculum Implementation Group	59%
Centre for Early Childhood & Development	56%
Committee on Educational Disadvantage	56%
Residential Institutions Redress Board	55%
National Council for Special Education	50%
Teaching Council	46%
Further Education Training Awards Council (FETAC)	44%
National Qualification Authority of Ireland (NQAI)	43%
Institutes of Technology (& DIT) Boards	41%
State Exams Commission	40%
Higher Education Authority (HEA)	37%
National Council for Curriculum & Assessment (NCCA)	32%
University Boards (7 Universities & NCAD)	30%
Higher Education Training Awards Council (HETAC)	29%
Education Sector Performance Verification Group	20%
Royal Irish Academy (RIA)	18%

☐ Female ■ Male

---

23 Source: The data given here on the gender composition of the boards of state agencies are compiled by the Gender Equality Unit of the Department of Education and Science. This information is forwarded regularly to the Department of Justice, Equality and Law Reform. See appendix table 8.17 for additional details.

Vocational education committees

The VECs are extremely important statutory providers of education at the local level, responsible for the provision of a significant amount of second-level education and the great majority of provision in further and adult education. These education and training programmes include adult, community and second-chance education, post-Leaving Certificate courses, prison education, Traveller education, and a variety of EU-funded and co-operative training schemes. VECs also have a range of other duties, which include the local administration of student supports for higher education.

There are thirty-three VEC areas in the country, with approximately seventeen members on each committee. While committees were traditionally composed almost entirely of local councillors, the Vocational Education (Amendment) Act (2001) revised their composition to extend representation to parents, staff members, and other local interests. A majority of members, however, are still local councillors, who are nominated and elected by the county council and the town councils within the VEC area.

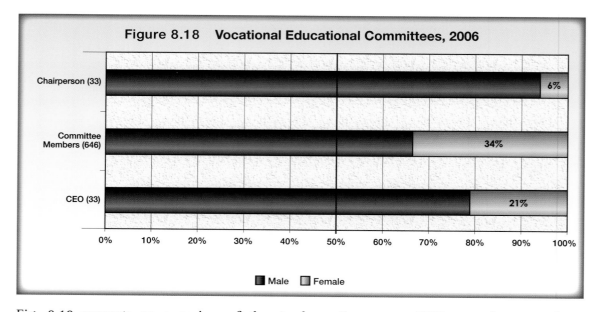

Figure 8.18   Vocational Educational Committees, 2006

Fig. 8.18 presents an overview of the gender ratios among VEC committee members, committee chairpersons and chief executive officers at the beginning of 2006. Women account at present for one-third of the total of 588 committee members and occupy the position of chairperson in only two of the thirty-three committees. Approximately one-fifth of all VEC areas have a female chief executive. These figures show that women are under-represented at the board level and the senior management level in our vocational education committees.

Personnel of selected agencies

By way of concluding this section on the administration of the education system, a breakdown of staff by gender and grade in a selection of publicly funded agencies is presented. The information refers to 2005 and covers the following educational agencies:

Higher Education Authority (HEA)
State Examinations Commission (SEC)
National Council for Special Education (NCSE)
National Council for Curriculum and Assessment (NCCA)
National Education Welfare Board (NEWB)
National Qualifications Authority of Ireland (NQAI)
Higher Education Training and Awards Council (HETAC)
Further Education Training and Awards Council (FETAC)
National Adult Literacy Agency (NALA)
Aontas (National Association of Adult Education)

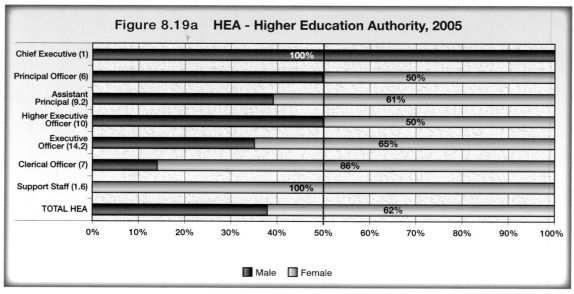

Figure 8.19a   HEA - Higher Education Authority, 2005

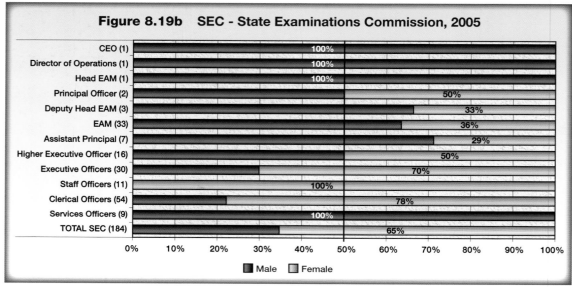

Figure 8.19b   SEC - State Examinations Commission, 2005

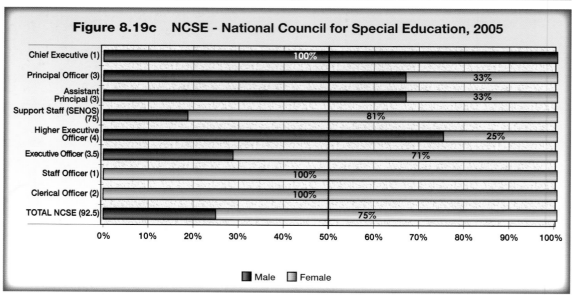

Figure 8.19c   NCSE - National Council for Special Education, 2005

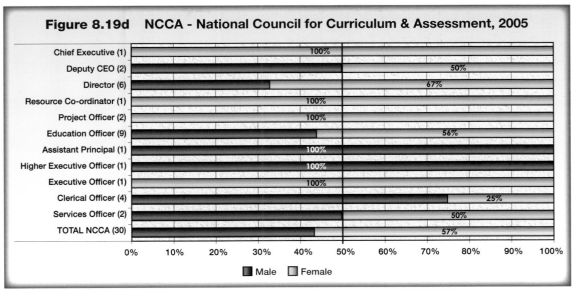

Figure 8.19d   NCCA - National Council for Curriculum & Assessment, 2005

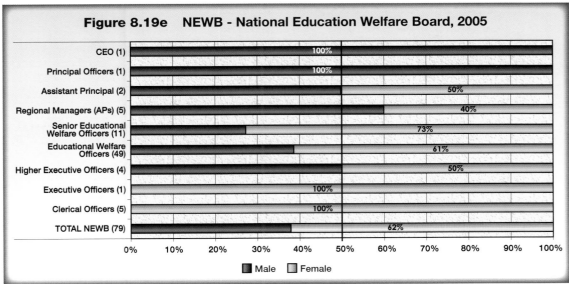

Figure 8.19e   NEWB - National Education Welfare Board, 2005

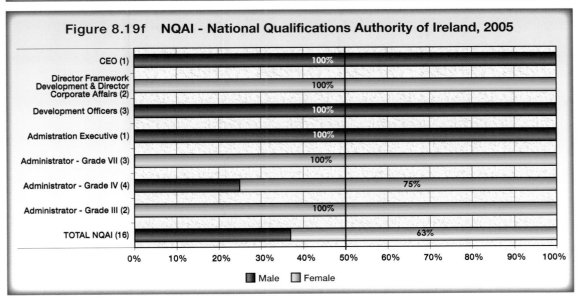

Figure 8.19f   NQAI - National Qualifications Authority of Ireland, 2005

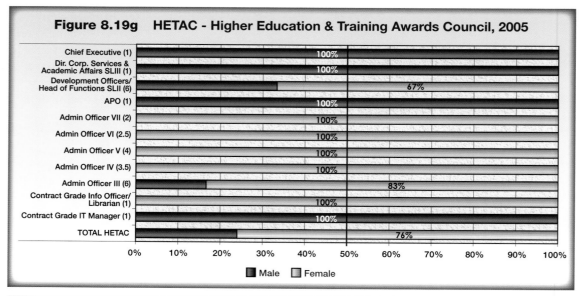

Figure 8.19g HETAC - Higher Education & Training Awards Council, 2005

Grade	Male	Female
Chief Executive (1)		100%
Dir. Corp. Services & Academic Affairs SLIII (1)		100%
Development Officers/ Head of Functions SLII (6)		67%
APO (1)	100%	
Admin Officer VII (2)	100%	
Admin Officer VI (2.5)	100%	
Admin Officer V (4)	100%	
Admin Officer IV (3.5)	100%	
Admin Officer III (6)		83%
Contract Grade Info Officer/ Librarian (1)	100%	
Contract Grade IT Manager (1)	100%	
TOTAL HETAC		76%

■ Male □ Female

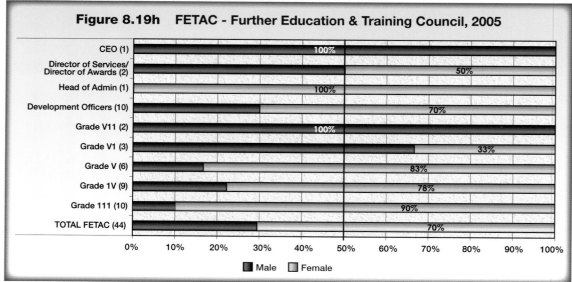

Figure 8.19h FETAC - Further Education & Training Council, 2005

Grade	Male	Female
CEO (1)	100%	
Director of Services/ Director of Awards (2)	50%	50%
Head of Admin (1)		100%
Development Officers (10)		70%
Grade V11 (2)	100%	
Grade V1 (3)		33%
Grade V (6)		83%
Grade 1V (9)		78%
Grade 111 (10)		90%
TOTAL FETAC (44)		70%

■ Male □ Female

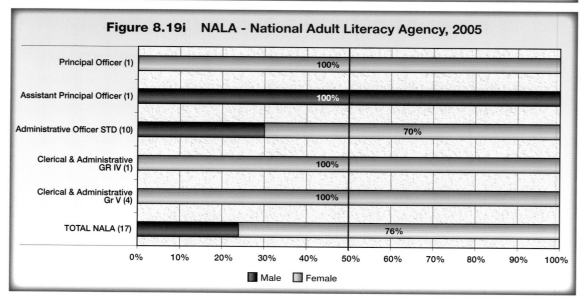

Figure 8.19i NALA - National Adult Literacy Agency, 2005

Grade	Male	Female
Principal Officer (1)		100%
Assistant Principal Officer (1)	100%	
Administrative Officer STD (10)		70%
Clerical & Administrative GR IV (1)		100%
Clerical & Administrative Gr V (4)		100%
TOTAL NALA (17)		76%

■ Male □ Female

Figure 8.19j   AONTAS, 2005

	Male	Female
Principal Officer (2)	100%	
Assistant Principal Officer (1)	100%	
Higher Executive Officer (1)	100%	
Executive Officer (5)	100%	
Clerical Officer (1)	100%	
TOTAL Aontas (10)	100%	

0%   10%   20%   30%   40%   50%   60%   70%   80%   90%   100%

■ Male   ☐ Female

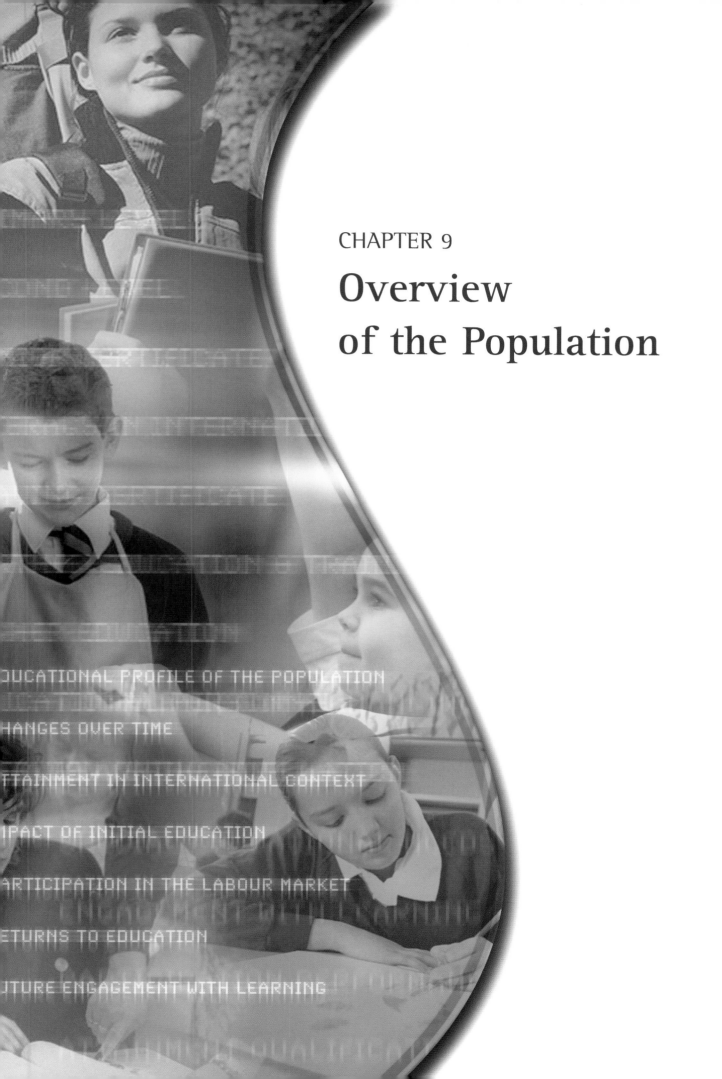

CHAPTER 9

Overview
of the Population

Overview of the Population

In this final chapter, readers will be presented with a summary overview of the educational profile of the Irish population. In addition to looking at our educational attainment in its international context, this chapter will explore the relationship between education and participation in the labour market and will provide some recent data on continuing engagement with learning by adults.

Changes over time in the educational profile of the population

Fig. 9.1[1] provides an overview of the proportions of those with low levels of educational attainment. These are adults who have not progressed beyond lower second-level education, i.e. adults whose highest level of educational attainment is either the Junior Certificate[2] or primary-level education. Although these data refer to the situation in 2004, the breakdown by age group provides a good insight into trends in educational attainment over recent decades.

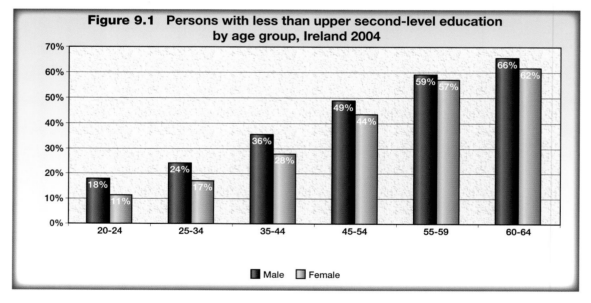

Figure 9.1   Persons with less than upper second-level education by age group, Ireland 2004

This chart demonstrates that Ireland has made steady and substantial progress in reducing the number of those who leave school with low levels of educational attainment. The proportion of those with these low levels of education has fallen from 64 per cent among those aged between 60 and 64 to 15 per cent among those aged between 20 and 24. In fact the majority of men (51.3 per cent) now aged between 60 and 64 did not even progress beyond primary-level education.[3] Looking at the gender differences, it is clear that men outnumber women among those with low levels of educational attainment in all age groups. This shows that women have achieved higher rates of participation and attainment in upper second-level education than men for at least fifty or sixty years. While the number of those with low levels of educational attainment has declined steadily among both sexes, the gap in favour of women has increased over time.

---

[1] Source: Central Statistics Office, Quarterly National Household Survey. Reference period: second quarter, March to May 2004. The Department of Education and Science is grateful to the Labour Market Section of the CSO for providing this data disaggregated by gender. Note: The small number of respondents whose highest level of education is classified as "other" have been omitted from this analysis.

[2] Previously known as the Intermediate Certificate.

[3] See appendix, table 9.1, for this additional detail.

Looking at the higher end of the attainment spectrum, fig. 9.2[4] presents data on the proportions of adults who have achieved third-level qualifications. Once again the results by age group show considerable improvements over time in the numbers of those benefiting from higher education. Although men have slightly higher rates of third-level educational attainment from the 35–44 age group upwards, a striking difference in favour of women is emerging among the younger cohort of 25 to 34-year-olds.

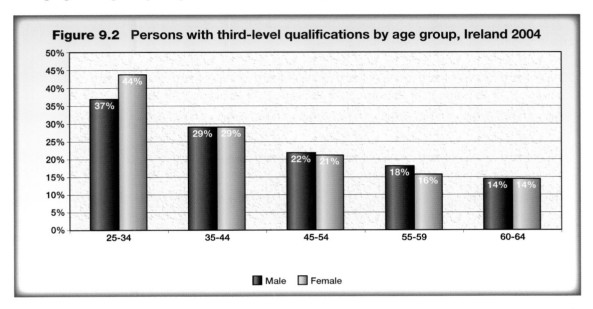

Figure 9.2 Persons with third-level qualifications by age group, Ireland 2004

The educational profile evident from these CSO surveys is entirely consistent with the trends in enrolment and graduation in higher education presented earlier in chapter 7.

Educational attainment in international comparison

An overview of the educational attainment of adult populations in the OECD countries is published annually in the OECD's publication Education at a Glance. When older age groups are compared there are striking differences between countries, but these differences are less pronounced for the younger age groups, demonstrating that many countries have made steady and substantial progress over recent decades. Ireland is among the countries that have made most progress in the expansion of educational opportunities over recent decades. Indeed the OECD includes Ireland in a small number of countries that are identified as having made "remarkable improvement" in the upper secondary attainment of the population over time.[5] Fig. 9.3[6] presents an overview of upper second-level attainment, comparing men and women in Ireland with the averages for all OECD countries.

4 Source: Central Statistics Office, Quarterly National Household Survey. Reference period: second quarter, March to May 2004. The Department of Education and Science is grateful to the Labour Market Section of the CSO for providing these data disaggregated by gender.
   Note: The small number of respondents whose highest level of education is classified as "other" have been omitted from this analysis.
5 Organisation for Economic Co-operation and Development, *Education at a Glance: OECD Indicators, 2005*, Paris: OECD, 2005, p. 31.
6 Source: OECD, *Education at a Glance, 2005*, table A1.2 (The gender breakdowns that were not published are available on the OECD web site.)

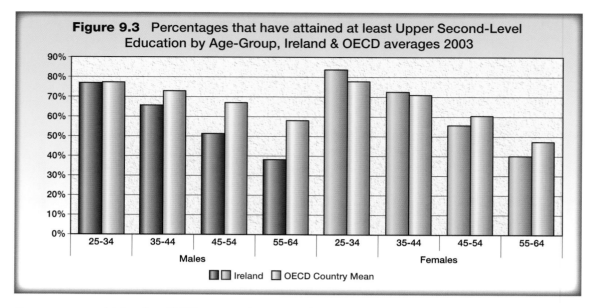

Figure 9.3 Percentages that have attained at least Upper Second-Level Education by Age-Group, Ireland & OECD averages 2003

On average within the OECD countries, men have traditionally outperformed women in upper second-level attainment. This can be seen in the substantially higher rates of educational attainment among males in the 55–64 age group and to a lessening extent among 45 to 54-year-olds and 35 to 44-year-olds throughout the OECD. With regard to OECD averages, it is only in the youngest adult cohort (25 to 34-year-olds) that women have overtaken men by 1 percentage point in the attainment of upper second-level education. In contrast to these international trends, women in Ireland display higher levels of second-level attainment in all age cohorts.

Although women in Ireland over the age of 45 are behind international averages in upper second-level education, their younger counterparts have moved ahead of international averages for women by 5 percentage points among 25 to 34-year-olds. Irish men, who lag well behind international averages for older age groups, have now equalled the OECD average for upper second-level attainment among 25 to 34-year-olds.

In general, the improvement in upper secondary attainment in Ireland was such that we have moved from a position well below the OECD average (for those aged over 45) to one where the educational profile of 25 to 34-year-olds compares more favourably with the OECD average. In ranking, Ireland has moved from 23rd out of 30 (for 45 to 54-year-olds) to 17th out of 30 (for 25 to 34-year-olds). While our progress and improvement over recent decades has been impressive, "the challenge now is to ensure that the remaining fraction is not left behind, with the risk of limited job prospects and social exclusion that this may entail."[7] Substantial continuing improvement will be required to match the performance of our northern European and Scandinavian neighbours or the performance of the United States, Canada, Japan, and South Korea.

[7] This quotation combines two phrases, one used in OECD, *Education at a Glance, 2003*, p. 35, and the other in *Education at a Glance, 2005*, p. 40.

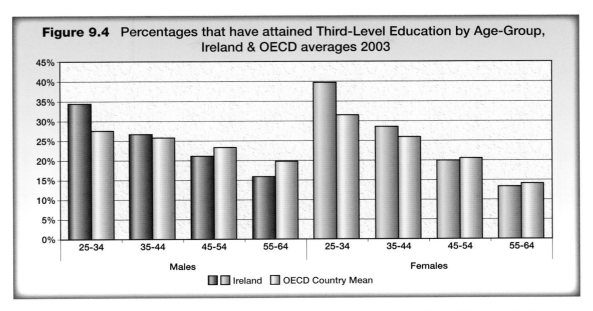

Figure 9.4 Percentages that have attained Third-Level Education by Age-Group, Ireland & OECD averages 2003

Fig. 9.4 presents data on the proportions of men and women in the adult population who have attained third-level education. This indicates steady improvement internationally in third-level educational attainment. Once again, in general Ireland has improved at a faster rate than international averages and has improved its ranking from 16th out of 30 (for those aged over 45) to 11th out of 30 (among the younger 25–34 age cohort).

The substantial expansion of higher education over recent decades throughout the OECD has resulted in steady improvements in the third-level educational attainment of both men and women. The international trends in higher education are similar to the international trends observed at second level, where women display lower levels of attainment among the middle to older age cohorts but have moved ahead of men among the younger 25–34 cohort. Ireland's rate of improvement is faster than international averages for both men and women, and the third-level educational attainment levels of young Irish women (aged 25–34) is particularly impressive by international standards.

Upon closer examination of the types of third-level qualification that people are now obtaining we see that Ireland has a relatively high proportion of those with certificates and diplomas [8], NFQ levels 6 and 7. The proportions graduating with primary and masters' degrees in Ireland (NFQ levels 8 and 9) have also risen above the OECD average over recent years, but our output of graduates from PhD courses (NFQ level 10) remains below average. [9]

---

[8] Certificates and Diplomas are now known as Higher Certificates and Ordinary Degrees.

[9] See OECD, *Education at a Glance, 2005*, indicator A3.1 (p. 55).

The impact of initial educational attainment

Initial educational attainment has a substantial and broad-ranging impact on many aspects of life from personal development to civic engagement and economic well-being.[10]

Having presented an overview of the educational profile of the Irish population, it is appropriate at this point that we explore the impact of initial educational attainment on important aspects of later life. While education has broad-ranging effects at the level of the individual, the community, and society, the analysis here is confined to the consequences of educational attainment for individuals in the form of participation in the labour market, financial returns to education, and future engagement with learning. It is important to remember that the individual benefits of education extend far beyond those that can be quantified statistically and financially. In addition, "society also benefits from the learning activities of its citizens in the form of active citizenship, cultural enrichment, technological innovation and taxation."[11]

Participation in the labour market

The total labour force in Ireland has increased substantially over the last decade, rising from 1.2 million in 1994 to over 1.8 million in 2004. In addition to the increases in the population of working age, higher female participation rates have contributed substantially to the rapid growth in the labour force over recent years. Ireland's female labour force participation rate reached 49.4 per cent in 2004, up substantially from 30 per cent in 1985. This figure of 49.4 per cent refers to the participation rate of all females aged fifteen and over and compares with a male labour force participation rate of 70.9 per cent in the same year (2004).[12] Fig. 9.5[13] provides an overview of labour force participation rates of 25 to 64-year-olds by age group. This suggests that the gap between male and female participation rates is narrowing among the younger age cohorts.

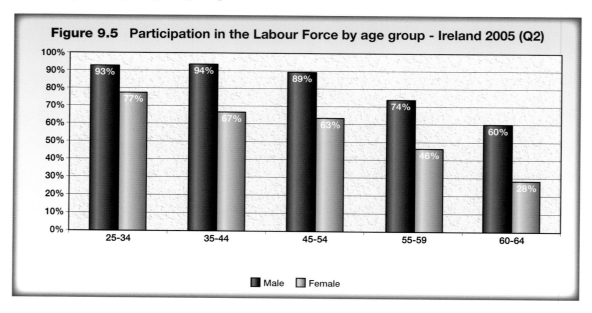

Figure 9.5 Participation in the Labour Force by age group - Ireland 2005 (Q2)

[10] Department of Education and Science, *Supporting Equity in Higher Education: A Report to the Minister for Education and Science*, 2003, p. 7.

[11] Department of Education and Science, *Supporting Equity in Higher Education*, p. 7.

[12] The figures referred to in this paragraph are taken from Central Statistics Office, *Statistical Yearbook of Ireland, 2005*, Dublin: CSO, 2005, p. 28–37.

[13] Source: CSO web site, data on labour force from the Quarterly National Household Survey (www.cso.ie/px/pxeirestat/temp/QNBQ42005113494249.xls). Data extracted 2 November 2005.

Of particular interest in the context of this publication is the relationship between educational attainment and employment rates for men and women. Fig. 9.6[14] presents data on employment rates by educational attainment and gender between 1991 and 2003. The most striking aspect of the information presented in fig. 9.6 is the dramatic impact that educational attainment has on the employment rates of women in Ireland (and throughout the OECD). For example, the employment rate for women with low levels of educational attainment in 2003 was only 38 per cent. This increased to 63 per cent for those with medium levels of education (i.e. Leaving Certificate or equivalent) and to 81 per cent for those with third-level education. This 81 per cent is within 10 percentage points of the equivalent employment rate for men with third-level education. By contrast, gender differences in employment rates are widest among the less educated groups, where men with low levels of education are twice as likely to be employed as their female counterparts. For men the gap in employment rates is particularly wide between those with at least the Leaving Certificate and those with less than upper second-level education.

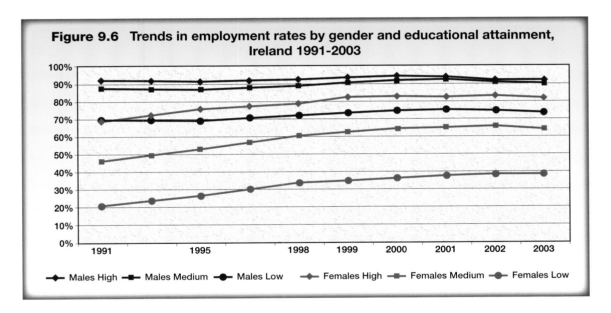

Figure 9.6   Trends in employment rates by gender and educational attainment, Ireland 1991-2003

Legend: Males High, Males Medium, Males Low, Females High, Females Medium, Females Low

The strong relationship between educational attainment and employment prospects is also apparent in the available data relating to rates of unemployment. Unemployment rates among 25 to 29-year-olds in Ireland are presented in fig. 9.7[15] by education level and gender. These data demonstrate that the risk of unemployment decreases steadily as education levels increase.

We know from the previous chart that women with low qualifications are unlikely to be in employment. In fact the labour force participation rate of women with low levels of education is very low in Ireland. While men of all education levels are likely to be included in the labour force, the risks of unemployment for young men with low levels of educational attainment are severe.

---

[14] Source: OECD, *Education at a Glance*, 2005, table A8.3a (p. 111). (The gender breakdowns that were not published are available on the OECD web site; see web tables A8.3b and A8.3c.) Note: For educational attainment, "low" = below upper secondary, "medium" = upper secondary and post-secondary non-tertiary, "high" = tertiary education.

[15] Source: OECD, *Education at a Glance*, 2005, table C4.3 (p. 292).

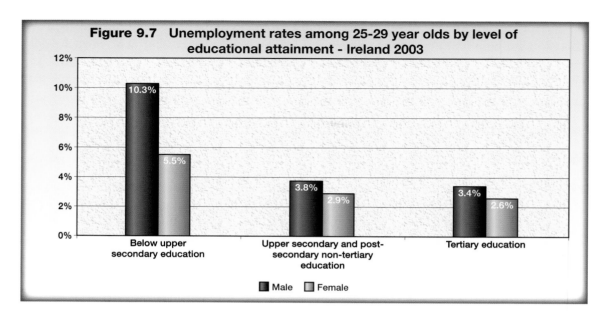

Figure 9.7 Unemployment rates among 25-29 year olds by level of educational attainment - Ireland 2003

In 2003, 10.3 per cent of men aged between 25 and 29 with a qualification less than the Leaving Certificate were unemployed. This was more than two-and-a-half times greater than the unemployment rate of men with the Leaving Certificate and more than three times greater than the rate for men with third-level qualifications. Given the substantial improvement in employment prospects for men who achieve at least upper second-level qualifications, these data emphasise the severe consequences of early school-leaving on the employment prospects of young men and on the labour market participation prospects of young women.

Returns to education

In general, the salaries that people earn from employment increase steadily with higher levels of educational attainment.

> Earnings differentials between those who have tertiary [third-level] education and those who have upper secondary education are generally more pronounced than the differentials between upper secondary and lower secondary or below, suggesting that in many countries upper secondary education forms a break-point beyond which additional education attracts a particularly high premium.[16]

With regard to gender, the average weekly income of all female employees in Ireland was approximately 74 per cent of that for male employees in 2004.[17] In Ireland and throughout the OECD countries women still earn less than men with a similar level of educational attainment. Nevertheless, educational attainment has a significant impact on female earnings, in that women with low skills earn substantially less than their male counterparts, while the average earnings of women with high educational attainment is much closer to that of men with similar qualification levels.

[16] OECD, *Education at a Glance, 2005*, p. 118.
[17] Central Statistics Office, *Statistical Yearbook of Ireland, 2005*, p. 361.

The impact of educational attainment on the average earnings of men and women is outlined with Irish data from 2000 below. This compares average earnings at the lower and the higher ends of the qualification spectrum with the average earnings of men and women with the Leaving Certificate or equivalent qualification (represented by the 100 per cent line).

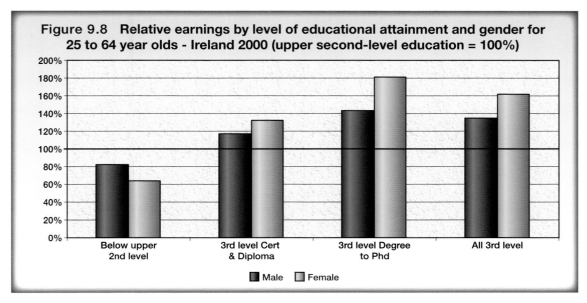

Figure 9.8   Relative earnings by level of educational attainment and gender for 25 to 64 year olds - Ireland 2000 (upper second-level education = 100%)

This comparison shows that the wages available to women with low levels of educational attainment are relatively very low, and that educational attainment has a particularly strong impact on the average earnings of women. Third-level education attracts a particularly high premium of 61 per cent for women relative to those whose highest level of education is upper second level. The individual rates of return from higher education are greater for women than for men. However, women continue to earn less on average than men in all levels of educational attainment. Recent research by the ESRI and by the HEA indicate that gender differences in earnings emerge very early in the career cycle. [18]

Future engagement with learning

In Ireland, and in all OECD countries, initial educational attainment has a very significant impact on future participation in education and training. Fig. 9.9 presents data on participation rates in formal and non-formal education among 25 to 64-year-olds in Ireland by level of initial educational attainment. This clearly demonstrates the strong link between initial and continuing education. Irish adults with third-level qualifications are almost four times more likely to participate in continuing education than their peers with less than upper second-level education.

[18] See HEA Statistics Section (2007), What do Graduates Do? The Class of 2005 and Russell, H., Smyth, E., O'Connell, P. (2005), Degrees of Equality: Gender Pay Differentials among Recent Graduates.

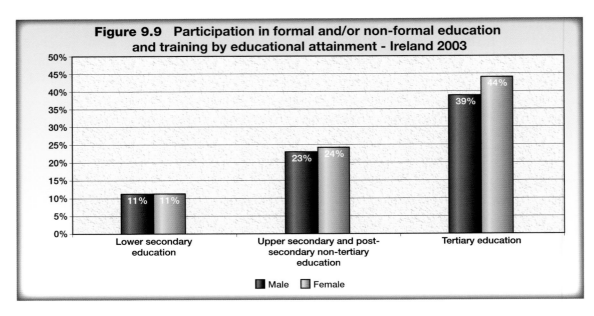

Figure 9.9 Participation in formal and/or non-formal education and training by educational attainment - Ireland 2003

With regard to gender and the participation of adults in formal and non-formal education, fig. 9.9 shows that there are small differences favouring women, and these differences appear to increase with the level of initial education. These data suggest that while participation rates in continuing education are very similar among men and women with low qualifications, women with a third-level education are 5 percentage points more likely to participate in continuing education than their male counterparts.

Fig. 9.10[19] presents some recent international data on participation in lifelong learning among 25 to 64-year-olds throughout the European Union.[20] Countries are ranked according to the total participation rates of all adults, and it is clear that there is very considerable variation in the extent to which member-states have succeeded in achieving participation in lifelong learning. The Scandinavian countries have achieved the highest participation rates; in the country with the highest performance, Sweden, it is estimated that more than a third of all adults were engaged in education or training in 2004. Britain, Slovenia, the Netherlands and, to a lesser extent, Austria have also achieved relatively high levels of participation in lifelong learning. In all other EU member-states the participation rate of adults in lifelong learning was below 10 per cent. In 2004 the participation rate among Irish adults was 7.2 per cent, which was below the EU average of 9.9 per cent.

---

[19] Source: European Commission Communication, Draft 2006 Progress Report on the Implementation of the "Education and Training 2010 work programme," 2005, p. 24.

[20] For this indicator, participation in lifelong learning is understood as the percentage of adults (25 to 64-year-olds) who participated in education or training in the four weeks before the EU Labour Force Survey (which in Ireland is the CSO Quarterly National Household Survey).

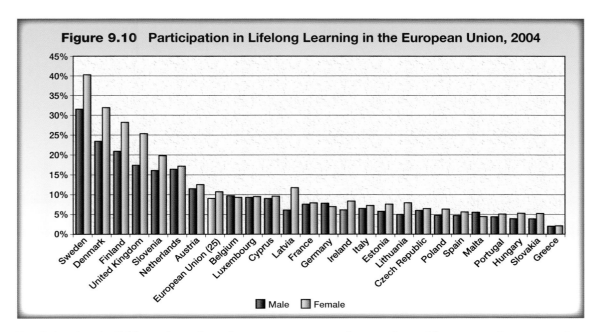

Figure 9.10   Participation in Lifelong Learning in the European Union, 2004

Participation in lifelong learning also appears to vary by gender, with women demonstrating higher rates of participation in almost all EU countries; the exceptions are Belgium, Germany, and Malta, where the participation rates of men are slightly higher than for women. Taking the European Union as a whole, an average of 10.7 per cent of women participated in lifelong learning in 2004 compares with 9.0 per cent of men. The differences in favour of women appear to be most stark in the countries with the highest total levels of participation. Nevertheless there are also gender differences in favour of women that exceed the EU average in Latvia, Lithuania, Estonia, and Ireland.

In general, however, the differences in participation rates by gender are dwarfed in comparison with the very strong differences observed earlier (figure 9.9) that arise from differences in initial levels of educational attainment. We know from the available international data that participation rates in continuing education are strongly linked to initial levels of educational attainment in every OECD country.

> These patterns suggest that initial education and continuing education are mutually reinforcing, and that education combines with other factors to make adult training least common among those who need it most.[21]

The fact that "all countries share inequalities in access to adult learning"[22] demonstrates a lack of success in promoting lifelong learning among those with low levels of education and emphasises the scale of the challenge that this presents.

Leabharlanna Fhine Gall

---

[21] OECD, *Education at a Glance, 2002*, p. 248–249.
[22] OECD, *Education at a Glance, 2005*, p. 312.

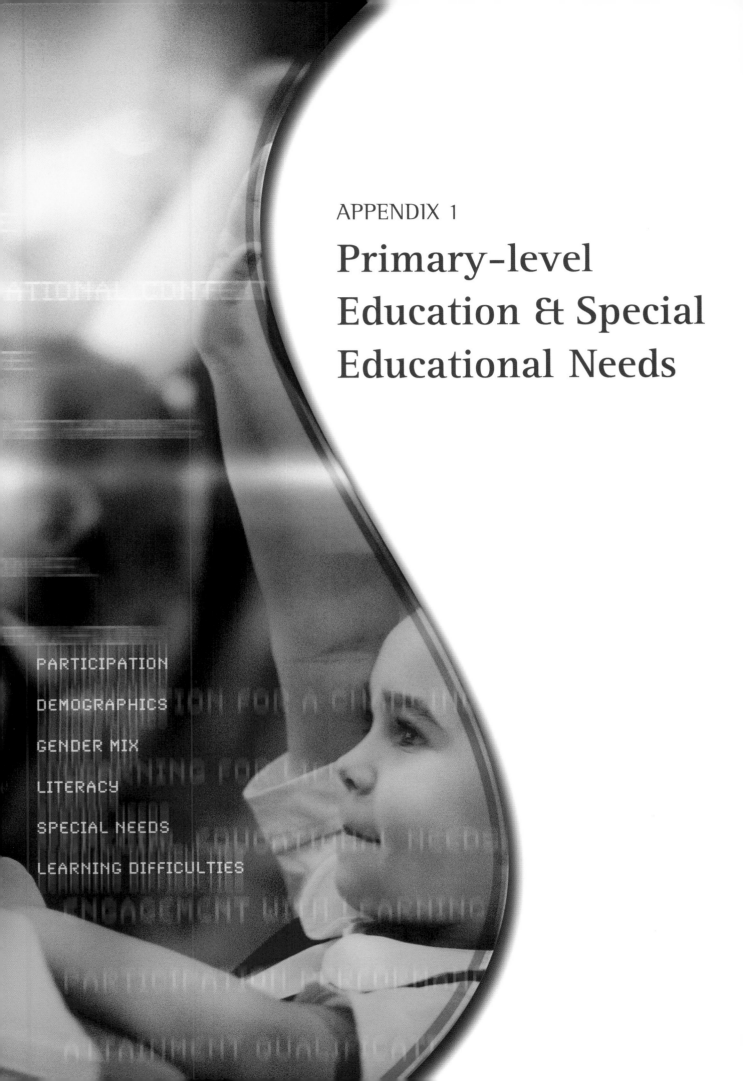

APPENDIX 1

Primary-level Education & Special Educational Needs

PARTICIPATION

DEMOGRAPHICS

GENDER MIX

LITERACY

SPECIAL NEEDS

LEARNING DIFFICULTIES

TABLE 1.1 PUPILS IN ORDINARY CLASSES IN PRIMARY SCHOOLS

| YEAR | PUPIL NUMBERS | | | GENDER BALANCE | |
	MALE	FEMALE	TOTAL	MALE	FEMALE
1980-81*	277,520	263,295	540,815	51.3%	48.7%
1985-86*	285,212	270,627	555,839	51.3%	48.7%
1990-91	272,969	259,271	532,240	51.3%	48.7%
1991-92	268,309	254,488	522,797	51.3%	48.7%
1992-93	261,637	248,375	510,012	51.3%	48.7%
1993-94	253,648	240,674	494,322	51.3%	48.7%
1994-95	245,847	233,279	479,126	51.3%	48.7%
1995-96	239,105	226,749	465,854	51.3%	48.7%
1996-97	233,661	222,433	456,094	51.2%	48.8%
1997-98	228,425	217,934	446,359	51.2%	48.8%
1998-99	223,645	213,090	436,735	51.2%	48.8%
1999-00	219,299	209,040	428,339	51.2%	48.8%
2000-01	216,854	206,490	423,344	51.2%	48.8%
2001-02	217,537	207,170	424,707	51.2%	48.8%
2002-03	218,905	208,624	427,529	51.2%	48.8%

Data Source: Department of Education & Science, Tuarascáil Staitistiúil (Annual Statistical Reports), Various years.

TABLE 1.2 AVERAGE ANNUAL BIRTHS BY SEX 1871-2003

YEAR	NUMBERS			GENDER BALANCE	
	MALE	FEMALE	MALES PER 1,000 FEMALES	MALE	FEMALE
1871-1880	53,604	50,775	1,056	51.36%	48.64%
1881-1890	43,077	40,685	1,059	51.43%	48.57%
1891-1900	37,982	36,013	1,055	51.33%	48.67%
1901-1910	36,666	34,714	1,056	51.37%	48.63%
1911-1920	34,206	32,301	1,056	51.43%	48.57%
1921-1930	30,983	29,423	1,053	51.29%	48.71%
1931-1940	29,279	27,826	1,052	51.27%	48.73%
1941-1950	33,495	31,515	1,063	51.52%	48.48%
1951-1960	31,606	30,058	1,052	51.26%	48.74%
1961-1970	32,053	30,364	1,056	51.35%	48.65%
1971-1980	35,715	33,724	1,059	51.43%	48.57%
1981-1990	31,747	29,882	1,062	51.51%	48.49%
1991	27,122	25,596	1,060	51.45%	48.55%
1992	26,307	24,782	1,062	51.49%	48.51%
1993	25,359	23,945	1,059	51.43%	48.57%
1994	24,957	23,298	1,071	51.72%	48.28%
1995	25,153	23,634	1,064	51.56%	48.44%
1996	26,350	24,305	1,084	52.02%	47.98%
1997	27,061	25,714	1,052	51.28%	48.72%
1998	27,848	26,121	1,066	51.60%	48.40%
1999	27,817	26,107	1,065	51.59%	48.41%
2000	28,175	26,614	1,059	51.42%	48.58%
2001	29,684	28,170	1,054	51.31%	48.69%
2002	31,001	29,520	1,050	51.22%	48.78%
2003	31,414	30,103	1,044	51.07%	48.93%

Data Source: CSO Vital Statistics

TABLE 1.3 PUPILS IN EARLY START PRE-SCHOOL PROGRAMMES

| | PUPIL NUMBERS | | | GENDER BALANCE | |
YEAR	MALE	FEMALE	TOTAL	MALE	FEMALE
1995-1996	806	790	1,596	50.5%	49.5%
1996-1997	750	818	1,568	47.8%	52.2%
1997-1998	816	743	1,559	52.3%	47.7%
1998-1999	787	748	1,535	51.3%	48.7%
1999-2000	792	822	1,614	49.1%	50.9%
2000-2001	824	793	1,617	51.0%	49.0%
2001-2002	758	766	1,524	49.7%	50.3%
2002-2003	805	693	1,498	53.7%	46.3%

Data Source: Department of Education & Science, Tuarascáil Staitistiúil (Annual Statistical Reports), Various years.

TABLE 1.4 PERCENTAGE OF BOYS & GIRLS IN SINGLE SEX & MIXED CLASSES - PRIMARY EDUCATION

| | SINGLE SEX CLASSES | | | MIXED CLASSES | | |
YEAR	MALE	FEMALE	TOTAL	MALE	FEMALE	TOTAL
1985-86	34.7%	35.9%	35.3%	65.3%	64.1%	64.7%
1990-91	31.7%	33.7%	32.6%	68.3%	66.3%	67.4%
1991-92	30.8%	32.8%	31.8%	69.2%	67.2%	68.2%
1992-93	30.3%	32.5%	31.4%	69.7%	67.5%	68.6%
1993-94	29.9%	32.2%	31.0%	70.1%	67.8%	69.0%
1994-95	29.5%	31.8%	30.6%	70.5%	68.2%	69.4%
1995-96	28.9%	31.2%	30.0%	71.1%	68.8%	70.0%
1996-97	28.1%	30.3%	29.2%	71.9%	69.7%	70.8%
1997-98	27.6%	29.8%	28.7%	72.4%	70.2%	71.3%
1998-99	26.9%	29.2%	28.0%	73.1%	70.8%	72.0%
1999-00	26.5%	28.9%	27.7%	73.5%	71.1%	72.3%
2000-01	25.8%	28.2%	27.0%	74.2%	71.8%	73.0%
2001-02	25.0%	27.4%	26.2%	75.0%	72.6%	73.8%
2002-03	24.5%	26.7%	25.6%	75.5%	73.3%	74.4%

Data Source: Department of Education & Science, Tuarascáil Staitistiúil (Annual Statistical Reports), Various years.

TABLE 1.5 READING STANDARD OF FIFTH CLASS PUPILS AS JUDGED BY TEACHERS, 1998

	WEAK/ INADEQUATE	BASIC	PROFICIENT	ADVANCED	TOTAL
MALES	12.4%	25.5%	40.6%	21.4%	100%
FEMALES	8.4%	24.1%	42.9%	24.6%	100%
TOTAL	10.5%	24.8%	41.7%	23.0%	100%

Source: Cosgrove, Kellaghan et al. (2000), The 1998 National Assessment of English Reading, ERC, p.37.
Note: Sample size = 3,856 pupils (1,962 males & 1,894 females).

TABLE 1.6 PUPILS IN ORDINARY CLASSES RETAINED IN THE SAME STANDARD

	PUPIL NUMBERS			GENDER BALANCE	
YEAR	MALE	FEMALE	TOTAL	MALE	FEMALE
1990-91	9,247	7,444	16,691	55.4%	44.6%
1991-92	8,250	6,748	14,998	55.0%	45.0%
1992-93	7,698	6,056	13,754	56.0%	44.0%
1993-94	7,396	5,988	13,384	55.3%	44.7%
1994-95	6,859	5,317	12,176	56.3%	43.7%
1995-96	6,289	4,769	11,058	56.9%	43.1%
1996-97	5,745	4,318	10,063	57.1%	42.9%
1997-98	5,332	3,820	9,152	58.3%	41.7%
1998-99	4,826	3,592	8,418	57.3%	42.7%
1999-00	4,186	3,321	7,507	55.8%	44.2%
2000-01	3,991	2,975	6,966	57.3%	42.7%
2001-02	3,112	2,366	5,478	56.8%	43.2%
2002-03	2,772	2,039	4,811	57.6%	42.4%

Data Source: Department of Education & Science, Tuarascáil Staitistiúil (Annual Statistical Reports), Various years.

TABLE 1.7 PUPILS WITH SPECIAL NEEDS IN ORDINARY NATIONAL SCHOOLS

YEAR	PUPIL NUMBERS			GENDER BALANCE	
	MALE	FEMALE	TOTAL	MALE	FEMALE
1994-95	1,040	781	1,821	57.1%	42.9%
1995-96	1,162	846	2,007	57.9%	42.1%
1996-97	1,323	967	2,289	57.8%	42.2%
1997-98	1,675	1,102	2,777	60.3%	39.7%
1998-99	1,933	1,433	3,366	57.4%	42.6%
1999-00	2,192	1,459	3,650	60.0%	40.0%
2000-01	2,216	1,378	3,594	61.7%	38.3%
2001-02	2,306	1,310	3,616	63.8%	36.2%
2002-03	2,240	1,266	3,505	63.9%	36.1%

Data Source: Department of Education & Science, Tuarascáil Staitistiúil (Annual Statistical Reports), Various years.

TABLE 1.8a GRADE REPETITION AND SPECIAL EDUCATIONAL NEEDS AMONG MALE PUPILS IN ORDINARY NATIONAL SCHOOLS

YEAR	MALE PUPIL NUMBERS				AS A PERCENTAGE OF ALL MALE PUPILS		
	RETAINED IN THE SAME STANDARD	SPECIAL NEEDS IN ORDINARY CLASSES	TOTAL RETAINED & SPECIAL NEEDS	OVERALL TOTAL IN ORDINARY NATIONAL SCHOOLS	RETAINED IN THE SAME STANDARD	SPECIAL NEEDS IN ORDINARY CLASSES	TOTAL RETAINED & SPECIAL NEEDS
1994-95	6,859	1,040	7,899	248,133	2.8%	0.4%	3.2%
1995-96	6,289	1,162	7,451	241,856	2.6%	0.5%	3.1%
1996-97	5,745	1,323	7,068	236,838	2.4%	0.6%	3.0%
1997-98	5,332	1,675	7,007	232,250	2.3%	0.7%	3.0%
1998-99	4,826	1,933	6,759	228,101	2.1%	0.8%	3.0%
1999-00	4,186	2,192	6,378	224,037	1.9%	1.0%	2.8%
2000-01	3,991	2,216	6,207	221,819	1.8%	1.0%	2.8%
2001-02	3,112	2,306	5,418	222,723	1.4%	1.0%	2.4%
2002-03	2,772	2,240	5,012	224,084	1.2%	1.0%	2.2%

Data Source: Department of Education & Science, Annual Census of National Schools

Note: The numbers of pupils with special needs in ordinary classes are as reported in Table 1.7. The overall total in Ordinary National Schools is the total number of pupils in National Schools minus the number of pupils in Special Schools. The numbers of pupils in Special Schools are reported in Table 1.10.

TABLE 1.8b GRADE REPETITION AND SPECIAL EDUCATIONAL NEEDS AMONG FEMALE PUPILS IN ORDINARY NATIONAL SCHOOLS

YEAR	FEMALE PUPIL NUMBERS				AS A PERCENTAGE OF ALL FEMALE PUPILS		
	RETAINED IN THE SAME STANDARD	SPECIAL NEEDS IN ORDINARY CLASSES	TOTAL RETAINED & SPECIAL NEEDS	OVERALL TOTAL IN ORDINARY NATIONAL SCHOOLS	RETAINED IN THE SAME STANDARD	SPECIAL NEEDS IN ORDINARY CLASSES	TOTAL RETAINED & SPECIAL NEEDS
1994-95	5,317	781	6,098	235,306	2.3%	0.3%	2.6%
1995-96	4,769	846	5,615	229,184	2.1%	0.4%	2.4%
1996-97	4,318	967	5,285	225,254	1.9%	0.4%	2.3%
1997-98	3,820	1,102	4,922	221,186	1.7%	0.5%	2.2%
1998-99	3,592	1,433	5,025	217,046	1.7%	0.7%	2.3%
1999-00	3,321	1,459	4,780	213,045	1.6%	0.7%	2.2%
2000-01	2,975	1,378	4,353	210,617	1.4%	0.7%	2.1%
2001-02	2,366	1,310	3,676	211,360	1.1%	0.6%	1.7%
2002-03	2,039	1,266	3,305	212,829	1.0%	0.6%	1.6%

Data Source: Department of Education & Science, Annual Census of National Schools

Note: The numbers of pupils with special needs in ordinary classes are as reported in Table 1.7. The overall total in Ordinary National Schools is the total number of pupils in National Schools minus the number of pupils in Special Schools. The numbers of pupils in Special Schools are reported in Table 1.10.

TABLE 1.9 PUPILS WITH SPECIAL EDUCATIONAL NEEDS IN ORDINARY NATIONAL SCHOOLS BY CATEGORY, 2002-03.

PUPIL TYPE	UNDER 12	12 AND OVER	TOTAL PUPILS
Mild Learning	1,827	539	2,366
Moderate Learning	80	48	128
Severe/Profound Learning	8	14	22
Hearing Impairment	27	5	32
Physical Disability	4	3	7
Speech & Language	388	30	418
Multiple Disabilities	23	0	23
Emotional Disturbance	21	5	26
Specific Learning	182	44	226
Severe Emotional	0	4	4
Autism/Autistic Spectrum	243	10	253
Total Pupils with Special Educational Needs	2,803	702	3,505
Traveller Children	5,190	689	5,879

Data Source: Department of Education & Science (Annual Census of National Schools).

TABLE 1.10 PUPILS IN SPECIAL SCHOOLS

	PUPIL NUMBERS			GENDER BALANCE	
YEAR	MALE	FEMALE	TOTAL	MALE	FEMALE
1980-81	4,788	3,380	8,168	58.6%	41.4%
1985-86	4,974	3,458	8,432	59.0%	41.0%
1990-91	4,988	3,281	8,269	60.3%	39.7%
1991-92	5,004	3,159	8,163	61.3%	38.7%
1992-93	4,977	3,107	8,084	61.6%	38.4%
1993-94	4,965	3,094	8,059	61.6%	38.4%
1994-95	4,848	2,969	7,817	62.0%	38.0%
1995-96	4,763	2,889	7,652	62.2%	37.8%
1996-97	4,678	2,858	7,536	62.1%	37.9%
1997-98	4,625	2,784	7,409	62.4%	37.6%
1998-99	4,645	2,741	7,386	62.9%	37.1%
1999-00	4,575	2,653	7,228	63.3%	36.7%
2000-01	4,514	2,610	7,124	63.4%	36.6%
2001-02	4,438	2,544	6,982	63.6%	36.4%
2002-03	4,383	2,424	6,807	64.4%	35.6%

Data Source: Department of Education & Science, Tuarascáil Staitistiúil (Annual Statistical Reports), Various years.

TABLE 1.11 PUPILS IN SPECIAL SCHOOLS BY AGE AND SEX (2002/2003)

PUPIL NUMBERS				GENDER BALANCE			
AGE	MALE	FEMALE	TOTAL	AGE	MALE	FEMALE	TOTAL
3	37	29	66	3	0.8%	1.2%	1.0%
4	61	38	99	4	1.4%	1.6%	1.5%
5	119	63	182	5	2.7%	2.6%	2.7%
6	181	88	269	6	4.1%	3.6%	4.0%
7	197	126	323	7	4.5%	5.2%	4.7%
8	231	109	340	8	5.3%	4.5%	5.0%
9	277	129	406	9	6.3%	5.3%	6.0%
10	340	185	525	10	7.8%	7.6%	7.7%
11	355	190	545	11	8.1%	7.8%	8.0%
12	395	181	576	12	9.0%	7.5%	8.5%
13	422	223	645	13	9.6%	9.2%	9.5%
14	435	270	705	14	9.9%	11.1%	10.4%
15	424	238	662	15	9.7%	9.8%	9.7%
16	413	212	625	16	9.4%	8.7%	9.2%
17	324	207	531	17	7.4%	8.5%	7.8%
18	143	102	245	18	3.3%	4.2%	3.6%
19	17	20	37	19	0.4%	0.8%	0.5%
20	4	9	13	20	0.1%	0.4%	0.2%
21	8	5	13	21	0.2%	0.2%	0.2%
TOTAL:	4,383	2,424	6,807	TOTAL:	100%	100%	100%

Data Source: Department of Education & Science (Annual Census of National Schools).

TABLE 1.12   PROFILE OF PUPILS IN SPECIAL SCHOOLS, 2002-03

PUPIL TYPE	UNDER 12	12 AND OVER	TOTAL PUPILS
Mild Learning	711	1,888	2,599
Moderate Learning	612	791	1,403
Severe/Profound Learning	385	341	726
Hearing Impairment	54	122	176
Visually Impairment	14	15	29
Physical Disability	67	42	109
Multiple Disabilities	164	210	374
Emotional Disturbance	138	26	164
Specific Learning	193	56	249
Young Offender	9	180	189
Emotional Disturbance	168	105	273
Profoundly Deaf	24	62	86
Autism/Autistic Spectrum	148	104	252
Out of Parental Control	2	13	15
Total Pupils in Special Schools	2,799	4,008	6,807
Traveller Children*	110	53	163

Data Source: Department of Education & Science (Annual Census of National Schools).

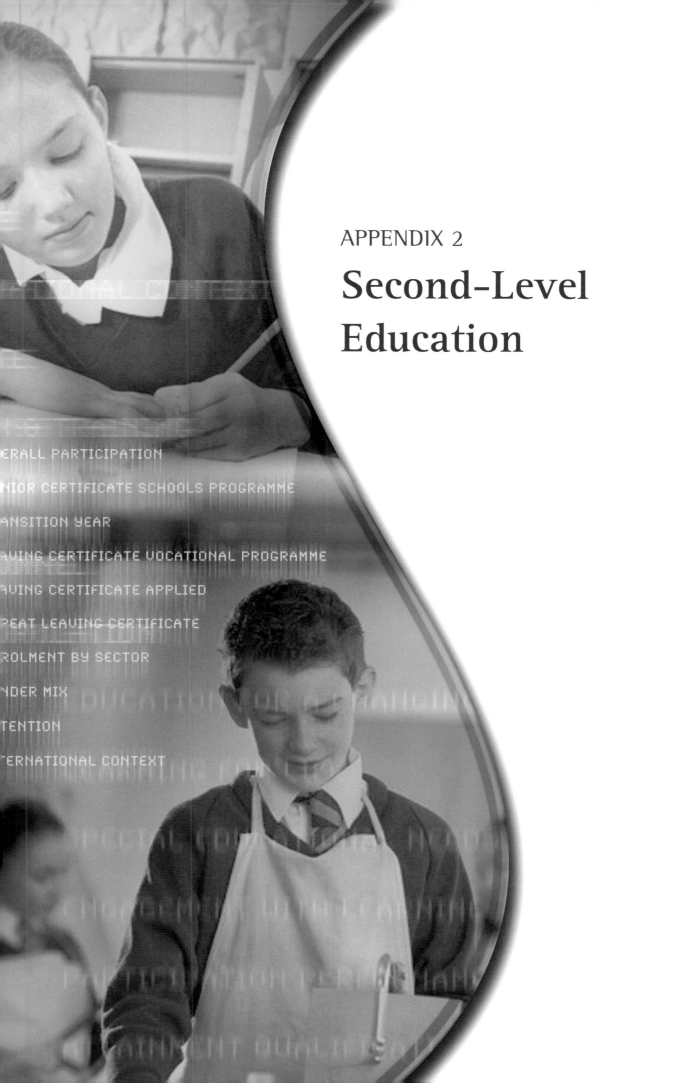

APPENDIX 2

Second–Level Education

OVERALL PARTICIPATION

JUNIOR CERTIFICATE SCHOOLS PROGRAMME

TRANSITION YEAR

LEAVING CERTIFICATE VOCATIONAL PROGRAMME

LEAVING CERTIFICATE APPLIED

REPEAT LEAVING CERTIFICATE

ENROLMENT BY SECTOR

GENDER MIX

RETENTION

INTERNATIONAL CONTEXT

TABLE 2.1 ENROLMENTS IN THE JUNIOR CYCLE OF SECOND-LEVEL EDUCATION

YEAR	MALE	FEMALE	TOTAL
1980-81	102,350	97,346	199,696
1985-86	108,066	104,252	212,318
1990-91	103,090	98,015	201,105
1991-92	103,467	99,910	203,377
1992-93	105,556	102,348	207,904
1993-94	106,791	103,471	210,262
1994-95	106,410	102,507	208,917
1995-96	104,695	100,722	205,417
1996-97	101,764	97,807	199,571
1997-98	98,686	94,258	192,944
1998-99	95,594	91,474	187,068
1999-00	93,357	90,526	183,883
2000-01	91,471	89,527	180,998
2001-02	88,825	87,609	176,434
2002-03	87,082	85,591	172,673

Data Source: Department of Education & Science, Tuarascáil Staitistiúil (Annual Statistical Reports), Various years.

TABLE 2.2 ENROLMENTS IN THE SENIOR CYCLE OF SECOND-LEVEL EDUCATION

YEAR	MALE	FEMALE	TOTAL
1980-81	38,674	47,783	86,457
1985-86	48,818	53,977	102,795
1990-91	55,056	59,211	114,267
1991-92	60,326	64,114	124,440
1992-93	62,884	65,893	128,777
1993-94	65,549	68,355	133,904
1994-95	68,266	72,268	140,534
1995-96	70,067	74,677	144,744
1996-97	73,340	78,567	151,907
1997-98	74,457	79,472	153,929
1998-99	72,842	78,318	151,160
1999-00	70,175	75,465	145,640
2000-01	66,875	72,101	138,976
2001-02	65,900	71,059	136,959
2002-03	66,457	71,452	137,909

Data Source: Department of Education & Science, Tuarascáil Staitistiúil (Annual Statistical Reports), Various years.

TABLE 2.3 JUNIOR CERTIFICATE SCHOOL PROGRAMME

	PUPIL NUMBERS			GENDER BALANCE	
YEAR	MALE	FEMALE	TOTAL	MALE	FEMALE
1996-97	752	299	1,051	71.6%	28.4%
1997-98	1,033	416	1,449	71.3%	28.7%
1998-99	1,366	813	2,179	62.7%	37.3%
1999-00	1,689	1,082	3,507	61.0%	39.0%
2000-01	2,091	1,416	2,771	59.6%	40.4%
2001-02	2,605	1,662	4,267	61.0%	39.0%
2002-03	2,970	1,909	4,879	60.9%	39.1%

Data Source: Department of Education & Science, Tuarascáil Staitistiúil (Annual Statistical Reports), Various years.

TABLE 2.4 TRANSITION YEAR STUDENTS

	PUPIL NUMBERS			GENDER BALANCE	
YEAR	MALE	FEMALE	TOTAL	MALE	FEMALE
1980-81	231	309	540	42.8%	57.2%
1985-86	218	266	484	45.0%	55.0%
1990-91	2,649	3,456	6,105	43.4%	56.6%
1991-92	3,699	4,351	8,050	46.0%	54.0%
1992-93	3,829	4,364	8,193	46.7%	53.3%
1993-94	4,046	4,453	8,499	47.6%	52.4%
1994-95	9,637	11,536	21,173	45.5%	54.5%
1995-96	11,162	12,987	24,149	46.2%	53.8%
1996-97	11,246	13,054	24,300	46.3%	53.7%
1997-98	11,361	13,304	24,665	46.1%	53.9%
1998-99	10,825	12,902	23,727	45.6%	54.4%
1999-00	10,338	12,416	22,754	45.4%	54.6%
2000-01	10,797	12,451	23,248	46.4%	53.6%
2001-02	10,268	12,505	22,773	45.1%	54.9%
2002-03	10,466	12,833	23,299	44.9%	55.1%

Data Source: Department of Education & Science, Tuarascáil Staitistiúil (Annual Statistical Reports), Various years.

TABLE 2.5 LEAVING CERTIFICATE VOCATIONAL PROGRAMME

YEAR	PUPIL NUMBERS			GENDER BALANCE	
	MALE	FEMALE	TOTAL	MALE	FEMALE
1996-97	9,257	7,254	16,511	56.1%	43.9%
1997-98	10,395	11,852	22,247	46.7%	53.3%
1998-99	11,411	14,736	26,147	43.6%	56.4%
1999-00	12,572	16,110	28,682	43.8%	56.2%
2000-01	13,307	17,021	30,328	43.9%	56.1%
2001-02	14,222	17,695	31,917	44.6%	55.4%
2002-03	14,637	18,238	32,875	44.5%	55.5%

Data Source: Department of Education & Science, Tuarascáil Staitistiúil (Annual Statistical Reports), Various years.

TABLE 2.6 LEAVING CERTIFICATE APPLIED PROGRAMME

YEAR	PUPIL NUMBERS			GENDER BALANCE	
	MALE	FEMALE	TOTAL	MALE	FEMALE
1996-97	2,041	1,554	3,595	56.8%	43.2%
1997-98	2,968	2,340	5,308	55.9%	44.1%
1998-99	3,347	2,926	6,273	53.4%	46.6%
1999-00	3,585	3,305	6,890	52.0%	48.0%
2000-01	3,583	3,610	7,193	49.8%	50.2%
2001-02	3,775	3,720	7,495	50.4%	49.6%
2002-03	4,163	3,814	7,977	52.2%	47.8%

Data Source: Department of Education & Science, Tuarascáil Staitistiúil (Annual Statistical Reports), Various years.

TABLE 2.7 REPEAT LEAVING CERTIFICATE STUDENTS (PUBLIC INSTITUTIONS)

	PUPIL NUMBERS			GENDER BALANCE	
YEAR	MALE	FEMALE	TOTAL	MALE	FEMALE
1990-91	4,441	3,256	7,697	57.7%	42.3%
1991-92	4,123	3,242	7,365	56.0%	44.0%
1992-93	4,048	3,194	7,242	55.9%	44.1%
1993-94	4,408	3,886	8,294	53.1%	46.9%
1994-95	4,423	4,091	8,514	51.9%	48.1%
1995-96	4,200	3,994	8,194	51.3%	48.7%
1996-97	2,828	2,356	5,184	54.6%	45.4%
1997-98	2,981	2,742	5,723	52.1%	47.9%
1998-99	2,796	2,694	5,490	50.9%	49.1%
1999-00	2,274	2,043	4,317	52.7%	47.3%
2000-01	1,658	1,425	3,083	53.8%	46.2%
2001-02	1,899	1,835	3,734	50.9%	49.1%
2002-03	1,809	1,819	3,628	49.9%	50.1%

Data Source: Department of Education & Science, Tuarascáil Staitistiúil (Annual Statistical Reports), Various years.

TABLE 2.8 OVERVIEW OF (FIFTH AND SIXTH YEAR) LEAVING CERTIFICATE STUDENTS BY PROGRAMME, 2002-03

	MALES	FEMALES	ALL LC STUDENTS
Leaving Cert.	63.2%	59.3%	61.2%
Leaving Cert. Voc. Programme	26.1%	31.1%	28.7%
Leaving Cert. Applied	7.4%	6.5%	7.0%
Repeat Leaving Cert.	3.2%	3.1%	3.2%
TOTAL	100%	100%	100%

Data Source: Department of Education & Science, Tuarascáil Staitistiúil (Annual Statistical Reports), 2002-2003.

TABLE 2.9 SECOND-LEVEL PUPILS IN SECOND-LEVEL SCHOOLS BY SCHOOL TYPE (EXCLUDING PLC STUDENTS)

NUMBER OF PUPILS

YEAR	SECONDARY		VOCATIONAL		COMMUNITY & COMPREHENSIVE		TOTAL	
	MALE	FEMALE	MALE	FEMALE	MALE	FEMALE	MALE	FEMALE
1980-'81	87,003	114,534	40,160	19,522	14,002	11,703	141,165	145,759
1985-'86	93,482	117,642	43,649	24,139	19,870	16,802	157,001	158,583
1990-'91	95,174	115,122	43,248	26,797	22,372	18,743	160,794	160,662
1995-'96	100,573	122,556	47,319	30,810	27,877	22,745	175,769	176,111
2000-'01	89,285	107,319	42,343	31,044	26,718	23,265	158,346	161,628
2002-'03	85,560	102,656	40,963	30,767	27,016	23,620	153,539	157,043

PERCENTAGE OF MALE AND FEMALE PUPILS (ACROSS THE SECTORS)

YEAR	SECONDARY		VOCATIONAL		COMMUNITY & COMPREHENSIVE		TOTAL	
	MALE	FEMALE	MALE	FEMALE	MALE	FEMALE	MALE	FEMALE
1980-'81	61.6%	78.6%	28.4%	13.4%	9.9%	8.0%	100%	100%
1985-'86	59.5%	74.2%	27.8%	15.2%	12.7%	10.6%	100%	100%
1990-'91	59.2%	71.7%	26.9%	16.7%	13.9%	11.7%	100%	100%
1995-'96	57.2%	69.6%	26.9%	17.5%	15.9%	12.9%	100%	100%
2000-'01	56.4%	66.4%	26.7%	19.2%	16.9%	14.4%	100%	100%
2002-'03	55.7%	65.4%	26.7%	19.6%	17.6%	15.0%	100%	100%

TABLE 2.9 (CONTD.) SECOND-LEVEL PUPILS IN SECOND-LEVEL SCHOOLS BY SCHOOL TYPE (EXCLUDING PLC STUDENTS)

GENDER BALANCE OF PUPILS WITHIN EACH SECTOR

YEAR	SECONDARY		VOCATIONAL		COMMUNITY & COMPREHENSIVE		TOTAL	
	MALE	FEMALE	MALE	FEMALE	MALE	FEMALE	MALE	FEMALE
1980-'81	43.2%	56.8%	67.3%	32.7%	54.5%	45.5%	100%	100%
1985-'86	44.3%	55.7%	64.4%	35.6%	54.2%	45.8%	100%	100%
1990-'91	45.3%	54.7%	61.7%	38.3%	54.4%	45.6%	100%	100%
1995-'96	45.1%	54.9%	60.6%	39.4%	55.1%	44.9%	100%	100%
2000-'01	45.4%	54.6%	57.7%	42.3%	53.5%	46.5%	100%	100%
2002-'03	45.5%	54.5%	57.1%	42.9%	53.4%	46.6%	100%	100%

Data Source: Department of Education & Science, Tuarascáil Staitistiúil (Annual Statistical Reports), Various years.

TABLE 2.10 GENDER-MIX OF PUPILS IN SECOND-LEVEL SCHOOLS

NUMBER OF PUPILS

YEAR	SINGLE SEX			MIXED			TOTAL		
	MALE	FEMALE	TOTAL	MALE	FEMALE	TOTAL	MALE	FEMALE	TOTAL
1980-'81	77,483	94,203	171,686	66,419	58,828	125,247	143,902	153,031	296,933
1985-'86	76,084	93,042	169,126	87,338	78,228	165,566	163,422	171,270	334,692
1990-'91	64,980	87,990	152,970	102,737	86,709	189,446	167,717	174,699	342,416
1995-'96	64,785	90,440	155,225	116,534	98,106	214,640	181,319	188,546	369,865
2000-'01	55,254	77,801	133,055	110,303	102,026	212,329	165,557	179,827	345,384
2002-'03	52,797	75,765	128,562	108,885	101,784	210,669	161,682	177,549	339,231

PERCENTAGE OF PUPILS

YEAR	SINGLE SEX			MIXED			TOTAL		
	MALE	FEMALE	TOTAL	MALE	FEMALE	TOTAL	MALE	FEMALE	TOTAL
1980-'81	53.8%	61.6%	57.8%	46.2%	38.4%	42.2%	100%	100%	100%
1985-'86	46.6%	54.3%	50.5%	53.4%	45.7%	49.5%	100%	100%	100%
1990-'91	38.7%	50.4%	44.7%	61.3%	49.6%	55.3%	100%	100%	100%
1995-'96	35.7%	48.0%	42.0%	64.3%	52.0%	58.0%	100%	100%	100%
2000-'01	33.4%	43.3%	38.5%	66.6%	56.7%	61.5%	100%	100%	100%
2002-'03	32.7%	42.7%	37.9%	67.3%	57.3%	62.1%	100%	100%	100%

Data Source: Department of Education & Science, Tuarascáil Statistiúil (Annual Statistical Reports), Various years.

TABLE 2.11a INDICATOR OF LOWER SECOND-LEVEL ATTAINMENT: TOTAL NUMBER OF JUNIOR/ INTER. CERTIFICATE EXAMINATION CANDIDATES IN ENGLISH, 1932 TO 2004

YEAR	MALES	FEMALES
1932	2,700	2,035
1935	3,262	2,531
1941	4,158	3,702
1946	4,452	4,356
1952	5,273	5,738
1957	6,272	7,286
1961	7,330	8,868
1966	9,450	11,277
1968	10,565	12,714
1975	21,188	23,699
1980	23,998	26,821
1983	26,298	28,108
1990	27,977	29,233
1995	34,049	33,466
2000	30,683	29,756
2004	28,191	28,026

Data Source: Department of Education & Science, Tuarascáil Staitistiúil (Annual Statistical Reports), Various years.

TABLE 2.11b INDICATOR OF UPPER SECOND-LEVEL ATTAINMENT: TOTAL NUMBER OF LEAVING CERTIFICATE EXAMINATION CANDIDATES IN ENGLISH, 1932 TO 2004

YEAR	MALES	FEMALES
1932	1,054	616
1935	1,323	839
1941	1,794	1,326
1946	1,992	1,703
1952	2,944	2,358
1957	3,484	3,168
1961	4,484	4,147
1966	6,256	6,215
1968	7,158	7,469
1975	13,054	15,504
1980	15,800	20,556
1983	19,075	23,649
1990	24,325	27,442
1995	29,248	31,074
2000	27,529	30,287
2004	25,235	27,545

Data Source: Department of Education & Science, Tuarascáil Staitistiúil (Annual Statistical Reports), Various years.

TABLE 2.12 SECOND-LEVEL SCHOOL LEAVERS BY LEVEL OF EDUCATION - 1982, 1993 & 2002

PUPIL NUMBERS

	1982		1993		2002	
	MALE	**FEMALE**	**MALE**	**FEMALE**	**MALE**	**FEMALE**
No Qualifications	2,640	2,300	2,300	1,100	1,600	900
Junior Certificate Only	10,150	5,660	5,900	3,900	6,900	3,800
Leaving Certificate	18,390	22,400	24,000	26,600	27,200	29,300

COLUMN PERCENTAGES

	1982		1993		2002	
	MALE	**FEMALE**	**MALE**	**FEMALE**	**MALE**	**FEMALE**
No Qualifications	9.0%	8.0%	7.1%	3.4%	3.5%	2.7%
Junior Certificate Only	33.0%	19.0%	18.3%	12.0%	18.3%	10.2%
Leaving Certificate	59.0%	74.0%	74.6%	84.7%	78.2%	87.0%

Note: ESRI data on those who left school in 2004 will be published in summer 2007.

TABLE 2.13 GENDER BALANCE BY LEVEL OF EDUCATION FOR SECOND-LEVEL SCHOOL LEAVERS

PUPIL NUMBERS

	NO QUALIFICATIONS			JUNIOR CERT. ONLY			LEAVING CERT.		
	2002	1993	1982	2002	1993	1982	2002	1993	1982
Males	1,600	2,300	2,640	6,900	5,900	10,150	27,200	24,000	18,390
Females	900	1,100	2,300	3,800	3,900	5,660	29,300	26,600	22,400

GENDER BALANCE

	NO QUALIFICATIONS			JUNIOR CERT. ONLY			LEAVING CERT.		
	2002	1993	1982	2002	1993	1982	2002	1993	1982
Males	64%	68%	53%	64%	60%	64%	48%	47%	45%
Females	36%	32%	47%	36%	40%	36%	52%	53%	55%

Note: ESRI data on those who left school in 2004 will be published in summer 2007.

TABLE 2.14 DEPARTURE FROM PUBLICLY-AIDED SECOND-LEVEL EDUCATION (AMONG THE 1994 COHORT OF 69,103 ENTRANTS)

| | PUPIL NUMBERS | | | GENDER BALANCE | | DEPARTURE RATES | | |
	MALE	FEMALE	ALL STUDENTS	MALE	FEMALE	MALE	FEMALE	ALL STUDENTS
Prior to sitting LC exam	2,474	1,819	4,293	57.6%	42.4%	27.5%	15.7%	21.7%
Prior to LC Year 1	4,775	1,990	6,765	70.6%	29.4%	20.5%	10.3%	15.5%
Prior to sitting JC exam	870	572	1,442	60.3%	39.7%	6.9%	4.4%	5.7%
Prior to JC Year 3	956	513	1,469	65.1%	34.9%	4.5%	2.7%	3.6%
Prior to JC Year 2	617	414	1,031	59.8%	40.2%	1.7%	1.2%	1.5%
Summary								
Departure Prior to Leaving Cert.	7,249	3,809	11,058	65.6%	34.4%	27.5%	15.7%	21.7%
Departure Prior to Junior Cert.	2,443	1,499	3,942	62.0%	38.0%	6.9%	4.4%	5.7%
Total Departures	9,692	5,308	15,000	64.6%	35.4%			

Data Source: Department of Education & Science, Retention Rates of Pupils in Post-primary Schools - 1994 Cohort (http://www.education.ie/servlet/blobservlet/pp_retention_1994_report.doc)

Note: Data on the 1995 and 1996 cohorts of post-primary pupils are published on the website of the Department of Education and Science at http://www.education.ie/servlet/blobservlet/pp_retention_1996_report.doc

TABLE 2.15 UPPER SECONDARY GRADUATION RATES (2002)

	MALES	FEMALES	TOTAL
Norway	89%	100%	97%
Germany	91%	96%	93%
Japan	90%	94%	92%
Poland	86%	93%	90%
Switzerland	90%	90%	90%
Ireland (revised)	**80%**	**94%**	**87%**
Finland	78%	93%	85%
Greece	74%	97%	85%
France	79%	86%	82%
Hungary	79%	86%	82%
Italy	79%	85%	82%
Czech Republic	80%	83%	81%
OECD mean	**75%**	**87%**	**81%**
Belgium	74%	83%	79%
Iceland	68%	89%	79%
Ireland (published)	**70%**	**84%**	**77%**
United States	69%	76%	73%
Sweden	69%	76%	72%
Luxembourg	64%	73%	68%
Spain	62%	75%	68%
Slovak Republic	57%	66%	61%

Data Source: OECD, Education at a Glance 2004, Indicator A2.1 (p.57)

TABLE 2.16   GENDER DIFFERENCES IN UPPER SECONDARY GRADUATION RATES (2002)

	FEMALES - MALES
Greece	22%
Iceland	21%
Finland	15%
Ireland (revised)	**15%**
Ireland (published)	**14%**
Spain	13%
OECD mean	**11%**
Norway	11%
Luxembourg	9%
Slovak Republic	9%
Belgium	9%
Hungary	7%
United States	7%
Poland	7%
France	7%
Sweden	6%
Italy	6%
Germany	5%
Japan	4%
Czech Republic	2%
Switzerland	0%

Data Source: OECD, Education at a Glance 2004, Indicator A2.1 (p.57)

TABLE 2.17 INTERNATIONAL DATA ON EXPECTED YEARS OF SCHOOLING FROM AGE 5 (2002)

	GENDER DIFFERENCE	EXPECTED YEARS OF SCHOOLING	
	FEMALES- MALES	MALES	FEMALES
United Kingdom	3.0	18.9	21.9
Sweden	2.9	18.7	21.6
New Zealand	1.9	17.3	19.2
Iceland	1.7	17.6	19.4
Finland	1.5	18.7	20.2
Norway	1.4	16.4	17.8
Belgium	1.2	18.8	20.0
Denmark	1.1	17.5	18.6
Ireland	**1.1**	**16.0**	**17.1**
Poland	1.0	16.5	17.5
Portugal	0.9	16.6	17.5
Spain	0.9	16.9	17.8
United States	0.8	16.5	17.3
Greece	0.7	15.9	16.7
OECD mean	**0.7**	**16.8**	**17.5**
Hungary	0.6	16.5	17.1
Italy	0.6	16.3	16.9
France	0.5	16.3	16.9
Australia	0.4	20.9	21.4
Mexico	0.2	12.8	13.1
Slovak Republic	0.2	15.0	15.2
Czech Republic	0.2	16.1	16.3
Luxembourg	0.1	13.8	13.9
Austria	0.1	16.0	16.1
Germany	-0.2	17.2	17.0
Netherlands	-0.3	17.3	17.1
Switzerland	-0.6	16.7	16.2
Korea	-1.9	17.1	15.3

Data Source: OECD (2004) Education at a Glance: OECD Indicators 2004, Table C1.1, p.277.

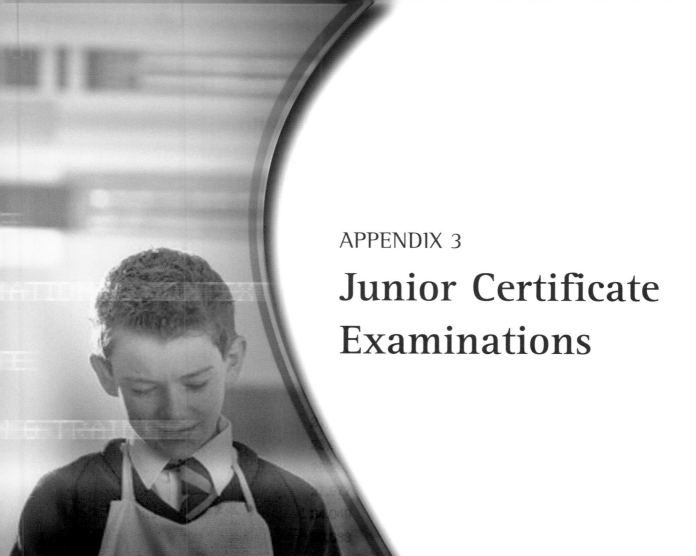

APPENDIX 3

Junior Certificate Examinations

EXAM CANDIDATES

SUBJECT TAKE-UP

HIGHER AND ORDINARY LEVEL

OVERALL PERFORMANCE

OVERVIEW BY SUBJECT

IRISH, ENGLISH, MATHS . . .

TABLE 3.1 JUNIOR CERTIFICATE CANDIDATES

| YEAR | PUPIL NUMBERS | | | GENDER BALANCE | |
	MALE	FEMALE	TOTAL	MALE	FEMALE
1991	30,045	30,349	60,394	49.7%	50.3%
1992	31,860	31,319	63,179	50.4%	49.6%
1993	33,168	32,895	66,063	50.2%	49.8%
1994	33,846	33,969	67,815	49.9%	50.1%
1995	34,352	33,733	68,085	50.5%	49.5%
1996	34,312	33,752	68,064	50.4%	49.6%
1997	33,740	33,313	67,053	50.3%	49.7%
1998	33,137	32,471	65,608	50.5%	49.5%
1999	31,773	30,886	62,659	50.7%	49.3%
2000	31,302	30,168	61,470	50.9%	49.1%
2001	30,308	29,816	60,124	50.4%	49.6%
2002	30,150	30,002	60,152	50.1%	49.9%
2003	29,855	29,485	59,340	50.3%	49.7%

Data Source: Department of Education & Science, Tuarascáil Staitistiúil (Annual Statistical Reports), Various years.

TABLE 3.2 JUNIOR CERTIFICATE EXAMINATION CANDIDATES BY SUBJECT 2003

	GENDER BALANCE		NUMBERS		
	MALE	FEMALE	MALE	FEMALE	ALL STUDENTS
Home Economics	12.4%	87.6%	2,511	17,713	20,224
Typewriting*	17.3%	82.7%	76	364	440
Music	22.8%	77.2%	1,916	6,486	8,402
Hebrew Studies***	33.3%	66.7%	2	4	6
Italian*	35.9%	64.1%	120	214	334
Art, Craft & Design	39.3%	60.7%	8,483	13,109	21,592
Spanish	39.5%	60.5%	1,087	1,663	2,750
Religious Education	44.1%	55.9%	2,552	3,235	5,787
Business Studies	46.0%	54.0%	17,160	20,155	37,315
French	46.2%	53.8%	18,159	21,164	39,323
German	48.9%	51.1%	5,565	5,820	11,385
History	49.4%	50.6%	26,387	27,066	53,453
Geography	49.6%	50.4%	26,665	27,121	53,786
Irish	49.6%	50.4%	26,791	27,188	53,979
Civic, Social & Political	50.2%	49.8%	28,859	28,667	57,526
English	50.3%	49.7%	29,530	29,186	58,716
Mathematics	50.4%	49.6%	29,431	29,010	58,441
Science	52.7%	47.3%	26,912	24,178	51,090
Environmental & Social Studies*	54.4%	45.6%	320	268	588
Classical Studies*	64.0%	36.0%	371	209	580
Latin*	73.0%	27.0%	367	136	503
Technology	73.1%	26.9%	2,331	857	3,188
Materials Technology	87.6%	12.4%	13,935	1,967	15,902
Technical Graphics	88.1%	11.9%	11,794	1,593	13,387
Metalwork	91.2%	8.8%	7,588	729	8,317
Ancient Greek**	97.4%	2.6%	38	1	39

Data Source: Department of Education & Science, Tuarascáil Staitistiúil (Annual Statistical Reports), 2003.
Note: * Less than 1,000 candidates ** Less than 100 candidates *** Less than 10 candidates excluded.

TABLE 3.3   JUNIOR CERTIFICATE EXAMINATION CANDIDATES BY SUBJECT 1993

	GENDER BALANCE		NUMBERS		
	MALE	FEMALE	MALE	FEMALE	ALL STUDENTS
Shorthand	2.3%	97.7%	7	302	309
Home Economics	8.4%	91.6%	1,742	18,971	20,713
Typewriting*	11.2%	88.8%	60	478	538
S.E.S.P.*	12.1%	87.9%	38	275	313
Music	22.2%	77.8%	1,985	6,955	8,940
Italian*	35.0%	65.0%	71	132	203
Art, Craft & Design	40.0%	60.0%	9,556	14,351	23,907
Spanish	43.0%	57.0%	885	1,175	2,060
German	43.6%	56.4%	7,775	10,057	17,832
French	44.4%	55.6%	20,376	25,543	45,919
Business Studies	44.9%	55.1%	19,779	24,279	44,058
History	49.0%	51.0%	28,453	29,638	58,091
Geography	49.2%	50.8%	28,776	29,742	58,518
Irish	49.9%	50.1%	31,253	31,428	62,681
English	50.3%	49.7%	32,346	31,990	64,336
Mathematics	50.5%	49.5%	32,810	32,177	64,987
Science	54.0%	46.0%	30,508	25,941	56,449
ESP-History*	56.7%	43.3%	203	155	358
Classical Studies*	58.6%	41.4%	311	220	531
Humanities 1 - English*	59.6%	40.4%	536	364	900
Humanities 3 - History*	59.7%	40.3%	534	361	895
Humanities 2 - Geography*	60.4%	39.6%	550	360	910
Technology	70.5%	29.5%	1,702	713	2,415
Latin*	70.8%	29.2%	631	260	891
ESP-Geography*	71.2%	28.8%	203	82	285
Greek**	86.8%	13.2%	33	5	38
Mechanical Drawing	92.3%	7.7%	17,460	1,458	18,918
Woodwork	93.7%	6.3%	13,633	913	14,546
Metalwork	95.3%	4.7%	8,838	437	9,275

Data Source: Department of Education & Science, Tuarascáil Statistiúil (Annual Statistical Reports), 1993.

TABLE 3.4 PROPORTIONS OF EXAMINATION CANDIDATES TAKING HIGHER LEVEL PAPERS: JUNIOR CERTIFICATE 2003

	% TAKING HIGHER LEVEL				NUMBERS TAKING HIGHER LEVEL		
	FEMALE/MALE RATIO	MALE	FEMALE	ALL STUDENTS	MALE	FEMALE	ALL STUDENTS
Italian	2.38	31.7%	75.2%	59.6%	38	161	199
Typewriting*	1.95	18.4%	36.0%	33.0%	14	131	145
Home Economics	1.76	45.1%	79.3%	75.1%	1,132	14,055	15,187
Irish	1.47	33.2%	48.7%	41.0%	8,886	13,250	22,136
Spanish	1.36	54.4%	74.1%	66.3%	591	1,233	1,824
Art,Craft & Design	1.29	51.5%	66.6%	60.7%	4,372	8,725	13,097
English	1.25	56.0%	70.1%	63.1%	16,551	20,472	37,023
German	1.20	64.3%	77.0%	70.8%	3,579	4,480	8,059
French	1.19	60.7%	72.4%	67.0%	11,019	15,318	26,337
Classical Studies*	1.18	70.1%	82.8%	74.7%	260	173	433
Science	1.17	59.1%	69.3%	63.9%	15,905	16,762	32,667
Religious Education	1.16	66.0%	76.6%	72.0%	1,685	2,479	4,164
Mathematics	1.11	38.6%	42.7%	40.6%	11,352	12,382	23,734
Music	1.10	72.7%	79.8%	78.2%	1,393	5,179	6,572
Ancient Greek**	1.09	92.1%	100.0%	92.3%	35	1	36
Business Studies	1.08	63.2%	67.9%	65.8%	10,843	13,692	24,535
History	1.07	62.4%	66.5%	64.5%	16,460	17,997	34,457
Geography	1.06	73.3%	77.5%	75.4%	19,537	21,026	40,563
Hebrew Studies***	1.00	100.0%	100.0%	100.0%	2	4	6
Latin*	0.95	90.2%	85.3%	88.9%	331	116	447
Technical Graphics	0.94	56.7%	53.1%	56.2%	6,684	846	7,530
Technology	0.90	75.4%	67.7%	73.3%	1,758	580	2,338
Environmental & Social Studies*	0.83	18.4%	15.3%	17.0%	59	41	100
Materials Technology	0.80	72.8%	58.1%	71.0%	10,147	1,143	11,290
Metalwork	0.76	71.0%	54.2%	69.5%	5,387	395	5,782

Data Source: Department of Education & Science, Tuarascáil Statistiúil (Annual Statistical Reports), 2003.
Note: * Less than 1,000 candidates ** Less than 100 candidates *** Less than 10 candidates.

TABLE 3.5 PROPORTIONS OF EXAMINATION CANDIDATES TAKING HIGHER LEVEL PAPERS: JUNIOR CERTIFICATE 1993

	% TAKING HIGHER LEVEL				NUMBERS TAKING HIGHER LEVEL			
	FEMALE/MALE RATIO	MALE	FEMALE	ALL STUDENTS	MALE	FEMALE	ALL STUDENTS
Typewriting*	7.03	5.0%	35.1%	31.8%	3	168	171
Hebrew Studies***	1.50	66.7%	100.0%	87.5%	2	5	7
Humanities 1 - English*	1.44	26.1%	37.6%	30.8%	140	137	277
Humanities 2 - Geography*	1.42	26.5%	37.8%	31.0%	146	136	282
Irish	1.42	30.8%	43.8%	37.3%	9,617	13,757	23,374
Humanities 3 - History*	1.35	27.9%	37.7%	31.8%	149	136	285
Art, Craft & Design	1.31	46.9%	61.5%	55.6%	4,479	8,819	13,298
English	1.25	50.1%	62.5%	56.3%	16,209	19,994	36,203
Home Economics	1.24	77.8%	96.6%	95.0%	1,355	18,328	19,683
Spanish	1.18	69.6%	82.3%	76.8%	616	967	1,583
Science	1.17	63.5%	74.6%	68.6%	19,383	19,344	38,727
French	1.17	66.6%	77.7%	72.8%	13,570	19,840	33,410
German	1.12	80.4%	89.9%	85.7%	6,250	9,039	15,289
Greek**	1.10	90.9%	100.0%	92.1%	30	5	35
ESP-Geography*	1.09	83.7%	91.5%	86.0%	170	75	245
ESP-History*	1.05	80.3%	84.5%	82.1%	163	131	294
History	1.05	72.5%	76.1%	74.3%	20,629	22,544	43,173
Geography	1.04	78.0%	80.8%	79.4%	22,435	24,045	46,480
Mathematics	1.01	31.2%	31.4%	31.3%	10,221	10,096	20,317
Latin*	1.01	90.6%	91.2%	90.8%	572	237	809
Business Studies	0.99	70.1%	69.2%	69.6%	13,860	16,789	30,649
Italian*	0.98	80.3%	78.8%	79.3%	57	104	161
Technology	0.97	82.3%	79.5%	81.4%	1,400	567	1,967
Classical Studies*	0.96	88.4%	85.0%	87.0%	275	187	462
Technical Graphics	0.86	53.3%	45.6%	52.7%	9,299	665	9,964
Woodwork	0.80	62.3%	49.9%	61.5%	8,497	456	8,953
Metalwork	0.74	65.8%	49.0%	65.0%	5,818	214	6,032

Data Source: Department of Education & Science, Tuarascáil Staitistiúil (Annual Statistical Reports), 1993.
Note: * Less than 1,000 candidates ** Less than 100 candidates *** Less than 10 candidates.

TABLE 3.6 SUMMARY OF HIGH PERFORMANCE IN THE JUNIOR CERTIFICATE, 1997 TO 2003

	VERY HIGH PERFORMANCE 6 'C'S AT HIGHER LEVEL, OF WHICH 3+ 'A'S				HIGH PERFORMANCE 6 'C'S AT HIGHER LEVEL			
	MALE	FEMALE	ALL STUDENTS	FEMALE MALE/RATIO	MALE	FEMALE	ALL STUDENTS	FEMALE MALE/RATIO
1997	6.7%	9.9%	8.3%	1.46	32.2%	46.1%	39.1%	1.43
1998	6.8%	10.8%	8.8%	1.60	32.2%	46.0%	39.0%	1.43
1999	6.7%	10.8%	8.7%	1.61	32.7%	47.5%	40.0%	1.45
2000	6.5%	11.3%	8.8%	1.75	31.6%	45.9%	38.6%	1.45
2001	6.7%	11.2%	8.9%	1.66	31.8%	44.9%	38.3%	1.41
2002	8.9%	14.9%	11.9%	1.67	37.4%	51.3%	44.3%	1.37
2003	8.8%	15.0%	11.9%	1.70	40.0%	54.0%	46.9%	1.35

Data Source: Department of Education & Science, Tuarascáil Staitistiúil (Annual Statistical Reports), Various years.

TABLE 3.7 LOW PERFORMANCE IN THE JUNIOR CERTIFICATE, 1997 TO 2003				
	< 5 'D'S AT ANY LEVEL			
	MALE	FEMALE	ALL STUDENTS	FEMALE MALE RATIO
1997	2.4%	1.1%	1.7%	0.44
1998	2.5%	1.1%	1.8%	0.45
1999	3.3%	1.3%	2.3%	0.39
2000	2.7%	1.4%	2.1%	0.51
2001	2.7%	1.5%	2.1%	0.56
2002	1.8%	0.9%	1.4%	0.51
2003	1.2%	0.6%	0.9%	0.50

Data Source: Department of Education & Science, Tuarascáil Staitistiúil (Annual Statistical Reports), Various years.

TABLE 3.8 OVERVIEW OF HIGH PERFORMANCE IN THE JUNIOR CERTIFICATE EXAMS, 1997 & 2003

	2003			1997		
	MALE	FEMALE	ALL STUDENTS	MALE	FEMALE	ALL STUDENTS
< 5 'D' at any level	1.2%	0.6%	0.9%	2.4%	1.1%	1.7%
5 'D's at any level & < 2 'C's at higher	24.1%	17.8%	21.0%	31.7%	24.6%	28.2%
6 'D's at any level & 2 to 4 'C's at higher level	20.9%	15.3%	18.1%	19.1%	14.6%	16.9%
6 'D's at any level & 4 to 6 'C's at higher level	13.8%	12.3%	13.1%	14.6%	13.5%	14.1%
6 'C's at higher level & < 3 'B's	7.0%	7.6%	7.3%	5.9%	8.9%	7.4%
6 'C's at higher level & 3+ 'B's but <3 'A's	24.2%	31.4%	27.7%	19.5%	27.4%	23.4%
6 'C's at higher level & 3+ 'A's	8.8%	15.0%	11.9%	6.7%	9.9%	8.3%
TOTAL	100.0%	100.0%	100.0%	100.0%	100.0%	100.0%

Data Source: Department of Education & Science, Tuarascáil Staitistiúil (Annual Statistical Reports), 1997 & 2003.

TABLE 3.9	TRENDS IN THE GENDER DIFFERENCE IN JUNIOR CERTIFICATE EXAM PERFORMANCE, 1992-2002

The figures below are the percentage of female candidates obtaining higher level honours minus the percentage of male candidates obtaining honours. Figures above 0% indicate that a higher proportion of females obtained honour and figures below 0% indicate that a higher proportion of males obtained honours in the particular subject.

	1992	1993	1994	1995	1996	1997	1998	1999	2000	2001	2002
English	16.0%	18.2%	18.5%	17.4%	19.3%	19.2%	18.3%	20.8%	21.2%	20.7%	20.1%
Irish	13.8%	14.3%	15.3%	15.0%	15.5%	15.7%	15.2%	16.8%	15.1%	17.3%	16.7%
French	15.9%	14.6%	15.0%	14.7%	16.6%	15.4%	15.3%	16.1%	14.0%	13.8%	14.6%
Science	11.2%	10.5%	11.6%	10.8%	8.6%	10.2%	11.8%	11.4%	12.5%	11.0%	10.3%
History	6.7%	5.7%	5.0%	4.8%	6.0%	3.8%	4.6%	5.4%	5.8%	3.9%	5.2%
Business Studies	-0.7%	1.5%	2.0%	4.4%	3.2%	4.0%	4.0%	6.7%	4.2%	3.7%	4.9%
Mathematics	-0.5%	1.2%	1.5%	2.3%	2.6%	1.4%	2.1%	2.8%	2.2%	3.1%	4.5%
Geography	-0.4%	0.6%	3.4%	3.2%	3.6%	6.1%	4.2%	4.3%	3.5%	4.8%	4.1%
TOP 8 AVERAGE	7.8%	8.3%	9.0%	9.1%	9.4%	9.5%	9.4%	10.5%	9.8%	9.8%	10.1%

Data Source: Department of Education & Science, Tuarascáil Staitistiúil (Annual Statistical Reports), Various years.

TABLE 3.10 AVERAGE GENDER DIFFERENCES IN THE OVERALL PERCENTAGES OBTAINING HIGHER LEVEL HONOURS

	1992-1994	2000-2002
Home Economics	35.3%	38.1%
Italian	4.8%	21.8%
English	17.6%	20.7%
German	21.2%	19.5%
Spanish	19.5%	18.9%
Art	16.3%	17.6%
Irish	14.5%	16.3%
French	15.1%	14.1%
Music	20.6%	12.4%
Science	11.1%	11.3%
Classical Studies*	13.2%	8.8%
History	5.8%	5.0%
Business Studies	1.0%	4.3%
Geography	1.2%	4.1%
Mathematics	0.8%	3.2%
Latin*	14.9%	0.0%
Technology	-1.6%	-1.2%
Environmental & Social Studies*	9.5%	-1.3%
Technical Graphics	-6.9%	-3.2%
Metalwork	-18.8%	-20.7%

Data Source: Department of Education & Science, Tuarascáil Staitistiúil (Annual Statistical Reports), Various years.

TABLE 3.11a IRISH

	1990	1991	1992	1993	1994	1995	1996	1997	1998	1999	2000	2001	2002
OVERALL NUMBER OF JUNIOR CERTIFICATE CANDIDATES TAKING THE SUBJECT													
Male	26,870	28,165	29,877	31,253	31,857	32,393	32,298	31,623	31,035	29,777	28,773	27,874	27,509
Female	28,724	29,393	29,894	31,428	32,594	32,274	32,250	31,767	30,858	29,318	28,287	27,982	27,924
PERCENTAGES TAKING THE SUBJECT AT HIGHER LEVEL													
Male	25.0%	25.0%	27.9%	30.8%	32.4%	32.6%	32.3%	33.3%	33.9%	33.7%	33.1%	32.4%	32.1%
Female	34.5%	35.2%	40.5%	43.8%	45.9%	46.5%	47.0%	47.9%	48.0%	48.4%	46.9%	48.3%	47.6%
PERCENTAGE OF HIGHER LEVEL CANDIDATES OBTAINING GRADE 'C' OR ABOVE													
Male	53.3%	54.8%	75.0%	71.0%	67.6%	64.5%	71.3%	66.6%	58.4%	69.8%	69.6%	69.9%	71.0%
Female	69.4%	67.6%	85.7%	82.7%	81.1%	77.6%	82.0%	79.0%	72.9%	83.3%	81.3%	82.6%	83.0%
CANDIDATES OBTAINING GRADE 'C' OR ABOVE AT HIGHER LEVEL AS A PERCENTAGE OF ALL CANDIDATES													
Male	13.3%	13.7%	20.9%	21.9%	21.9%	21.0%	23.1%	22.2%	19.8%	23.5%	23.1%	22.6%	22.8%
Female	23.9%	23.8%	34.7%	36.2%	37.2%	36.1%	38.6%	37.9%	35.0%	40.3%	38.1%	39.9%	39.5%

TABLE 3.11b ENGLISH

	1990	1991	1992	1993	1994	1995	1996	1997	1998	1999	2000	2001	2002
OVERALL NUMBER OF JUNIOR CERTIFICATE CANDIDATES TAKING THE SUBJECT													
Male	27,977	29,433	31,102	32,346	33,538	34,049	33,966	33,419	32,816	31,499	30,683	29,974	29,877
Female	29,233	29,882	30,404	31,990	33,726	33,466	33,420	33,014	32,203	30,666	29,756	29,521	29,713
PERCENTAGES TAKING THE SUBJECT AT HIGHER LEVEL													
Male	47.1%	47.6%	46.4%	50.1%	49.9%	52.3%	53.0%	53.3%	54.3%	55.4%	55.5%	54.9%	54.8%
Female	56.3%	58.2%	60.1%	62.5%	63.9%	66.5%	66.7%	67.7%	68.1%	70.5%	69.0%	69.2%	69.3%
PERCENTAGE OF HIGHER LEVEL CANDIDATES OBTAINING GRADE 'C' OR ABOVE													
Male	53.1%	53.1%	49.5%	47.5%	55.4%	56.9%	59.8%	58.3%	60.4%	65.5%	60.8%	62.8%	68.3%
Female	65.9%	64.2%	64.9%	67.2%	72.2%	70.9%	76.6%	74.2%	74.9%	80.9%	79.7%	79.7%	83.1%
CANDIDATES OBTAINING GRADE 'C' OR ABOVE AT HIGHER LEVEL AS A PERCENTAGE OF ALL CANDIDATES													
Male	25.1%	25.3%	23.0%	23.8%	27.6%	29.8%	31.7%	31.1%	32.7%	36.3%	33.7%	34.4%	37.5%
Female	37.1%	37.4%	39.0%	42.0%	46.2%	47.1%	51.1%	50.3%	51.0%	57.0%	55.0%	55.2%	57.6%

TABLE 3.11c MATHEMATICS

	1990	1991	1992	1993	1994	1995	1996	1997	1998	1999	2000	2001	2002
OVERALL NUMBER OF JUNIOR CERTIFICATE CANDIDATES TAKING THE SUBJECT													
Male	28,461	29,928	31,588	32,810	33,426	33,929	33,799	33,288	32,702	31,352	30,530	29,875	29,778
Female	29,559	30,268	30,671	32,177	33,507	33,197	33,182	32,745	31,881	30,393	29,489	29,309	29,517
PERCENTAGES TAKING THE SUBJECT AT HIGHER LEVEL													
Male	33.0%	32.0%	29.8%	31.2%	32.8%	34.0%	34.4%	34.7%	34.4%	34.5%	35.7%	34.3%	35.2%
Female	29.5%	29.4%	29.9%	31.4%	33.5%	35.6%	36.8%	36.6%	36.3%	37.5%	37.4%	37.1%	38.4%
PERCENTAGE OF HIGHER LEVEL CANDIDATES OBTAINING GRADE 'C' OR ABOVE													
Male	69.7%	71.2%	64.8%	70.8%	78.4%	72.2%	66.6%	74.2%	68.0%	75.2%	65.0%	75.8%	71.1%
Female	67.8%	71.0%	63.2%	74.0%	81.5%	75.4%	69.4%	74.3%	70.2%	76.7%	67.9%	78.3%	76.8%
CANDIDATES OBTAINING GRADE 'C' OR ABOVE AT HIGHER LEVEL AS A PERCENTAGE OF ALL CANDIDATES													
Male	23.0%	22.8%	19.3%	22.1%	25.8%	24.5%	22.9%	25.8%	23.4%	26.0%	23.2%	26.0%	25.0%
Female	20.0%	20.9%	18.9%	23.2%	27.3%	26.9%	25.5%	27.1%	25.5%	28.8%	25.4%	29.0%	29.5%

TABLE 3.11d HISTORY

	1992	1993	1994	1995	1996	1997	1998	1999	2000	2001	2002
OVERALL NUMBER OF JUNIOR CERTIFICATE CANDIDATES TAKING THE SUBJECT											
Male	27,045	28,453	28,978	30,122	30,051	29,847	29,457	28,166	27,369	26,785	26,412
Female	27,913	29,638	31,122	31,162	31,062	30,735	29,977	28,553	27,570	27,481	27,384
PERCENTAGES TAKING THE SUBJECT AT HIGHER LEVEL											
Male	73.5%	n\a	72.8%	71.2%	71.7%	70.9%	69.4%	68.2%	68.4%	66.6%	65.6%
Female	77.4%	76.1%	76.8%	75.7%	76.0%	75.3%	74.0%	73.0%	71.5%	70.5%	67.6%
PERCENTAGE OF HIGHER LEVEL CANDIDATES OBTAINING GRADE 'C' OR ABOVE											
Male	71.9%	80.6%	69.9%	78.9%	72.1%	75.0%	71.1%	69.1%	78.9%	68.6%	67.7%
Female	77.0%	84.3%	72.8%	80.6%	75.9%	75.8%	72.9%	71.9%	83.5%	70.4%	73.4%
CANDIDATES OBTAINING GRADE 'C' OR ABOVE AT HIGHER LEVEL AS A PERCENTAGE OF ALL CANDIDATES											
Male	52.8%	58.4%	50.9%	56.2%	51.7%	53.2%	49.3%	47.1%	54.0%	45.7%	44.4%
Female	59.5%	64.1%	55.9%	61.0%	57.7%	57.0%	53.9%	52.5%	59.7%	49.6%	49.6%

TABLE 3.11e GEOGRAPHY

	1992	1993	1994	1995	1996	1997	1998	1999	2000	2001	2002
OVERALL NUMBER OF JUNIOR CERTIFICATE CANDIDATES TAKING THE SUBJECT											
Male	27,755	28,776	29,715	30,496	30,427	31,603	29,711	28,282	27,735	26,972	26,951
Female	28,019	29,742	31,327	31,305	31,306	30,811	30,121	28,511	27,504	27,408	27,495
PERCENTAGES TAKING THE SUBJECT AT HIGHER LEVEL											
Male	74.3%	78.0%	75.2%	76.0%	75.7%	72.5%	75.8%	76.9%	77.1%	75.5%	75.8%
Female	78.1%	80.8%	78.8%	80.1%	79.6%	79.3%	79.1%	81.7%	81.0%	79.2%	79.2%
PERCENTAGE OF HIGHER LEVEL CANDIDATES OBTAINING GRADE 'C' OR ABOVE											
Male	81.2%	74.5%	78.8%	72.7%	74.7%	82.7%	81.6%	82.8%	74.4%	78.9%	80.5%
Female	76.7%	72.6%	79.5%	73.0%	75.6%	83.3%	83.6%	83.2%	75.2%	81.2%	82.2%
CANDIDATES OBTAINING GRADE 'C' OR ABOVE AT HIGHER LEVEL AS A PERCENTAGE OF ALL CANDIDATES											
Male	60.3%	58.1%	59.3%	55.3%	56.5%	60.0%	61.8%	63.7%	57.4%	59.6%	61.0%
Female	59.9%	58.7%	62.7%	58.4%	60.2%	66.1%	66.1%	68.0%	60.9%	64.3%	65.0%

TABLE 3.11f FRENCH

	1992	1993	1994	1995	1996	1997	1998	1999	2000	2001	2002
OVERALL NUMBER OF JUNIOR CERTIFICATE CANDIDATES TAKING THE SUBJECT											
Male	19,315	20,376	21,150	22,203	21,490	21,760	21,088	20,378	19,456	19,282	18,543
Female	23,961	25,543	26,552	26,369	26,065	25,783	24,722	23,425	22,606	22,427	21,980
PERCENTAGES TAKING THE SUBJECT AT HIGHER LEVEL											
Male	68.3%	66.6%	65.2%	63.4%	62.2%	62.6%	63.0%	61.3%	62.5%	58.6%	60.7%
Female	77.9%	77.7%	76.3%	74.2%	74.4%	75.1%	75.7%	74.5%	73.0%	71.1%	72.3%
PERCENTAGE OF HIGHER LEVEL CANDIDATES OBTAINING GRADE 'C' OR ABOVE											
Male	62.8%	70.6%	62.5%	64.6%	63.1%	63.3%	66.1%	62.4%	65.6%	64.8%	61.8%
Female	75.4%	79.3%	73.0%	75.0%	75.0%	73.3%	75.2%	73.0%	75.4%	72.8%	72.1%
CANDIDATES OBTAINING GRADE 'C' OR ABOVE AT HIGHER LEVEL AS A PERCENTAGE OF ALL CANDIDATES											
Male	42.9%	47.0%	40.8%	40.9%	39.3%	39.7%	41.6%	38.2%	41.0%	38.0%	37.5%
Female	58.8%	61.6%	55.7%	55.6%	55.8%	55.0%	57.0%	54.3%	55.0%	51.7%	52.1%

TABLE 3.11g GERMAN

	1992	1993	1994	1995	1996	1997	1998	1999	2000	2001	2002
OVERALL NUMBER OF JUNIOR CERTIFICATE CANDIDATES TAKING THE SUBJECT											
Male	6,938	7,775	8,195	8,085	8,040	7,294	7,079	6,617	6,578	6,152	5,956
Female	9,741	10,057	10,447	10,097	9,478	8,972	8,507	7,803	7,176	6,867	6,321
PERCENTAGES TAKING THE SUBJECT AT HIGHER LEVEL											
Male	80.1%	80.4%	76.7%	75.7%	72.9%	72.4%	70.5%	68.0%	65.4%	63.7%	61.6%
Female	89.9%	89.9%	88.4%	86.5%	84.7%	84.9%	82.9%	82.0%	78.6%	75.3%	74.6%
PERCENTAGE OF HIGHER LEVEL CANDIDATES OBTAINING GRADE 'C' OR ABOVE											
Male	69.0%	63.2%	61.3%	59.4%	63.6%	63.2%	60.8%	65.3%	61.8%	66.9%	63.7%
Female	82.2%	80.6%	79.4%	76.9%	79.0%	79.1%	77.9%	78.9%	77.3%	80.8%	79.4%
CANDIDATES OBTAINING GRADE 'C' OR ABOVE AT HIGHER LEVEL AS A PERCENTAGE OF ALL CANDIDATES											
Male	55.3%	50.8%	47.0%	44.9%	46.4%	45.8%	42.9%	44.4%	40.4%	42.6%	39.2%
Female	73.9%	72.5%	70.2%	66.5%	66.9%	67.1%	64.5%	64.7%	60.8%	60.8%	59.2%

TABLE 3.11h   SPANISH

	1992	1993	1994	1995	1996	1997	1998	1999	2000	2001	2002
OVERALL NUMBER OF JUNIOR CERTIFICATE CANDIDATES TAKING THE SUBJECT											
Male	819	885	905	912	1,057	886	1,021	857	1,042	785	1,004
Female	1,124	1,175	1,075	1,191	1,218	1,121	1,259	1,274	1,254	1,095	1,341
PERCENTAGES TAKING THE SUBJECT AT HIGHER LEVEL											
Male	69.8%	69.6%	65.0%	63.9%	55.2%	60.9%	59.5%	60.2%	58.5%	57.3%	57.6%
Female	78.9%	82.3%	79.0%	77.3%	75.3%	79.9%	70.8%	69.5%	71.8%	72.6%	76.1%
PERCENTAGE OF HIGHER LEVEL CANDIDATES OBTAINING GRADE 'C' OR ABOVE											
Male	74.7%	57.1%	56.1%	59.0%	59.0%	64.3%	44.0%	58.3%	60.5%	66.4%	69.6%
Female	84.9%	72.9%	75.7%	69.5%	73.3%	71.1%	66.0%	73.3%	68.2%	80.0%	83.1%
CANDIDATES OBTAINING GRADE 'C' OR ABOVE AT HIGHER LEVEL AS A PERCENTAGE OF ALL CANDIDATES											
Male	52.1%	39.8%	36.5%	37.7%	32.5%	39.2%	26.2%	35.1%	35.4%	38.1%	40.0%
Female	67.0%	60.0%	59.8%	53.7%	55.2%	56.8%	46.7%	50.9%	49.0%	58.1%	63.2%

TABLE 3.11i ITALIAN

	1992	1993	1994	1995	1996	1997	1998	1999	2000	2001	2002
OVERALL NUMBER OF JUNIOR CERTIFICATE CANDIDATES TAKING THE SUBJECT											
Male	34	71	88	54	128	101	49	89	56	68	98
Female	78	132	154	134	155	165	101	158	74	124	170
PERCENTAGES TAKING THE SUBJECT AT HIGHER LEVEL											
Male	91.2%	80.3%	71.6%	50.0%	44.5%	44.6%	46.9%	49.4%	53.6%	57.4%	37.8%
Female	88.5%	78.8%	66.9%	67.9%	67.7%	69.7%	66.3%	60.8%	75.7%	76.6%	76.5%
PERCENTAGE OF HIGHER LEVEL CANDIDATES OBTAINING GRADE 'C' OR ABOVE											
Male	74.2%	38.6%	47.6%	88.9%	40.4%	60.0%	65.2%	75.0%	96.7%	92.3%	62.2%
Female	79.7%	47.1%	59.2%	78.0%	58.1%	63.5%	68.7%	76.0%	91.1%	95.8%	66.9%
CANDIDATES OBTAINING GRADE 'C' OR ABOVE AT HIGHER LEVEL AS A PERCENTAGE OF ALL CANDIDATES											
Male	67.6%	31.0%	34.1%	44.4%	18.0%	26.7%	30.6%	37.1%	51.8%	52.9%	23.5%
Female	70.5%	37.1%	39.6%	53.0%	39.4%	44.2%	45.5%	46.2%	68.9%	73.4%	51.2%

TABLE 3.11n MATERIALS TECHNOLOGY

	1994	1995	1996	1997	1998	1999	2000	2001	2002
OVERALL NUMBER OF JUNIOR CERTIFICATE CANDIDATES TAKING THE SUBJECT									
Male	13,457	13,484	14,161	14,664	14,580	14,442	13,757	13,907	13,889
Female	1,038	1,183	1,338	1,678	1,685	1,776	1,816	1,815	1,786
PERCENTAGES TAKING THE SUBJECT AT HIGHER LEVEL									
Male	61.8%	64.8%	66.2%	67.5%	74.1%	69.2%	68.5%	67.2%	70.9%
Female	44.1%	47.3%	45.7%	52.1%	58.8%	54.4%	51.4%	48.6%	52.2%
PERCENTAGE OF HIGHER LEVEL CANDIDATES OBTAINING GRADE 'C' OR ABOVE									
Male	73.8%	76.7%	84.7%	84.4%	83.9%	83.3%	83.1%	85.9%	87.2%
Female	69.7%	75.5%	85.8%	82.0%	84.5%	82.7%	80.8%	86.6%	86.3%
CANDIDATES OBTAINING GRADE 'C' OR ABOVE AT HIGHER LEVEL AS A PERCENTAGE OF ALL CANDIDATES									
Male	45.6%	49.7%	56.0%	57.0%	62.2%	57.6%	56.9%	57.7%	61.8%
Female	30.7%	35.8%	39.2%	42.7%	49.7%	45.0%	41.6%	42.1%	45.1%

TABLE 3.11o METALWORK

	1992	1993	1994	1995	1996	1997	1998	1999	2000	2001	2002
OVERALL NUMBER OF JUNIOR CERTIFICATE CANDIDATES TAKING THE SUBJECT											
Male	8,949	8,838	8,665	8,751	8,806	8,585	8,387	7,734	7,542	7,330	7,820
Female	391	437	423	518	558	564	575	531	607	553	695
PERCENTAGES TAKING THE SUBJECT AT HIGHER LEVEL											
Male	61.0%	65.8%	65.9%	67.5%	67.5%	66.4%	66.8%	70.8%	68.0%	71.6%	68.4%
Female	47.6%	49.0%	48.7%	51.9%	48.6%	52.1%	45.9%	56.5%	49.4%	48.3%	49.2%
PERCENTAGE OF HIGHER LEVEL CANDIDATES OBTAINING GRADE 'C' OR ABOVE											
Male	82.1%	82.4%	91.8%	86.4%	90.1%	88.1%	90.4%	85.8%	87.2%	90.9%	90.9%
Female	74.2%	69.2%	81.1%	77.7%	90.4%	83.3%	88.3%	71.3%	79.7%	87.3%	87.3%
CANDIDATES OBTAINING GRADE 'C' OR ABOVE AT HIGHER LEVEL AS A PERCENTAGE OF ALL CANDIDATES											
Male	50.1%	54.3%	60.6%	58.3%	60.8%	58.5%	60.4%	60.8%	59.3%	65.1%	62.2%
Female	35.3%	33.9%	39.5%	40.3%	43.9%	43.4%	40.5%	40.3%	39.4%	42.1%	42.9%

TABLE 3.11p TECHNICAL GRAPHICS

	1992	1993	1994	1995	1996	1997	1998	1999	2000	2001	2002
OVERALL NUMBER OF JUNIOR CERTIFICATE CANDIDATES TAKING THE SUBJECT											
Male	17,507	17,460	17,655	17,402	16,864	15,640	15,197	14,529	13,551	12,715	12,783
Female	1,390	1,458	1,722	1,768	1,901	1,753	1,775	1,619	1,477	1,566	1,627
PERCENTAGES TAKING THE SUBJECT AT HIGHER LEVEL											
Male	62.4%	53.3%	52.6%	49.3%	47.6%	53.1%	53.5%	52.4%	54.6%	54.6%	51.3%
Female	51.7%	45.6%	46.1%	42.1%	45.2%	47.5%	48.5%	47.8%	46.2%	49.3%	51.8%
PERCENTAGE OF HIGHER LEVEL CANDIDATES OBTAINING GRADE 'C' OR ABOVE											
Male	54.1%	70.2%	60.1%	64.6%	77.7%	73.7%	73.1%	80.5%	81.7%	86.7%	78.0%
Female	47.6%	64.2%	61.5%	62.2%	71.9%	70.7%	73.3%	83.3%	81.7%	86.3%	81.1%
CANDIDATES OBTAINING GRADE 'C' OR ABOVE AT HIGHER LEVEL AS A PERCENTAGE OF ALL CANDIDATES											
Male	33.8%	37.4%	31.6%	31.8%	37.0%	39.1%	39.1%	42.2%	44.6%	47.3%	40.0%
Female	24.6%	29.3%	28.3%	26.2%	32.5%	33.6%	35.5%	39.8%	37.7%	42.5%	42.0%

TABLE 3.11q TECHNOLOGY

	1992	1993	1994	1995	1996	1997	1998	1999	2000	2001	2002
OVERALL NUMBER OF JUNIOR CERTIFICATE CANDIDATES TAKING THE SUBJECT											
Male	929	1,702	1,964	2,436	2,163	2,458	2,450	2,228	2,261	2,208	2,070
Female	487	713	865	876	966	958	1,045	936	827	767	851
PERCENTAGES TAKING THE SUBJECT AT HIGHER LEVEL											
Male	87.5%	82.3%	84.8%	82.4%	74.3%	75.0%	71.3%	72.6%	73.2%	78.1%	79.0%
Female	80.9%	79.5%	76.6%	74.7%	69.8%	64.6%	66.6%	67.9%	69.2%	71.8%	71.3%
PERCENTAGE OF HIGHER LEVEL CANDIDATES OBTAINING GRADE 'C' OR ABOVE											
Male	66.1%	67.6%	77.9%	70.0%	74.1%	73.4%	78.5%	77.9%	80.5%	77.4%	77.5%
Female	70.1%	69.7%	81.6%	72.2%	77.7%	81.1%	85.1%	87.9%	82.7%	86.0%	81.2%
CANDIDATES OBTAINING GRADE 'C' OR ABOVE AT HIGHER LEVEL AS A PERCENTAGE OF ALL CANDIDATES											
Male	57.8%	55.6%	66.0%	57.7%	55.1%	55.0%	56.0%	56.5%	58.9%	60.5%	61.2%
Female	56.7%	55.4%	62.5%	53.9%	54.2%	52.4%	56.7%	59.7%	57.2%	61.8%	57.9%

TABLE 3.11r ART, CRAFT & DESIGN

	1992	1993	1994	1995	1996	1997	1998	1999	2000	2001	2002
OVERALL NUMBER OF JUNIOR CERTIFICATE CANDIDATES TAKING THE SUBJECT											
Male	9,468	9,556	10,038	9,828	9,687	9,530	9,389	8,956	8,605	8,377	8,484
Female	13,871	14,351	14,393	14,193	14,069	14,036	13,677	12,931	12,697	13,077	13,052
PERCENTAGES TAKING THE SUBJECT AT HIGHER LEVEL											
Male	52.2%	46.9%	46.9%	49.8%	49.1%	50.5%	50.8%	53.1%	49.5%	48.1%	51.0%
Female	66.1%	61.5%	60.8%	61.1%	62.3%	60.3%	63.6%	65.4%	62.9%	62.2%	63.6%
PERCENTAGE OF HIGHER LEVEL CANDIDATES OBTAINING GRADE 'C' OR ABOVE											
Male	52.2%	66.7%	72.8%	71.7%	66.8%	73.5%	72.8%	68.5%	67.0%	74.8%	75.5%
Female	64.7%	78.2%	83.4%	83.1%	79.0%	86.7%	83.5%	83.7%	81.5%	85.5%	88.1%
CANDIDATES OBTAINING GRADE 'C' OR ABOVE AT HIGHER LEVEL AS A PERCENTAGE OF ALL CANDIDATES											
Male	27.3%	31.3%	34.2%	35.7%	32.8%	37.1%	36.9%	36.4%	33.2%	36.0%	38.5%
Female	42.8%	48.1%	50.7%	50.8%	49.2%	52.2%	53.1%	54.7%	51.3%	53.2%	56.1%

TABLE 3.11s MUSIC

	1994	1995	1996	1997	1998	1999	2000	2001	2002
OVERALL NUMBER OF JUNIOR CERTIFICATE CANDIDATES TAKING THE SUBJECT									
Male	1,829	1,915	2,035	1,916	1,868	1,718	1,844	1,871	1,906
Female	6,858	6,893	6,785	6,875	6,809	6,991	6,899	6,875	6,785
PERCENTAGES TAKING THE SUBJECT AT HIGHER LEVEL									
Male	62.5%	66.4%	67.2%	71.1%	72.3%	70.5%	71.4%	67.6%	76.2%
Female	80.3%	80.8%	81.8%	82.9%	79.9%	80.8%	80.8%	78.5%	77.9%
PERCENTAGE OF HIGHER LEVEL CANDIDATES OBTAINING GRADE 'C' OR ABOVE									
Male	68.7%	80.0%	82.1%	79.9%	63.3%	77.1%	78.7%	69.4%	76.3%
Female	79.2%	88.2%	91.6%	86.9%	77.3%	84.8%	84.9%	81.0%	85.3%
CANDIDATES OBTAINING GRADE 'C' OR ABOVE AT HIGHER LEVEL AS A PERCENTAGE OF ALL CANDIDATES									
Male	43.0%	53.2%	55.2%	56.8%	45.7%	54.4%	56.2%	46.9%	58.1%
Female	63.6%	71.3%	74.9%	72.1%	61.8%	68.5%	68.6%	63.6%	66.4%

TABLE 3.11t LATIN

	1992	1993	1994	1995	1996	1997	1998	1999	2000	2001	2002
OVERALL NUMBER OF JUNIOR CERTIFICATE CANDIDATES TAKING THE SUBJECT											
Male	599	631	577	547	483	463	372	415	424	458	343
Female	254	260	262	262	221	257	225	208	190	160	151
PERCENTAGES TAKING THE SUBJECT AT HIGHER LEVEL											
Male	92.0%	90.6%	90.1%	92.9%	91.9%	93.5%	90.6%	91.1%	92.7%	90.4%	91.3%
Female	95.3%	91.2%	92.4%	93.9%	90.0%	88.7%	88.4%	85.1%	91.6%	91.3%	74.2%
PERCENTAGE OF HIGHER LEVEL CANDIDATES OBTAINING GRADE 'C' OR ABOVE											
Male	76.8%	74.0%	75.6%	77.8%	82.9%	84.8%	76.0%	86.0%	78.6%	85.0%	79.6%
Female	90.9%	81.9%	96.7%	95.1%	91.0%	86.0%	85.9%	94.9%	81.0%	89.7%	89.3%
CANDIDATES OBTAINING GRADE 'C' OR ABOVE AT HIGHER LEVEL AS A PERCENTAGE OF ALL CANDIDATES											
Male	70.6%	67.0%	68.1%	72.2%	76.2%	79.3%	68.8%	78.3%	72.9%	76.9%	72.6%
Female	86.6%	74.6%	89.3%	89.3%	81.9%	76.3%	76.0%	80.8%	74.2%	81.9%	66.2%

TABLE 3.11u CLASSICAL STUDIES

	1992	1993	1994	1995	1996	1997	1998	1999	2000	2001	2002
OVERALL NUMBER OF JUNIOR CERTIFICATE CANDIDATES TAKING THE SUBJECT											
Male	318	311	316	418	433	375	328	347	370	367	347
Female	198	220	231	227	264	238	204	192	172	191	256
PERCENTAGES TAKING THE SUBJECT AT HIGHER LEVEL											
Male	77.4%	88.4%	92.1%	87.1%	83.1%	87.7%	88.4%	84.1%	77.3%	86.9%	76.7%
Female	86.9%	85.0%	85.7%	85.0%	84.5%	81.1%	89.2%	76.0%	77.3%	82.2%	81.6%
PERCENTAGE OF HIGHER LEVEL CANDIDATES OBTAINING GRADE 'C' OR ABOVE											
Male	66.3%	69.1%	64.3%	73.6%	64.2%	73.3%	66.9%	63.4%	68.9%	68.0%	68.0%
Female	69.8%	90.4%	85.9%	85.0%	80.7%	81.3%	72.5%	74.0%	81.2%	79.0%	77.5%
CANDIDATES OBTAINING GRADE 'C' OR ABOVE AT HIGHER LEVEL AS A PERCENTAGE OF ALL CANDIDATES											
Male	51.3%	61.1%	59.2%	64.1%	53.3%	64.3%	59.1%	53.3%	53.2%	59.1%	52.2%
Female	60.6%	76.8%	73.6%	72.2%	68.2%	66.0%	64.7%	56.3%	62.8%	64.9%	63.3%

APPENDIX 4

Literacy in International Context

TABLE 4.1 READING LITERACY: MEAN SCORES ON THE COMBINED READING LITERACY SCALE - PISA 2000

	MALE	FEMALE	OVERALL	RANKING 2000
Finland	520	571	546	1
Canada	519	551	534	2
New Zealand	507	553	529	3
Australia	513	546	528	4
Ireland	**513**	**542**	**527**	**5**
Korea	519	533	525	6
United Kingdom	512	537	523	7
Japan	507	537	522	8
Sweden	499	536	516	9
Austria	495	520	507	10
Belgium	492	525	507	11
Iceland	488	528	507	12
Norway	486	529	505	13
France	490	519	505	14
United States	490	518	504	15
OECD average	**485**	**517**	**500**	
Denmark	485	510	497	16
Switzerland	480	510	494	17
Spain	481	505	493	18
Czech Republic	473.	510	492	19
Italy	469	507	487	20
Germany	468	502	484	21
Hungary	465	496	480	22
Poland	461	498	479	23
Greece	456	493	474	24
Portugal	458	482	470	25
Luxembourg	429	456	441	26
Mexico	411	432	422	27

Data Source: OECD (2001) Knowledge and Skills for Life - First Results from PISA 2000, Table 5.1a (p.276)

TABLE 4.1(b) READING LITERACY: MEAN SCORES ON THE COMBINED READING LITERACY SCALE - PISA 2003

	MALE	FEMALE	OVERALL	RANKING 2003
Finland	521	565	543	1
Korea	525	547	534	2
Canada	514	546	528	3
Australia	506	545	525	4
New Zealand	508	535	522	5
Ireland	**501**	**530**	**515**	**6**
Sweden	496	533	514	7
Netherlands	503	524	513	8
Belgium	489	526	507	9
Norway	475	525	500	10
Switzerland	482	517	499	11
Japan	487	509	498	12
Poland	477	516	497	13
France	476	514	496	14
United States	479	511	495	15
OECD average	**477**	**511**	**494**	
Denmark	479	505	492	16
Iceland	464	522	492	17
Germany	471	513	491	18
Austria	467	514	491	19
Czech Republic	473	504	489	20
Hungary	467	498	482	21
Spain	461	500	481	22
Luxembourg	463	496	479	23
Portugal	459	495	478	24
Italy	455	495	476	25
Greece	453	490	472	26
Slovak Republic	453	486	469	27
Turkey	426	459	441	28
Mexico	389	410	400	29

Data Source: OECD (2004) Learning for Tomorrow's World - First Results from PISA 2003, Table 6.2 & Table 6.3 (p.444-445)

TABLE 4.2 GENDER DIFFERENCES IN READING LITERACY - PISA 2000

	FEMALE MINUS MALE	CORRELATION BETWEEN GENDER & READING LITERACY	REGRESSION OF GENDER ON READING LITERACY PERFORMANCE
Finland	51	0.29	51.25
New Zealand	46	0.21	45.83
Norway	43	0.21	43.20
Iceland	40	0.22	39.68
Italy	38	0.21	38.17
Czech Republic	37	0.20	37.44
Greece	37	0.19	37.04
Sweden	37	0.20	36.96
Poland	36	0.18	36.13
Germany	35	0.16	34.65
Australia	34	0.17	33.61
Belgium	33	0.15	32.81
Canada	32	0.17	32.21
OECD average	**32**	**0.20**	**37.04**
Hungary	32	0.17	31.62
Switzerland	30	0.15	29.97
Japan	30	0.17	29.66
France	29	0.16	28.76
Ireland	**29**	**0.15**	**28.68**
United States	29	0.14	28.57
Luxembourg	27	0.13	26.88
United Kingdom	26	0.13	25.63
Austria	26	0.14	25.63
Denmark	25	0.13	24.84
Portugal	25	0.13	24.67
Spain	24	0.14	24.14
Mexico	20	0.12	20.27
Korea	14	0.10	14.21

Data Source: OECD (2001) Knowledge and Skills for Life - First Results from PISA 2000, Table 5.1a (p.276) & OECD (2002) Reading for Change: Performance and Engagement across Countries - Results from PISA 2000, Table 6.2a (p.222)

Note: Positive differences indicate that females perform better than males. The above gender differences in reading performance were statistically significant in all OECD countries.

TABLE 4.2(b) GENDER DIFFERENCES IN READING LITERACY - PISA 2003

	FEMALE MINUS MALE
Iceland	58
Norway	49
Austria	47
Finland	44
Germany	42
Poland	40
Italy	39
Australia	39
Spain	39
France	38
Greece	37
Belgium	37
Sweden	37
Portugal	36
Switzerland	35
OECD average	**34**
Turkey	33
Luxembourg	33
Slovak Republic	33
United States	32
Canada	32
Czech Republic	31
Hungary	31
Ireland	**29**
New Zealand	28
Denmark	25
Japan	22
Mexico	21
Korea	21
Netherlands	21

Data Source: OECD (2004) Learning for Tomorrow's World - First Results from PISA 2003, Table 6.3 (p.445)

TABLE 4.3 PISA 2000: READING DIFFICULTIES - PERFORMANCE AT LEVEL 1 AND BELOW

	MALE	FEMALE	ALL STUDENTS	RANKING	MALE / FEMALE RATIO
Korea	7.3%	3.8%	5.8%	1	2.0
Finland	11.0%	3.2%	7.0%	2	3.5
Canada	12.7%	6.0%	9.6%	3	2.1
Japan	14.2%	6.0%	10.1%	4	2.4
Ireland	13.5%	8.3%	11.0%	5	1.6
Australia	16.0%	8.4%	12.5%	6	1.9
Sweden	16.8%	7.8%	12.6%	7	2.2
United Kingdom	15.3%	9.8%	12.9%	8	1.6
New Zealand	18.5%	8.3%	13.7%	9	2.2
Iceland	20.1%	8.0%	14.5%	10	2.5
Austria	17.8%	11.1%	14.6%	11	1.6
France	19.9%	10.5%	15.2%	12	1.9
Spain	20.4%	11.5%	16.3%	13	1.8
Norway	23.2%	10.4%	17.5%	14	2.2
Czech Republic	23.6%	11.5%	17.5%	15	2.0
OECD average	22.3%	13.1%	17.9%		1.7
Denmark	21.8%	13.3%	17.9%	16	1.6
United States	23.0%	13.2%	17.9%	17	1.7
Italy	24.6%	12.6%	18.9%	18	2.0
Belgium	22.8%	14.1%	19.0%	19	1.6
Switzerland	24.7%	15.7%	20.4%	20	1.6
Germany	26.6%	18.2%	22.6%	21	1.5
Hungary	27.2%	17.9%	22.7%	22	1.5
Poland	30.4%	15.9%	23.2%	23	1.9
Greece	30.9%	17.7%	24.4%	24	1.7
Portugal	31.3%	21.2%	26.3%	25	1.5
Luxembourg	40.1%	29.1%	35.1%	26	1.4
Mexico	49.8%	38.9%	44.1%	27	1.3

Data Source: OECD (2001) Knowledge and Skills for Life - First Results from PISA 2000, Table 5.2a (p.278)

TABLE 4.3(b)   PISA 2003: READING DIFFICULTIES - PERFORMANCE AT LEVEL 1 AND BELOW

	MALE	FEMALE	ALL STUDENTS	RANKING	MALE / FEMALE RATIO
Finland	9.0%	2.4%	5.7%	1	3.8
Korea	8.4%	4.4%	6.8%	2	1.9
Canada	13.3%	5.6%	9.5%	3	2.4
Ireland	**14.3%**	**7.7%**	**11.0%**	**4**	**1.9**
Netherlands	14.3%	8.6%	11.5%	5	1.7
Australia	16.5%	7.1%	11.8%	6	2.3
Sweden	17.7%	8.8%	13.3%	7	2.0
New Zealand	17.9%	11.1%	14.5%	8	1.6
Denmark	20.5%	12.7%	16.5%	9	1.6
Switzerland	21.2%	11.8%	16.7%	10	1.8
Poland	23.4%	10.3%	16.8%	11	2.3
France	23.5%	12.1%	17.5%	12	1.9
Belgium	22.4%	13.0%	17.9%	13	1.7
Norway	24.8%	11.3%	18.1%	14	2.2
Iceland	26.9%	9.5%	18.5%	15	2.8
OECD average	**24.2%**	**13.8%**	**19.0%**		**1.7**
Japan	23.2%	15.1%	19.0%	16	1.5
Czech Republic	23.5%	15.0%	19.3%	17	1.6
United States	24.3%	14.4%	19.4%	18	1.7
Hungary	25.5%	14.9%	20.5%	19	1.7
Austria	28.2%	13.1%	20.7%	20	2.1
Spain	27.9%	14.5%	21.1%	21	1.9
Portugal	29.5%	15.1%	21.9%	22	2.0
Germany	28.1%	16.3%	22.3%	23	1.7
Luxembourg	28.5%	17.1%	22.7%	24	1.7
Italy	31.1%	17.2%	23.9%	25	1.8
Slovak Republic	30.9%	18.6%	24.9%	26	1.7
Greece	32.5%	18.5%	25.3%	27	1.8
Turkey	44.1%	27.8%	36.8%	28	1.6
Mexico	57.0%	47.4%	52.0%	29	1.2

Data Source: OECD (2004) Learning for Tomorrow's World - First Results from PISA 2003, Table 6.1 & Table 6.5 (p.443-447)

TABLE 4.4 READING LITERACY PERFORMANCE BY LEVEL - PISA 2000

	IRELAND			OECD		
	MALES	FEMALES	ALL STUDENTS: IRELAND	MALES	FEMALES	ALL STUDENTS: OECD MEAN
Below Level 1	4.0%	2.0%	3.0%	8.0%	3.7%	6.0%
Level 1	9.5%	6.3%	7.9%	14.2%	9.3%	11.9%
Level 2	21.3%	14.3%	17.8%	23.3%	20.0%	21.7%
Level 3	29.9%	29.6%	29.7%	27.9%	29.6%	28.7%
Level 4	24.1%	30.4%	27.3%	19.4%	25.4%	22.3%
Level 5	11.2%	17.4%	14.3%	7.2%	11.9%	9.5%

Data Source: Shiel, Cosgrove et al. [2001], Ready for Life, ERC [p.59]. OECD [2004], Education at a Glance, OECD Indicators 2004, [p.105]. OECD (2001) Knowledge and Skills for Life - First Results from PISA 2000, Table 5.1a (p.278)

TABLE 4.5 MATHEMATICAL LITERACY IN OECD COUNTRIES: PISA 2003

	MALE	FEMALE	ALL STUDENTS	RANKING 2003
Finland	548	541	544	1
Korea	552	528	542	2
Netherlands	540	535	538	3
Japan	539	530	534	4
Canada	541	530	532	5
Belgium	533	525	529	6
Switzerland	535	518	527	7
Australia	527	522	524	8
New Zealand	531	516	523	9
Czech Republic	524	509	516	10
Iceland	508	523	515	11
Denmark	523	506	514	12
France	515	507	511	13
Sweden	512	506	509	14
Austria	509	502	506	15
Germany	508	499	503	16
Ireland	**510**	**495**	**503**	**17**
OECD average	**506**	**494**	**500**	
Slovak Republic	507	489	498	18
Norway	498	492	495	19
Luxembourg	502	485	493	20
Poland	493	487	490	21
Hungary	494	486	490	22
Spain	490	481	485	23
United States	486	480	483	24
Portugal	472	460	466	25
Italy	475	457	466	26
Greece	455	436	445	27
Turkey	430	415	423	28
Mexico	391	380	385	29

Data Source: OECD(2004) Learning for Tomorrow's World - First Results from PISA 2003, Table 2.5c (p.356)

TABLE 4.5(B)
MATHEMATICAL LITERACY IN OECD COUNTRIES: PISA 2000

	MALE	FEMALE	OVERALL	RANKING 2000
Japan	561	553	557	1
Korea	559	532	547	2
New Zealand	536	539	537	3
Finland	537	536	536	4
Australia	539	527	533	5
Canada	539	529	533	6
Switzerland	537	523	529	7
United Kingdom	534	526	529	8
Belgium	524	518	520	9
France	525	511	517	10
Austria	530	503	515	11
Denmark	522	507	514	12
Iceland	513	518	514	13
Sweden	514	507	510	14
Ireland	**510**	**497**	**503**	**15**
Norway	506	495	499	16
Czech Republic	504	492	498	17
OECD mean	**506**	**495**	**498**	
United States	497	490	493	18
Germany	498	483	490	19
Hungary	492	485	488	20
Spain	487	469	476	21
Poland	472	468	470	22
Italy	462	454	457	23
Portugal	464	446	454	24
Greece	451	444	447	25
Luxembourg	454	439	446	26
Mexico	393	382	387	27

Data Source: OECD (2001) Knowledge and Skills for Life - First Results from PISA 2000, Table 5.1a (p.276)

TABLE 4.6 GENDER DIFFERENCES IN MATHEMATICAL LITERACY - PISA 2003

	FEMALE MINUS MALE
Iceland	15.4
Netherlands	-5.1
Australia	-5.3
Poland	-5.6
Norway	-6.2
United States	-6.3
Sweden	-6.5
Finland	-7.4
Belgium	-7.5
Austria	-7.6
Hungary	-7.8
Japan	-8.4
France	-8.5
Spain	-8.9
Germany	-9.0
Mexico	-10.9
OECD average	**-11.1**
Canada	-11.2
Portugal	-12.2
New Zealand	-14.5
Ireland	**-14.8**
Czech Republic	-15.0
Turkey	-15.1
Denmark	-16.6
Switzerland	-16.6
Luxembourg	-17.2
Italy	-17.8
Slovak Republic	-18.7
Greece	-19.4
Korea	-23.4

Data Source: OECD (2004) Learning for Tomorrow's World - First Results from PISA 2003, Table 2.5c (p.356)

TABLE 4.6(b) GENDER DIFFERENCES IN MATHEMATICAL LITERACY - PISA 2000

	FEMALE MINUS MALE
Iceland	4.6
New Zealand	2.7
Finland	-1.0
Poland	-4.8
Belgium	-6.2
Greece	-6.5
Hungary	-7.0
United States	-7.1
Sweden	-7.5
United Kingdom	-8.0
Japan	-8.2
Italy	-8.4
Canada	-10.3
Norway	-10.5
Mexico	-10.6
OECD average	**-11.3**
Czech Republic	-11.7
Australia	-12.0
Ireland	**-12.9**
France	-14.1
Switzerland	-14.2
Germany	-14.6
Denmark	-14.8
Luxembourg	-15.0
Spain	-18.2
Portugal	-18.5
Korea	-26.6
Austria	-27.1

Data Source: OECD (2001) Knowledge and Skills for Life - First Results from PISA 2000, Table 5.1a (p.276)

Positive differences indicate that females perform better than males while negative differences indicate that males perform better than females.

TABLE 4.7 PISA 2003: MATHEMATICAL DIFFICULTIES - PERFORMANCE AT LEVEL 1 AND BELOW

	MALES	FEMALES	ALL STUDENTS	RANKING 2003	MALE/ FEMALE RATIO
Finland	7.3%	6.2%	6.8%	1	1.2
Korea	8.5%	11.0%	9.5%	2	0.8
Canada	10.3%	9.4%	10.1%	3	1.1
Netherlands	10.2%	11.7%	10.9%	4	0.9
Japan	14.2%	12.4%	13.3%	5	1.1
Australia	14.9%	13.8%	14.3%	6	1.1
Switzerland	13.4%	15.7%	14.5%	7	0.9
Iceland	18.3%	11.5%	15.0%	8	1.6
New Zealand	14.5%	15.6%	15.1%	9	0.9
Denmark	13.4%	17.4%	15.4%	10	0.8
Belgium	17.2%	15.7%	16.5%	11	1.1
Czech Republic	15.1%	18.1%	16.6%	12	0.8
France	16.8%	16.5%	16.6%	13	1.0
Ireland	**15.0%**	**18.7%**	**16.8%**	**14**	**0.8**
Sweden	16.7%	17.9%	17.3%	15	0.9
Austria	19.2%	18.4%	18.8%	16	1.0
Slovak Republic	18.0%	22.0%	19.9%	17	0.8
Norway	20.6%	21.1%	20.8%	18	1.0
OECD average	**20.7%**	**22.2%**	**21.4%**		**0.9**
Germany	21.4%	21.4%	21.6%	19	1.0
Luxembourg	20.0%	23.4%	21.7%	20	0.9
Poland	22.7%	21.4%	22.0%	21	1.1
Spain	22.5%	23.4%	23.0%	22	1.0
Hungary	22.2%	23.9%	23.0%	23	0.9
United States	25.2%	26.3%	25.7%	24	1.0
Portugal	28.7%	31.3%	30.1%	25	0.9
Italy	29.7%	34.0%	31.9%	26	0.9
Greece	35.8%	41.9%	38.9%	27	0.9
Turkey	49.3%	55.8%	52.2%	28	0.9
Mexico	63.1%	68.5%	65.9%	29	0.9

Data Source: OECD (2004) Learning for Tomorrow's World - First Results from PISA 2003, Table 2.5a & Table 2.5b (pp.354-355)

TABLE 4.8 MATHEMATICAL LITERACY PERFORMANCE BY LEVEL, IRELAND AND OECD 2003.				
	IRELAND		OECD	
	MALE	FEMALE	MALE	FEMALE
Below Level 1	4.2%	5.2%	8.1%	8.4%
Level 1	10.8%	13.5%	12.6%	13.8%
Level 2	22.5%	24.7%	20.0%	22.1%
Level 3	27.8%	28.2%	22.9%	24.5%
Level 4	21.0%	19.4%	19.5%	18.8%
Level 5	10.8%	7.4%	11.8%	9.5%
Level 6	2.9%	1.6%	5.1%	2.9%

Data Source: Cosgrove, Shiel, Sofroniou et al. [2005], Education for Life, ERC [p.101]. OECD [2004], Learning for Tomorrow's World: First Results from PISA 2003, [pp.354-355].

TABLE 4.9 SCIENTIFIC LITERACY IN OECD COUNTRIES: PISA 2003

	MALES	FEMALES	ALL STUDENTS	RANKING 2003
Finland	548	545	551	1
Japan	548	550	546	2
Korea	538	546	527	3
Australia	525	525	525	4
Netherlands	524	527	522	5
Czech Republic	523	526	520	6
New Zealand	521	529	513	7
Canada	519	527	516	8
Switzerland	513	518	508	9
France	511	511	511	10
Belgium	509	509	509	11
Sweden	506	509	504	12
Ireland	**505**	**506**	**504**	**13**
Hungary	503	503	504	14
Germany	502	506	500	15
OECD average	**500**	**503**	**497**	
Poland	498	501	494	16
Slovak Republic	495	502	487	17
Iceland	495	490	500	18
United States	491	494	489	19
Austria	491	490	492	20
Spain	487	489	485	21
Italy	486	490	484	22
Norway	484	485	483	23
Luxembourg	483	489	477	24
Greece	481	487	475	25
Denmark	475	484	467	26
Portugal	468	471	465	27
Turkey	434	434	434	28
Mexico	405	410	400	29

Data Source: OECD (2004) Learning for Tomorrow's World - First Results from PISA 2003, Table 6.6 & 6.7 (pp.448-449)

TABLE 4.9(b) SCIENTIFIC LITERACY IN OECD COUNTRIES: PISA 2000

	MALES	FEMALES	ALL STUDENTS	RANKING 2003
Korea	561	541	552	1
Japan	547	554	550	2
Finland	534	541	538	3
United Kingdom	535	531	532	4
Canada	529	531	529	5
New Zealand	523	535	528	6
Australia	526	529	528	7
Austria	526	514	519	8
Ireland	**511**	**517**	**513**	**9**
Sweden	512	513	512	10
Czech Republic	512	511	511	11
France	504	498	500	12
Norway	499	505	500	13
OECD average	**501**	**501**	**500**	
United States	497	502	499	14
Hungary	496	497	496	15
Iceland	495	499	496	16
Belgium	496	498	496	17
Switzerland	500	493	496	18
Spain	492	491	491	19
Germany	489	487	487	20
Poland	486	480	483	21
Denmark	488	476	481	22
Italy	474	483	478	23
Greece	457	464	461	24
Portugal	456	462	459	25
Luxembourg	441	448	443	26
Mexico	423	419	422	27

Data Source: OECD(2004) Learning for Tomorrow's World - First Results from PISA 2003, Table 2.5c (pp.356)

TABLE 4.10
GENDER DIFFERENCES IN SCIENTIFIC LITERACY: PISA 2003

	FEMALE MINUS MALE
Denmark	9
Canada	9
New Zealand	8
Korea	7
Slovak Republic	7
Luxembourg	6
Greece	6
Switzerland	5
Mexico	5
Poland	3
Germany	3
Portugal	3
Italy	3
OECD average	**3**
Czech Republic	3
Netherlands	2
United States	2
Sweden	2
Japan	2
Spain	2
Ireland	**1**
Norway	1
Turkey	0
Belgium	0
France	0
Australia	0
Hungary	-1
Austria	-1
Finland	-3
Iceland	-5

Data Source: OECD (2004) Learning for Tomorrow's World - First Results from PISA 2003, Table 6.6 (p449)

TABLE 4.10 (b) GENDER DIFFERENCES IN SCIENTIFIC LITERACY: PISA 2000	
	MALE MINUS FEMALE
New Zealand	12
Italy	9
Japan	7
Greece	7
Norway	7
Luxembourg	7
Finland	6
Portugal	6
Ireland	**6**
United States	5
Iceland	5
Australia	3
Belgium	2
Canada	2
Hungary	2
Sweden	0
OECD average	**0**
Czech Republic	-1
Spain	-1
Germany	-3
United Kingdom	-4
Mexico	-4
France	-6
Poland	-6
Switzerland	-7
Denmark	-12
Austria	-12
Korea	-19

TABLE 4.11(a) PERCENTAGE OF STUDENTS SCORING BELOW 400 POINTS ON THE SCIENCE SCALE: PISA 2003

	MALES	FEMALES	ALL STUDENTS	RANKING
Finland	6.9%	4.6%	5.7%	1
Korea	8.6%	10.0%	9.2%	2
Japan	11.0%	8.4%	9.7%	3
Netherlands	10.6%	11.6%	11.1%	4
Australia	12.9%	10.2%	11.6%	5
Czech Republic	11.2%	12.1%	11.6%	6
Canada	11.5%	11.6%	12.0%	7
Ireland	**13.4%**	**12.8%**	**13.1%**	**8**
New Zealand	12.5%	14.6%	13.5%	9
Hungary	15.5%	14.0%	14.8%	10
Switzerland	15.3%	15.8%	15.6%	11
Sweden	15.7%	16.6%	16.1%	12
Iceland	18.7%	13.5%	16.2%	13
Belgium	17.5%	15.4%	16.5%	14
France	17.7%	15.6%	16.6%	15
Slovak Republic	16.1%	17.6%	16.9%	16
Poland	17.9%	17.4%	17.7%	17
OECD average	**18.0%**	**17.7%**	**17.9%**	
Austria	20.2%	16.7%	18.5%	18
Germany	19.0%	18.2%	18.8%	19
Spain	19.6%	18.7%	19.1%	20
United States	19.1%	19.4%	19.3%	21
Italy	21.6%	20.9%	21.2%	22
Norway	22.0%	20.5%	21.3%	23
Luxembourg	21.1%	21.8%	21.4%	24
Greece	21.0%	22.3%	21.7%	25
Denmark	20.6%	24.7%	22.7%	26
Portugal	23.9%	23.1%	23.5%	27
Turkey	38.9%	38.3%	38.6%	28
Mexico	46.7%	50.5%	48.7%	29

Data Source: OECD (2004) Learning for Tomorrow's World - First Results from PISA 2003, Table 6.8 (p450)

TABLE 4.11(b) PERCENTAGE OF STUDENTS SCORING ABOVE 600 POINTS ON THE SCIENCE SCALE: PISA 2003

	MALES	FEMALES	ALL STUDENTS	RANKING
Japan	35.8%	31.2%	33.4%	1
Finland	29.2%	29.2%	29.2%	2
Korea	31.2%	23.4%	28.1%	3
Netherlands	25.5%	23.4%	24.5%	4
Australia	24.9%	22.5%	23.7%	5
New Zealand	27.0%	20.3%	23.7%	6
Czech Republic	24.2%	22.1%	23.2%	7
France	23.6%	21.5%	22.5%	8
Switzerland	23.6%	19.0%	21.4%	9
Canada	25.3%	19.3%	21.0%	10
Belgium	22.5%	19.1%	20.9%	11
Germany	21.9%	18.0%	19.9%	12
Sweden	20.3%	18.7%	19.5%	13
OECD average	**19.3%**	**16.0%**	**17.6%**	
Hungary	17.3%	15.4%	16.4%	14
Poland	18.1%	14.7%	16.4%	15
Ireland	**16.5%**	**15.2%**	**15.8%**	**16**
Slovak Republic	17.3%	12.8%	15.1%	17
United States	16.3%	13.1%	14.7%	18
Italy	16.4%	12.7%	14.5%	19
Austria	14.9%	12.0%	13.4%	20
Iceland	13.4%	13.4%	13.4%	21
Norway	13.9%	11.9%	12.9%	22
Luxembourg	15.8%	10.0%	12.9%	23
Spain	14.5%	11.1%	12.7%	24
Greece	14.6%	9.8%	12.1%	25
Denmark	12.4%	9.3%	10.8%	26
Portugal	9.1%	6.0%	7.5%	27
Turkey	6.2%	5.0%	5.7%	28
Mexico	1.8%	1.0%	1.4%	29

Data Source: OECD (2004)Learning for Tomorrow's World - First Results from PISA 2003, Table 6.8 (p450)

254

APPENDIX 5

Leaving Certificate Examinations

EXAM CANDIDATES

SUBJECT TAKE-UP

HIGHER AND ORDINARY LEVEL

OVERALL PERFORMANCE

EXTENDED TIME-SERIES ANALYSIS

OVERVIEW BY SUBJECT

IRISH, ENGLISH, MATHS . . .

TABLE 5.1 LEAVING CERTIFICATE CANDIDATES

YEAR	NUMBERS			GENDER BALANCE	
	MALE	FEMALE	TOTAL	MALE	FEMALE
1991	26,603	29,038	55,641	47.8%	52.2%
1992	26,631	28,548	55,179	48.3%	51.7%
1993	27,977	29,253	57,230	48.9%	51.1%
1994	30,912	33,122	64,034	48.3%	51.7%
1995	31,874	34,431	66,305	48.1%	51.9%
1996	28,616	30,560	59,176	48.4%	51.6%
1997	29,995	33,239	63,234	47.4%	52.6%
1998	31,333	34,589	65,922	47.5%	52.5%
1999	30,811	34,125	64,936	47.4%	52.6%
2000	30,138	33,281	63,419	47.5%	52.5%
2001	28,176	31,361	59,537	47.3%	52.7%
2002	27,716	30,684	58,400	47.5%	52.5%
2003	28,532	31,004	59,536	47.9%	52.1%

Data Source: Department of Education & Science, Tuarascáil Staitistiúil (Annual Statistical Reports), Various years.

TABLE 5.2 LEAVING CERTIFICATE EXAMINATION CANDIDATES BY SUBJECT 2003

	GENDER BALANCE		NUMBERS		
	MALE	FEMALE	MALE	FEMALE	ALL STUDENTS
Hebrew***	0.0%	100.0%	0	1	1
Home Economics (General)**	12.1%	87.9%	7	51	58
Home Economics (S & S)	13.7%	86.3%	2,474	15,581	18,055
Music	22.6%	77.4%	889	3,047	3,936
Biology	31.6%	68.4%	7,166	15,505	22,671
Portuguese***	33.3%	66.7%	3	6	9
Italian*	35.3%	64.7%	59	108	167
Art	36.1%	63.9%	3,557	6,291	9,848
Spanish	36.3%	63.7%	563	988	1,551
Arabic**	37.5%	62.5%	9	15	24
French	40.8%	59.2%	13,263	19,228	32,491
German	42.8%	57.2%	3,720	4,972	8,692
Modern Greek***	42.9%	57.1%	3	4	7
Business Studies	45.0%	55.0%	10,585	12,946	23,531
Chemistry	46.1%	53.9%	3,085	3,613	6,698
Russian**	46.6%	53.4%	27	31	58
Irish	47.2%	52.8%	23,527	26,301	49,828
Accounting	47.5%	52.5%	3,184	3,515	6,699
English	47.9%	52.1%	25,624	27,836	53,460
Mathematics	48.3%	51.7%	26,222	28,034	54,256
Swedish***	50.0%	50.0%	4	4	8
Japanese***	50.0%	50.0%	4	4	8
Geography	52.1%	47.9%	15,094	13,857	28,951
Classical Studies*	55.9%	44.1%	486	383	869
Latin*	56.4%	43.6%	66	51	117
History	56.5%	43.5%	6,695	5,147	11,842
Arabic*	61.9%	38.1%	83	51	134
Economics	63.5%	36.5%	3,073	1,770	4,843
Economic History*	64.2%	35.8%	208	116	324

Contd.

TABLE 5.2   LEAVING CERTIFICATE EXAMINATION CANDIDATES BY SUBJECT 2003 (CONTD).

	GENDER BALANCE		NUMBERS		
	MALE	FEMALE	MALE	FEMALE	ALL STUDENTS
Physics & Chemistry*	67.4%	32.6%	629	304	933
Agricultural Economics*	70.9%	29.1%	83	34	117
Ancient Greek**	71.4%	28.6%	10	4	14
Physics	75.4%	24.6%	6,637	2,169	8,806
Agricultural Science	75.5%	24.5%	2,244	728	2,972
Applied Mathematics	78.8%	21.2%	1,098	296	1,394
Construction Studies	93.8%	6.2%	8,342	556	8,898
Technical Drawing	94.1%	5.9%	6,086	385	6,471
Engineering	95.3%	4.7%	4,757	232	4,989
Danish***	100.0%	0.0%	2	0	2
Finnish***	100.0%	0.0%	1	0	1

NOTE: * = Less than 1,000 candidates; ** = Less than 100 candidates; *** Less than 10 candidates.

Data Source: Department of Education & Science, Tuarascáil Staitistiúil (Annual Statistical Report, 2002/2003).

TABLE 5.3 LEAVING CERTIFICATE EXAMINATION CANDIDATES BY SUBJECT 1993

	GENDER BALANCE		NUMBERS		
	MALE	FEMALE	MALE	FEMALE	ALL STUDENTS
Home Economics (General)*	5.4%	94.6%	39	685	724
Home Economics (S&S)	14.4%	85.6%	2,751	16,386	19,137
Music	17.9%	82.1%	208	953	1,161
Spanish	32.4%	67.6%	411	857	1,268
Biology	33.3%	66.7%	8,849	17,694	26,543
German	38.6%	61.4%	3,026	4,816	7,842
Art	38.7%	61.3%	4,115	6,522	10,637
French	39.1%	60.9%	13,265	20,702	33,967
Italian*	41.1%	58.9%	46	66	112
Irish	46.3%	53.7%	22,732	26,403	49,135
Business Studies	46.3%	53.7%	10,407	12,050	22,457
Accounting	46.7%	53.3%	6,542	7,470	14,012
English	48.8%	51.2%	27,502	28,853	56,355
Mathematics	49.0%	51.0%	27,585	28,737	56,322
Geography	55.6%	44.4%	12,636	10,075	22,711
Chemistry	55.8%	44.2%	4,191	3,320	7,511
History	56.7%	43.3%	8,229	6,278	14,507
Latin*	63.9%	36.1%	168	95	263
Economic History	66.3%	33.7%	691	352	1,043
Classical Studies*	67.1%	32.9%	289	142	431
Economics	67.1%	32.9%	4,441	2,175	6,616
Physics & Chemistry	73.0%	27.0%	1,160	430	1,590
Ancient Greek***	75.0%	25.0%	6	2	8
Physics	75.9%	24.1%	8,409	2,665	11,074
Hebrew***	83.3%	16.7%	5	1	6
Applied Mathematics	85.7%	14.3%	1,087	181	1,268
Agricultural Science	87.4%	12.6%	2,033	293	2,326
Agricultural Economics*	91.8%	8.2%	167	15	182
Technical Drawing	95.9%	4.1%	8,009	341	8,350
Engineering	97.3%	2.7%	4,877	134	5,011
Construction Studies	97.4%	2.6%	6,086	160	6,246

NOTE: * = Less than 1,000 candidates; ** = Less than 100 candidates; *** Less than 10 candidates.
Data Source: Department of Education & Science, Tuarascáil Staitistiúil (Annual Statistical Report, 1992/1993).

TABLE 5.4 PROPORTIONS OF EXAMINATION CANDIDATES TAKING HIGHER LEVEL PAPERS: LEAVING CERTIFICATE 2003

	RATIO: FEMALE/MALE	% TAKING HIGHER LEVEL			NUMBERS TAKING HIGHER LEVEL		
		MALE	FEMALE	ALL STUDENTS	MALE	FEMALE	ALL STUDENTS
Irish	1.69	22.3%	37.5%	30.3%	5,235	9,867	15,102
Italian*	1.40	45.8%	63.9%	57.5%	27	69	96
Physics	1.24	66.2%	82.2%	70.1%	4,392	1,783	6,175
English	1.23	54.1%	66.5%	60.6%	13,852	18,524	32,376
Physics & Chemistry	1.22	68.5%	83.9%	73.5%	431	255	686
German	1.21	52.2%	63.0%	58.4%	1,941	3,133	5,074
French	1.21	41.3%	49.8%	46.3%	5,474	9,580	15,054
Biology	1.19	53.7%	64.1%	60.8%	3,849	9,934	13,783
Technical Drawing	1.18	51.9%	61.3%	52.4%	3,156	236	3,392
Spanish	1.18	52.6%	61.9%	58.5%	296	612	908
Art	1.17	64.2%	75.1%	71.2%	2,285	4,727	7,012
Home Economics (S&S)	1.15	62.6%	71.8%	70.5%	1,548	11,186	12,734
History	1.12	58.7%	66.1%	61.9%	3,933	3,401	7,334
Chemistry	1.12	80.5%	89.9%	85.6%	2,483	3,248	5,731
Agricultural Science	1.08	67.1%	72.7%	68.4%	1,505	529	2,034
Geography	1.08	72.3%	78.4%	75.2%	10,918	10,859	21,777
Latin*	1.06	93.9%	100.0%	96.6%	62	51	113
Economics	1.06	75.8%	80.5%	77.5%	2,328	1,425	3,753
Applied Mathematics	1.06	91.2%	96.3%	92.3%	1,001	285	1,286

Continued

TABLE 5.4 PROPORTIONS OF EXAMINATION CANDIDATES TAKING HIGHER LEVEL PAPERS: LEAVING CERTIFICATE 2003 (CONT'D)

	RATIO: FEMALE/MALE	% TAKING HIGHER LEVEL			NUMBERS TAKING HIGHER LEVEL		
		MALE	FEMALE	ALL STUDENTS	MALE	FEMALE	ALL STUDENTS
Business Studies	1.04	66.6%	69.4%	68.1%	7,045	8,982	16,027
Agricultural Economics*	1.02	97.6%	100.0%	98.3%	81	34	115
Economic History*	1.01	92.8%	94.0%	93.2%	193	109	302
Classical Studies*	1.01	90.1%	90.6%	90.3%	438	347	785
Music	1.00	89.5%	89.7%	89.7%	796	2,733	3,529
Ancient Greek**	1.00	100.0%	100.0%	100.0%	10	4	14
Dutch**	1.00	100.0%	100.0%	100.0%	9	15	24
Portuguese***	1.00	100.0%	100.0%	100.0%	3	6	9
Modern Greek***	1.00	100.0%	100.0%	100.0%	3	4	7
Swedish***	1.00	100.0%	100.0%	100.0%	4	4	8
Japanese***	1.00	100.0%	100.0%	100.0%	4	4	8
Russian**	0.97	96.3%	93.5%	94.8%	26	29	55
Accounting	0.95	71.9%	68.4%	70.1%	2,290	2,404	4,694
Construction Studies	0.94	74.1%	69.6%	73.8%	6,182	387	6,569
Engineering	0.90	70.9%	63.8%	70.6%	3,372	148	3,520
Arabic*	0.87	96.4%	84.3%	91.8%	80	43	123
Mathematics	0.78	19.6%	15.3%	17.4%	5,150	4,303	9,453
Home Economics (General)**	0.52	71.4%	37.3%	41.4%	5	19	24

NOTE: * = Less than 1,000 candidates; ** = Less than 100 candidates; *** Less than 10 candidates.
Data Source: Department of Education & Science. Tuarascáil Statitistiúil (Annual Statistical Report. 2002/2003).

TABLE 5.5 PROPORTIONS OF EXAMINATION CANDIDATES TAKING HIGHER LEVEL PAPERS: LEAVING CERTIFICATE 1993

	RATIO: FEMALE/MALE	% TAKING HIGHER LEVEL			NUMBERS TAKING HIGHER LEVEL		
		MALE	FEMALE	ALL STUDENTS	MALE	FEMALE	ALL STUDENTS
Irish	1.50	19.6%	29.4%	24.9%	4,446	7,767	12,213
Physics	1.33	60.0%	80.1%	64.8%	5,046	2,134	7,180
Italian*	1.29	60.9%	78.8%	71.4%	28	52	80
Physics & Chemistry	1.24	61.8%	76.7%	65.8%	717	330	1,047
Home Economics (General)*	1.24	30.8%	38.1%	37.7%	12	261	273
German	1.22	60.0%	73.4%	68.3%	1,817	3,537	5,354
English	1.21	45.2%	54.8%	50.1%	12,438	15,799	28,237
Home Economics(S & S)	1.18	62.1%	73.2%	71.6%	1,709	11,990	13,699
Biology	1.17	53.2%	62.3%	59.3%	4,707	11,026	15,733
Chemistry	1.13	74.0%	83.7%	78.3%	3,100	2,780	5,880
Art	1.13	57.2%	64.6%	61.7%	2,355	4,212	6,567
History	1.11	55.1%	61.4%	57.9%	4,538	3,856	8,394
Agricultural Economics*	1.11	71.9%	80.0%	72.5%	120	12	132
Technical Drawing	1.07	39.6%	42.2%	39.7%	3,169	144	3,313
Agricultural Science	1.05	67.5%	71.0%	67.9%	1,372	208	1,580
French	1.05	46.2%	48.5%	47.6%	6,129	10,047	16,176
Geography	1.03	65.2%	66.9%	65.9%	8,238	6,736	14,974

Continued

TABLE 5.5 PROPORTIONS OF EXAMINATION CANDIDATES TAKING HIGHER LEVEL PAPERS: LEAVING CERTIFICATE 1993 (CONT'D)

	RATIO: FEMALE/MALE	% TAKING HIGHER LEVEL			NUMBERS TAKING HIGHER LEVEL		
		MALE	FEMALE	ALL STUDENTS	MALE	FEMALE	ALL STUDENTS
Economic History	1.02	95.1%	97.4%	95.9%	657	343	1,000
Economics	1.01	65.4%	65.9%	65.5%	2,903	1,433	4,336
Classical Studies*	1.00	85.8%	85.9%	85.8%	248	122	370
Ancient Greek***	1.00	100.0%	100.0%	100.0%	6	2	8
Latin*	0.98	97.6%	95.8%	97.0%	164	91	255
Business Studies	0.98	56.7%	55.5%	56.0%	5,900	6,686	12,586
Applied Mathematics	0.97	81.2%	79.0%	80.9%	883	143	1,026
Spanish*	0.95	61.6%	58.3%	59.4%	253	500	753
Music*	0.93	82.7%	76.8%	77.9%	172	732	904
Engineering	0.81	61.7%	50.0%	61.4%	3,011	67	3,078
Accounting	0.81	67.1%	54.0%	60.1%	4,388	4,036	8,424
Construction Studies	0.76	61.3%	46.9%	60.9%	3,730	75	3,805
Mathematics	0.56	14.3%	8.0%	11.1%	3,942	2,298	6,240
Hebrew***	0.00	80.0%	0.0%	66.7%	4	0	4

NOTE: * = Less than 1,000 candidates; ** = Less than 100 candidates; *** = Less than 10 candidates.
Data Source: Department of Education & Science, Tuarascáil Statistiúil (Annual Statistical Reports 1992/1993).

TABLE 5.6 SUMMARY OF HIGH PERFORMANCE IN THE LEAVING CERTIFICATE, 1991 TO 2003

| YEAR | HIGH PERFORMANCE 6 'C'S AT HIGHER LEVEL | | | | VERY HIGH PERFORMANCE 6 'C'S AT HIGHER LEVEL & 3+ 'A'S | | | |
	MALE	FEMALE	ALL STUDENTS	RATIO: FEMALE/MALE	MALE	FEMALE	ALL STUDENTS	RATIO: FEMALE/MALE
1991	8.5%	10.0%	9.3%	1.18	1.4%	1.5%	1.4%	1.09
1992	8.6%	11.2%	9.9%	1.30	1.6%	1.4%	1.5%	0.91
1993	9.8%	12.8%	11.3%	1.31	1.8%	1.9%	1.8%	1.02
1994	10.5%	14.6%	12.6%	1.40	2.3%	2.5%	2.4%	1.06
1995	11.5%	16.1%	13.8%	1.40	2.3%	3.0%	2.7%	1.27
1996	12.4%	17.3%	14.9%	1.39	2.7%	3.2%	3.0%	1.16
1997	12.3%	18.1%	15.3%	1.47	2.8%	3.7%	3.2%	1.33
1998	13.3%	19.6%	16.6%	1.47	3.2%	4.4%	3.8%	1.35
1999	14.0%	20.3%	17.3%	1.45	3.7%	5.0%	4.4%	1.36
2000	13.6%	20.2%	17.1%	1.48	3.4%	5.2%	4.3%	1.52
2001	13.7%	21.4%	17.8%	1.56	4.2%	5.9%	5.1%	1.42
2002	14.1%	22.2%	18.3%	1.57	3.8%	6.1%	5.0%	1.60
2003	15.2%	22.4%	18.9%	1.48	4.7%	6.5%	5.6%	1.39

Data Source: Department of Education & Science, Tuarascáil Staitistiúil (Annual Statistical Reports, various years).

TABLE 5.7 LOW PERFORMANCE IN THE LEAVING CERTIFICATE, 1991 TO 2003

YEAR	< 5 'D'S AT ANY LEVEL			
	MALE	FEMALE	ALL STUDENTS	RATIO: FEMALE/MALE
1991	15.8%	11.8%	13.7%	0.74
1992	12.7%	9.5%	11.0%	0.75
1993	10.9%	8.0%	9.4%	0.73
1994	13.2%	8.5%	10.8%	0.64
1995	14.2%	9.6%	11.8%	0.67
1996	10.4%	6.6%	8.5%	0.63
1997	9.7%	6.8%	8.2%	0.71
1998	9.9%	7.5%	8.6%	0.76
1999	8.9%	6.2%	7.5%	0.70
2000	7.6%	5.2%	6.4%	0.69
2001	7.6%	5.7%	6.6%	0.75
2002	7.1%	5.1%	6.1%	0.71
2003	6.2%	4.3%	5.2%	0.70

Data Source: Department of Education & Science, Tuarascáil Staitistiúil (Annual Statistical Reports, various years).

TABLE 5.8 OVERVIEW OF PERFORMANCE IN THE LEAVING CERTIFICATE EXAMS, 1993 & 2003

	2003			1993		
	MALE	FEMALE	ALL STUDENTS	MALE	FEMALE	ALL STUDENTS
< 5 'D' at any level	6.2%	4.3%	5.2%	10.9%	8.0%	9.4%
5 'D's at any level & < 2 'C's at higher level	37.5%	32.5%	34.9%	43.7%	41.5%	42.6%
6 'D's at any level & 2 to 4 'C's at higher level	23.3%	19.7%	21.4%	21.5%	20.7%	21.1%
6 'D's at any level & 4 to 6 'C's at higher level	17.8%	21.1%	19.5%	14.1%	17.0%	15.6%
At least 6 'C's at higher level	15.2%	22.4%	18.9%	9.8%	12.8%	11.3%
TOTAL	100%	100%	100%	100%	100%	100%

Data Source: Department of Education & Science, Tuarascáil Staitistiúil (Annual Statistical Reports, 1992/1993 & 2002/2003).

TABLE 5.9 LEAVING CERTIFICATE RESULTS NOMINAL POINTS SCORE, 2005

POINTS	NUMBERS			GENDER BALANCE			CUMULATIVE PERCENT		
	MALE	FEMALE	PERSONS	MALE	FEMALE	PERSONS	MALE	FEMALE	PERSONS
600	64	94	158	0.3%	0.3%	0.3%	0.3%	0.3%	0.3%
550-599	444	744	1,188	1.7%	2.6%	2.2%	2.0%	2.9%	2.5%
500-549	1,107	1,855	2,962	4.3%	6.5%	5.5%	6.3%	9.4%	8.0%
450-499	1,871	3,075	4,946	7.3%	10.8%	9.1%	13.7%	20.2%	17.1%
400-449	2,632	3,747	6,379	10.3%	13.1%	11.8%	24.0%	33.4%	28.9%
350-399	3,114	3,823	6,937	12.2%	13.4%	12.8%	36.2%	46.8%	41.8%
300-349	3,352	3,436	6,788	13.1%	12.0%	12.6%	49.3%	58.8%	54.3%
250-299	2,859	2,722	5,581	11.2%	9.5%	10.3%	60.5%	68.4%	64.6%
200-249	2,556	2,206	4,762	10.0%	7.7%	8.8%	70.5%	76.1%	73.4%
150-199	2,260	2,015	4,275	8.9%	7.1%	7.9%	79.3%	83.2%	81.4%
100-149	2,034	1,757	3,791	8.0%	6.2%	7.0%	87.3%	89.3%	88.4%
<100	3,242	3,047	6,289	12.7%	10.7%	11.6%	100.0%	100.0%	100.0%
Total	25,535	28,521	54,056	100%	100%	100%			

Data Source: Seán McDonagh and Vivienne Patterson, Discipline Choices and Trends for High Points CAO Acceptors, 2005, p.3 (data originating from the Central Applications Office).

TABLE 5.10 TRENDS IN THE GENDER DIFFERENCE IN LEAVING CERTIFICATE EXAM PERFORMANCE, 1990-2002

The figures below are the percentage of female candidates obtaining higher level honours minus the percentage of male candidates obtaining honours. Figures above 0% indicate that a higher proportion of females obtained honours and figures below 0% indicate that a higher proportion of males obtained honours in the particular subject.

	1990	1991	1992	1993	1994	1995	1996	1997	1998	1999	2000	2001	2002
Mathematics	-5.4%	-5.0%	-4.8%	-3.7%	-4.1%	-3.6%	-2.2%	-2.2%	-2.7%	-3.1%	-2.4%	-2.3%	-2.5%
English	7.4%	6.8%	8.6%	10.2%	12.2%	10.3%	11.3%	12.1%	11.5%	11.5%	11.4%	13.4%	13.9%
Irish	8.1%	8.2%	8.9%	9.0%	10.9%	12.5%	11.5%	12.6%	13.1%	13.2%	13.5%	14.0%	13.4%
French	2.5%	4.6%	4.5%	6.3%	7.1%	8.3%	6.7%	8.2%	8.0%	8.0%	8.2%	9.7%	9.7%
Geography	-0.6%	4.9%	4.8%	5.6%	8.9%	5.8%	8.0%	8.0%	7.3%	5.9%	8.2%	7.1%	8.6%
Business Studies	-4.9%	-1.2%	-3.5%	-3.8%	0.7%	0.9%	-1.0%	0.2%	-0.1%	4.2%	3.5%	4.2%	4.9%
Biology	3.9%	4.1%	4.1%	5.0%	7.3%	5.7%	8.6%	7.8%	4.8%	7.0%	7.3%	6.8%	8.4%
Home Economics (S&S)	22.0%	22.4%	21.2%	19.4%	17.9%	18.5%	15.9%	13.2%	11.2%	15.2%	12.4%	17.0%	15.7%
TOP 8 AVERAGE	**4.1%**	**5.6%**	**5.5%**	**6.0%**	**7.6%**	**7.3%**	**7.3%**	**7.5%**	**6.6%**	**7.7%**	**7.8%**	**8.7%**	**9.0%**

Data Source: Department of Education & Science, Tuarascáil Staitistiúil (Annual Statistical Reports, various years).

TABLE 5.11 AVERAGE GENDER DIFFERENCE IN THE OVERALL PERCENTAGES OBTAINING GRADE C OR HIGHER BY SUBJECT (FEMALES MINUS MALES)

	1990-1992	2000-2002
Physics & Chemistry	20.3%	27.4%
Physics	11.7%	19.0%
German	16.5%	16.0%
Art	5.6%	15.1%
Home Economics (S&S)	21.9%	15.1%
Irish	8.4%	13.6%
English	7.6%	12.9%
Chemistry	2.2%	11.4%
Italian	19.2%	9.8%
French	3.9%	9.2%
History	4.1%	8.9%
Technical Drawing	0.3%	8.5%
Geography	3.0%	8.0%
Spanish	1.0%	7.5%
Biology	4.0%	7.5%
Classical Studies*	19.5%	6.9%
Applied Mathematics	-9.1%	4.8%
Business Organisation	-3.2%	4.2%
Agricultural Economics	20.6%	3.3%
Economics	-0.9%	2.7%
Music	3.3%	1.0%
Agricultural Science	-3.8%	0.8%
Accounting	-11.1%	-1.7%
Mathematics	-5.1%	-2.4%
Economic History	1.8%	-2.7%
Engineering	-11.3%	-7.4%
Construction Studies	-10.7%	-8.2%
Home Economics(Gen)**	9.5%	-14.6%

Data Source: Department of Education & Science, Tuarascáil Staitistiúil (Annual Statistical Reports, various years).

TABLE 5.12a IRISH - HISTORICAL TIME-SERIES

	1932	1935	1941	1946	1952	1957	1961	1966	1968	1975	1980	1983
OVERALL NUMBER OF LEAVING CERTIFICATE CANDIDATES TAKING THE SUBJECT												
Male	987	1,325	1,800	2,001	2,950	3,482	4,503	6,221	7,097	12,510	14,345	17,480
Female	595	840	1,327	1,707	2,362	3,169	4,151	6,205	7,417	15,124	19,384	22,199
PERCENTAGES TAKING THE SUBJECT AT HIGHER LEVEL												
Male	62.5%	70.3%	80.9%	51.6%	62.4%	58.9%	54.1%	51.7%	48.7%	30.3%	25.7%	21.8%
Female	76.5%	82.4%	89.9%	69.9%	73.4%	67.6%	63.6%	56.5%	50.7%	31.4%	29.2%	28.6%
PERCENTAGE OF HIGHER LEVEL CANDIDATES OBTAINING GRADE 'C' OR ABOVE												
Male	78.1%	78.2%	74.9%	52.4%	67.7%	58.6%	64.8%	61.7%	51.6%	59.8%	64.6%	61.4%
Female	57.6%	78.0%	78.4%	50.7%	70.9%	64.4%	71.4%	67.0%	66.5%	65.6%	76.8%	68.2%
CANDIDATES OBTAINING GRADE 'C' OR ABOVE AT HIGHER LEVEL AS A PERCENTAGE OF ALL CANDIDATES												
Male	48.8%	54.9%	60.6%	27.1%	42.2%	34.5%	35.1%	31.9%	25.1%	18.1%	16.6%	13.4%
Female	44.0%	64.3%	70.5%	35.4%	52.0%	43.5%	45.4%	37.9%	33.7%	20.6%	22.4%	19.5%

TABLE 5.12b ENGLISH - HISTORICAL TIME-SERIES

	1932	1935	1941	1946	1952	1957	1961	1966	1968	1975	1980	1983
OVERALL NUMBER OF LEAVING CERTIFICATE CANDIDATES TAKING THE SUBJECT												
Male	1,054	1,323	1,794	1,992	2,944	3,484	4,484	6,256	7,158	13,054	15,800	19,075
Female	616	839	1,326	1,703	2,358	3,168	4,147	6,215	7,469	15,504	20,556	23,649
PERCENTAGES TAKING THE SUBJECT AT HIGHER LEVEL												
Male	64.3%	98.8%	98.6%	57.2%	65.1%	66.2%	58.4%	62.7%	63.4%	39.3%	47.3%	44.5%
Female	70.3%	96.9%	97.7%	73.7%	76.3%	76.2%	70.9%	69.3%	69.0%	41.2%	45.9%	46.1%
PERCENTAGE OF HIGHER LEVEL CANDIDATES OBTAINING GRADE 'C' OR ABOVE												
Male	70.8%	62.8%	61.1%	55.4%	34.1%	47.1%	38.3%	38.6%	41.4%	46.8%	44.3%	50.2%
Female	76.0%	59.9%	56.0%	48.8%	35.7%	33.9%	39.2%	41.6%	42.4%	55.8%	53.3%	58.1%
CANDIDATES OBTAINING GRADE 'C' OR ABOVE AT HIGHER LEVEL AS A PERCENTAGE OF ALL CANDIDATES												
Male	45.5%	62.0%	60.2%	31.7%	22.2%	31.2%	22.3%	24.2%	26.3%	18.4%	20.9%	22.4%
Female	53.4%	58.0%	54.7%	36.0%	27.3%	25.8%	27.8%	28.8%	29.3%	23.0%	24.5%	26.8%

TABLE 5.12c   MATHEMATICS - HISTORICAL TIME-SERIES

	1932	1935	1941	1946	1952	1957	1961	1966	1968	1975	1980	1983
OVERALL NUMBER OF LEAVING CERTIFICATE CANDIDATES TAKING THE SUBJECT												
Male	989	1,285	1,767	1,966	2,948	3,429	4,433	5,836	7,143	13,084	15,603	19,478
Female	494	700	1,134	1,468	2,046	2,642	3,150	4,177	5,308	13,265	19,227	23,282
PERCENTAGES TAKING THE SUBJECT AT HIGHER LEVEL												
Male	21.3%	28.9%	25.7%	23.0%	23.9%	25.9%	27.4%	34.9%	26.8%	18.2%	15.8%	17.5%
Female	3.0%	4.3%	5.0%	1.6%	1.0%	0.7%	1.8%	4.1%	3.0%	4.2%	4.4%	6.1%
PERCENTAGE OF HIGHER LEVEL CANDIDATES OBTAINING GRADE 'C' OR ABOVE												
Male	80.1%	34.0%	44.9%	54.6%	69.2%	38.5%	49.6%	48.2%	47.8%	59.3%	75.2%	62.2%
Female	40.0%	26.7%	40.4%	41.7%	81.0%	33.3%	46.4%	36.0%	39.1%	58.3%	80.4%	67.9%
CANDIDATES OBTAINING GRADE 'C' OR ABOVE AT HIGHER LEVEL AS A PERCENTAGE OF ALL CANDIDATES												
Male	17.1%	9.8%	11.5%	12.6%	16.5%	10.0%	13.6%	16.8%	12.8%	10.8%	11.9%	10.9%
Female	1.2%	1.1%	2.0%	0.7%	0.8%	0.2%	0.8%	1.5%	1.2%	2.5%	3.5%	4.1%

TABLE 5.12d HISTORY - HISTORICAL TIME-SERIES

	1932	1935	1941	1946	1952	1957	1961	1966	1968	1975	1980	1983
OVERALL NUMBER OF LEAVING CERTIFICATE CANDIDATES TAKING THE SUBJECT												
Male	854	1,158	1,485	1,436	2,303	2,514	3,492	3,663	3,672	5,827	5,958	7471
Female	548	777	1,245	1,506	1,975	2,479	3,281	4,133	3,566	5,949	6,997	7,993
PERCENTAGES TAKING THE SUBJECT AT HIGHER LEVEL												
Male	62.4%	73.7%	76.6%	53.3%	59.3%	56.0%	46.6%	62.7%	65.7%	53.3%	53.3%	53.5%
Female	67.5%	70.7%	85.1%	76.0%	64.6%	66.5%	63.2%	68.4%	72.3%	47.0%	52.7%	50.3%
PERCENTAGE OF HIGHER LEVEL CANDIDATES OBTAINING GRADE 'C' OR ABOVE												
Male	38.1%	45.9%	76.9%	34.7%	26.8%	26.0%	33.8%	32.1%	44.7%	53.3%	50.8%	49.7%
Female	17.8%	62.1%	76.0%	37.9%	34.9%	34.3%	27.4%	36.7%	44.1%	54.3%	57.2%	48.2%
CANDIDATES OBTAINING GRADE 'C' OR ABOVE AT HIGHER LEVEL AS A PERCENTAGE OF ALL CANDIDATES												
Male	23.8%	33.9%	58.9%	18.5%	15.9%	14.6%	15.8%	20.1%	29.4%	28.4%	27.1%	26.6%
Female	12.0%	43.9%	64.6%	28.8%	22.5%	22.8%	17.3%	25.1%	31.9%	25.5%	30.1%	24.3%

TABLE 5.12e   PHYSICS - HISTORICAL TIME-SERIES

	1932	1935	1941	1946	1952	1957	1961	1966	1968	1975	1980	1983
OVERALL NUMBER OF LEAVING CERTIFICATE CANDIDATES TAKING THE SUBJECT												
Male	92	73	118	236	445	747	1,139	2,102	2,225	3,063	4,408	6,921
Female	2	0	0	0	10	12	30	90	130	373	694	1,357
PERCENTAGES TAKING THE SUBJECT AT HIGHER LEVEL												
Male	56.5%	89.0%	76.3%	66.5%	49.7%	58.1%	57.9%	58.3%	65.3%	55.3%	56.2%	53.6%
Female	100.0%	0.0%	0.0%	0.0%	40.0%	25.0%	63.3%	52.2%	70.0%	70.5%	70.6%	76.0%
PERCENTAGE OF HIGHER LEVEL CANDIDATES OBTAINING GRADE 'C' OR ABOVE												
Male	44.2%	23.1%	71.1%	18.5%	55.2%	47.0%	35.8%	42.3%	41.0%	52.4%	55.9%	62.6%
Female	50.0%	0.0%	0.0%	0.0%	50.0%	66.7%	10.5%	36.2%	45.1%	47.9%	44.7%	54.4%
CANDIDATES OBTAINING GRADE 'C' OR ABOVE AT HIGHER LEVEL AS A PERCENTAGE OF ALL CANDIDATES												
Male	25.0%	20.6%	54.2%	12.3%	27.4%	27.3%	20.7%	24.6%	26.7%	29.0%	31.4%	33.6%
Female	50.0%	0.0%	0.0%	0.0%	20.0%	16.7%	6.7%	18.9%	31.5%	33.8%	31.6%	41.3%

TABLE 5.13a IRISH

	1990	1991	1992	1993	1994	1995	1996	1997	1998	1999	2000	2001	2002
OVERALL NUMBER OF LEAVING CERTIFICATE CANDIDATES TAKING THE SUBJECT													
Male	21,040	21,197	21,979	22,732	23,767	24,703	23,240	25,256	26,842	26,411	25,537	23,806	22,965
Female	25,778	25,849	26,066	26,403	27,620	28,568	25,748	28,728	30,714	30,015	29,016	27,019	26,120
PERCENTAGES TAKING THE SUBJECT AT HIGHER LEVEL													
Male	20.3%	19.8%	18.2%	19.6%	21.3%	22.3%	21.4%	22.2%	23.5%	23.0%	23.2%	22.7%	22.3%
Female	27.7%	27.1%	27.1%	29.4%	32.6%	35.2%	34.2%	35.3%	37.2%	37.1%	38.0%	38.2%	37.4%
PERCENTAGE OF HIGHER LEVEL CANDIDATES OBTAINING GRADE 'C' OR ABOVE													
Male	63.9%	65.0%	68.3%	73.0%	69.9%	69.4%	79.2%	75.5%	77.3%	77.7%	76.0%	74.0%	80.5%
Female	76.1%	77.9%	78.7%	79.0%	79.2%	79.7%	84.2%	83.7%	85.4%	84.7%	82.8%	81.8%	85.5%
CANDIDATES OBTAINING GRADE 'C' OR ABOVE AT HIGHER LEVEL AS A PERCENTAGE OF ALL CANDIDATES													
Male	13.0%	12.9%	12.4%	14.3%	14.9%	15.5%	17.0%	16.7%	18.2%	17.9%	17.6%	16.8%	17.9%
Female	21.1%	21.1%	21.3%	23.2%	25.9%	28.0%	28.8%	29.6%	31.8%	31.4%	31.5%	31.2%	32.0%

TABLE 5.13b ENGLISH

	1990	1991	1992	1993	1994	1995	1996	1997	1998	1999	2000	2001	2002
OVERALL NUMBER OF LEAVING CERTIFICATE CANDIDATES TAKING THE SUBJECT													
Male	24,325	24,639	25,984	27,502	28,377	29,248	25,754	27,564	29,057	28,400	27,529	25,186	25,193
Female	27,442	27,463	27,937	28,853	29,963	31,074	27,135	30,506	32,247	31,404	30,287	28,097	27,804
PERCENTAGES TAKING THE SUBJECT AT HIGHER LEVEL													
Male	45.3%	46.3%	45.5%	45.2%	45.7%	46.9%	47.7%	46.2%	49.2%	49.5%	49.0%	52.4%	52.7%
Female	51.0%	52.1%	53.2%	54.8%	56.5%	58.7%	59.0%	58.6%	60.4%	60.7%	60.9%	64.6%	65.7%
PERCENTAGE OF HIGHER LEVEL CANDIDATES OBTAINING GRADE 'C' OR ABOVE													
Male	54.2%	56.0%	57.7%	58.8%	58.8%	59.1%	60.9%	59.1%	60.7%	62.4%	61.6%	71.5%	72.6%
Female	62.7%	62.9%	65.6%	67.3%	69.2%	64.8%	68.4%	67.2%	68.4%	69.8%	68.2%	78.8%	79.3%
CANDIDATES OBTAINING GRADE 'C' OR ABOVE AT HIGHER LEVEL AS A PERCENTAGE OF ALL CANDIDATES													
Male	24.6%	25.9%	26.2%	26.6%	26.8%	27.7%	29.0%	27.3%	29.9%	30.9%	30.2%	37.5%	38.2%
Female	32.0%	32.8%	34.9%	36.8%	39.1%	38.0%	40.4%	39.4%	41.3%	42.3%	41.6%	50.9%	52.1%

TABLE 5.13g FRENCH

	1990	1991	1992	1993	1994	1995	1996	1997	1998	1999	2000	2001	2002
OVERALL NUMBER OF LEAVING CERTIFICATE CANDIDATES TAKING THE SUBJECT													
Male	13,249	13,528	13,815	13,265	13,615	14,332	12,342	13,290	14,501	14,554	14,332	13,647	12,908
Female	21,354	21,282	20,891	20,702	20,869	21,943	19,068	21,059	22,584	22,317	21,642	20,171	19,208
PERCENTAGES TAKING THE SUBJECT AT HIGHER LEVEL													
Male	47.4%	47.1%	45.7%	46.2%	44.6%	45.2%	48.0%	44.3%	44.0%	44.7%	42.5%	42.5%	42.7%
Female	44.8%	46.2%	46.9%	48.5%	50.7%	51.4%	53.0%	49.4%	49.8%	51.3%	49.4%	50.8%	50.5%
PERCENTAGE OF HIGHER LEVEL CANDIDATES OBTAINING GRADE 'C' OR ABOVE													
Male	56.5%	55.7%	58.3%	58.9%	57.4%	58.3%	58.1%	64.4%	63.0%	63.9%	63.6%	64.3%	62.4%
Female	65.4%	66.6%	66.4%	69.1%	64.6%	67.4%	65.2%	74.3%	71.6%	71.1%	71.3%	72.8%	71.9%
CANDIDATES OBTAINING GRADE 'C' OR ABOVE AT HIGHER LEVEL AS A PERCENTAGE OF ALL CANDIDATES													
Male	26.8%	26.2%	26.7%	27.2%	25.6%	26.4%	27.9%	28.5%	27.7%	28.5%	27.1%	27.3%	26.6%
Female	29.3%	30.8%	31.1%	33.5%	32.8%	34.7%	34.6%	36.7%	35.7%	36.5%	35.2%	37.0%	36.3%

TABLE 5.13h GERMAN

	1990	1991	1992	1993	1994	1995	1996	1997	1998	1999	2000	2001	2002
OVERALL NUMBER OF LEAVING CERTIFICATE CANDIDATES TAKING THE SUBJECT													
Male	922	1,374	1,886	3,026	4,280	4,665	4,358	4,450	4,760	4,680	4,299	4,020	3,789
Female	2,298	2,853	3,450	4,816	6,619	6,765	5,677	6,357	6,612	6,148	5,941	5,359	4,933
PERCENTAGES TAKING THE SUBJECT AT HIGHER LEVEL													
Male	60.1%	64.1%	63.6%	60.0%	58.1%	59.2%	58.6%	57.5%	55.3%	57.3%	55.3%	55.4%	51.9%
Female	72.7%	74.4%	74.2%	73.4%	69.6%	72.1%	72.5%	70.5%	69.6%	68.8%	67.9%	68.1%	64.9%
PERCENTAGE OF HIGHER LEVEL CANDIDATES OBTAINING GRADE 'C' OR ABOVE													
Male	61.9%	66.5%	66.3%	60.9%	57.4%	59.3%	63.2%	72.0%	70.0%	68.8%	76.0%	69.7%	73.5%
Female	74.9%	79.4%	78.4%	75.5%	71.5%	76.2%	76.3%	82.2%	80.0%	80.7%	83.7%	80.5%	85.0%
CANDIDATES OBTAINING GRADE 'C' OR ABOVE AT HIGHER LEVEL AS A PERCENTAGE OF ALL CANDIDATES													
Male	37.2%	42.6%	42.2%	36.6%	33.3%	35.1%	37.0%	41.4%	38.7%	39.4%	42.1%	38.6%	38.1%
Female	54.4%	59.0%	58.1%	55.5%	49.8%	54.9%	55.3%	57.9%	55.7%	55.5%	56.8%	54.8%	55.2%

TABLE 5.13i SPANISH

	1990	1991	1992	1993	1994	1995	1996	1997	1998	1999	2000	2001	2002
OVERALL NUMBER OF LEAVING CERTIFICATE CANDIDATES TAKING THE SUBJECT													
Male	342	401	451	411	476	570	538	515	650	575	542	508	659
Female	724	810	885	857	865	1,007	765	792	1,024	984	881	975	1,043
PERCENTAGES TAKING THE SUBJECT AT HIGHER LEVEL													
Male	59.9%	56.1%	67.8%	61.6%	62.4%	54.2%	56.9%	48.2%	52.9%	61.7%	56.1%	55.7%	49.5%
Female	58.3%	58.5%	59.8%	58.3%	64.2%	64.9%	64.1%	65.5%	63.0%	66.3%	58.6%	60.3%	61.1%
PERCENTAGE OF HIGHER LEVEL CANDIDATES OBTAINING GRADE 'C' OR ABOVE													
Male	66.3%	77.8%	65.7%	76.3%	72.4%	67.6%	75.2%	69.4%	63.4%	65.4%	61.8%	74.6%	79.4%
Female	70.9%	77.0%	74.9%	72.4%	72.6%	75.5%	78.8%	72.8%	74.1%	79.8%	70.7%	80.3%	79.0%
CANDIDATES OBTAINING GRADE 'C' OR ABOVE AT HIGHER LEVEL AS A PERCENTAGE OF ALL CANDIDATES													
Male	39.8%	43.6%	44.6%	47.0%	45.2%	36.7%	42.8%	33.4%	33.5%	40.3%	34.7%	41.5%	39.3%
Female	41.3%	45.1%	44.7%	42.2%	46.6%	49.1%	50.5%	47.7%	46.7%	52.8%	41.4%	48.4%	48.2%

TABLE 5.13j ITALIAN

	1990	1991	1992	1993	1994	1995	1996	1997	1998	1999	2000	2001	2002
OVERALL NUMBER OF LEAVING CERTIFICATE CANDIDATES TAKING THE SUBJECT													
Male	40	19	29	46	51	50	69	59	54	78	67	51	64
Female	55	60	52	66	61	75	74	97	106	132	133	91	109
PERCENTAGES TAKING THE SUBJECT AT HIGHER LEVEL													
Male	70.0%	84.2%	51.7%	60.9%	78.4%	58.0%	65.2%	50.8%	66.7%	53.8%	56.7%	68.6%	56.3%
Female	83.6%	90.0%	86.5%	78.8%	88.5%	73.3%	70.3%	69.1%	60.4%	72.7%	71.4%	73.6%	72.5%
PERCENTAGE OF HIGHER LEVEL CANDIDATES OBTAINING GRADE 'C' OR ABOVE													
Male	53.6%	81.3%	73.3%	71.4%	65.0%	79.3%	75.6%	76.7%	61.1%	73.8%	92.1%	82.9%	80.6%
Female	63.0%	77.8%	91.1%	67.3%	79.6%	67.3%	84.6%	77.6%	76.6%	85.4%	86.3%	85.1%	82.3%
CANDIDATES OBTAINING GRADE 'C' OR ABOVE AT HIGHER LEVEL AS A PERCENTAGE OF ALL CANDIDATES													
Male	37.5%	68.4%	37.9%	43.5%	51.0%	46.0%	49.3%	39.0%	40.7%	39.7%	52.2%	56.9%	45.3%
Female	52.7%	70.0%	78.8%	53.0%	70.5%	49.3%	59.5%	53.6%	46.2%	62.1%	61.7%	62.6%	59.6%

TABLE 5.13k PHYSICS

	1990	1991	1992	1993	1994	1995	1996	1997	1998	1999	2000	2001	2002
OVERALL NUMBER OF LEAVING CERTIFICATE CANDIDATES TAKING THE SUBJECT													
Male	8,055	8,148	8,252	8,409	8,462	8,283	6,817	6,792	7,120	6,822	6,480	6,312	6,505
Female	2,460	2,563	2,772	2,665	2,771	2,808	2,376	2,431	2,539	2,290	2,108	2,099	2,146
PERCENTAGES TAKING THE SUBJECT AT HIGHER LEVEL													
Male	61.9%	60.1%	61.2%	60.0%	61.6%	64.9%	65.7%	64.1%	64.8%	64.6%	63.6%	62.5%	64.8%
Female	77.6%	77.3%	79.1%	80.1%	81.2%	82.6%	82.1%	82.3%	82.2%	80.8%	81.9%	80.8%	82.4%
PERCENTAGE OF HIGHER LEVEL CANDIDATES OBTAINING GRADE 'C' OR ABOVE													
Male	66.3%	62.8%	60.3%	65.8%	59.6%	63.5%	61.1%	62.5%	61.9%	68.4%	70.9%	63.1%	63.9%
Female	67.6%	62.5%	63.0%	68.9%	61.2%	68.7%	62.6%	65.1%	66.4%	74.2%	75.8%	72.5%	75.6%
CANDIDATES OBTAINING GRADE 'C' OR ABOVE AT HIGHER LEVEL AS A PERCENTAGE OF ALL CANDIDATES													
Male	41.0%	37.8%	36.9%	39.5%	36.7%	41.2%	40.2%	40.1%	40.1%	44.2%	45.1%	39.5%	41.4%
Female	52.4%	48.3%	49.9%	55.2%	49.7%	56.7%	51.3%	53.6%	54.5%	60.0%	62.0%	58.6%	62.3%

TABLE 5.13I CHEMISTRY

	1990	1991	1992	1993	1994	1995	1996	1997	1998	1999	2000	2001	2002
OVERALL NUMBER OF LEAVING CERTIFICATE CANDIDATES TAKING THE SUBJECT													
Male	4,900	4,661	4,317	4,191	4,209	4,412	3,783	3,446	3,592	3,324	3,165	2,924	3,017
Female	3,806	3,502	3,224	3,320	3,743	4,050	3,533	3,524	3,733	3,639	3,546	3,431	3,480
PERCENTAGES TAKING THE SUBJECT AT HIGHER LEVEL													
Male	70.7%	70.1%	73.0%	74.0%	75.1%	76.0%	76.5%	78.2%	78.9%	79.4%	77.9%	78.1%	80.1%
Female	79.1%	78.4%	81.9%	83.7%	82.6%	83.6%	85.6%	85.5%	86.2%	87.1%	86.5%	85.4%	90.4%
PERCENTAGE OF HIGHER LEVEL CANDIDATES OBTAINING GRADE 'C' OR ABOVE													
Male	66.5%	65.4%	63.7%	66.7%	64.2%	62.1%	63.9%	66.0%	67.1%	67.0%	69.4%	71.4%	74.2%
Female	58.7%	61.3%	62.9%	68.5%	62.7%	63.2%	64.2%	68.3%	72.4%	71.1%	75.4%	77.9%	79.3%
CANDIDATES OBTAINING GRADE 'C' OR ABOVE AT HIGHER LEVEL AS A PERCENTAGE OF ALL CANDIDATES													
Male	47.0%	45.8%	46.5%	49.4%	48.2%	47.1%	48.9%	51.6%	52.9%	53.2%	54.0%	55.8%	59.4%
Female	46.5%	48.1%	51.5%	57.3%	51.7%	52.9%	55.0%	58.4%	62.4%	62.0%	65.2%	66.5%	71.8%

TABLE 5.13m   PHYSICS & CHEMISTRY

	1990	1991	1992	1993	1994	1995	1996	1997	1998	1999	2000	2001	2002
OVERALL NUMBER OF LEAVING CERTIFICATE CANDIDATES TAKING THE SUBJECT													
Male	1,260	1,150	1,266	1,160	1,170	1,095	875	884	869	946	733	720	669
Female	563	489	468	430	474	436	363	339	371	424	320	304	300
PERCENTAGES TAKING THE SUBJECT AT HIGHER LEVEL													
Male	55.5%	62.1%	60.2%	61.8%	53.5%	59.6%	59.1%	62.0%	62.9%	63.5%	69.2%	68.1%	60.7%
Female	82.1%	82.0%	81.2%	76.7%	82.7%	82.1%	84.0%	85.3%	89.5%	84.2%	87.2%	87.2%	82.7%
PERCENTAGE OF HIGHER LEVEL CANDIDATES OBTAINING GRADE 'C' OR ABOVE													
Male	54.8%	52.9%	50.7%	47.3%	62.6%	57.0%	61.3%	65.3%	70.4%	58.4%	58.6%	59.6%	57.1%
Female	62.6%	63.6%	62.9%	61.2%	77.6%	79.9%	70.2%	82.0%	81.0%	81.0%	79.2%	74.3%	77.4%
CANDIDATES OBTAINING GRADE 'C' OR ABOVE AT HIGHER LEVEL AS A PERCENTAGE OF ALL CANDIDATES													
Male	30.4%	32.9%	30.5%	29.2%	33.5%	34.0%	36.2%	40.5%	44.3%	37.1%	40.5%	40.6%	34.7%
Female	51.3%	52.1%	51.1%	47.0%	64.1%	65.6%	59.0%	69.9%	72.5%	68.2%	69.1%	64.8%	64.0%

TABLE 5.13n BIOLOGY

	1990	1991	1992	1993	1994	1995	1996	1997	1998	1999	2000	2001	2002
OVERALL NUMBER OF LEAVING CERTIFICATE CANDIDATES TAKING THE SUBJECT													
Male	9,138	8,766	8,552	8,849	9,654	10,842	9,733	9,787	10,350	9,438	8,884	7,736	6,920
Female	17,942	17,496	17,191	17,694	19,121	20,617	17,959	19,245	20,263	19,312	17,776	16,324	15,144
PERCENTAGES TAKING THE SUBJECT AT HIGHER LEVEL													
Male	53.6%	51.6%	51.1%	53.2%	52.7%	55.0%	56.5%	55.3%	57.4%	55.5%	55.5%	55.5%	56.7%
Female	58.6%	59.1%	58.4%	62.3%	62.8%	64.4%	64.5%	63.0%	64.5%	62.6%	63.3%	63.0%	65.0%
PERCENTAGE OF HIGHER LEVEL CANDIDATES OBTAINING GRADE 'C' OR ABOVE													
Male	64.0%	62.8%	70.7%	58.8%	67.1%	61.3%	61.5%	63.5%	63.5%	68.1%	67.0%	67.0%	69.9%
Female	65.1%	61.7%	68.7%	58.3%	67.9%	61.1%	67.2%	68.0%	64.0%	71.4%	70.3%	69.9%	73.8%
CANDIDATES OBTAINING GRADE 'C' OR ABOVE AT HIGHER LEVEL AS A PERCENTAGE OF ALL CANDIDATES													
Male	34.3%	32.4%	36.1%	31.3%	35.4%	33.7%	34.8%	35.1%	36.5%	37.8%	37.2%	37.2%	39.7%
Female	38.2%	36.5%	40.2%	36.3%	42.6%	39.4%	43.3%	42.9%	41.3%	44.8%	44.5%	44.0%	48.0%

TABLE 5.13o AGRICULTURAL SCIENCE

	1990	1991	1992	1993	1994	1995	1996	1997	1998	1999	2000	2001	2002
OVERALL NUMBER OF LEAVING CERTIFICATE CANDIDATES TAKING THE SUBJECT													
Male	1,839	1,986	1,897	2,033	1,992	2,156	1,961	2,248	2,386	2,484	2,387	2,297	2,246
Female	298	310	278	293	206	296	278	363	461	515	583	618	644
PERCENTAGES TAKING THE SUBJECT AT HIGHER LEVEL													
Male	55.7%	57.6%	59.2%	56.7%	57.8%	58.2%	59.7%	57.3%	61.0%	70.5%	67.8%	66.8%	67.0%
Female	49.2%	51.1%	54.6%	55.5%	57.6%	58.0%	57.2%	57.2%	60.1%	71.1%	70.0%	68.5%	70.2%
PERCENTAGE OF HIGHER LEVEL CANDIDATES OBTAINING GRADE 'C' OR ABOVE													
Male	65.7%	61.8%	65.3%	63.1%	66.1%	74.0%	68.8%	71.4%	68.8%	68.6%	58.6%	64.3%	69.2%
Female	71.5%	63.9%	63.4%	61.1%	59.2%	74.8%	73.5%	73.6%	72.4%	67.5%	62.9%	60.8%	68.3%
CANDIDATES OBTAINING GRADE 'C' OR ABOVE AT HIGHER LEVEL AS A PERCENTAGE OF ALL CANDIDATES													
Male	37.6%	39.8%	43.0%	42.6%	44.0%	50.3%	51.3%	50.7%	50.5%	48.5%	44.3%	47.0%	49.3%
Female	34.6%	37.7%	36.7%	43.3%	45.1%	52.0%	55.8%	51.5%	57.9%	50.5%	50.3%	46.0%	46.9%

TABLE 5.13p BUSINESS ORGANISATION

	1990	1991	1992	1993	1994	1995	1996	1997	1998	1999	2000	2001	2002
OVERALL NUMBER OF LEAVING CERTIFICATE CANDIDATES TAKING THE SUBJECT													
Male	9,819	9,991	10,025	10,407	10,450	10,596	9,564	10,021	10,987	11,144	11,360	10,762	10,439
Female	12,254	12,530	12,477	12,050	12,322	11,905	10,589	11,813	13,068	13,439	13,899	13,477	13,166
PERCENTAGES TAKING THE SUBJECT AT HIGHER LEVEL													
Male	87.7%	80.4%	76.6%	85.8%	93.0%	87.3%	86.0%	86.1%	82.4%	84.3%	90.3%	89.0%	88.8%
Female	80.7%	87.9%	94.6%	85.9%	94.3%	94.0%	91.2%	89.1%	85.5%	89.5%	87.0%	90.0%	89.7%
PERCENTAGE OF HIGHER LEVEL CANDIDATES OBTAINING GRADE 'C' OR ABOVE													
Male	54.9%	54.1%	58.0%	64.3%	60.3%	64.6%	64.8%	65.3%	66.7%	65.0%	63.9%	66.1%	67.4%
Female	52.2%	58.5%	56.5%	58.9%	61.7%	66.5%	65.9%	65.7%	67.5%	70.4%	67.0%	70.6%	71.3%
CANDIDATES OBTAINING GRADE 'C' OR ABOVE AT HIGHER LEVEL AS A PERCENTAGE OF ALL CANDIDATES													
Male	30.6%	31.1%	34.3%	36.5%	34.9%	37.6%	38.7%	37.4%	40.7%	45.8%	43.3%	44.2%	45.1%
Female	25.7%	29.9%	30.9%	32.7%	35.5%	38.6%	37.7%	37.5%	40.6%	50.0%	46.9%	48.3%	50.1%

TABLE 5.13q ECONOMICS

	1990	1991	1992	1993	1994	1995	1996	1997	1998	1999	2000	2001	2002
OVERALL NUMBER OF LEAVING CERTIFICATE CANDIDATES TAKING THE SUBJECT													
Male	4,846	4,621	4,380	4,441	4,065	3,804	3,103	3,179	3,348	3,301	3,229	3,074	2,982
Female	2,481	2,452	2,180	2,175	1,921	2,024	1,634	1,820	2,046	1,899	1,898	1,863	1,745
PERCENTAGES TAKING THE SUBJECT AT HIGHER LEVEL													
Male	60.5%	62.7%	65.2%	65.4%	68.1%	69.3%	71.0%	72.6%	74.7%	73.8%	73.8%	74.0%	77.5%
Female	55.1%	58.8%	67.6%	65.9%	73.3%	72.5%	74.6%	75.2%	76.8%	78.7%	77.1%	77.5%	81.0%
PERCENTAGE OF HIGHER LEVEL CANDIDATES OBTAINING GRADE 'C' OR ABOVE													
Male	56.6%	54.9%	57.2%	58.7%	60.3%	63.1%	66.1%	69.9%	71.3%	69.2%	73.9%	72.5%	69.5%
Female	56.4%	57.9%	56.6%	62.2%	64.3%	64.4%	67.9%	68.5%	73.3%	69.6%	71.8%	74.6%	70.6%
CANDIDATES OBTAINING GRADE 'C' OR ABOVE AT HIGHER LEVEL AS A PERCENTAGE OF ALL CANDIDATES													
Male	34.3%	34.4%	37.3%	38.3%	41.1%	43.7%	46.9%	50.7%	53.2%	51.1%	54.6%	53.7%	53.9%
Female	31.0%	34.0%	38.3%	41.0%	47.1%	46.7%	50.7%	51.5%	56.3%	54.8%	55.3%	57.8%	57.2%

TABLE 5.13r ACCOUNTING

	1990	1991	1992	1993	1994	1995	1996	1997	1998	1999	2000	2001	2002
OVERALL NUMBER OF LEAVING CERTIFICATE CANDIDATES TAKING THE SUBJECT													
Male	7,490	6,894	6,676	6,542	5,691	5,376	4,484	4,333	4,674	4,336	4,124	3,401	3,287
Female	8,373	7,965	7,821	7,470	6,538	6,287	5,032	5,070	5,214	4,988	4,470	3,998	3,783
PERCENTAGES TAKING THE SUBJECT AT HIGHER LEVEL													
Male	66.1%	65.9%	67.9%	67.1%	67.8%	69.7%	71.8%	69.4%	69.0%	69.1%	67.7%	69.0%	68.7%
Female	52.6%	51.3%	53.5%	54.0%	57.2%	58.0%	60.7%	60.4%	63.2%	61.1%	64.3%	64.9%	64.7%
PERCENTAGE OF HIGHER LEVEL CANDIDATES OBTAINING GRADE 'C' OR ABOVE													
Male	63.9%	69.0%	64.5%	63.0%	65.9%	65.6%	71.5%	66.6%	64.5%	72.3%	72.2%	75.5%	74.5%
Female	64.4%	63.1%	59.9%	63.3%	64.8%	68.3%	72.2%	67.5%	67.9%	73.3%	74.8%	77.1%	76.0%
CANDIDATES OBTAINING GRADE 'C' OR ABOVE AT HIGHER LEVEL AS A PERCENTAGE OF ALL CANDIDATES													
Male	42.2%	45.4%	43.8%	42.2%	44.7%	45.7%	51.4%	46.2%	44.5%	50.0%	48.9%	52.1%	51.2%
Female	33.9%	32.3%	32.0%	34.2%	37.1%	39.7%	43.8%	40.8%	42.9%	44.8%	48.1%	50.0%	49.1%

TABLE 5.13s AGRICULTURAL ECONOMICS

	1990	1991	1992	1993	1994	1995	1996	1997	1998	1999	2000	2001	2002
OVERALL NUMBER OF LEAVING CERTIFICATE CANDIDATES TAKING THE SUBJECT													
Male	199	184	137	167	208	208	196	180	197	224	188	148	130
Female	30	22	24	15	40	72	103	82	83	103	132	84	57
PERCENTAGES TAKING THE SUBJECT AT HIGHER LEVEL													
Male	52.8%	52.2%	71.5%	71.9%	84.1%	71.6%	86.7%	88.3%	95.4%	89.3%	91.0%	91.9%	93.8%
Female	80.0%	72.7%	87.5%	80.0%	92.5%	91.7%	98.1%	100.0%	96.4%	99.0%	99.2%	98.8%	98.2%
PERCENTAGE OF HIGHER LEVEL CANDIDATES OBTAINING GRADE 'C' OR ABOVE													
Male	53.3%	55.2%	56.1%	64.2%	51.4%	72.5%	63.5%	77.4%	57.4%	83.5%	58.5%	52.9%	55.7%
Female	79.2%	62.5%	57.1%	75.0%	59.5%	59.1%	71.3%	75.6%	52.5%	78.4%	51.9%	51.8%	62.5%
CANDIDATES OBTAINING GRADE 'C' OR ABOVE AT HIGHER LEVEL AS A PERCENTAGE OF ALL CANDIDATES													
Male	28.1%	28.8%	40.1%	46.1%	43.3%	51.9%	55.1%	68.3%	54.8%	74.6%	53.2%	48.6%	52.3%
Female	63.3%	45.5%	50.0%	60.0%	55.0%	54.2%	69.9%	75.6%	50.6%	77.7%	51.5%	51.2%	61.4%

TABLE 5.13t HOME ECONOMICS (S&S)

	1990	1991	1992	1993	1994	1995	1996	1997	1998	1999	2000	2001	2002
OVERALL NUMBER OF LEAVING CERTIFICATE CANDIDATES TAKING THE SUBJECT													
Male	2,126	2,287	2,614	2,751	3,328	3,445	3,439	3,510	3,945	3,741	3,541	2,912	2,599
Female	15,170	15,434	15,723	16,386	17,147	18,253	16,775	18,752	20,236	19,216	18,175	16,493	15,748
PERCENTAGES TAKING THE SUBJECT AT HIGHER LEVEL													
Male	56.9%	57.1%	58.6%	62.1%	63.4%	65.5%	65.1%	60.7%	66.2%	66.1%	62.0%	62.4%	62.1%
Female	66.5%	70.6%	71.2%	73.2%	75.9%	76.8%	73.5%	71.0%	74.2%	73.9%	72.4%	74.5%	73.5%
PERCENTAGE OF HIGHER LEVEL CANDIDATES OBTAINING GRADE 'C' OR ABOVE													
Male	39.1%	42.4%	45.9%	50.5%	47.1%	50.4%	51.0%	53.5%	56.2%	49.8%	58.6%	52.1%	55.0%
Female	66.6%	66.0%	67.5%	69.4%	62.9%	67.1%	66.7%	64.3%	65.2%	65.2%	67.4%	66.5%	67.8%
CANDIDATES OBTAINING GRADE 'C' OR ABOVE AT HIGHER LEVEL AS A PERCENTAGE OF ALL CANDIDATES													
Male	22.2%	24.2%	26.9%	31.4%	29.9%	33.0%	33.2%	32.5%	37.2%	32.9%	36.3%	32.5%	34.1%
Female	44.3%	46.6%	48.1%	50.8%	47.8%	51.5%	49.1%	45.7%	48.4%	48.2%	48.8%	49.5%	49.9%

TABLE 5.13u CONSTRUCTION STUDIES

	1990	1991	1992	1993	1994	1995	1996	1997	1998	1999	2000	2001	2002
OVERALL NUMBER OF LEAVING CERTIFICATE CANDIDATES TAKING THE SUBJECT													
Male	4,236	4,721	5,364	6,086	6,553	7,073	6,596	7,813	8,129	8,145	8,168	7,887	7,993
Female	86	108	131	160	207	305	271	480	479	503	531	524	519
PERCENTAGES TAKING THE SUBJECT AT HIGHER LEVEL													
Male	53.0%	53.7%	59.4%	61.3%	65.8%	67.7%	67.4%	69.1%	71.4%	72.4%	74.7%	74.7%	73.3%
Female	50.0%	40.7%	53.4%	46.9%	52.7%	63.3%	60.1%	55.2%	66.4%	69.4%	67.0%	60.9%	64.5%
PERCENTAGE OF HIGHER LEVEL CANDIDATES OBTAINING GRADE 'C' OR ABOVE													
Male	84.4%	90.5%	90.2%	87.5%	87.7%	85.1%	85.5%	85.7%	86.0%	84.3%	86.4%	86.4%	82.8%
Female	81.4%	75.0%	81.4%	80.0%	84.4%	82.9%	81.0%	81.9%	79.6%	82.2%	86.0%	89.3%	82.4%
CANDIDATES OBTAINING GRADE 'C' OR ABOVE AT HIGHER LEVEL AS A PERCENTAGE OF ALL CANDIDATES													
Male	47.7%	48.6%	53.6%	53.6%	57.7%	57.7%	57.6%	59.3%	61.4%	61.0%	64.5%	64.5%	60.7%
Female	40.7%	30.6%	43.5%	37.5%	44.4%	52.5%	48.7%	45.2%	52.8%	57.1%	57.6%	54.4%	53.2%

TABLE 5.13v ENGINEERING

	1990	1991	1992	1993	1994	1995	1996	1997	1998	1999	2000	2001	2002
	OVERALL NUMBER OF LEAVING CERTIFICATE CANDIDATES TAKING THE SUBJECT												
Male	3,569	3,993	4,339	4,877	5,095	5,354	4,563	5,004	4,952	4,851	4,821	4,421	4,563
Female	80	97	57	134	176	189	162	192	194	216	190	211	183
	PERCENTAGES TAKING THE SUBJECT AT HIGHER LEVEL												
Male	52.1%	54.2%	59.3%	61.7%	61.9%	64.9%	62.7%	65.0%	63.2%	66.6%	70.3%	69.9%	66.8%
Female	35.0%	41.2%	49.1%	50.0%	45.5%	57.7%	53.7%	58.3%	58.8%	69.9%	61.1%	65.9%	61.7%
	PERCENTAGE OF HIGHER LEVEL CANDIDATES OBTAINING GRADE 'C' OR ABOVE												
Male	88.8%	77.3%	80.3%	75.6%	71.3%	71.2%	70.6%	65.2%	80.7%	78.8%	78.4%	78.5%	73.4%
Female	82.1%	75.0%	85.7%	77.6%	65.0%	63.3%	56.3%	61.6%	75.4%	70.2%	78.4%	72.7%	66.4%
	CANDIDATES OBTAINING GRADE 'C' OR ABOVE AT HIGHER LEVEL AS A PERCENTAGE OF ALL CANDIDATES												
Male	46.3%	41.9%	47.6%	46.7%	44.1%	46.2%	44.3%	42.4%	51.0%	52.5%	55.2%	54.8%	49.0%
Female	28.8%	30.9%	42.1%	38.8%	29.5%	36.5%	30.2%	35.9%	44.3%	49.1%	47.9%	47.9%	41.0%

TABLE 5.13w   TECHNICAL DRAWING

	1990	1991	1992	1993	1994	1995	1996	1997	1998	1999	2000	2001	2002
OVERALL NUMBER OF LEAVING CERTIFICATE CANDIDATES TAKING THE SUBJECT													
Male	6,786	7,071	7,313	8,009	8,100	7,913	6,858	7,179	7,049	7,094	6,369	5,992	5,691
Female	230	226	245	341	314	352	336	425	431	423	392	388	348
PERCENTAGES TAKING THE SUBJECT AT HIGHER LEVEL													
Male	36.2%	36.9%	40.1%	39.6%	42.0%	43.0%	42.6%	44.4%	45.3%	49.0%	48.8%	49.2%	50.9%
Female	37.0%	42.0%	47.3%	42.2%	47.5%	46.0%	53.0%	49.6%	54.3%	57.0%	61.0%	63.9%	61.5%
PERCENTAGE OF HIGHER LEVEL CANDIDATES OBTAINING GRADE 'C' OR ABOVE													
Male	59.4%	59.8%	62.5%	65.4%	62.7%	67.1%	71.5%	70.4%	71.4%	70.7%	72.3%	75.1%	74.1%
Female	55.3%	55.8%	54.3%	60.4%	65.1%	67.3%	73.0%	69.2%	73.9%	72.2%	69.5%	73.4%	75.2%
CANDIDATES OBTAINING GRADE 'C' OR ABOVE AT HIGHER LEVEL AS A PERCENTAGE OF ALL CANDIDATES													
Male	21.5%	22.0%	25.1%	25.9%	26.3%	28.9%	30.5%	31.3%	32.3%	34.6%	35.3%	37.0%	37.7%
Female	20.4%	23.5%	25.7%	25.5%	30.9%	31.0%	38.7%	34.4%	40.1%	41.1%	42.3%	46.9%	46.3%

TABLE 5.13x ART

	1990	1991	1992	1993	1994	1995	1996	1997	1998	1999	2000	2001	2002
	OVERALL NUMBER OF LEAVING CERTIFICATE CANDIDATES TAKING THE SUBJECT												
Male	3,596	3,717	3,978	4,115	4,106	3,989	3,632	4,086	4,272	4,050	4,011	3,482	3,528
Female	6,228	6,303	6,452	6,522	6,140	6,201	5,360	6,074	6,051	5,919	5,902	5,556	5,696
	PERCENTAGES TAKING THE SUBJECT AT HIGHER LEVEL												
Male	57.4%	55.8%	57.4%	57.2%	58.6%	62.0%	59.0%	61.7%	63.0%	65.4%	64.9%	64.9%	65.4%
Female	58.9%	59.1%	63.7%	64.6%	67.4%	70.9%	68.6%	70.5%	73.5%	73.2%	74.1%	75.4%	73.7%
	PERCENTAGE OF HIGHER LEVEL CANDIDATES OBTAINING GRADE 'C' OR ABOVE												
Male	53.3%	57.5%	54.3%	59.3%	60.6%	59.6%	59.1%	57.4%	58.5%	55.3%	60.5%	67.7%	79.5%
Female	60.0%	63.4%	59.6%	65.8%	65.9%	70.6%	68.0%	67.0%	70.7%	68.6%	74.2%	80.8%	87.9%
	CANDIDATES OBTAINING GRADE 'C' OR ABOVE AT HIGHER LEVEL AS A PERCENTAGE OF ALL CANDIDATES												
Male	30.6%	32.1%	31.2%	33.9%	35.5%	37.0%	34.9%	35.4%	36.9%	36.2%	39.3%	43.9%	52.0%
Female	35.3%	37.5%	38.0%	42.5%	44.4%	50.1%	46.6%	47.2%	51.9%	50.2%	54.9%	60.9%	64.8%

TABLE 5.13y MUSIC

	1990	1991	1992	1993	1994	1995	1996	1997	1998	1999	2000	2001	2002
OVERALL NUMBER OF LEAVING CERTIFICATE CANDIDATES TAKING THE SUBJECT													
Male	187	196	175	208	189	207	200	283	305	557	658	697	713
Female	988	952	868	953	936	962	968	1,270	1,488	2,438	2,628	2,605	2,732
PERCENTAGES TAKING THE SUBJECT AT HIGHER LEVEL													
Male	74.9%	74.5%	74.9%	82.7%	83.1%	84.5%	76.5%	82.0%	82.6%	84.2%	90.1%	88.5%	89.1%
Female	78.4%	76.7%	79.4%	76.8%	79.9%	84.8%	87.2%	85.8%	85.3%	85.4%	87.5%	89.8%	88.4%
PERCENTAGE OF HIGHER LEVEL CANDIDATES OBTAINING GRADE 'C' OR ABOVE													
Male	58.6%	67.8%	77.1%	73.8%	78.3%	80.6%	73.9%	73.7%	76.6%	95.9%	96.6%	93.7%	93.2%
Female	60.5%	66.7%	80.0%	70.2%	77.3%	78.1%	77.3%	79.4%	79.7%	97.9%	97.5%	95.9%	95.8%
CANDIDATES OBTAINING GRADE 'C' OR ABOVE AT HIGHER LEVEL AS A PERCENTAGE OF ALL CANDIDATES													
Male	43.9%	50.5%	57.7%	61.1%	65.1%	68.1%	56.5%	60.4%	63.3%	80.8%	87.1%	82.9%	83.0%
Female	47.5%	51.2%	63.5%	53.9%	61.8%	66.2%	67.4%	68.1%	67.9%	83.6%	85.4%	86.0%	84.7%

TABLE 5.13z CLASSICAL STUDIES

	1990	1991	1992	1993	1994	1995	1996	1997	1998	1999	2000	2001	2002
OVERALL NUMBER OF LEAVING CERTIFICATE CANDIDATES TAKING THE SUBJECT													
Male	154	153	248	289	415	529	421	375	551	477	434	418	536
Female	83	58	93	142	265	382	351	358	449	381	385	389	495
PERCENTAGES TAKING THE SUBJECT AT HIGHER LEVEL													
Male	87.7%	80.4%	76.6%	85.8%	93.0%	87.3%	86.0%	86.1%	82.4%	84.3%	90.3%	89.0%	88.8%
Female	80.7%	87.9%	94.6%	85.9%	94.3%	94.0%	91.2%	89.1%	85.5%	89.5%	87.0%	90.0%	89.7%
PERCENTAGE OF HIGHER LEVEL CANDIDATES OBTAINING GRADE 'C' OR ABOVE													
Male	50.4%	56.9%	62.1%	69.8%	60.6%	47.0%	41.2%	53.6%	52.4%	63.9%	60.5%	68.3%	53.4%
Female	74.6%	78.4%	70.5%	71.3%	67.6%	52.4%	54.7%	60.5%	62.0%	73.0%	74.0%	71.4%	61.0%
CANDIDATES OBTAINING GRADE 'C' OR ABOVE AT HIGHER LEVEL AS A PERCENTAGE OF ALL CANDIDATES													
Male	44.2%	45.8%	47.6%	59.9%	56.4%	41.0%	35.4%	46.1%	43.2%	53.9%	54.6%	60.8%	47.4%
Female	60.2%	69.0%	66.7%	61.3%	63.8%	49.2%	49.9%	53.9%	53.0%	65.4%	64.4%	64.3%	54.7%

POST LEAVING
CERTIFICATE COURSES

VOCATIONAL TRAINING
OPPORTUNITIES SCHEME

OUTREACH

SENIOR TRAVELLER
TRAINING PROGRAMME

ADULT LITERACY

BACK-TO-EDUCATION
INITIATIVE

APPRENTICESHIP

FETAC AWARDS

COMMUNITY EDUCATION

PART-TIME COURSES

APPENDIX 6

Further Education & Training

TABLE 6.1 ENROLMENT IN POST LEAVING CERTIFICATE (VPT2) COURSES

	PUPIL NUMBERS			GENDER BALANCE	
YEAR	MALE	FEMALE	TOTAL	MALE	FEMALE
1991-92	4,542	10,670	15,212	30%	70%
1992-93	5,235	11,279	16,514	32%	68%
1993-94	5,681	11,997	17,678	32%	68%
1994-95	5,437	12,207	17,644	31%	69%
1995-96	5,550	12,435	17,985	31%	69%
1996-97	5,720	13,001	18,721	31%	69%
1997-98	6,363	14,924	21,287	30%	70%
1998-99	6,960	16,863	23,823	29%	71%
1999-00	6,779	17,558	24,337	28%	72%
2000-01	7,211	18,199	25,410	28%	72%
2001-02	7,603	19,082	26,685	28%	72%
2002-03	8,143	20,506	28,649	28%	72%

TABLE 6.2 TOTAL VTOS PARTICIPATION ON 1 JANUARY (FULL-TIME STUDENTS)

	PUPIL NUMBERS			GENDER BALANCE	
YEAR	MALE	FEMALE	TOTAL	% MALE	% FEMALE
1995	2,031	2,106	4,137	49.1%	50.9%
1996	2,123	2,259	4,382	48.4%	51.6%
1997	2,030	2,377	4,407	46.1%	53.9%
1998	2,070	2,504	4,574	45.3%	54.7%
1999	1,873	2,707	4,580	40.9%	59.1%
2000	1,827	3,344	5,171	35.3%	64.7%
2001	1,786	3,519	5,305	33.7%	66.3%
2002	1,724	3,719	5,443	31.7%	68.3%
2003	1,880	3,821	5,701	33.0%	67.0%
2004	1,758	3,881	5,639	31.2%	68.8%

TABLE 6.3 NUMBER OF STUDENTS ENROLLED IN YOUTHREACH PROGRAMMES BY SEX AND AGE (2003)					
	PUPIL NUMBERS			GENDER BALANCE	
AGE	MALE	FEMALE	TOTAL	MALE	FEMALE
under 16	63	33	96	65.6%	34.4%
16	594	349	943	63.0%	37.0%
17	324	325	649	49.9%	50.1%
18	189	258	447	42.3%	57.7%
19+	128	387	515	24.9%	75.1%
Total	**1,299**	**1,354**	**2,653**	**49.0%**	**51.0%**
of which:					
Foundation Level	871	732	1,603	54.3%	45.7%
Progression Level	428	622	1,050	40.8%	59.2%

TABLE 6.4 NUMBER OF STUDENTS ENROLLED IN SENIOR TRAVELLER TRAINING COURSES BY SEX AND AGE (2003)					
	PUPIL NUMBERS			GENDER BALANCE	
AGE	MALE	FEMALE	TOTAL	MALE	FEMALE
15-17	113	166	279	40.5%	59.5%
18-19	17	60	77	22.1%	77.9%
20-24	13	140	153	8.5%	91.5%
25-44	25	324	349	7.2%	92.8%
45-49	3	46	49	6.1%	93.9%
50+	2	72	74	2.7%	97.3%
Total	**173**	**808**	**981**	**17.6%**	**82.4%**
of which:					
Foundation Level	101	486	587	17.2%	82.8%
Progression Level	72	322	394	18.3%	81.7%

TABLE 6.5 PARTICIPANTS IN ADULT LITERACY PROGRAMMES (DECEMBER RETURNS)

	PUPIL NUMBERS			GENDER BALANCE	
YEAR	MALE	FEMALE	TOTAL	% MALE	% FEMALE
2004	12,290	16,359	28,649	43%	57%
2003	10,968	15,717	26,685	41%	59%
2002	10,367	15,043	25,410	41%	59%
2001	9,272	15,065	24,337	38%	62%
2000	8,743	15,080	23,823	37%	63%

Data source: Data supplied by NALA - National Adult Literacy Agency.

TABLE 6.6 PARTICIPANTS IN BACK TO EDUCATION INITIATIVE - PART-TIME PROGRAMMES (JANUARY TO DECEMBER 2004)

	NUMBERS			GENDER BALANCE	
REGION	MALE	FEMALE	TOTAL	MALE	FEMALE
BMW region	1,105	4,619	5,724	19%	81%
S&E region	3,222	9,489	12,708	25%	75%
National	4,327	14,108	18,432	23%	77%

Data source: BTEI - Report on Implementation January to December 2004, Further Education Development Unit, Dept of Education & Science.

TABLE 6.7   FÁS APPRENTICES 2004

| | NUMBERS | | | GENDER BALANCE | |
AGE	MALE	FEMALE	TOTAL	% MALE	% FEMALE
16	205	0	205	100.0%	0.0%
17	932	3	935	99.7%	0.3%
18	2,439	5	2,443	99.8%	0.2%
19	3,633	9	3,642	99.8%	0.2%
20	4,306	18	4,324	99.6%	0.4%
21	4,289	14	4,303	99.7%	0.3%
22	3,972	19	3,991	99.5%	0.5%
23	3,086	16	3,102	99.5%	0.5%
24	1,872	11	1,883	99.4%	0.6%
25	1,051	8	1,059	99.2%	0.8%
26	597	2	599	99.7%	0.3%
27	407	5	412	98.7%	1.3%
28	264	4	268	98.6%	1.4%
29	154	3	157	98.3%	1.7%
30 +	608	3	611	99.6%	0.4%
TOTAL	**27,816**	**119**	**27,935**	**99.6%**	**0.4%**

Data Source: The figures here use data supplied by FAS on the age and gender breakdown or Apprentices applied on a pro-rata basis to the total number of Apprentices of 27,935 - as published in the 2004 FÁS Annual Report - http://www.fas.ie/annual_report/annual_report04/appendices2.htm

TABLE 6.8   FETAC AWARDS: JANUARY - DECEMBER 2005

	NUMBERS			
	MALE	**FEMALE**	**TOTAL**	**% FEMALE**
FÁS NCC & NSC Awards	4,788	24	4,812	0%
Teagasc	2,411	377	2,788	14%
FAS Spefic Skills-IVS Awards	29,003	12,115	41,118	29%
Fáilte Ireland Awards	853	1,255	2,108	60%
NCVA Records of Achievement	16,449	40,000	56,449	71%
NCEA	60	149	209	71%
NCVA Awards	2,853	10,527	13,380	79%
TOTAL FETAC AWARDS	**56,417**	**64,447**	**120,864**	**53%**

Data Source: Data supplied by FETAC - Further Education & Training Awards Council.

TABLE 6.9   NUMBER OF PART-TIME STUDENTS ENROLLED IN DAY-TIME ADULT EDUCATION COURSES IN VOCATIONAL AND COMMUNITY & COMPREHENSIVE SCHOOLS

	NUMBERS			GENDER BALANCE	
YEAR	**DAY-TIME MALE**	**DAY-TIME FEMALE**	**DAY-TIME TOTAL**	**% MALE**	**% FEMALE**
1995/1996	6,334	23,815	30,149	21.0%	79.0%
1996/1997	6,200	22,479	28,679	21.6%	78.4%
1997/1998	5,532	21,621	27,153	20.4%	79.6%
1998/1999	5,904	22,946	28,850	20.5%	79.5%
1999/2000	7,012	20,065	27,077	25.9%	74.1%
2000/2001	8,214	25,698	33,912	24.2%	75.8%
2001/2002	9,146	26,695	35,841	25.5%	74.5%
2002/2003	7,200	20,291	27,491	26.2%	73.8%
2003/2004	6,175	18,785	24,960	24.7%	75.3%

Data Source: Department of Education & Science, Tuarascáil Staitistiúil (Annual Statistical Reports), Various years.

TABLE 6.10 NUMBER OF PART-TIME STUDENTS ENROLLED IN EVENING-TIME ADULT EDUCATION COURSES IN VOCATIONAL AND COMMUNITY & COMPREHENSIVE SCHOOLS

YEAR	NUMBERS			GENDER BALANCE	
	NIGHT-TIME MALE	NIGHT-TIME FEMALE	NIGHT-TIME TOTAL	% MALE	% FEMALE
1995/1996	29,962	75,031	104,993	28.5%	71.5%
1996/1997	30,447	74,847	105,294	28.9%	71.1%
1997/1998	29,700	75,006	104,706	28.4%	71.6%
1998/1999	30,041	74,911	104,952	28.6%	71.4%
1999/2000	32,019	81,313	113,332	28.3%	71.7%
2000/2001	30,685	80,666	111,351	27.6%	72.4%
2001/2002	31,525	84,892	116,417	27.1%	72.9%
2002/2003	33,597	90,746	124,343	27.0%	73.0%
2003/2004	32,684	89,060	121,744	26.8%	73.2%

TABLE 6.11 PERCENTAGE OF EMPLOYEES (ALL ENTERPRISES) PARTICIPATING IN CONTINUING VOCATIONAL TRAINING (CVT) COURSES BY SEX: 1999-2000

	PERCENTAGE OF TOTAL PARTICIPATING IN CVT			AVERAGE HOURS SPENT (PER ANNUM)		
	MALE	FEMALE	TOTAL	MALE	FEMALE	TOTAL
Sweden	60%	61%	61%	32	29	31
Denmark	52%	54%	53%	31	54	41
Finland	48%	53%	50%	38	32	36
United Kingdom	50%	46%	49%	27	25	26
Norway	40%	66%	48%	32	35	33
France	48%	44%	46%	38	33	36
Czech Republic	46%	35%	42%	24	27	25
Belgium	-	-	41%	-	-	31
Ireland	**40%**	**43%**	**41%**	**40**	**41**	**40**
Netherlands	44%	35%	41%	38	36	37
European Union (15)	41%	38%	40%	31	29	31
European Union (25)	**40%**	**36%**	**39%**	**31**	**29**	**30**
Luxembourg	34%	39%	36%	42	34	39
Germany	34%	29%	32%	28	25	27
Slovenia	32%	33%	32%	27	21	24
Austria	31%	32%	31%	28	31	29
Italy	27%	23%	26%	33	29	32
Spain	25%	26%	25%	42	41	42
Estonia	18%	20%	19%	31	31	31
Portugal	17%	17%	17%	39	37	38
Poland	17%	15%	16%	26	31	28
Greece	14%	16%	15%	40	38	39
Latvia	13%	12%	12%	35	31	34
Hungary	13%	11%	12%	38	38	38
Lithuania	10%	9%	10%	42	40	41

Data Source: Eurostat CVTS 2000 -
http://epp.eurostat.cec.eu.int/portal/page?_pageid=0,1136184,0_45572595&_dad=portal&_schema=PORTAL

TABLE 7.5 PART-TIME ENROLMENT IN THIRD-LEVEL COURSES IN INSTITUTIONS AIDED BY THE DEPARTMENT OF EDUCATION & SCIENCE

YEAR	UNIVERSITIES (HEA)			IOTS, DIT & OTHER TECHNOLOGICAL			OTHER DES AIDED COLLEGES			ALL AIDED THIRD LEVEL		
	MALE	FEMALE	TOTAL	MALE	FEMALE	TOTAL	MALE	FEMALE	TOTAL	MALE	FEMALE	TOTAL
1994-95			0	7,344	5,275	12,619	527	1,007	1,534		10,400	0
1995-96	3,863	4,063	7,926	7,044	5,186	12,230	603	1,151	1,754	11,510	10,400	21,910
1996-97	3,890	4,536	8,426	6,820	5,741	12,561	621	1,187	1,808	11,331	11,464	22,795
1997-98	4,108	5,257	9,365	7,236	5,921	13,157	1,002	1,915	2,917	12,346	13,093	25,439
1998-99	4,583	6,344	10,927	7,562	6,274	13,836	1,031	1,970	3,001	13,176	14,588	27,764
1999-00	4,607	6,698	11,305	8,683	7,821	16,504	1,430	2,230	3,660	14,720	16,749	31,469
2000-01	4,581	6,732	11,313	8,982	8,718	17,700	990	2,262	3,252	14,553	17,712	32,265
2001-02	5,579	8,247	13,826	9,018	9,024	18,042	913	2,184	3,097	15,510	19,455	34,965
2002-03	5,403	8,633	14,036	8,367	9,037	17,404	879	3,240	4,119	14,649	20,910	35,559

Note: Figures in red italics are estimates.

TABLE 7.6 GRADUATES FROM THIRD-LEVEL INSTITUTIONS, 1993

	PUPIL NUMBERS			GENDER BALANCE	
	MALE	FEMALE	TOTAL	MALE	FEMALE
NFQ levels 6&7 Certificate & Diploma	6,002	4,987	10,989	55%	45%
NFQ level 8 Undergraduate Degree	6,712	7,392	14,104	48%	52%
NFQ level 9 Postgraduate	1,340	1,122	2,462	54%	46%
NFQ level 10 PhD	241	103	344	70%	30%
Total All Graduates	**14,295**	**13,604**	**27,899**	**51%**	**49%**

TABLE 7.7 GRADUATES FROM THIRD-LEVEL INSTITUTIONS, 2003

	PUPIL NUMBERS			GENDER BALANCE	
	MALE	FEMALE	TOTAL	MALE	FEMALE
NFQ levels 6&7 Higher Cert. & Ord. Degree	8,556	9,470	18,026	47%	53%
NFQ level 8 Honours Degree	10,095	14,820	24,915	41%	59%
NFQ level 9 Postgraduate	3,817	6,382	10,199	37%	63%
NFQ level 10 PhD	330	338	668	49%	51%
Total All Graduates	**22,798**	**31,010**	**53,808**	**42%**	**58%**

TABLE 7.8 RETENTION AND COMPLETION RATES OF 1995 ENTRANTS TO INSTITUTES OF TECHNOLOGY (AB-INITIO COURSES)

FIELD OF STUDY	NUMBER COMMENCING			GRADUATING ON TIME			GRADUATING LATE			STILL ATTENDING			NOT COMPLETING COURSE		
	M	F	T	M	F	T	M	F	T	M	F	T	M	F	T
Business Studies	1,685	2,586	4,271	53.3%	62.1%	58.6%	4.3%	3.2%	3.6%	1.7%	0.8%	1.2%	40.8%	33.9%	36.6%
Engineering	3,228	310	3,538	43.9%	44.5%	43.9%	3.0%	3.5%	3.1%	2.1%	1.6%	2.1%	51.0%	50.3%	50.9%
Science	866	1,125	1,991	51.4%	55.6%	53.8%	3.6%	3.9%	3.8%	4.8%	1.1%	2.7%	40.2%	39.4%	39.7%
Computing	580	327	907	41.7%	46.8%	43.5%	7.1%	5.2%	6.4%	0.0%	0.0%	0.0%	51.2%	48.0%	50.0%
Humanities	97	371	468	47.4%	67.1%	63.0%	0.0%	2.4%	1.9%	9.3%	1.1%	2.8%	43.3%	29.4%	32.3%
TOTAL	**6,456**	**4,719**	**11,175**										**46.8%**	**36.9%**	**42.6%**

Data Source: Flanagan, R., Morgan, M. & Kellaghan, T. (2000) A Study of Non-Completion in Institute of Technology Courses, Table 5.1, p.17.

Note: More recent data on the issue of non-completion in institutes of technology suggests that retention rates have improved somewhat in more recent years. This more up-to-date information is available at http://www.councilofdirectors.ie/documents/301_Completion%20Report%20Final.pdf

TABLE 7.9 RETENTION AND COMPLETION OF 1992/93 ENTRANTS TO UNDERGRADUATE PROGRAMMES IN UNIVERSITIES

FIELD OF STUDY	NUMBER COMMENCING			GRADUATING ON TIME			GRADUATING LATE			NOT COMPLETING COURSE		
	MALE	FEMALE	TOTAL	MALE	FEMALE	TOTAL	MALE	FEMALE	TOTAL	MALE	FEMALE	TOTAL
Arts/European Studies/Education	1,621	2,939	4,560	62.6%	62.3%	62.4%	18.4%	20.9%	20.0%	19.0%	16.8%	17.6%
Business Economics & Social Studies/Commerce	1,101	994	2,095	75.7%	82.4%	78.9%	11.7%	6.9%	9.4%	12.5%	10.7%	11.6%
Communications & Information Studies	39	112	151	79.5%	66.1%	69.5%	7.7%	23.2%	19.2%	12.8%	10.7%	11.3%
Computer Studies	344	165	509	58.7%	60.0%	59.1%	15.1%	11.5%	13.9%	26.2%	28.5%	26.9%
Engineering/Architecture	899	177	1,076	62.6%	70.0%	63.8%	17.1%	13.6%	16.5%	20.2%	16.4%	19.6%
Law	175	219	394	86.9%	89.5%	88.6%	5.7%	3.2%	4.3%	7.4%	6.8%	7.1%
Medicine/Dentistry/Veterinary Medicine	246	413	659	79.3%	86.9%	84.0%	13.0%	6.0%	8.6%	7.7%	7.0%	7.3%
Science/Agric. Science/Food Science & Technology	1,004	1,064	2,068	61.5%	65.2%	63.4%	14.1%	14.5%	14.3%	24.3%	20.3%	22.2%
Social Science	23	216	239	73.9%	70.4%	70.7%	17.4%	14.8%	15.1%	8.7%	14.8%	14.2%
TOTAL	**5,452**	**6,299**	**11,751**							**18.4%**	**15.5%**	**16.8%**

Data Source: Morgan, M., Flanagan, R. & Kellaghan, T. (2000) A Study of Non-Completion in Undergraduate University Courses, Table 5.1, p.30.

TABLE 7.10 TOTAL GRADUATES 1993: FULL-TIME AND PART-TIME FROM PUBLIC AND PRIVATE INSTITUTIONS AT THIRD LEVEL

	MALES	FEMALES	TOTAL
Home economics (domestic science)* (ISC 66)	10%	90%	249
Service trades* (ISC 78)	20%	80%	585
Education science & teacher training (ISC 14)	26%	74%	1,530
Mass communication & documentation* (ISC 84)	36%	64%	290
Fine and applied arts* (ISC 18)	36%	64%	767
Social & behavioural sciences (ISC 30)	39%	61%	1,529
Humanities, religion & theology (ISC 22,26)	39%	61%	4,159
Medical science & health related (ISC 50)	43%	57%	1,088
Law (ISC 38)	44%	56%	1,051
Commercial & business administration (ISC 34)	46%	54%	6,093
Natural science (ISC 42)	48%	52%	3,384
TOTAL: ALL GRADUATES 1993	**51%**	**49%**	**27,899**
Mathematics & computer science (ISC 46)	59%	41%	1,699
Agriculture, forestry & fishery** (ISC 62)	65%	35%	416
Other fields of study** (ISC 89)	84%	16%	32
Trade, craft, & industrial programmes** (ISC 52)	85%	15%	48
Architecture & town planning (ISC 58)	86%	14%	1,050
Engineering (ISC 54)	90%	10%	3,929

* = Less than 1,000 grads; ** = Less than 100 grads.

TABLE 7.11 TOTAL GRADUATES 2003: FULL-TIME AND PART-TIME FROM PUBLIC AND PRIVATE INSTITUTIONS AT THIRD LEVEL

	MALES	FEMALES	TOTAL
Social services (ISC 76)	11.4%	88.6%	1,435
Health (ISC 72)	18.4%	81.6%	5,249
Teacher training (ISC 141)	19.2%	80.8%	3,513
Social and behavioural science (ISC 31)	30.5%	69.5%	1,685
Education science* (ISC 142)	30.6%	69.4%	281
Arts (ISC 21)	32.0%	68.0%	4,822
Veterinary* (ISC 64)	32.6%	67.4%	135
Humanities (ISC 22)	32.6%	67.4%	2,741
Personal services* (ISC 81)	33.9%	66.1%	614
Law (ISC 38)	34.6%	65.4%	1,325
Life sciences (ISC 42)	36.0%	64.0%	2,266
Journalism and information* (ISC 32)	38.9%	61.1%	316
Business and administration (ISC 34)	40.5%	59.5%	13,200
TOTAL: ALL GRADUATES 2003	**42.4%**	**57.6%**	**53,808**
Environmental protection** (ISC 85)	47.0%	53.0%	83
Physical sciences (ISC 44)	47.7%	52.3%	1,242
Agriculture, forestry and fishery* (ISC 62)	62.1%	37.9%	589
Computing (ISC 48)	63.2%	36.8%	5,687
Manufacturing and processing* (ISC 54)	63.4%	36.6%	757
Mathematics and statistics* (ISC 46)	65.3%	34.7%	268
Security services* (ISC 86)	65.6%	34.4%	889
Architecture and building (ISC 58)	82.3%	17.7%	2,491
Engineering & engineering trades (ISC 52)	84.9%	15.1%	3,033

* = Less than 1,000 grads; ** = Less than 100 grads.

TABLE 7.12 CERTIFICATE AND DIPLOMA GRADUATES FROM THIRD-LEVEL INSTITUTIONS, 2003

	PUPIL NUMBERS			GENDER BALANCE	
	MALE	FEMALE	TOTAL	MALE	FEMALE
Social Sciences, Business & Law	2,139	3,970	6,109	35%	65%
Engineering	2,999	408	3,407	88%	12%
Science	1,783	1,556	3,339	53%	47%
Health and Welfare	358	2,029	2,387	15%	85%
Services	687	616	1,303	53%	47%
Humanities & Arts	381	701	1,082	35%	65%
Agriculture*	174	130	304	57%	43%
Education**	20	48	68	29%	71%
Unspecified**	15	12	27	56%	44%
TOTAL CERT & DIPLOMA GRADS	**8,556**	**9,470**	**18,026**	**47%**	**53%**

* = Less than 1,000 grads; ** = Less than 100 grads.

TABLE 7.13 UNDERGRADUATE GRADUATES FROM THIRD-LEVEL INSTITUTIONS, 2003

	PUPIL NUMBERS			GENDER BALANCE	
	MALE	FEMALE	TOTAL	MALE	FEMALE
Social Sciences, Business & Law	2,883	4,469	7,352	39%	61%
Humanities & Arts	1,651	3,718	5,369	31%	69%
Science	2,458	2,029	4,487	55%	45%
Health and Welfare	494	2,035	2,529	20%	80%
Engineering	1,694	533	2,227	76%	24%
Education	201	1,181	1,382	15%	85%
Unspecified	478	656	1134	42%	58%
Agriculture*	145	120	265	55%	45%
Services*	91	79	170	54%	46%
TOTAL UNDERGRADUATES DEGREES	**10,095**	**14,820**	**24,915**	**41%**	**59%**

* = Less than 1,000 grads; ** = Less than 100 grads.

TABLE 7.14 POSTGRADUATES FROM THIRD-LEVEL INSTITUTIONS, 2003

	PUPIL NUMBERS			GENDER BALANCE	
	MALE	FEMALE	TOTAL	MALE	FEMALE
Social Sciences, Business & Law	1,393	1,619	3,012	46%	54%
Education	537	1,801	2,338	23%	77%
Health and Welfare	242	1,453	1,695	14%	86%
Science	805	528	1,333	60%	40%
Humanities & Arts*	346	638	984	35%	65%
Engineering*	361	209	570	63%	37%
Agriculture*	78	58	136	57%	43%
Services*	52	61	113	46%	54%
Unspecified**	3	15	18	17%	83%
TOTAL POSTGRADUATE DEGREES	**3,817**	**6,382**	**10,199**	**37%**	**63%**

* = Less than 1,000 grads; ** = Less than 100 grads.

TABLE 7.15 PHD GRADUATES FROM THIRD-LEVEL INSTITUTIONS, 2003					
PUPIL NUMBERS				GENDER BALANCE	
	MALE	FEMALE	TOTAL	MALE	FEMALE
Science	132	172	304	43%	57%
Humanities & Arts	60	68	128	47%	53%
Engineering	53	24	77	69%	31%
Health and Welfare	36	37	73	49%	51%
Social Sciences, Business & Law	28	25	53	53%	47%
Agriculture	13	6	19	68%	32%
Unspecified	5	3	8	63%	38%
Education	3	3	6	50%	50%
TOTAL P.H.D.	330	338	668	49%	51%

TABLE 7.16 ANALYSIS OF PERFORMANCE IN FINAL UNIVERSITY EXAMINATIONS: GRADUATES 2004

		1ST CLASS HONOURS	2ND CLASS HONOURS (GRADE 1)	2ND CLASS HONOURS (GRADE 2)	OTHER HONOURS	PASS	NOT APPLICABLE	GRAND TOTAL		GENDER BALANCE AMONG GRADS
		1ST	2.1	2.2	OTHER	PASS	N/A	%	GRADS	
1 Undergraduate Degree (total)	M	15%	36%	24%	12%	13%	0%	100%	6,324	40%
	F	12%	41%	25%	13%	9%	0%	100%	9,630	60%
2 Postgraduate Degrees & Diplomas (total = 3+4+5)	M	17%	43%	7%	13%	20%	0%	100%	3,943	38%
	F	17%	42%	7%	10%	24%	0%	100%	6,416	62%
3 Postgraduate Certificate & Diploma	M	12%	39%	10%	12%	27%	0%	100%	1,235	27%
	F	14%	40%	8%	10%	29%	0%	100%	3,268	73%
4 MA Degrees - Taught	M	21%	50%	6%	5%	18%	0%	100%	2,428	45%
	F	21%	47%	6%	6%	21%	0%	100%	2,925	55%
5 MA Degree - Research	M	4%	3%	0%	85%	6%	3%	100%	280	56%
	F	6%	7%	0%	83%	3%	1%	100%	223	44%
6 PhD (total)	M	0%	0%	0%	88%	5%	6%	100%	369	54%
	F	0%	0%	0%	86%	6%	7%	100%	309	46%

Data source: Statistics Section, Higher Education Authority (HEA)

TABLE 7.17 ANALYSIS OF PERFORMANCE IN FINAL UNIVERSITY EXAMINATIONS: GRADUATES 2004 PROGRAMME TYPE(S) : UNDERGRADUATE GENERAL DEGREE, UNDERGRADUATE HONOURS DEGREE

		1ST CLASS HONOURS	2ND CLASS HONOURS (GRADE 1)	2ND CLASS HONOURS (GRADE 2)	OTHER HONOURS	PASS	NOT APPLICABLE	GRAND TOTAL		GENDER BALANCE AMONG GRADS
		1ST	2.1	2.2	OTHER	PASS	N/A	%	GRADS	
Education	M	11%	38%	37%	0%	14%	0%	100%	177	16%
	F	7%	46%	39%	0%	8%	0%	100%	957	84%
Humanities & Arts	M	7%	23%	13%	53%	5%	0%	100%	889	34%
	F	6%	30%	17%	42%	5%	0%	100%	1,734	66%
Social Sciences, Business and Law	M	12%	50%	25%	4%	9%	0%	100%	1,494	40%
	F	15%	54%	21%	7%	4%	0%	100%	2,285	60%
Services	M								0	
	F								0	
Engineering, Manufacturing & Construction	M	24%	32%	26%	2%	16%	0%	100%	975	75%
	F	24%	36%	32%	1%	6%	0%	100%	324	25%
Agriculture & Veterinary	M	7%	40%	32%	6%	14%	0%	100%	155	57%
	F	15%	32%	40%	0%	12%	0%	100%	117	43%
Health & Welfare	M	5%	22%	11%	16%	46%	0%	100%	371	19%
	F	6%	29%	27%	16%	22%	0%	100%	1,561	81%

Continued on next page.

TABLE 7.17 ANALYSIS OF PERFORMANCE IN FINAL UNIVERSITY EXAMINATIONS: GRADUATES 2004 PROGRAMME TYPE(S) : UNDERGRADUATE GENERAL DEGREE, UNDERGRADUATE HONOURS DEGREE

		1ST CLASS HONOURS	2ND CLASS HONOURS (GRADE 1)	2ND CLASS HONOURS (GRADE 2)	OTHER HONOURS	PASS	NOT APPLICABLE	GRAND TOTAL		GENDER BALANCE AMONG GRADS
		1ST	2.1	2.2	OTHER	PASS	N/A	%	GRADS	
Combined Science	M	17%	37%	18%	5%	23%	0%	100%	305	44%
	F	19%	46%	16%	3%	17%	0%	100%	386	56%
Life Science	M	19%	41%	28%	5%	7%	0%	100%	177	32%
	F	25%	49%	19%	1%	5%	0%	100%	382	68%
Physical Science	M	24%	33%	21%	10%	11%	0%	100%	254	53%
	F	24%	37%	28%	6%	4%	0%	100%	225	47%
Mathematics and Statistics	M	46%	26%	14%	5%	9%	0%	100%	85	57%
	F	44%	38%	11%	5%	3%	0%	100%	64	43%
Computing	M	20%	34%	27%	5%	14%	0%	100%	812	74%
	F	25%	41%	16%	5%	13%	0%	100%	283	26%
Combination across different fields	M	11%	39%	32%	8%	10%	0%	100%	630	32%
	F	9%	44%	35%	6%	5%	0%	100%	1,312	68%
Undergraduate Degree (total)	M	15%	36%	24%	12%	13%	0%	100%	6,324	40%
	F	12%	41%	25%	13%	9%	0%	100%	9,630	60%

Data source: Statistics Section, Higher Education Authority (HEA)

TABLE 7.18 ANALYSIS OF PERFORMANCE IN FINAL UNIVERSITY EXAMINATIONS: GRADUATES 2004 POST-GRADUATE DIPLOMAS & CERTIFICATES, MASTERS DEGREES (TAUGHT AND RESEARCH)

		1ST CLASS HONOURS	2ND CLASS HONOURS (GRADE 1)	2ND CLASS HONOURS (GRADE 2)	OTHER HONOURS	PASS	NOT APPLICABLE	GRAND TOTAL		GENDER BALANCE AMONG GRADS
		1ST	2.1	2.2	OTHER	PASS	N/A	%	GRADS	
Education	M	19%	61%	7%	1%	13%	0%	100%	437	21%
	F	23%	58%	8%	4%	7%	0%	100%	1,627	79%
Humanities & Arts	M	20%	46%	11%	11%	11%	0%	100%	419	37%
	F	20%	48%	9%	10%	14%	0%	100%	711	63%
Social Sciences, Business and Law	M	15%	50%	7%	8%	20%	0%	100%	1,725	48%
	F	17%	51%	7%	9%	16%	0%	100%	1,896	52%
Services	M	13%	45%	11%	9%	21%	0%	100%	53	49%
	F	13%	48%	21%	7%	11%	0%	100%	56	51%
Engineering, Manufacturing & Construction	M	14%	30%	4%	31%	20%	0%	100%	339	62%
	F	15%	24%	4%	35%	22%	0%	100%	208	38%
Agriculture & Veterinary	M	11%	26%	2%	54%	7%	0%	100%	46	52%
	F	12%	45%	7%	36%	0%	0%	100%	42	48%
Health & Welfare	M	8%	16%	5%	21%	50%	0%	100%	207	13%
	F	6%	15%	4%	11%	63%	0%	100%	1,387	87%

Continued on next page.

TABLE 7.18 ANALYSIS OF PERFORMANCE IN FINAL UNIVERSITY EXAMINATIONS: GRADUATES 2004 POST-GRADUATE DIPLOMAS & CERTIFICATES, MASTERS DEGREES (TAUGHT AND RESEARCH)

		1ST CLASS HONOURS	2ND CLASS HONOURS (GRADE 1)	2ND CLASS HONOURS (GRADE 2)	OTHER HONOURS	PASS	NOT APPLICABLE	GRAND TOTAL		GENDER BALANCE AMONG GRADS
		1ST	2.1	2.2	OTHER	PASS	N/A	%	GRADS	
Combined Science	M	27%	32%	0%	12%	29%	0%	100%	41	71%
	F	35%	47%	0%	12%	6%	0%	100%	17	29%
Life Science	M	16%	42%	6%	16%	19%	0%	100%	67	46%
	F	23%	23%	3%	28%	25%	0%	100%	80	54%
Physical Science	M	17%	38%	6%	37%	2%	0%	100%	52	50%
	F	16%	43%	8%	29%	2%	2%	100%	51	50%
Mathematics and Statistics	M	19%	17%	5%	19%	39%	2%	100%	64	47%
	F	16%	14%	5%	34%	30%	0%	100%	73	53%
Computing	M	26%	28%	7%	21%	17%	1%	100%	393	69%
	F	22%	35%	7%	14%	22%	0%	100%	174	31%
Combination across different fields	M	19%	21%	0%	14%	46%	0%	100%	100	52%
	F	24%	35%	0%	11%	30%	0%	100%	94	48%
Postgraduate Degrees & Diplomas (total)	M	17%	43%	7%	13%	20%	0%	100%	3,943	38%
	F	17%	42%	7%	10%	24%	0%	100%	6,416	62%

Data source: Statistics Section, Higher Education Authority (HEA)

TABLE 7.19   PERCENTAGE OF PERSONS AGED 25 TO 34 WITH THIRD LEVEL QUALIFICATIONS CLASSIFIED BY SEX, 1999 TO 2003

	MALE	FEMALE	ALL PERSONS
1999	26.7%	27.5%	27.1%
2000	27.5%	30.5%	29.0%
2001	29.8%	34.0%	31.9%
2002	31.3%	37.7%	34.5%
2003	34.2%	39.0%	36.6%
2004	36.0%	42.7%	39.4%
2005	34.9%	43.7%	39.2%

Data source: CSO QNHS Special Module on Education (Table 5a), 1999-2003, available at http://www.cso.ie/qnhs/documents/qnhseducation.xls & CSO QNHS Module on Educational Attainment 2002-2005, available at http://www.cso.ie/releasespublications/documents/labour_market/current/qnhs_educationalattainment.pdf

TABLE 7.20(a) POPULATION AGED 25-34 THAT HAS ATTAINED TERTIARY EDUCATION (2004) PERCENTAGE OF THE POPULATION THAT HAS ATTAINED TERTIARY-TYPE B EDUCATION OR TERTIARY-TYPE A AND ADVANCED RESEARCH PROGRAMMES

RANKING	COUNTRY	ALL HIGHER EDUCATION			CERTIFICATES & DIPLOMAS (NOW KNOWN AS ADVANCED CERTIFICATES & ORDINARY DEGREES)			UNDERGRADUATE DEGREES & HIGHER LEVEL POSTGRADUATE AWARDS		
		MALE	FEMALE	TOTAL	MALE	FEMALE	TOTAL	MALE	FEMALE	TOTAL
1	Canada	47%	60%	53%	22%	29%	26%	24%	31%	27%
2	Japan	49%	54%	52%	14%	36%	25%	35%	18%	26%
3	Korea	50%	48%	49%	18%	19%	18%	33%	29%	31%
4	Sweden	38%	47%	42%	16%	16%	16%	21%	31%	26%
5	Belgium	36%	45%	41%	17%	26%	22%	19%	19%	19%
6	Ireland	37%	44%	40%	13%	16%	15%	24%	27%	26%
7	Norway	33%	46%	39%	2%	2%	2%	31%	44%	37%
8	United States	36%	42%	39%	8%	9%	9%	28%	32%	30%
9	Spain	34%	42%	38%	12%	11%	12%	22%	31%	27%
10	France	35%	41%	38%	15%	17%	16%	20%	24%	22%
11	Finland	30%	47%	38%	10%	18%	14%	20%	28%	24%
12	Australia	32%	41%	36%	8%	10%	9%	23%	31%	27%

Continued on next page.

TABLE 7.20(b) POPULATION AGED 25-64 THAT HAS ATTAINED TERTIARY EDUCATION (2004) PERCENTAGE OF THE POPULATION THAT HAS ATTAINED TERTIARY-TYPE B EDUCATION OR TERTIARY-TYPE A AND ADVANCED RESEARCH PROGRAMME

RANKING	COUNTRY	ALL HIGHER EDUCATION			CERTIFICATES & DIPLOMAS (NOW KNOWN AS ADVANCED CERTIFICATES & ORDINARY DEGREES)			UNDERGRADUATE DEGREES & HIGHER LEVEL POSTGRADUATE AWARDS		
		MALE	FEMALE	TOTAL	MALE	FEMALE	TOTAL	MALE	FEMALE	TOTAL
14	Switzerland	37%	19%	28%	14%	6%	10%	23%	13%	18%
15	Iceland	26%	30%	28%	3%	6%	4%	23%	24%	24%
16	Spain	26%	26%	26%	8%	6%	7%	18%	20%	19%
17	New Zealand	22%	28%	25%	4%	11%	8%	18%	17%	18%
18	Germany	29%	21%	25%	12%	8%	10%	17%	12%	15%
19	France	23%	25%	24%	9%	11%	10%	14%	14%	14%
20	Luxembourg	26%	19%	23%	9%	9%	9%	17%	10%	13%
21	Greece	22%	19%	21%	6%	6%	6%	16%	14%	15%
22	Austria	22%	15%	18%	11%	7%	9%	11%	8%	9%
23	Mexico	19%	14%	16%	2%	2%	2%	17%	12%	14%
24	Slovak Republic	13%	12%	12%	0%	1%	1%	12%	11%	12%
	OECD average	26%	25%	25%	9%	10%	9%	20%	18%	19%
EU19	average	23%	23%	23%	9%	10%	9%	18%	16%	17%

Data Source: OECD (2006), Education at a Glance 2006, Indicator A1.3a, A1.3b & A1.3c, p.39 (Gender breakdowns not published but available on the web at http://dx.doi.org/10.1787/701655207564

TABLE 7.21 GENDER DIFFERENCES IN THE PERCENTAGE OF THE POPULATION THAT HAS ATTAINED TERTIARY EDUCATION (2004) – FEMALES MINUS MALES; AGE GROUPS 25-34 & 25-6

ALL HIGHER EDUCATION

	YOUNGER ADULT POPULATION (AGED 25-34)					ADULT POPULATION AGED 25-64		
		MALE	FEMALE	GENDER DIFFERENCE (FEMALE MINUS MALE)			MALE	FEMALE	GENDER DIFFERENCE (FEMALE MINUS MALE)
1	Finland	30%	47%	17%	1	Finland	30%	38%	8%
2	Norway	33%	46%	13%	2	Canada	41%	48%	6%
3	Canada	47%	60%	13%	3	Sweden	32%	38%	6%
4	Iceland	25%	38%	13%	4	New Zealand	22%	28%	6%
5	Sweden	38%	47%	9%	5	Denmark	30%	35%	4%
6	Australia	32%	41%	9%	6	Norway	30%	34%	4%
7	Denmark	30%	40%	9%	7	Iceland	26%	30%	4%
8	Belgium	36%	45%	9%	8	Australia	29%	33%	4%
9	Spain	34%	42%	8%	9	France	23%	25%	2%
10	Ireland	37%	44%	7%	10	Belgium	29%	31%	2%
11	France	35%	41%	7%	11	Ireland	27%	29%	2%
12	New Zealand	25%	31%	6%	12	United States	38%	40%	1%
13	Greece	22%	27%	6%	13	Spain	26%	26%	0%
14	United States	36%	42%	6%	14	Slovak Republic	13%	12%	0%
15	Japan[1]	49%	54%	5%	15	United Kingdom	29%	29%	-1%
16	Netherlands	33%	36%	3%	16	Greece	22%	19%	-3%
17	Slovak Republic	13%	15%	2%	17	Japan[1]	39%	35%	-4%
18	Luxembourg	31%	31%	0%	18	Netherlands	32%	27%	-5%
19	United Kingdom	35%	35%	0%	19	Mexico	19%	14%	-6%
20	Austria	20%	20%	0%	20	Austria	22%	15%	-7%
21	Germany	23%	23%	-1%	21	Luxembourg	26%	19%	-7%
22	Mexico	20%	18%	-2%	22	Germany	29%	21%	-9%
23	Korea	50%	48%	-2%	23	Korea	36%	25%	-11%
24	Switzerland	38%	23%	-14%	24	Switzerland	37%	19%	-18%
	OECD average	29%	34%	5%		OECD average	26%	25%	-1%
	EU19 average	26%	31%	6%		EU19 average	23%	23%	0%

Data Source: OECD (2006), Education at a Glance 2006, Indicator A1.3a, A1.3b & A1.3c, p.39 (Gender breakdowns not published but available on the web at http://dx.doi.org/10.1787/701165207564

SÉ SÍ GENDER IN IRISH EDUCATION

TABLE 8.1 TOTAL NUMBER OF PRIMARY TEACHERS IN SERVICE BY GENDER, 1930 TO 2003					
PUPIL NUMBERS				GENDER BALANCE	
YEAR	MALE	FEMALE	TOTAL	MALE	FEMALE
1930	3,852	5,399	9,251	42%	58%
1940	4,064	5,707	9,771	42%	58%
1950	4,196	8,674	12,870	33%	67%
1960	4,409	9,457	13,866	32%	68%
1970	4,677	10,182	14,859	31%	69%
1975	4,877	12,211	17,088	29%	71%
1980	5,062	13,940	19,002	27%	73%
1985	5,129	15,804	20,933	25%	75%
1990	4,865	15,456	20,321	24%	76%
1995	4,622	16,279	20,901	22%	78%
2000	4,370	17,480	21,850	20%	80%
2003	4,490	20,210	24,700	18%	82%

Data Source: Department of Education & Science, Tuarascáil Staitistiúil – Annual Statistical Reports and Annual Reports, various years 1929-30 to 2002-03.

TABLE 8.2 & 8.4 INTERNATIONAL DATA ON PRIMARY TEACHERS AND HEADTEACHERS (PRINCIPALS), 2003

	PRIMARY LEVEL 2003		RATIO OF FEMALE HEADS TO FEMALE TEACHERS
	TEACHERS % FEMALE	HEADTEACHERS % FEMALE	
Turkey	44.1%	:	
Japan	65.0%	19.5%	0.30
Denmark	65.3%	:	
Luxembourg	69.3%	:	
Spain	70.5%	:	
Norway	72.6%	47.9%	0.66
Finland	74.8%	35.2%	0.47
Belgium	77.7%	40.3%	0.52
Iceland	78.2%	79.8%	1.02
Portugal	78.9%	:	
Sweden	80.4%	:	
France	80.6%	80.6%	1.00
Netherlands	81.0%	28.8%	0.36
United Kingdom	81.4%	:	
Germany	82.8%	:	
Cyprus	83.2%	60.6%	0.73
Czech Republic	84.0%	:	
Hungary	84.3%	:	
Poland	84.7%	78.3%	0.92
Malta	85.2%	62.5%	0.73
Ireland	86.5%	51.2%	0.59
Romania	87.2%	:	
United States	88.2%	:	
Croatia	89.9%	:	
Austria	90.1%	60.7%	0.67
Slovakia	92.1%	78.1%	0.85
Bulgaria	92.3%	76.0%	0.82
Italy	95.3%	:	
Slovenia	96.5%	:	
Latvia	96.9%	:	
Lithuania	97.6%	:	
Average for available countries	**81.8%**	**57.1%**	**0.69**

Data Source: Eurostat website indicators on Educational Personnel - s06_2 & s01_2 (http://epp.eurostat.cec.eu.int/portal/page?_pageid=0,1136184,0_45572595&_dad=portal&_schema=PORTAL) Data updated - Sept. 15, 2005; Date of extraction - Oct. 10, 2005

TABLE 8.3 PRINCIPALS, POSTS OF RESPONSIBILITY AND TEACHERS AT PRIMARY LEVEL, 1990 TO 2005			
	YEAR	MALE	FEMALE
Principal	1990	52.5%	47.5%
	1995	51.1%	48.9%
	2000	50.0%	50.0%
	2005	46.6%	53.4%
Deputy/ Vice Principal	1990	16.5%	83.5%
	1995	16.9%	83.1%
	2000	15.7%	84.3%
	2005	14.9%	85.1%
Asst. Principal/ Grade A	1990	33.9%	66.1%
	1995	31.2%	68.8%
	2000	24.7%	75.3%
	2005	22.2%	77.8%
Special Duties/ Grade B	1990	25.0%	75.0%
	1995	23.7%	76.3%
	2000	18.0%	82.0%
	2005	14.7%	85.3%
Class Teacher	1990	15.5%	84.5%
	1995	14.4%	85.6%
	2000	11.6%	88.4%
	2005	10.2%	89.8%
Total	1990	23.2%	76.8%
	1995	21.9%	78.1%
	2000	19.6%	80.4%
	2005	17.0%	83.0%

TABLE 8.5 TOTAL TEACHERS AT SECOND LEVEL 1980 - 2003

Numbers

	TOTAL SECOND LEVEL TEACHERS				SECONDARY TEACHERS (NUMBERS)				VOCATIONAL TEACHERS (NUMBERS)				C&C TEACHERS NUMBERS		
	MALE	FEMALE	TOTAL		MALE	FEMALE	TOTAL		MALE	FEMALE	TOTAL		MALE	FEMALE	TOTAL
1980	6,064	6,951	13,015	1980	5,214	6,256	11,470	1980	..	..	4,633	1980	850	695	1,545
1985	9,525	9,502	19,027	1985	5,415	6,487	11,902	1985	2,943	2,006	4,949	1985	1,167	1,009	2,176
1990	9,242	9,506	18,748	1990	5,219	6,411	11,630	1990	2,783	2,042	4,825	1990	1,240	1,053	2,293
1995	9,447	11,193	20,640	1995	5,275	7,360	12,635	1995	2,753	2,433	5,186	1995	1,419	1,400	2,819
2000	9,029	12,072	21,101	2000	5,054	7,364	12,418	2000	2,608	3,017	5,625	2000	1,367	1,691	3,058
2003	9,016	13,046	22,062	2003	4,890	7,557	12,447	2003	2,544	3,389	5,933	2003	1,582	2,100	3,682

Percentages

	TOTAL SECOND LEVEL TEACHERS %				SECONDARY TEACHERS %				VOCATIONAL TEACHERS %				C&C TEACHERS %		
	MALE	FEMALE	TOTAL		MALE	FEMALE	TOTAL		MALE	FEMALE	TOTAL		MALE	FEMALE	TOTAL
1985	50.1%	49.9%	100.0%	1985	45.5%	54.5%	100.0%	1985	59.5%	40.5%	100.0%	1985	53.6%	46.4%	100.0%
1990	49.3%	50.7%	100.0%	1990	44.9%	55.1%	100.0%	1990	57.7%	42.3%	100.0%	1990	54.1%	45.9%	100.0%
1995	45.8%	54.2%	100.0%	1995	41.7%	58.3%	100.0%	1995	53.1%	46.9%	100.0%	1995	50.3%	49.7%	100.0%
2000	42.8%	57.2%	100.0%	2000	40.7%	59.3%	100.0%	2000	46.4%	53.6%	100.0%	2000	44.7%	55.3%	100.0%
2003	40.9%	59.1%	100.0%	2003	39.3%	60.7%	100.0%	2003	42.9%	57.1%	100.0%	2003	43.0%	57.0%	100.0%

TABLE 8.6 & 8.8   INTERNATIONAL DATA ON SECOND-LEVEL TEACHERS AND HEADTEACHERS (PRINCIPALS), 2003

	SECOND LEVEL 2003		RATIO OF FEMALE HEADS TO FEMALE TEACHERS
	TEACHERS % FEMALE	HEADTEACHERS % FEMALE	
Japan	32.3%	5.3%	0.16
Turkey	40.0%	:	
Luxembourg	43.0%	:	
Netherlands	43.5%	17.6%	0.40
Malta	45.2%	31.7%	0.70
Iceland	48.3%	31.3%	0.65
Germany	51.5%	:	
Spain	54.2%	:	
Sweden	56.6%	:	
Belgium	57.7%	26.2%	0.45
France	58.3%	52.4%	0.90
Austria	58.4%	21.5%	0.37
Norway	59.5%	41.0%	0.69
United Kingdom	59.6%	:	
Ireland	59.6%	32.2%	0.54
Cyprus	59.9%	44.9%	0.75
United States	60.1%	:	
Finland	64.4%	36.7%	0.57
Romania	65.7%	:	
Italy	66.6%	25.6%	0.38
Croatia	67.1%	:	
Czech Republic	68.8%	:	
Portugal	69.0%	:	
Poland	69.2%	57.5%	0.83
Slovenia	71.0%	52.4%	0.74
Slovakia	72.5%	44.6%	0.62
Hungary	72.7%	:	
Bulgaria	77.2%	63.5%	0.82
Latvia	80.8%	:	
Lithuania	81.7%	:	
Average for available countries	**60.5%**	**36.5%**	**0.60**

Source: Eurostat website indicators on Educational Personnel - s06_3,4 & s01_3
(http://epp.eurostat.cec.eu.int/portal/page?_pageid=0,1136184,0_45572595&_dad=portal&_schema=PORTAL) Data updated - Sept. 15, 2005; Date of extraction - Oct. 10, 2005
Note: Since lower second-level education and upper second-level education are delivered in separate institutions in many European countries, the total second-level gender balance of teachers has been calculated as an average of the gender balance at lower and upper second level to establish comparability with the Irish system.

TABLE 8.7 GENDER BREAKDOWN OF POSTS OF RESPONSIBILITY IN SECONDARY AND COMMUNITY & COMPREHENSIVE SCHOOLS, MAY 2005

	TOTAL SECONDARY & C&C		SECONDARY		COMMUNITY & COMPREHENSIVE	
	MALE	FEMALE	MALE	FEMALE	MALE	FEMALE
Principals	366	178	280	157	86	21
Deputy/Vice principal	319	233	253	180	66	53
Assistant Principal/A Post	1,733	1,753	1,309	1,378	424	375
Special Duties/B Post	1,918	3,471	1,467	2,725	451	746
Special Functions	4	3	4	1	0	2
	4,340	5,638	3,313	4,441	1,027	1,197
	TOTAL SECONDARY & C&C		**SECONDARY**		**COMMUNITY & COMPREHENSIVE**	
	MALE	FEMALE	MALE	FEMALE	MALE	FEMALE
Principals	67.3%	32.7%	64.1%	35.9%	80.4%	19.6%
Deputy/Vice principal	57.8%	42.2%	58.4%	41.6%	55.5%	44.5%
Assistant Principal/A Post	49.7%	50.3%	48.7%	51.3%	53.1%	46.9%
Special Duties/B Post	35.6%	64.4%	35.0%	65.0%	37.7%	62.3%
Special Functions	57.1%	42.9%	80.0%	20.0%	0.0%	100.0%
	43.5%	56.5%	42.7%	57.3%	46.2%	53.8%

Data Source: Department of Education & Science, Payroll Division (Primary Substitution and IT Liaison), Athlone.

8.9 OVERALL GENDER BREAKDOWN FOR ALL STAFF - TOTAL IOTS

	ACADEMIC STAFF		MANAGEMENT & ADMIN STAFF		SUPPORT STAFF		TOTAL STAFF NUMBERS	
	MALE	FEMALE	MALE	FEMALE	MALE	FEMALE	MALE	FEMALE
1997-98	77%	23%	24%	76%	76%	24%	67%	33%
1998-99	75%	25%	23%	77%	74%	26%	65%	35%
1999-00	72%	28%	23%	77%	73%	27%	63%	37%
2000-01	70%	30%	23%	77%	74%	26%	62%	38%
2001-02	69%	31%	22%	78%	73%	27%	61%	39%
2002-03	67%	33%	22%	78%	74%	26%	60%	40%
2003-04	66%	34%	21%	79%	74%	26%	58%	42%

TABLE 8.10 GENDER BREAKDOWN BY GRADE - MANAGEMENT AND ADMINISTRATION

	MANAGEMENT		PO - AP LEVEL		LIBRARY STAFF		OTHER ADMIN		PART TIME HOURS	
	MALE	FEMALE	MALE	FEMALE	MALE	FEMALE	MALE	FEMALE	MALE	FEMALE
1997-98	92%	8%	68%	32%	19%	81%	13%	87%	28%	72%
1998-99	93%	7%	65%	35%	18%	82%	10%	90%	19%	81%
1999-00	88%	13%	66%	34%	21%	79%	11%	89%	25%	75%
2000-01	90%	10%	66%	34%	23%	77%	11%	89%	23%	77%
2001-02	90%	10%	63%	37%	22%	78%	10%	90%	23%	77%
2002-03	86%	14%	64%	36%	21%	79%	12%	88%	17%	83%
2003-04	85%	15%	66%	34%	26%	74%	11%	89%	24%	76%

TABLE 8.11 GENDER BREAKDOWN OF FULL-TIME ACADEMIC STAFF IN INSTITUTES OF TECHNOLOGY

		% PERCENTAGE		NUMBERS	
		MALE	FEMALE	MALE	FEMALE
Senior Lecturer III	2003-04	84%	16%	69	13
Senior Lecturer II	2003-04	77%	23%	129	39
L1& L2 Structured	2003-04	89%	11%	43	6
Senior Lecturer (Tch)	2003-04	83%	17%	196	41
Lecturer Grade	2003-04	73%	27%	1,040	378
Lecturer II	2003-04	81%	19%	254	60
Lecturer I	2003-04	52%	48%	327	307
Assistant Lecturer	2003-04	59%	41%	468	327
College Teacher	2003-04	92%	8%	11	1
TOTAL ACADEMIC	**2003-04**	**68%**	**32%**	**2,537**	**1,172**
Senior Lecturer III	1998-99	91%	9%	61	6
Senior Lecturer II	1998-99	88%	12%	102	14
L1& L2 Structured	1998-99	87%	13%	53	8
Senior Lecturer (Tch)	1998-99	91%	9%	40	4
Lecturer Grade	1998-99	86%	14%	341	54
Lecturer II	1998-99	82%	18%	564	121
Lecturer I	1998-99	65%	35%	826	436
Assistant Lecturer	1998-99	59%	41%	10	7
College Teacher	1998-99	54%	46%	25	21
TOTAL ACADEMIC	**1998-99**	**75%**	**25%**	**2,022**	**671**

TABLE 8.12 GENDER BREAKDOWN OF FULL-TIME ACADEMIC STAFF IN HEA INSTITUTIONS

		% PERCENTAGE		NUMBERS	
		MALE	FEMALE	MALE	FEMALE
Professor	2002-03	92.5%	7.5%	319	26
Associate Professor	2002-03	87.5%	12.5%	225	32
Statutory/Senior Lecturer	2002-03	75.2%	24.8%	568	187
College Lecturer	2002-03	59.9%	40.1%	1,087	728
Assistant Lecturer	2002-03	49.1%	50.9%	158	164
Other Teaching Staff	2002-03	47.5%	52.5%	267	295
Other	2002-03	45.0%	55.0%	459	562
Total Full-time Academic	**2002-03**	**60.7%**	**39.3%**	**3,083**	**1,994**
Professor	1997-98	93.9%	6.1%	293	19
Associate Professor	1997-98	92.4%	7.6%	171	14
Statutory/Senior Lecturer	1997-98	83.7%	16.3%	498	97
College Lecturer	1997-98	67.1%	32.9%	894	438
Assistant Lecturer	1997-98	56.0%	44.0%	108	85
Other Teaching Staff	1997-98	53.2%	46.8%	74	65
Other	1997-98	0.0%	0.0%	0	0
Total Full-time Academic	**1997-98**	**73.9%**	**26.1%**	**2,038**	**718**

Data Source: These data are supplied annually by the HEA to the statistics section of the Department of Education & Science. They are used as inputs into the Department's annual data submissions to Eurostat and the OECD on Educational Personnel.

TABLE 8.13 GENDER BREAKDOWN OF FULL-TIME ACADEMIC STAFF IN HIGHER EDUCATION INSTITUTIONS, 2003

	% PERCENTAGE		NUMBERS		
	MALES	FEMALES	MALES	FEMALES	TOTAL
Switzerland	88%	12%	3,297	447	3,744
Japan	83%	17%	141,685	28,291	169,976
Netherlands	81%	19%	17,989	4,149	22,138
Malta	77%	23%	228	68	296
Germany	75%	25%	103,367	34,796	138,163
Austria	71%	29%	6,335	2,550	8,885
Slovenia	71%	29%	1,263	524	1,787
United Kingdom	68%	32%	55,120	26,130	81,250
Italy	67%	33%	58,855	28,360	87,215
France	66%	34%	87,668	44,530	132,198
Norway	64%	36%	7,154	4,067	11,221
Ireland	64%	36%	6,219	3,548	9,767
Turkey	63%	37%	47,215	28,102	75,317
Sweden	62%	38%	16,957	10,381	27,338
United States	62%	38%	397,860	248,581	646,441
Hungary	61%	39%	10,295	6,635	16,930
Croatia	60%	40%	3,534	2,310	5,844
Belgium	60%	40%	9,299	6,084	15,383
Spain	60%	40%	59,138	38,882	98,020
Cyprus	59%	41%	553	377	930
Albania	59%	41%	1,006	693	1,699
Slovakia	59%	41%	6,210	4,354	10,564
Romania	59%	41%	17,298	12,234	29,532
Iceland	58%	42%	455	326	781
Portugal	58%	42%	13,489	9,805	23,294
Macedonia	56%	44%	1,483	1,146	2,629
Bulgaria	55%	45%	6,175	5,045	11,220
Finland	55%	45%	9,213	7,576	16,789
Lithuania	47%	53%	3,170	3,606	6,776
Latvia	45%	55%	1,277	1,583	2,860
Country average	64%	36%			
Average of staff in all countries	**66%**	**34%**	**1,093,807**	**565,180**	**1,658,987**

Source: Eurostat website indicators on Educational Personnel - pers2_t
(http://epp.eurostat.cec.eu.int/portal/page?_pageid=0,1136184,0_45572595&_dad=portal&_schema=PORTAL) Data
updated - Sept. 14, 2005; Date of extraction - Dec. 21, 2005

TABLE 8.14 EMPLOYEES OF THE DEPARTMENT OF EDUCATION & SCIENCE, APRIL 2005

ADMINISTRATIVE GRADES

GRADE	MALE	%	FEMALE	%	TOTAL
Secretary General	0	0%	1	100%	1
Assistant Secretary	6	100%	0	0%	6
Director	1	100%	0	0%	1
Principal Officer	22	69%	10	31%	32
Assistant Principal	41	63%	24	37%	65
Higher Executive Officer	63	40%	93	60%	156
Administrative Officer	1	20%	4	80%	5
Executive Officer	85	27%	229	73%	314
Staff Officer	4	8%	47	92%	51
Clerical Officer	68	20%	269	80%	337
Total Administraive Staff	**291**	**30%**	**677**	**70%**	**968**

NON-ADMINISTRATIVE GRADES

(INSPECTORATE)

GRADE	MALE	%	FEMALE	%	TOTAL
Chief Inspector	1	100%	0	0%	1
Deputy Chief Inspector	2	100%	0	0%	2
Asst Chief Inspector	7	64%	4	36%	11
Divisional Inspector	26	70%	11	30%	37
District Inspector	15	42%	21	58%	36
Senior Inspector PP	13	65%	7	35%	20
Post Primary Inspector	17	40%	26	60%	43
Total Inspectorate	**81**	**54%**	**69**	**46%**	**150**

NEPS (NATIONAL EDUCATIONAL PSYCHOLOGICAL SERVICE)

GRADE	MALE	%	FEMALE	%	TOTAL
Acting Director	0	0%	1	100%	1
Regional Director	3	38%	5	63%	8
Senior Psychologist	14	30%	32	70%	46
Psychologists	13	19%	57	81%	70
Total NEPS	**30**	**24%**	**95**	**76%**	**125**

BUILDING UNIT (NON-ADMIN.)

GRADE	MALE	%	FEMALE	%	TOTAL
Manager	3	100%	0	0%	3
Project Planner	2	100%	0	0%	2
Senior Architect	5	83%	1	17%	6
Architect	2	67%	1	33%	3
Arch Asst	11	100%	0	0%	11
Engineer G1	3	100%	0	0%	3
Total Building Unit (Non-Admin)	**26**	**93%**	**2**	**7%**	**28**

Continued on next page

TABLE 8.14 EMPLOYEES OF THE DEPARTMENT OF EDUCATION & SCIENCE, APRIL 2005

SERVICE GRADES					
GRADE	MALE	%	FEMALE	%	TOTAL
Head Service Officer	1	100%	0	0%	1
Service Officer in charge	3	100%	0	0%	3
Service Officer	12	86%	2	14%	14
Service Attendant	1	100%	0	0%	1
Nightwatchmen	2	100%	0	0%	2
General Operative	1	100%	0	0%	1
Supervisor of Cleaners	0	0%	1	100%	1
Cleaners	1	17%	5	83%	6
Telephonists	2	67%	1	33%	3
Total Service Grades	**23**	**72%**	**9**	**28%**	**32**

OTHER					
GRADE	MALE	%	FEMALE	%	TOTAL
Civilian Driver	2	100%	0	0%	2
Senior Statistician	1	100%	0	0%	1
Statistician	1	50%	1	50%	2
Temp Accountant	1	100%	0	0%	1
Temp Barrister at Law	0	0%	1	100%	1
Employee Assistance	0	0%	1	100%	1
Total Other	5	63%	3	38%	8
Total Administrative	**291**	**30%**	**677**	**70%**	**968**
Total Non-Administrative	**165**	**48%**	**178**	**52%**	**343**
Total All Grades	**456**	**35%**	**855**	**65%**	**1311**

Data Source: Personnel Section, Department of Education & Science.

TABLE 8.15   EMPLOYEES OF THE CIVIL SERVICE, DECEMBER 2003

ADMINISTRATION GRADES

	MALE		FEMALE		TOTAL
Secretary General	15	94%	1	6%	16
Assistant Secretary	123	90%	14	10%	137
Principal Officer	477	80%	122	20%	599
Assistant Principal Officer	1,370	67%	663	33%	2,033
Higher Executive Officer	1,993	54%	1,730	46%	3,723
Administrative Officer	108	45%	132	55%	240
Executive Officer	1,804	37%	3,049	63%	4,853
Staff Officer	310	20%	1,209	80%	1,519
Clerical Officer	2,292	21%	8,819	79%	11,111
Total (24,231)	**8,492**	**35%**	**15,739**	**65%**	**24,231**

Data Source: Data supplied by the Department of Finance,
Note: These figures exclude the Irish Prison Service, Garda Civilians, State Exams Commission, National Council for Special Education and Foreign Affairs Local Recruits Serving Abroad.

TABLE 8.16 DEPARTMENT OF EDUCATION & SCIENCE 1995, 1996

ADMINISTRATION GRADES 1996

GRADE	MALE	%	FEMALE	%	TOTAL
Secretary General	1	100%	0	0%	1
Assistant Secretary	5	100%	0	0%	5
Director	1	100%	0	0%	1
Principal Officer	19	83%	4	17%	23
Assistant Principal Officer	36	80%	9	20%	45
Higher Executive Officer	53	55%	44	45%	97
Administrative Officer	2	50%	2	50%	4
Executive Officer	69	40%	102	60%	171
Staff Officer	8	14%	50	86%	58
Clerical Officer	24	18%	109	82%	133
Clerical Assistant Typist	1	3%	38	97%	39
Clerical Assistant	26	23%	85	77%	111
Total	**245**	**36%**	**443**	**64%**	**688**

INSPECTORATE 1995

GRADE	MALE	%	FEMALE	%	TOTAL
Chief Inspector	1	100%	0	0%	1
Deputy Chief Inspector	2	100%	0	0%	2
Asst Chief Inspector	8	100%	0	0%	8
Divisional Inspector	18	95%	1	5%	19
District Inspector	37	84%	7	16%	44
District Inspector Post Primary	2	50%	2	50%	4
Senior Inspector PP	16	94%	1	6%	17
Post Primary Inspector	26	79%	7	21%	33
Total Inspectorate	**110**	**86%**	**18**	**14%**	**128**

Data Source: Department of Education and Science, Personnel Section & IPA Diary 1996.

TABLE 8.17 MEMBERSHIP OF SELECTED STATE BOARDS AND COMMITTEES RELATING TO EDUCATION, 30 JUNE 2005

BOARD	APPOINTMENTS			GOVT./MINISTERIAL APPOINTMENTS			CHAIRS		
	TOTAL	WOMEN NUMBER	WOMEN %	TOTAL	WOMEN NUMBER	WOMEN %	MALE	FEMALE	% FEMALE
SET (Committee to encourage females into Science, Engineering & Technology)	11	10	91%	1	1	100%	0	1	100%
New Schools Advisory Committee	6	5	83%	0			0	1	100%
Modern Languages (Primary) Initiative Consultative Management Group	16	13	81%	0			1	0	0%
Education Equality Initiative (EEI)	17	11	65%	3	3	100%	0	1	100%
Modern Languages (Primary) Initiative Project Management Group	8	5	63%	0			1	0	0%
Advisory Committee on Traveller Education	21	13	62%	0			1	0	100%
Leargas	10	6	60%	10	6	60%	1	0	0%
Steering Committee of the Post-Primary Languages Initiative	10	6	60%	0			1	0	0%
Social Personal and Health Education Management Committee	10	6	60%	0			1	0	0%
Primary Curriculum Implementation Group	22	13	59%	0			1	0	0%
Committee on Educational Disadvantage (EDDIS)	18	10	56%	18	10	56%	0	1	100%
Centre for Early Childhood and Development (CECDE) Steering Committee	9	5	56%	0			0	1	100%
ACELS (Advisory Council for English Language)	11	6	55%	1	0	0%	0	1	100%
Residential Institutions Redress Board	11	6	55%	11	6	55%	1	0	0%
National Council for Special Education	12	6	50%	12	6	50%	1	0	0%
Task Force on Student Behaviour	12	6	50%	12	6	50%	0	1	100%
Teaching Council	37	17	46%	5	1	20%	0	1	100%
Further Education Training Awards Council (FETAC)	16	7	44%	9	5	56%	0	1	100%
Section 29 Appeals Board	30	13	43%	30	13	43%	Rotating Chair		

TABLE 8.17 MEMBERSHIP OF SELECTED STATE BOARDS AND COMMITTEES RELATING TO EDUCATION, 30 JUNE 2005

BOARD	APPOINTMENTS			GOVT./MINISTERIAL APPOINTMENTS			CHAIRS		
	TOTAL	WOMEN NUMBER	WOMEN %	TOTAL	WOMEN NUMBER	WOMEN %	MALE	FEMALE	% FEMALE
National Qualification Authority of Ireland (NQAI)	14	6	43%	4	1	25%	1	0	0%
NCTE (National Centre for Technology in Education)	7	3	43%	0			1	0	0%
Institutes of Technology (& DIT) Boards	259	106	41%	18	2	11%	14	0	0%
State Exams Commission	5	2	40%	5	2	40%	1	0	0%
National Adult Learning Council (NALC)	25	10	40%	4	2	50%	1	0	0%
Steering Committee of the Leadership Development for Schools	10	4	40%	0			0	1	100%
Council for Irish Language Education	23	9	39%	1	0	0%	1	0	0%
Irish Research Council for Science, Engineering and Technology (IRCSET)	23	9	39%				0	1	100%
Royal Irish Academy of Music (RIAM)	35	13	37%	0			1	0	0%
Higher Education Authority (HEA)	19	7	37%	19	7	37%	1	0	0%
Steering Group of the Commission on School Accommodation	30	11	37%	3	1	33%	1	0	0%
Irish Research Council for the Humanities and Social Sciences (IRCHSS)	11	4	36%				1	0	0%
International Education Board of Ireland (IEBI)	20	7	35%	1	1	100%	1	0	0%
National University of Ireland (NUI)	38	13	34%	4	2	50%	1	0	0%
National Council for Curriculum and Assessment (NCCA)	25	8	32%	1	1	100%	0	1	100%
University Boards (7 Universities & NCAD)	244	74	30%	25	13	52%	7	1	13%
Higher Education Training Awards Council (HETAC)	14	4	29%	4	2	50%	1	0	0%
National Educational Welfare Board (NEWB)	13	3	23%	12	3	25%	0	1	100%
Primary Schools Sports Initiative Taskforce Committee	13	3	23%	0	0	52%	1	0	0%
Education Sector Performance Verification Group	10	2	20%	7	2	29%	1	0	0%
Royal Irish Academy (RIA)	22	4	18%	0			1	0	0%
TOTAL OF ALL AGENCIES LISTED ABOVE	**1147**	**466**	**41%**	**220**	**96**	**44%**	**45**	**14**	**24%**

Data Source: The above data on the gender composition of the boards of state agencies is collected and compiled by the Gender Equality Unit within the Department of Education and Science.

TABLE 8.18 VOCATIONAL EDUCATIONAL COMMITTEES, 2006

	PERCENTAGES			NUMBERS		
	MALE	FEMALE	TOTAL	MALE	FEMALE	TOTAL
Chairperson	94%	6%	100%	31	2	33
Committee Members	66%	34%	100%	388	200	588
CEO	79%	21%	100%	26	7	33

Data Source: IPA Directory 2006, internet searches & telephone contact.

TABLE 8.19 SELECTED STATE AGENCIES WITH RESPONSIBILITY FOR ADMINISTRATION AND/OR EDUCATION POLICY, 2005

HEA - HIGHER EDUCATION AUTHORITY

GRADE	MALE	%	FEMALE	%	TOTAL
Chief Executive	1	100%	0	0%	1
Principal Officer	3	50%	3	50%	6
Assistant Principal	3.6	39%	5.6	61%	9.2
Higher Executive Officer	5	50%	5	50%	10
Executive Officer	5	35%	9.2	65%	14.2
Clerical Officer	1	14%	6	86%	7
Support Staff	0	0%	1.6	100%	1.6
TOTAL HEA	**18.6**	**38%**	**30.4**	**62%**	**49**

SEC - STATE EXAMINATIONS COMMISSION

GRADE	MALE	%	FEMALE	%	TOTAL
CEO	1	100%	0	0%	1
Director of Operations	1	100%	0	0%	1
Head EAM	1	100%	0	0%	1
Principal Officer	1	50%	1	50%	2
Deputy Head EAM	2	67%	1	33%	3
EAM	21	64%	12	36%	33
Assistant Principal	5	71%	2	29%	7
Higher Executive Officer	8	50%	8	50%	16
Executive Officers	9	30%	21	70%	30
Staff Officers	0	0%	11	100%	11
Clerical Officers	12	22%	42	78%	54
Services Officers	9	100%	0	0%	9
Night Watchmen	3	100%	0	0%	3
Cleaners	3	23%	10	77%	13
TOTAL SEC	**76**	**41%**	**108**	**59%**	**184**

NCSE - NATIONAL COUNCIL FOR SPECIAL EDUCATION

GRADE	MALE	%	FEMALE	%	TOTAL
Chief Executive	1	100%	0	0%	1
Principal Officer	2	67%	1	33%	3
Assistant Principal	2	67%	1	33%	3
Support Staff (SENOs)	14	19%	61	81%	75
Higher Executive Officer	3	75%	1	25%	4
Executive Officer	1	29%	2.5	71%	3.5
Staff Officer	0	0%	1	100%	1
Clerical Officer	0	0%	2	100%	2
TOTAL NCSE	**23**	**25%**	**69.5**	**75%**	**92.5**

TABLE 8.19 SELECTED STATE AGENCIES WITH RESPONSIBILITY FOR ADMINISTRATION AND/OR EDUCATION POLICY, 2005

NCCA - NATIONAL COUNCIL FOR CURRICULUM & ASSESSMENT

GRADE	MALE	%	FEMALE	%	TOTAL
Chief Executive	0	0%	1	100%	1
Deputy CEO	1	50%	1	50%	2
Director	2	33%	4	67%	6
Resource Co-ordinator	0	0%	1	100%	1
Project Officer	0	0%	2	100%	2
Education Officer	4	44%	5	56%	9
Assistant Principal	1	100%	0	0%	1
Higher Executive Officer	1	100%	0	0%	1
Executive Officer	0	0%	1	100%	1
Clerical Officer	3	75%	1	25%	4
Services Officer	1	50%	1	50%	2
TOTAL NCCA	**13**	**43%**	**17**	**57%**	**30**

NEWB - NATIONAL EDUCATION WELFARE BOARD

GRADE	MALE	%	FEMALE	%	TOTAL
CEO	1	100%	0	0%	1
Principal Officers	1	100%	0	0%	1
Assistant Principal	1	50%	1	50%	2
Regional Managers (APs)	3	60%	2	40%	5
Senior Educational Welfare Officers	3	27%	8	73%	11
Educational Welfare Officers	19	39%	30	61%	49
Higher Executive Officers	2	50%	2	50%	4
Executive Officers	0	0%	1	100%	1
Clerical Officers	0	0%	5	100%	5
TOTAL NEWB	**30**	**38%**	**49**	**62%**	**79**

NQAI - NATIONAL QUALIFICATIONS AUTHORITY OF IRELAND

GRADE	MALE	%	FEMALE	%	TOTAL
CEO	1	100%	0	0%	1
Director Framework Development & Director Corporate Affairs	0	0%	2	100%	2
Development Officers	3	100%	0	0%	3
Admistration Executive	1	100%	0	0%	1
Administrator - Grade VII	0	0%	3	100%	3
Administrator - Grade IV	1	25%	3	75%	4
Administrator - Grade III	0	0%	2	100%	2
TOTAL NQAI	**6**	**37%**	**10**	**63%**	**16**

TABLE 8.19   SELECTED STATE AGENCIES WITH RESPONSIBILITY FOR ADMINISTRATION AND/OR EDUCATION POLICY, 2005

HETAC

GRADE	MALE	%	FEMALE	%	TOTAL
Chief Executive	1	100%	0	0%	1
Director Corporate Services & Director Academic Affairs SLIII	1	100%	0	0%	1
Development Officers/Head of Functions SLII	2	33%	4	67%	6
APO	1	100%	0	0%	1
Admin Officer VII	0	0%	2	100%	2
Admin Officer VI	0	0%	2.5	100%	2.5
Admin Officer V	0	0%	4	100%	4
Admin Officer IV	0	0%	3.5	100%	3.5
Admin Officer III	1	17%	5	83%	6
Contract Grade Info Officer/ Librarian	0	0%	1	100%	1
Contract Grade IT Manager	1	100%	0	0%	1
TOTAL HETAC	**7**	**24%**	**22**	**76%**	**29**

FETAC

GRADE	MALE	%	FEMALE	%	TOTAL
CEO	1	100%	0	0%	1
Director of Services/ Director of Awards	1	50%	1	50%	2
Head of Admin	0	0%	1	100%	1
Development Officers	3	30%	7	70%	10
Grade VII	2	100%	0	0%	2
Grade VI	2	67%	1	33%	3
Grade V	1	17%	5	83%	6
Grade IV	2	22%	7	78%	9
Grade III	1	10%	9	90%	10
TOTAL FETAC	**13**	**30%**	**31**	**70%**	**44**

NALA - NATIONAL ADULT LITERACY AGENCY

GRADE	MALE	%	FEMALE	%	TOTAL
Principal Officer	0	0%	1	100%	1
Assistant Principal Officer	1	100%	0	0%	1
Asdministrative Officer STD	3	30%	7	70%	10
Clerical & Administrative GR IV	0	0%	1	100%	1
Clerical & Administrative Gr V	0	0%	4	100%	4
TOTAL NALA	**4**	**24%**	**13**	**76%**	**17**

AONTAS

GRADE	MALE	%	FEMALE	%	TOTAL
Principal Officer	0	0%	2	100%	2
Assistant Principal Officer	0	0%	1	100%	1
Higher Executive Officer	0	0%	1	100%	1
Executive Officer	0	0%	5	100%	5
Clerical Officer	0	0%	1	100%	1
TOTAL AONTAS	**0**	**0%**	**10**	**100%**	**10**

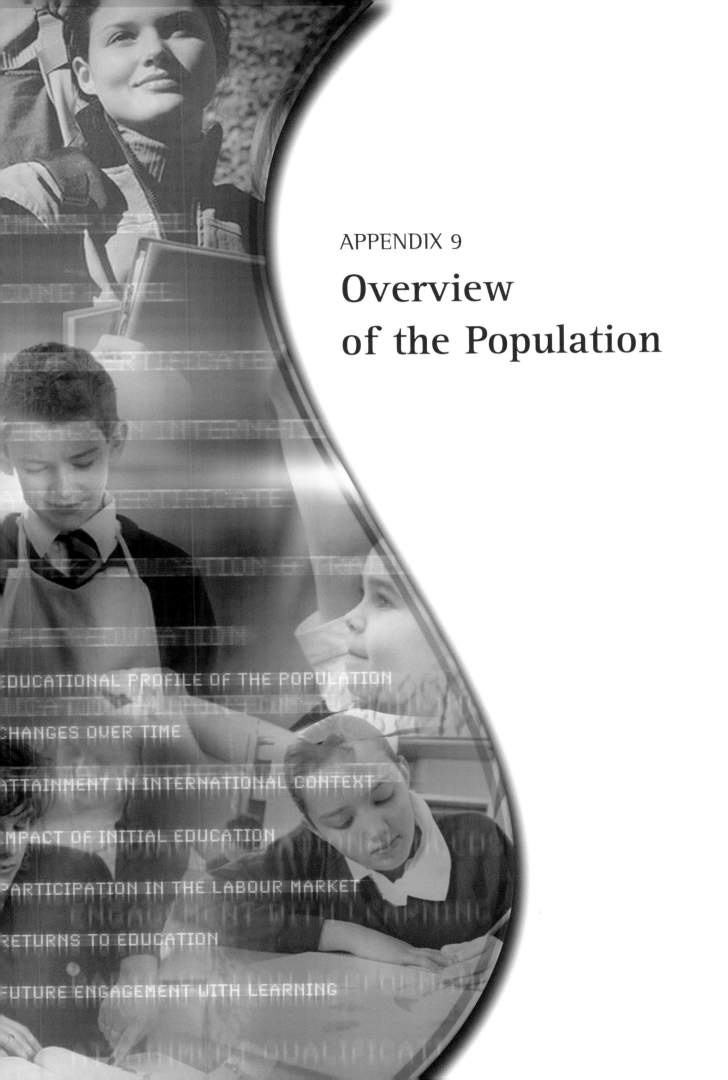

APPENDIX 9

Overview
of the Population

EDUCATIONAL PROFILE OF THE POPULATION

CHANGES OVER TIME

ATTAINMENT IN INTERNATIONAL CONTEXT

IMPACT OF INITIAL EDUCATION

PARTICIPATION IN THE LABOUR MARKET

RETURNS TO EDUCATION

FUTURE ENGAGEMENT WITH LEARNING

TABLE 9.1 PERCENTAGES OF PERSONS WITH LOW LEVELS OF EDUCATIONAL ATTAINMENT BY AGE GROUP AND GENDER

		AGE GROUP						
	HIGHEST LEVEL OF EDUCATION ATTAINED	**20-24**	**25-34**	**35-44**	**45-54**	**55-59**	**60-64**
Males	Primary or below	4.2%	6.7%	10.9%	25.7%	42.9%	51.3%
	Lower Second Level	13.6%	17.5%	24.7%	23.2%	16.2%	14.5%
	Lower 2nd level and below	**17.9%**	**24.2%**	**35.7%**	**48.9%**	**59.1%**	**65.7%**
Females	Primary or below	3.2%	5.1%	9.5%	22.7%	37.8%	44.1%
	Lower Second Level	8.2%	11.9%	18.3%	20.8%	19.3%	17.6%
	Lower 2nd level and below	**11.4%**	**17.1%**	**27.9%**	**43.6%**	**57.1%**	**61.7%**
All persons	Primary or below	3.8%	5.9%	10.2%	24.2%	40.4%	47.8%
	Lower Second Level	10.9%	14.7%	21.5%	22.0%	17.8%	16.0%
	Lower 2nd level and below	**14.7%**	**20.6%**	**31.8%**	**46.2%**	**58.1%**	**63.8%**

Data Source: Quarterly National Household Survey, Central Statistics Office. Reference period: Q2 - March to May, 2004. The Department is grateful to the Labour Market Section of the CSO for providing these data disaggregated by gender.

Note: The small numbers of respondents whose highest level of education is classified as "other" have been omitted from this analysis.

TABLE 9.2 PERCENTAGES OF PERSONS WITH THIRD-LEVEL QUALIFICATIONS BY AGE GROUP AND GENDER

| | HIGHEST LEVEL OF EDUCATION ATTAINED | AGE GROUP | | | | | |
		25-34	35-44	45-54	55-59	60-64
Males	Third Level non degree	12.6%	10.2%	7.4%	4.6%	4.7%
	Degree or above	24.4%	19.0%	14.5%	13.5%	9.8%
	Total Third Level	**37.0%**	**29.1%**	**21.9%**	**18.1%**	**14.5%**
Females	Third Level non degree	16.5%	11.7%	9.4%	7.0%	6.5%
	Degree or above	27.3%	16.9%	11.8%	8.8%	7.3%
	Total Third Level	**43.8%**	**28.6%**	**21.2%**	**15.8%**	**13.8%**
All persons	Third Level non degree	14.6%	10.9%	8.4%	5.8%	5.6%
	Degree or above	25.8%	17.9%	13.1%	11.2%	8.6%
	Total Third Level	**40.4%**	**28.9%**	**21.5%**	**16.9%**	**14.2%**

Data Source: Quarterly National Household Survey, Central Statistics Office. Reference period: Q2 - March to May, 2004. The Department is grateful to the Labour Market Section of the CSO for providing these data disaggregated by gender.

Note: The small numbers of respondents whose highest level of education is classified as "other" have been omitted from this analysis.

TABLE 9.3 PERCENTAGES THAT HAVE ATTAINED AT LEAST UPPER SECOND-LEVEL EDUCATION BY AGE-GROUP, IRELAND & OECD AVERAGES 2003

	MALES				FEMALES				PERSONS				25-64 YEAR OLDS		
	25-34	35-44	45-54	55-64	25-34	35-44	45-54	55-64	25-34	35-44	45-54	55-64	Males	Females	Persons
Ireland	75%	63%	50%	37%	81%	71%	54%	39%	78%	67%	52%	38%	59%	64%	62%
OECD Country mean	75%	70%	65%	56%	76%	69%	59%	46%	75%	70%	62%	51%	68%	64%	66%

Data Source: OECD (2005) Education at a Glance: OECD Indicators 2005, Table A1.2 [The gender breakdowns which were not published in hard-copy are available on the OECD website]

TABLE 9.4 PERCENTAGES THAT HAVE ATTAINED THIRD-LEVEL EDUCATION BY AGE-GROUP, IRELAND & OECD AVERAGES 2003

	MALES				FEMALES				PERSONS				25-64 YEAR OLDS		
	25-34	35-44	45-54	55-64	25-34	35-44	45-54	55-64	25-34	35-44	45-54	55-64	Males	Females	Persons
Ireland	34%	27%	21%	16%	40%	28%	20%	13%	37%	27%	20%	15%	26%	27%	26%
OECD Country Mean	28%	26%	23%	20%	32%	25%	21%	14%	29%	26%	22%	17%	25%	24%	24%

Data Source: OECD (2005) Education at a Glance: OECD Indicators 2005, Table A1.3 [The gender breakdowns which were not published in hard-copy are available on the OECD website]

TABLE 9.5 ILO PARTICIPATION RATE IN THE LABOUR FORCE BY AGE GROUP - IRELAND 2005 (Q2)

AGE GROUP	MALE	FEMALE	ALL PERSONS
25-34	93%	77%	85%
35-44	94%	67%	80%
45-54	89%	63%	76%
55-59	74%	46%	60%
60-64	60%	28%	44%

Data source: CSO website data on Labour Force from the QNHS
(http://www.cso.ie/px/pxeirestat/temp/QNBQ42005113494249.xls) Data extracted 2 November 2005

TABLE 9.6 TRENDS IN EMPLOYMENT RATES BY EDUCATIONAL ATTAINMENT (1991-2003)

Number of 25-to-64-year-olds in employment as a percentage of the population aged 25 to 64, by level of educational attainment

	GENDER	EDUCATIONAL ATTAINMENT**	1991	1995	1998	1999	2000	2001	2002	2003
Ireland	Males	Low	69%	68%	71%	73%	74%	74%	74%	73%
		Medium	87%	86%	88%	90%	91%	92%	90%	89%
		High	91%	91%	92%	93%	93%	93%	91%	91%
	Females	Low	21%	26%	33%	34%	36%	37%	38%	38%
		Medium	46%	52%	60%	62%	64%	64%	65%	63%
		High	68%	75%	78%	82%	82%	82%	82%	81%
	Total	Low	46%	49%	53%	54%	56%	57%	57%	57%
		Medium	63%	67%	72%	75%	77%	77%	77%	76%
		High	81%	83%	85%	87%	88%	87%	87%	86%
OECD Country Mean	Males	Low	75%	71%	71%	70%	70%	70%	70%	68%
		Medium	86%	84%	84%	85%	85%	84%	84%	83%
		High	91%	89%	90%	90%	90%	90%	89%	88%
	Females	Low	45%	44%	45%	45%	46%	46%	46%	46%
		Medium	63%	63%	64%	65%	65%	65%	66%	65%
		High	78%	78%	78%	78%	79%	79%	79%	78%
	Total	Low	59%	57%	57%	57%	57%	57%	57%	56%
		Medium	76%	73%	75%	76%	75%	75%	75%	74%
		High	86%	84%	85%	85%	85%	85%	84%	83%

Data Source: OECD (2005) Education at a Glance: OECD Indicators 2005, Table A8.3a, p.111 [The gender breakdowns which were not published in hard-copy are available on the OECD website, see web tables A8.3b & A8.3c].

Note: **For Educational Attainment, Low = Below upper secondary; Medium = Upper secondary and post-secondary non-tertiary; High = Tertiary education

TABLE 9.7 UNEMPLOYMENT RATES AMONG 25-29 YEAR OLDS BY LEVEL OF EDUCATIONAL ATTAINMENT (IRELAND AND OECD COUNTRY MEAN, 2003)

		Below upper secondary education	Upper secondary and post-secondary non-tertiary education	Tertiary education	All levels of education
Ireland	Males	10.3%	3.8%	3.4%	5.0%
	Females	5.5%	2.9%	2.6%	3.1%
	M & F	8.3%	3.4%	3.0%	4.1%
OECD Country mean	Males	13.0%	6.0%	4.6%	6.7%
	Females	9.5%	6.4%	4.9%	6.1%
	M & F	11.2%	6.2%	4.7%	6.4%

Data Source: OECD (2005) Education at a Glance: OECD Indicators 2005, Table C4.3, p.292.

TABLE 9.8 RELATIVE EARNINGS OF THE POPULATION WITH INCOME FROM EMPLOYMENT BY LEVEL OF EDUCATIONAL ATTAINMENT AND GENDER FOR 25 TO 64 YEAR OLDS AND 30 TO 44 YEAR OLDS - IRELAND 2000 (UPPER SECOND-LEVEL EDUCATION=100%

	AGE 25-64			AGE 30-44		
	MALES	FEMALES	TOTAL	MALES	FEMALES	TOTAL
Below upper 2nd level	82%	64%	87%	77%	61%	83%
3rd level Cert & Diploma	117%	132%	124%	123%	126%	130%
3rd level Degree to PhD	143%	181%	163%	140%	155%	152%
All 3rd level	135%	161%	149%	133%	144%	143%

Data Source: OECD (2005) Education at a Glance: OECD Indicators 2005, Table A9.1a, p.130.

TABLE 9.9 PARTICIPATION IN FORMAL AND/OR NON-FORMAL EDUCATION AND TRAINING, BY EDUCATIONAL ATTAINMENT AND GENDER (IRELAND 2003)

	Lower secondary education	Upper secondary and post-secondary non-tertiary education	Tertiary education	All levels of education
Males	11%	23%	39%	23%
Females	11%	24%	44%	26%
M & F	11%	24%	42%	24%

Data Source: OECD (2005) Education at a Glance: OECD Indicators 2005, Table C6.1a, p.321.

9.10 PARTICIPATION IN LIFELONG LEARNING, 2004

	MALES	FEMALES	PERSONS	GENDER DIFFERENCE (Females minus Males)	GENDER DIFFERENCE (Females/Males)
Sweden	31.5%	40.3%	35.8%	8.8%	1.3
Denmark	23.4%	31.9%	27.6%	8.5%	1.4
Finland	20.9%	28.2%	24.6%	7.3%	1.3
UK	17.4%	25.3%	21.2%	7.9%	1.5
Slovenia	16.1%	19.8%	17.9%	3.7%	1.2
Netherlands	16.4%	17.2%	16.8%	0.8%	1.0
Austria	11.5%	12.5%	12.0%	1.0%	1.1
EU 25	**9.0%**	**10.7%**	**9.9%**	**1.7%**	**1.2**
Belgium	9.7%	9.3%	9.5%	-0.4%	1.0
Luxembourg	9.3%	9.5%	9.4%	0.2%	1.0
Cyprus	9.0%	9.6%	9.3%	0.6%	1.1
Latvia	6.1%	11.8%	9.1%	5.7%	1.9
France	7.6%	7.9%	7.8%	0.3%	1.0
Germany	7.8%	7.0%	7.4%	-0.8%	0.9
Ireland	**6.1%**	**8.4%**	**7.2%**	**2.3%**	**1.4**
Italy	6.5%	7.2%	6.8%	0.7%	1.1
Estonia	5.8%	7.6%	6.7%	1.8%	1.3
Lithuania	5.0%	7.9%	6.5%	2.9%	1.6
Czech Republic	6.0%	6.5%	6.3%	0.5%	1.1
Poland	4.7%	6.3%	5.5%	1.6%	1.3
Spain	4.7%	5.6%	5.1%	0.9%	1.2
Malta	5.5%	4.4%	5.0%	-1.1%	0.8
Portugal	4.4%	5.1%	4.8%	0.7%	1.2
Hungary	3.9%	5.3%	4.6%	1.4%	1.4
Slovakia	3.9%	5.2%	4.6%	1.3%	1.3
Greece	2.0%	2.1%	3.9%	0.1%	1.1

Data Source: European Commission Communication (2005), Draft 2006 Progress Report on the implementation of the "Education and Training 2010 work programme", p.24.

APPENDIX 10

Bibliography

PRIMARY LEVEL

SECOND LEVEL

JUNIOR CERTIFICATE

LITERACY IN INTERNATIONAL CONTEXT

LEAVING CERTIFICATE

FURTHER EDUCATION & TRAINING

HIGHER EDUCATION

EDUCATIONAL PERSONNEL

OVERVIEW OF THE POPULATION

Bibliography

AONTAS. 2004. *Community Education.* Dublin: AONTAS

ATKINSON, T., CANTILLON, B., MARLIER, E., NOLAN, B. 2002. *Social Indicators: The EU and Social Inclusion.* Oxford: Oxford University Press

BARRY, U. 2000. *Building the Picture: The Role of Data in Achieving Equality.* Dublin: The Equality Authority

BYRNE, A., LENTIN, R. 2000. *(Re) searching Women: Feminist Research Methodologies in the Social Sciences in Ireland.* Dublin: Institute of Public Administration

CENTRAL STATISTICS OFFICE. 2006. *Quarterly National Household Survey, Educational Attainment 2002-2005.* Dublin: Central Statistics Office (available at http://www.cso.ie/releasespublications/documents/labour_market/current/qnhs_educationalattainment.pdf)

CENTRAL STATISTICS OFFICE. 2005. *Statistical Yearbook of Ireland 2005.* Dublin: The Stationary Office

CENTRAL STATISTICS OFFICE. 2004. *Quarterly National Household Survey (QNHS), Special Module on Education, 1999–2003.* Dublin: Central Statistics Office (tables available at www.cso.ie/qnhs/documents/qnhseducation.xls)

CENTRAL STATISTICS OFFICE. 2004. *Census 2002: Volume 7- Education and Qualifications.* Dublin: The Stationary Office

CENTRAL STATISTICS OFFICE. 2003. *Census 2002: Principle Demographic Results.* Dublin: The Stationary Office

CENTRAL STATISTICS OFFICE. 2003. *[The SPAR Report] Statistical Potential of Administrative Records in Six Government Departments.* Dublin: CSO. Website: http://www.cso.ie/releasespublications/documents/other_releases/spar.pdf

CLANCY, P. 2001. *College Entry in Focus.* Dublin: Higher Education Authority

COOLAHAN, J. 1981, Reprinted 2005. *Irish Education – History and Structure.* Dublin: Institute of Public Administration

CORI EDUCATION COMMISSION. 2001. *Learning for Life: White Paper on Adult Education: An Analysis,* Dublin: CORI

COSGROVE, J., SHIEL, G., SOFRONIOU, N., ZASTRUTZKI, S., SHORTT, F. 2005. *Education for Life: The Achievements of 15-Year-Olds in Ireland in the Second Cycle of PISA.* Dublin: Educational Research Centre

COSGROVE, J., KELLAGHAN, T., FORDE, P., MORGAN, M. 2000. *The 1998 National Assessment of English Reading (with Comparative Data from the 1993 National Assessment.,* Dublin: Educational Research Centre

DEPARTMENT OF EDUCATION AND SCIENCE. 2007. *Education Trends: Key Indicators on Education in Ireland and Europe.*
Website: http://www.education.ie/admin/servlet/blobservlet/des_educ_trends_intro.htm

DEPARTMENT OF EDUCATION AND SCIENCE. 1929 to 2006, *Tuarascáil Staitistiúil: Annual Statistical Reports and Annual Reports.* Dublin: The Stationary Office

DEPARTMENT OF EDUCATION AND SCIENCE, Higher Education Technology and Training Section. 1998 to 2005. *Annual Returns from IOTs (THAS Reports).* Unpublished.

DEPARTMENT OF EDUCATION AND SCIENCE. 2004. *The Senior Cycle in Second-Level Schools.* Dublin: Department of Education and Science.
Website: http://www.education.ie/servlet/blobservlet/senior_cycle_options.pdf?language=EN

DEPARTMENT OF EDUCATION AND SCIENCE. 2005. Retention Rates of Pupils in Post-Primary Schools – 1996 cohort. Website
http://www.education.ie/servlet/blobservlet/pp_retention_1996_report.doc

DEPARTMENT OF EDUCATION AND SCIENCE. 2003. Retention Rates of Pupils in Post-Primary Schools – 1994 cohort. Website
http://www.education.ie/servlet/blobservlet/pp_retention_1994_report.doc

DEPARTMENT OF EDUCATION AND SCIENCE. 2003. *Supporting Equity in Higher Education: A Report to the Minister for Education and Science.* Dublin: Department of Education and Science

DEPARTMENT OF EDUCATION AND SCIENCE. 2000. *Learning for Life: White Paper on Adult Education.* Dublin: The Stationary Office

DRUDY, S., MARTIN, M., WOODS, M., O'FLYNN, J. 2000. *Gender Differences at Entry to Colleges of Education: A Report to the Department of Education and Science.* Unpublished

ECONOMIC AND SOCIAL RESEARCH INSTITUTE (ESRI). 1982 to 2005. *Annual School-Leavers' Surveys.* Dublin: Department of Education and Science

EIVERS, E., SHIEL, G., PERKINS, R., COSGROVE, J. 2005. *Succeeding in Reading? Reading standards in Irish Primary Schools.* Dublin: Educational Research Centre

EIVERS, E., SHIEL, G., SHORTT, F., SOFRONIOU, N. 2004. *Reading Literacy in Disadvantaged Primary Schools.* Dublin: Educational Research Centre

ELWOOD, J., CARLISLE, K. 2003. Examining Gender: *Gender and Achievement in the Junior and Leaving Certificate Examinations 2000/2001.* Dublin: National Council for Curriculum and Assessment

EUROPEAN COMMISSION. 2005. *Draft 2006 Progress Report on the Implementation of the Education and Training 2010 work programme.* Brussels: European Commission

EUROPEAN COMMISSION. 2003. *European Benchmarks in Education and Training: Follow-up to the Lisbon European Council.* Brussels: European Commission

EUROPEAN COMMISSION. 2003. *"She Figures" – Women and Science Statistics and Indicators.* Brussels: European Commission

EUROSTAT. 2005. *Key Data on Education in Europe 2005.* Luxembourg: Office for Official Publications of the European Communities

EUROSTAT. 2002. *The Life of Women and Men in Europe: A Statistical Portrait – Data 1980-2000.* Luxembourg: Office for Official Publications of the European Communities

HANNAN, D., SMYTH, E., McCULLAGH, J., O'LEARY, R., McMAHON, D. 1996. *Co-education & Gender Equality.* Dublin: Oak Tree Press

HIGHER EDUCATION AUTHORITY. 2007. What do Graduates Do? The Class of 2005. Dublin: HEA Statistics Section

HUTMACHER, W., COCHRANE, D., BOTTANI, N. (eds). 2001. *In Pursuit of Equity in Education: Using International Indicators to Compare Equity Policies.* Dordrecht: Kluwer Academic Publishers

INSTITUTE OF PUBLIC ADMINISTRATION. 2006. *Administration Yearbook & Diary 2006.* Dublin: IPA

INSTITUTE OF PUBLIC ADMINISTRATION. 1996. *Administration Yearbook & Diary 1996.* Dublin: IPA

INTERNATIONAL ASSOCIATION FOR THE EVALUATION OF EDUCATIONAL ACHIEVEMENT (IEA). 1997. *Mathematics Achievement in the Primary School Years: Third International Mathematics and Science Stud.,* Amsterdam: IEA.

KING, P., O'DRISCOLL, S., HOLDEN, S. 2002. *Gender and Learning.* Dublin: Shannon Curriculum Development Centre, Commissioned by AONTAS on behalf of the Department of Education and Science.

MCDONAGH, S., PATTERSON, V. 2005. *Discipline Choices and Trends for High Points CAO Acceptors.* Unpublished

MCDONAGH, S., PATTERSON, V. 2006. *The Institutes of Technology and Future Skills.* Unpublished

MORGAN, M., FLANAGAN, R., KELLAGHAN, T. 2001. *A Study of Non-Completion in Undergraduate University Courses.* Dublin: Higher Education Authority

MORGAN, M., FLANAGAN, R., KELLAGHAN, T. 2000. *A Study of Non-Completion in Institute of Technology Courses.* Dublin: Higher Education Authority

Morgan, M., HICKEY, B., KELLAGHAN, T., CRONIN, A., MILLAR, D. 1997. *Education 2000: International Adult Literacy Survey: Results for Ireland,* Dublin: The Stationary Office

NATIONAL ECONOMIC AND SOCIAL COUNCIL (NESC). 2002. *National Progress Indicators.* Dublin: NESC

NATIONAL STATISTICS BOARD. 2003. *Developing Irish Social and Equality Statistics to meet Policy Needs: Report of the Steering Group for Social and Equality Statistics.* Dublin: The Stationary Office. Website: http://www.taoiseach.gov.ie/attached_files/Pdf%20files/SocialAndEqualityStatisticsReport.pdf

NATIONAL STATISTICS BOARD. 2003. *Strategy for Statistics 2003-2008.* Dublin: The Stationary Office. Website: http://www.nsb.ie/pdf_docs/StrategyforStatistics2003-2008.pdf

O'CONNELL, P., CLANCY, D., McCOY, S. 2006. *Who Went to College in 2004? A National Survey of New Entrants to Higher Education.* Dublin: Higher Education Authority

ORGANISATION FOR ECONOMIC CO-OPERATION AND DEVELOPMENT. 2006. *Education at a Glance: OECD Indicators 2006.* Paris: OECD

ORGANISATION FOR ECONOMIC CO-OPERATION AND DEVELOPMENT. 2005. *Education at a Glance: OECD Indicators 2005.* Paris: OECD

ORGANISATION FOR ECONOMIC CO-OPERATION AND DEVELOPMENT. 2004. *Education at a Glance: OECD Indicators 2004.* Paris: OECD

ORGANISATION FOR ECONOMIC CO-OPERATION AND DEVELOPMENT. 2004. *Learning for Tomorrow's World: First Results from PISA 2003.* Paris: OECD

ORGANISATION FOR ECONOMIC CO-OPERATION AND DEVELOPMENT. 2003. *The PISA 2003 Assessment Framework: Mathematics, Reading, Science and Problem Solving Knowledge and SkillS.* Paris: OECD

ORGANISATION FOR ECONOMIC CO-OPERATION AND DEVELOPMENT. 2003. *Education at a Glance: OECD Indicators 2003.* Paris: OECD

ORGANISATION FOR ECONOMIC CO-OPERATION AND DEVELOPMENT. 2001. *Knowledge and Skills for Life: First Results from PISA 2000.* Paris: OECD

OWENS, T. 2000. *Men on the Move.* Dublin: AONTAS

RUSSELL, H., SMYTH, E., O'CONNELL, P. 2005. Degrees of Equality: Gender Pay Differentials among Recent Graduates. Dublin: ESRI (books and monographs no. 184)

RUSSELL, H., SMYTH, E., LYONS, M., O'CONNELL, P. 2002. *"Getting out of the House" – Women Returning to Employment, Education and Training.* Dublin: The Liffey Press in association with the ESRI

SHIEL, G., COSGROVE, J., SOFRONIOU, N., KELLY, A. 2001. Ready for Life?: *The Literacy Achievements of Irish 15-Year-Olds with Comparative International Data.* Dublin: Educational Research Centre

WARREN, L., O'CONNOR, E. 1999. *Stepping out of the Shadows: Women in Educational Management in Ireland.* Dublin: Oak Tree Press.